# Great

# RACETRACKS

## of the World

Published in 2012 by Hardie Grant Books

Hardie Grant Books (Australia)
Ground Floor, Building 1
658 Church Street
Richmond, Victoria 3121
www.hardiegrant.com.au

Hardie Grant Books (UK)
Dudley House, North Suite
34–35 Southampton Street
London WC2E 7HF
www.hardiegrant.co.uk

Cataloguing-in-Publication data is available from the National Library of Australia.
Great Racetracks of the World
ISBN 978-174270461-6

Publisher: Pam Brewster
Cover and text designer: Peter Daniel
Colour reproduction: Splitting Image Colour Studio
Printed in China by 1010 Printing International Ltd.

# Great
# RACETRACKS
## of the World

TREVOR MARMALADE & JIM A McGRATH

**hardie grant** books

MELBOURNE · LONDON

| CONVERSION TABLE | |
|---|---|
| 100lb = 45kg | |
| 1ft = 0.3m | |
| 1yd (3ft) = 0.90m | |
| ¹⁄₁₀ mile = 0.16km | |
| ⅛ mile = 0.20km | |
| ¼ mile = 0.40km | |
| ½ mile = 0.80km | |
| 1 mile = 1760yds = 1.61km | |
| 1 acre = 0.40ha | |

# CONTENTS

# INTRODUCTION

*Thoroughbred racing is a unique sport with a language all its own. When racing people get together they rarely discuss anything else, and when they do it is always related in racing parlance and terminology.*

It is a game rich in colourful characters, prepared to chance their arm and back their opinions, who bounce between the penthouse and the poor house with no visible change to their demeanor.

More than 20 years ago it occurred to me that nobody had ever written a book covering all of the tracks that run Group or Listed races.

Since then the evolution of technology has transformed racing into a global sport, with races beamed live into loungerooms from all over the world. Not only did the idea of a comprehensive illustrated 'guide' become too hard to resist, but it appeared obvious that there had never been a better time for it.

Within these pages are more than 270 tracks arranged by country, beginning with the home of racing in England, and traversing all parts of the globe that run stakes races.

But not every legendary race is a stakes race, or run at a traditional course, and many of these have been included as well. It is hoped that this publication will fill the gap in current literature, and also assist in the never-ending search to back a winner.

Among the names of the notable winners there will be many to evoke memories, some to discover and others whose deeds stand the test of time, though their legends may have dimmed.

What can be guaranteed is that by the time you have finished reading this book there will be many places that you intend to visit.

# EPSOM DOWNS

Epsom Downs, Epsom, Surrey, England, UK. www.epsomdowns.co.uk

*A farmer was herding his cattle across the Epsom Downs in 1614 when he chanced upon a mineral spring. It was a discovery that would transform the area. Just 15 miles from London, The Downs soon became a popular destination for weekenders and day outings and many recreational activities were organised.*

Naturally it was not long before somebody had the idea to untie a couple of horses and race them off. In fact, racing thrived here for well over a century before the introduction of the races that would make The Downs famous.

Epsom Downs is the venue for the world's most celebrated and influential horse race – The Derby, first run in 1780. Every winner of The Derby is an instant legend in its own right.

The course is set on Common Land, so while it is permissible to charge admission to the grandstands and enclosures, entry to the inner section of the course has always been free to the public.

Consequently the event is one of the most well-attended sporting events in England as punters, party goers, campers and travellers sprawl across the infield in their tens of thousands, providing a vibrant, colourful and noisy carnival atmosphere.

For those who can't back a winner or have reason to rejoice, on the inside of the course is a pub called the Rubbing House, only a furlong past the winning post.

Part of Epsom folklore surrounds the local Amato Inn – named after Amato, who won The Derby in 1838 at his only appearance on a racetrack. The night before The Derby every year, a ghost is said to appear and writes its prediction of the winner in chalk on the post outside. The ghost has been right on occasion though some may argue it would be preferable to have a ghost that gets better mail. Or at least does the videos.

Epsom is also home to The Oaks. Named after the Epsom estate of Lord Derby, and predecessor to The Derby by a year, it was the success of the inaugural running of The Oaks in 1779 that led to the establishment of The Derby.

## THE TRACK

There is nothing like Epsom. No designer starting from scratch would dare come up with such a bizarre track. The Derby course was laid out in 1872 and is horseshoe shaped.

The start at the mile and a half is on a steep incline and it is a run of about 250yds before turning appreciably right. Runners then cut the corner before moving across to the left-hand side of the course by the mile and a quarter. The searching uphill climb continues until almost a furlong before the mile mark, which is the highest point on the course – 134ft above the start.

The track flattens out for 300yds then turns left for the long, very steep descent down Tattenham Hill, which at one point dips 40ft in 300yds, and continues downhill to the sharp left-hand bend into the straight at Tattenham Corner. There, the runners are met by a home straight that is adversely cambered because it runs along the foot of a hill, so the ground at the stands rail is, for the most part, 5ft higher than that by the inside rail.

It is a run home of just under 4 furlongs that continues to descend until the half furlong where the track again rises slightly until the post.

Epsom also features the world's fastest 5-furlong straight course with the start from a chute perched on a hill adjoining the straight. It is a very steep run downhill until linking up with the straight on the course proper, enabling blistering times to be set. Separate chutes are also used for the 6-furlong and 7-furlong starts, both of which join the course proper on the run down to Tattenham Corner.

The camber of the straight means rainwater runs quickly towards the inside of the track so riders tend to steer well towards the stands rail when the ground is soft.

| FEATURE RACES | | | | | | | |
|---|---|---|---|---|---|---|---|
| THE DERBY | G1 | 1M4F10Y | TURF | 3YOC&F | SW | 1780 | JUNE |
| THE OAKS | G1 | 1M4F10Y | TURF | 3YOF | SW | 1779 | JUNE |
| CORONATION CUP | G1 | 1M4F10Y | TURF | 4YO+ | WFA | 1902 | JUNE |

## FEATURE RACES

### THE DERBY

It is racing folklore that a toss of a coin between Lord Derby and Sir Charles Bunbury in 1779 decided the name for a new race for 3yos. Neither could have known that they were tossing for the honour of the world's most famous race or that the winner's name would become permanently and indelibly synonymous with Classic racing the world over. Though Bunbury lost the toss, his horse Diomed won the inaugural running, staged over a mile.

Notable winners include **SERJEANT (1784)**, who won the first running at the now classic mile and a half distance; **CHAMPION (1800)** was the first horse to win The Derby and the St Leger; **ELEANOR (1801)** also owned by Bunbury, became the first filly to win The Derby and The Oaks; **WHALEBONE (1810)**; Bunbury's **SMOLENSKO (1813)** became the first to claim the 2000 Guineas–Derby double; **MIDDLETON (1825)** also won The Derby at his only start.

Eternally linked legends **THE FLYING DUTCHMAN (1849)** and **VOLTIGEUR (1850)**; **WEST AUSTRALIAN (1853)** was the first horse to win the 2000 Guineas, Derby and St Leger – now known as the Triple Crown – **GLADIATEUR (1865)**

became the second Triple Crown winner and the first French-bred horse to do so.

**ORMONDE (1856)** was undefeated in his 16-start career, which included the Triple Crown. He could win at any distance. Having captured the Dewhurst over 7 furlongs as a 2yo, he returned after his triumphant 3yo campaign to make all in the July Cup. One of the all-time greats of the turf.

**BLINK BONNY (1857)**; **THORMANBY (1860)**; **CREMORNE (1872)**; **GALOPIN (1875)**; **BEND OR (1880)**; **ISINGLASS (1893)**; **LADAS (1894)** for Lord Roseberry, making him the first prime minister to win The Derby; **PERSIMMON (1896)**, owned by the Prince of Wales, later King Edward VII, who would win it twice more with **DIAMOND JUBILEE (1900)** and as King with **MINORU (1909)**.

The 100 to 1 outsider **SIGNORINETTA (1908)** became the third filly to take the Derby–Oaks double; **CORONACH (1926)**; **BLENHEIM (1930)**; **HYPERION (1933)**; **BAHRAM (1935)**; **TULYAR (1952)**; **NEVER SAY DIE (1954)**; **ST PADDY (1960)**; **RELKO (1962)**; **SEA BIRD (1965)** was one of the greatest racehorses of the 20th century. His 6-length win in the Arc as a 3yo propelled his annual Timeform rating to a record 145 in 1965. This remained the highest ever awarded until the win of Frankel in the Queen Anne Stakes at Ascot in 2012 earned that horse a rating of 147. **SIR IVOR (1968)**

had a stellar season, also winning the 2000 Guineas, Champion Stakes and the Washington DC International. He would have a successful stud career in the USA.

The start of the 1970s heralded a golden era beginning with **NIJINSKY (1970)**, **MILL REEF (1971)** and **ROBERTO (1972)** – each among the all-time greats and enormous influences on the breeding landscape. Vincent O'Brien had travelled to America on behalf of a client to inspect a horse which had left him unimpressed. However, as the story often goes, he was taken with a horse in an adjoining paddock which he considered to be a nice mover. The horse was Nijinsky, who earned British Horse of the Year honours in 1970 for winning the Triple Crown, the Irish Derby and beating the older horses in the King George VI & Queen Elizabeth Stakes. His arrival in Europe from America shone the spotlight on the Northern Dancer line now so dominant in the breeding world. Mill Reef won 12 of his 14 starts. As a 3yo he won The Derby, Eclipse, King Edward VI & Queen Elizabeth Stakes, and the Arc. One of his only two defeats – both seconds – was at the hands of the legendary Brigadier Gerard in the 2000 Guineas. Roberto, along with his win in this race, is best remembered for defeating Brigadier Gerard, previously unbeaten at all 15 starts, in the International Stakes at York in 1972. **THE MINSTREL (1977)** for Robert Sangster, sire of Palace Music, in turn sire

The Derby

of Cigar; **TROY (1979)** is considered one of the great winners, having streeted a top field by 7 lengths; **SHERGAR (1981)** was a headline horse all the way from his record 10-length Derby win, and victories in the Irish Derby and King George VI & Queen Elizabeth Stakes to his subsequent disappearance, which remains a matter of intrigue.

**LAMMTARRA (1994)** had a remarkable unde-feated 4-start career, which included The Derby, the Arc and the King George VI & Queen Elizabeth Stakes; **GALILEO (2001)**, out of Arc-winning mare Urban Sea, also claimed victory in the Irish Derby, King George VI & Queen Elizabeth Stakes (2001) and is the sire of Frankel; **HIGH CHAPARRAL (2002)**; **NEW APPROACH (2008)**.

**SEA THE STARS (2009)**, also out of Urban Sea, captured the imagination of the press and the public in his remarkable 2009 campaign when he also won the 2000 Guineas, Eclipse Stakes, International Stakes, Irish Champion Stakes and the Arc.

Lester Piggott rode the winner on nine occasions.

## THE OAKS

The inaugural winner was **BRIDGET (1779)**, owned by Lord Derby. After **ELEANOR (1801)**, **BLINK BONNY (1857)** became only the second filly to win the Derby–Oaks double. **FORMOSA (1868)** took the 1000 Guineas, 2000 Guineas, The Oaks and St Leger to become the first fillies' Triple Crown winner and the first horse to win four Classic races. **LA FLECHE (1891)** was a top filly who won 16 of her 24 starts, including the fillies' Triple Crown, the Ascot Gold Cup and the Coronation Stakes in 1894. **SCEPTRE (1902)** followed in the footsteps of Formosa by winning the same four Classics. She also ran second in The Derby. **PRETTY POLLY (1904)**; **SAUCY SUE (1925)**; **QUASHED (1935)** won the Ascot Gold Cup; **SUN CHARIOT (1942)**.

**MELD (1955)** was a Triple Crown winner who became a top broodmare and producer whose progeny included Derby winner Charlottown (1966), Lysander II and Mellay.

**PETITE ETOILE (1959)** was named British Horse of the Year; **SNOW BRIDE (1989)**, dam of Lammtarra, was awarded the race after the disqual-ification of the Aga Khan's horse Aliysa; **USER FRIENDLY (1992)** en route to being crowned Euro-pean Horse of the Year; **OUIJA BOARD (2004)**; and **SNOW FAIRY (2010)** was also a Group 1 winner in Ireland, Japan, Hong Kong and France.

## CORONATION CUP

The Coronation Cup was inaugurated in 1902 to mark the coronation of King Edward VII. It is a weight-for-age race for 4yos and up, run over the Derby distance.

Watching Hyperion, 1933

The Derby, 1931

Tattenham Corner, 1935

**PRETTY POLLY (1905, 06)** was the first horse to win it twice, a feat repeated by **WHITE KNIGHT (1907, 08)**.

**LEMBERG (1911)** had 24 starts for 17 wins. He was a dual Group 1 winner as a 2yo, and his 3yo wins included The Derby, Eclipse Stakes, St James's Palace Stakes (1910) and two Champion Stakes (1910, 11).

**PRINCE PALATINE (1913)** was a two-time British Horse of the Year (1912, 13).

**POMMERN (1916)** had won the Triple Crown the year before; **SOLARIO (1926)** would go on to sire two Derby winners in Mid-day Sun (1937) and Straight Deal (1943); **CORONACH (1927)** also won The Derby and St Leger; **REIGH COUNT (1929)** achieved a unique double following his triumph in the Kentucky Derby of 1928; **WINDSOR LAD (1935)** won The Derby and St Leger in 1934; **ARDAN (1946)** was a champion French horse who won 16 races from 23 starts including the Prix du Jockey Club and the Arc.

**TANTIEME (1951)** was a dual Arc winner (1950, 51) and twice leading sire in France; Her Majesty's **AUREOLE (1954)** went on to become a successful sire.

**BALLYMOSS (1958)**, trained by Vincent O'Brien, also won the Arc that year and retired as all-time leading money winner in Britain and Ireland, where he was commemorated on a postage stamp. He also won the St Leger, Irish Derby (1957), Eclipse Stakes and King George VI & Queen Elizabeth Stakes (1958).

**PETITE ETOILE (1960, 61)** also won the Oaks; **EXBURY (1963)** won the Arc; **RELKO (1964)**, **CHARLOTTOWN (1967)** and **ROYAL PALACE (1968)** all took out the Derby; **LUPE (1971)** followed up her win in The Oaks the previous season; **MILL REEF (1972)**; **ROBERTO (1973)**.

**EXCELLER (1977)** is a US Hall of Famer who won the Grand Prix de Paris (1976), Canadian Inter-national (1977), Hollywood Gold Cup (1978) and the Jockey Club Gold Cup of 1978, where he defeated Triple Crown winners Seattle Slew and Affirmed.

**RAINBOW QUEST (1985)** also won the Arc; **TRIPTYCH (1987, 88)** made it back-to-back victories. and was also a dual winner of the Cham-pion Stakes. **IN THE WINGS (1990)** also won the Breeders' Cup Turf (1990) and would sire champion **SINGSPIEL (1997)**, winner of the Canadian Inter-national, Japan Cup (1996), Dubai World Cup, Interna-tional Stakes (1997). **DAYLAMI (1999)** captured the race on his way to being European Horse of the Year and also took the Breeders Cup Turf that year. **YEATS (2005)**; **SHIROCCO (2006)** was a winner of the Deutsches Derby (2004) and Breeders' Cup Turf (2005); **FAME AND GLORY (2010)** won the Ascot Gold Cup the following year; **ST NICHOLAS ABBEY** won it three times (2011–13) and won the Breeders' Cup Turf (2011) and Dubai Sheema Classic (2013).

Lester Piggott won the race nine times, first with **ZUCCHERO (1953)** and finally with **BE MY NATIVE (1983)**.

# NEWMARKET

Westfield House, The Links, Newmarket, England, UK. www.newmarketracecourses.co.uk

*I*n *the early 17th century, King James I attended the Newmarket course for the first time and set it on its path as the major centre for racing. Newmarket has received the benefit of royal patronage ever since.*

King Charles II is listed as winning the prestigious Newmarket Town Plate as a rider on two occasions in the mid 1660s, and remains the only monarch to have ridden a winner on the Flat. It is a record that may stand a while.

Queen Anne rebuilt her house here and when the Jockey Club made Newmarket its permanent base in 1751, its status as the home of British racing was assured for all time.

Newmarket is also England's largest training centre with more than 3000 horses in work under the care of some of racing's leading trainers.

Newmarket contains two tracks.

## THE TRACKS

### ROWLEY MILE COURSE

The Rowley Mile is actually a straight course of a mile and a quarter. It is an extremely wide, enormously expansive course that can leave horses harshly exposed to the elements when conditions are inclement.

It has to be said that it was laid out specifically as a test of the horse rather than with spectator comfort in mind, although exactly what spectator comfort entailed in the early 17th century is unclear. But several millions have been spent in recent years to remedy the problem and upgrade facilities at both tracks.

The track is mainly flat until 'The Bushes' 2 furlongs out where the ground dips for a furlong before a stiff uphill rise for the last furlong home. A unique feature is the parallel strip of track that runs directly along the inside of the course proper that, in days of

## FEATURE RACES

### ROWLEY MILE COURSE

| | | | | | | | |
|---|---|---|---|---|---|---|---|
| **1000 GUINEAS** | G1 | 1M | TURF | 3YOF | SW | 1814 | APR–MAY |
| **2000 GUINEAS** | G1 | 1M | TURF | 3YOC&F | SW | 1809 | APR–MAY |
| **CHEVELEY PARK STAKES** | G1 | 6F | TURF | 2YOF | SW | 1899 | SEPT |
| **DEWHURST STAKES** | G1 | 7F | TURF | 2YOC&F | SW | 1875 | OCT |
| **FILLIES' MILE** | G1 | 1M | TURF | 2YOF | SW | 1973 | SEPT |
| **MIDDLE PARK STAKES** | G1 | 6F | TURF | 2YOC | SW | 1866 | OCT |
| **SUN CHARIOT STAKES** | G1 | 1M | TURF | 3YO+F&M | SW | 1966 | SEPT |
| CHALLENGE STAKES | G2 | 7F | TURF | 3YO+ | SWP | 1878 | OCT |
| JOCKEY CLUB STAKES | G2 | 1M4F | TURF RH | 4YO+ | SWP | 1894 | APR–MAY |
| ROYAL LODGE STAKES | G2 | 1M | TURF | 2YOC&G | SWP | 1946 | SEPT |
| Cambridgeshire Hcp | HCP | 9F | TURF | 3YO+ | HCP | 1839 | SEPT |
| Cesarewitch Hcp | HCP | 2M2F | TURF RH | 3YO+ | HCP | 1839 | OCT |

### JULY COURSE

| | | | | | | | |
|---|---|---|---|---|---|---|---|
| **FALMOUTH STAKES** | G1 | 1M | TURF | 3YO+F&M | SW | 1911 | JUL |
| **JULY CUP** | G1 | 6F | TURF | 3YO+ | WFA | 1876 | JUL |
| CHERRY HINTON STAKES | G2 | 6F | TURF | 2YOF | SWP | 1947 | JUL |
| JULY STAKES | G2 | 6F | TURF | 2YOC&G | SWP | 1786 | JUL |
| PRINCESS OF WALES'S STAKES | G2 | 1M4F | TURF RH | 3YO+ | SWP | 1894 | JUL |
| SUPERLATIVE STAKES | G2 | 7F | TURF | 2YO | SWP | 1986 | JUL |

At the gallops, Newmarket

yore, provided a spectacular sight as mounted spectators, connections, officials and carriages galloped in alongside the racers to the winning post.

In its entirety, the Newmarket course is an irregular Y-shape configuration. Races longer than 10 furlongs take in the adjoining tail of the Y. Though rarely used, the optimum distance is 2½ miles, providing a straight run of a mile before a very sharp right-hand bend into the straight.

The Cesarewitch is run over a distance of 2¼ miles, so the race starts in Cambridgeshire and finishes in Sussex.

## JULY COURSE

Though it is adjacent to the Rowley Course, the July Course is an entirely different environment with lots of trees and leafy areas sheltering the paddock and surrounds. The beautiful old thatched-roof grandstands, restored at great cost, give the July meeting a delightful garden-party atmosphere with

patrons suitably attired for such an occasion.

The straight course is a mile long. From the 6-furlong mark the ground descends gradually until the final furlong, where it rises sharply to the post.

For races longer than 1 mile, the start is situated around the bend, catering for races up to 2 miles. This allows for a run of a mile until a sharp right-hand turn, similar to that of the Rowley Mile, is encountered 1 mile from home.

## FEATURE RACES

### ROWLEY COURSE

#### 1000 GUINEAS

Notable winners include **CHARLOTTE (1814)**, the inaugural winner; **CRUCIFIX (1840)** also took out the 2000 Guineas and The Oaks; **VIRAGO (1854)** won 10 of her 11 starts as a 3yo filly, including the Goodwood Cup and the Doncaster Cup; **ACHIEVE-MENT (1867)** also won the Coronation Stakes and the St Leger in the same year; **FORMOSA (1868)**; **APOLOGY (1874)** won the Triple Crown and

the Ascot Gold Cup; Oaks winner **WHEEL OF FORTUNE (1879)** had 11 starts for 10 wins; **LA FLECHE (1892)**; **SCEPTRE (1902)**; **PRETTY POLLY (1904)**; **TAGALIE (1912)** won The Derby; **SAUCY SUE (1925)**; **SUN CHARIOT (1942)**; **MELD (1955)**; **BELLA PAOLA (1958)** also won The Oaks, Prix Vermeille and Champion Stakes; **PETITE ETOILE (1959)**; **HULA DANCER (1963)** also won the Champion Stakes as well as four Group 1s in France. **HIGHCLERE (1974)** was owned by Queen Elizabeth II.

**PEBBLES (1984)** became the first British-trained winner of a Breeders' Cup race when she claimed the Breeders' Cup Turf in 1985; **OH SO SHARP (1985)** was the first Classic winner for Sheik Mohammed and went on to take out the fillies' Triple Crown. Champion French filly **MIESQUE (1987)** became the first horse to win two Breeders' Cup races with consecutive victories in the Breeders' Cup Mile (1987, 88); **KAZZIA (2002)** also won The Oaks and the Flower Bowl Invitational at Belmont, dam of Dubai Sheema Classic winner Eastern Anthem.

#### 2000 GUINEAS

The 2000 Guineas is the first leg of the English Triple Crown for 3yos. It is run over a mile. The Derby and the St Leger make up the remaining legs.

Fifteen horses have won the Triple Crown. **WEST**

Uphill finish, Newmarket

AUSTRALIAN (1853), GLADIATEUR (1863), LORD LYON (1866), ORMONDE (1886), COMMON (1891), ISINGLASS (1893), GALTEE MORE (1897), FLYING FOX (1899), DIAMOND JUBILEE (1900), ROCK SAND (1903), POMMERN (1915), GAY CRUSADER (1917), GAINSBOROUGH (1918), BAHRAM (1935) and NIJINSKY (1970).

Those to complete the 2000 Guineas Derby double include CADLAND (1828), BAY MIDDLETON (1836), COTHERSTONE (1843), MACARONI (1863), SHOTOVER (1882), AYRSHIRE (1888), LADAS (1894), ST AMANT (1903), MINORU (1909), SUNSTAR (1911), MANNA (1925), CAMERONIAN (1931), BLUE PETER (1939), NIMBUS (1949), CREPELLO (1957), ROYAL PALACE (1967), SIR IVOR (1968), NASHWAN (1989), SEA THE STARS (2009), and CAMELOT (2012).

Other notable winners include inaugural winner WIZARD (1809); SMOLENSKO (1813); seven-time leading sire in Germany CHAMANT (1877); ST FRUSQUIN (1896) was twice leading sire in England; FORMOSA (1868); SCEPTRE (1902); DJEBEL (1940) won the Arc (1942) and went on to be leading sire in France on four occasions; BIG GAME (1942), owned by King George II; TUDOR MINSTREL (1947) was ranked equal second alongside Brigadier Gerard and only 1 point behind Sea Bird in Timeform's

assessment of the greatest European horses of the 20th century; DANCING BRAVE (1986) won the Arc and the Eclipse in the same year; ROCK OF GIBRALTAR (2002), in the colours of Sir Alex Ferguson; and FRANKEL (2011).

## CHEVELEY PARK STAKES

Named after the Cheveley Park estate, it is a 6-furlong race for 2yo fillies. It has been won by a number of horses that went on to win the 1000 Guineas, including HUMBLE DUTY (1969), SAYYEDATI (1992), NATAGORA (2007) and SPECIAL DUTY (2009).

Other notable winners include LUTETIA (1899) who won the inaugural running; champion PRETTY POLLY (1903); FIFINELLA (1915) won The Derby and The Oaks in 1916, both held at Newmarket; and TIFFIN (1928) was unbeaten at all eight runs and won a July Cup (1929).

## DEWHURST STAKES

The Dewhurst is a 7-furlong event for 2yos that has announced the arrival of many coming Classic winners.

Several have progressed to win The Derby, including KISBER (1875); DONOVAN (1888), who also won the St Leger; LEMBERG (1909); HYPERION (1932); PINZA (1952); CREPELLO (1956);

GRUNDY (1974); THE MINSTREL (1976); GENEROUS (1990); DR DEVIOUS (1991); SIR PERCY (2005) and NEW APPROACH (2007). Those to have won the 2000 Guineas as well include CHAMANT (1876), Grand Prix de Paris winner PARADOX (1884), ST FRUSQUIN (1895), WOLLOW (1975), EL GRAN SENOR (1973) and ROCK OF GIBRALTAR (2001).

Other notables include champions ORMONDE (1885), ROCK SAND (1902), NIJINSKY (1969), MILL REEF (1970); FRANKEL (2010); WHEEL OF FORTUNE (1878); ORME (1891) won 14 of 18 starts and sired Triple Crown winner Flying Fox.

BAYARDO (1908) won 22 from 25 starts, including the Middle Park Stakes, Dewhurst Stakes (1908), Prince of Wales's Stakes, Eclipse Stakes, Champion Stakes, St Leger (1909) and Ascot Gold Cup (1910). MIGOLI (1946) went on to win the Arc (1948), and SHAMARDAL (2004) won the Prix du Jockey Club the same year.

## FILLIES' MILE

The Fillies' Mile was transferred from Ascot in 2011. Established in 1973 and upgraded to Group 1 level in 1990, the race got off to a flying start when Queen Elizabeth II's ESCORIAL won the first edition.

Since then notables include fillies' Triple Crown winner OH SO SHARP (1984) BOSRA SHAM

**(1995)**, who won the 1000 Guineas, Champion Stakes (1996); Oaks winner **REAMS OF VERSE (1996)**; and top filly **SOVIET SONG (2002)**.

## MIDDLE PARK STAKES

The Middle Park Stakes is a historic 2yo race over 6 furlongs.

**THE RAKE (1866)** took out the inaugural running, and the race's honour roll is littered with champions including **ORME (1891)**, **ISINGLASS (1892)**, **LADAS (1893)**, **ST FRUSQUIN (1895)**, **GALTEE MORE (1896)**, **PRETTY POLLY (1903)**, **BAYARDO (1908)**, **LEMBERG (1909)**, **BAHRAM (1934)**, **DJEBEL (1939)**, **SUN CHARIOT (1941)**, and **BRIGADIER GERARD (1970)**.

**TETRATEMA (1919)**; **ORWELL (1931)**; **OUR BABU (1954)**; **RIGHT TACK (1968)**; **KNOWN FACT (1979)**; and **RODRIGO DE TRIANO (1991)** would all win the 2000 Guineas; **CALL BOY (1926)** and **DANTE (1944)** both won The Derby; **PETRARCH (1875)** won the 2000 Guineas, St Leger (1876) and Ascot Gold Cup (1877); **BUSYBODY (1883)** won the 1000 Guineas and The Oaks 1884; **MELTON (1884)** won The Derby, St Leger (1885) and the Ascot Gold Cup (1886); **MINTING (1885)** also took out the Grand Prix de Paris that same year. **ABERNANT (1948)** was arguably the greatest British sprinter of the 20th century, winning both the July Cup and the Nunthorpe in 1949 and 1950 as well as two King George Stakes and a King's Stand Stakes in a 17-start career yielding 14 wins.

**JOHANNESBURG (2001)** was also successful in the Breeders' Cup Juvenile.

Other winners notable in the breeding barn include **CHAMANT (1876)**, **PHARAMOND (1927)**, **KHALED (1945)**, **DIESIS (1982)**, **ROYAL APPLAUSE (1995)** and **OASIS DREAM (2002)**.

## SUN CHARIOT STAKES

Sun Chariot

In a 9-start career that produced eight wins, Sun Chariot won the fillies' Triple Crown in 1942, defeating Derby-winner Watling Street in the St Leger. This is a mile race for fillies and mares.

Winners include **POPKINS (1970)**, dam of Cherry Hinton; **TIME CHARTER (1982)** followed up her Oaks win; and **INDIAN SKIMMER (1988)** won three Group 1s in France including the Prix de

Diane. In addition she won the Champion Stakes and the Irish Champion Stakes; **ATTRACTION (2004)** won the 1000 Guineas; **FREE GUEST (1984, 85)** won it twice; and **SAHPRESA (2009–11)** made it a hat-trick.

## CAMBRIDGESHIRE HANDICAP

Established in 1839, the Cambridgeshire forms the first leg of the autumn handicap double. The Cesarewitch, also established in 1839, forms the second leg.

Notable winners include **ROSEBERRY (1876)**, the first horse to claim the Cambridgeshire–Cesarewitch double.

Great champion **ISONOMY (1878)** won the Goodwood Cup, Ebor Hcp (1879), two Ascot Gold Cups (1879, 80) and was sire of Triple Crown winners Isinglass and Common. **FOXHALL (1881)** also won the Cesarewitch, Grand Prix de Paris (1881) and Ascot Gold Cup (1882).

Champion French filly **PLAISENTERIE (1888)** took out the Cambridgeshire–Cesarewitch double; **LA FLECHE (1892)**; **POLYMELUS (1906)** went on to become a great sire of Classic winners including Triple Crown winner Pommern and Fifinella; **HALLING (1994)** was a dual winner of both the Eclipse Stakes and the International Stakes.

Six horses have been victorious twice: **HACKLER'S PRIDE (1903, 04)**, **CHRISTMAS DAISY (1909, 10)**, **SHEROPE (1948, 49)**, **PRINCE DE GALLES (1969, 70)**, **BARONET (1978, 80)** and **RAMBO'S HALL (1989, 92)**.

## CESAREWITCH HANDICAP

Notable winners include **FAUGH – A – BALLAGH (1844)** and **THE BARON (1845)**, who both earlier took out the St Leger.

**ROBERT THE DEVIL (1880)** won the Grand Prix de Paris, St Leger (1880), Champion Stakes (1881), Ascot Gold Cup (1882); **ST GATIEN (1884)** would win The Derby (1884), Ascot Gold Cup (1885) and three Jockey Club Gold Cups (1884–86); **SON-IN-LAW (1915)** won two Jockey Club Gold Cups (1914, 15); **VINTAGE CROP (1992)** won the Melbourne Cup (1993), Irish St Leger twice (1993, 94). **DETROIT CITY (2006)** won two Grade 1 hurdles.

## JULY COURSE

### JULY CUP

The July Cup is the oldest of Britain's famous sprint races and always has a major influence in deciding best European sprinter. **SPRINGFIELD (1876, 77)** bred by Queen Victoria, won the first two editions.

**TRISTAN (1882)** was a remarkable horse. A

winner of 27 races from 51 starts, he had the speed to win the July Cup and the following year won the Ascot Gold Cup (1883). He also won the Champion Stakes three times (18824) and the Coronation Cup twice (1882, 83).

Other notable winners include **MELTON (1886)**; **ORMONDE (1887)**; **SUNRIDGE (1903–05)** won it three times in succession and was a dual winner of the King's Stand (1903, 04).

Back-to-back winners include **SPANISH PRINCE (1912, 13)**; **DIADEM (1919, 20)**; **ABERNANT (1949, 50)**; and **RIGHT BOY (1958, 59)**, who would also win two Nunthorpes (1958, 59) and two Diamond Jubilee Stakes (1958, 59).

**THATCH (1973)**; **MOORESTYLE (1980)**; **SHARPO (1982)** also won the Nunthorpe three times in succession (1980–82); and mighty 3yo filly **HABIBTI (1983)** beat the older horses four times in a row in major Group 1 sprint races – the July Cup, Nunthorpe Stakes, Sprint Cup and Prix de l'Abbaye – to claim European Horse of the Year in 1983. An outstanding achievement for a 3yo filly, let alone a sprinter.

**ROYAL ACADEMY (1990)** won a Breeders' Cup Mile and is grandsire of Black Caviar; 3yo colt **SAKHEE'S SECRET (2007)**; **MARCHAND D'OR (2008)**; **STARSPANGLEDBANNER (2010)** arrived from Australia having won the Oakleigh Plate and Caulfield Guineas and claimed the Golden Jubilee as well. Lester Piggott rode the winner on ten occasions.

## FALMOUTH STAKES

Named after prominent 19th-century owner and breeder the 6th Viscount Falmouth, the Falmouth Stakes mile race for fillies and mares was established in 1911 and upgraded to Group 1 status in 2004.

**SOVIET SONG** won the first two editions at Group 1 level and star mare **GOLDIKOVA** won in 2009. The 1984 Breeders' Cup Mile winner **ROYAL HEROINE** won the race in 1983.

# ASCOT

Ascot, Berkshire, England, UK. www.ascot.co.uk

*Queen Anne was renowned as a keen devotee of all things equine, in particular hunting and racing. It was at her behest that the course was laid out on Ascot Heath in 1711 and her patronage of the meeting gave it instant popularity and prestige. To this day it is the only course owned by the Crown and it is the continued presence and support of the Royal Family that makes Royal Ascot unique and special.*

The Royal Procession was founded by the 'First Gentleman of Europe', later King George IV, around 1820. Wooden posts at the course entrance were replaced by the Golden Gates in 1878. The daily arrival of the Queen and her entourage, which makes its way down the home straight by horse-drawn carriage, remains a highlight. Guests invited to the royal enclosure must adhere to a strict dress code of black or grey morning suits with top hats for the gentlemen and brimmed hats for the ladies.

Up until the 1960s divorcees were forbidden.

The royal meeting now takes place over five days.

## THE TRACK

Ascot is a very undulating, triangularshaped, right-handed course with a circumference of 1m6f34yds.

From the judge it is a very sharp right-hand turn out of the straight before a downhill run to the mile where the track levels out for the right-hand bend. Then it is a straight uphill run of about 3 furlongs before the right-hand bend into the uphill straight of just under 3 furlongs, considered to be a short run home in this part of the world.

Races of up to a mile are run on a very wide, expansive straight course that is uphill and rises steadily the whole way except for slight dips for the first furlong and between the 5- and 4-furlong marks. The sheer width of the track can often see fields break up into three or four divisions.

The second or 'old mile' start is on the round course. Starting at Swinley Bottom, it is a straight uphill run of 5 furlongs before the bend into the home straight.

## FEATURE RACES

| | | | | | | | |
|---|---|---|---|---|---|---|---|
| QUEEN ANNE STAKES | G1 | 1M | TURF | 4YO+ | SW | 1840 | JUN |
| KING'S STAND STAKES | G1 | 5F | TURF | 3YO+ | SW | 1860 | JUN |
| ST JAMES'S PALACE STAKES | G1 | 1M | TURF | 3YOC | SW | 1834 | JUN |
| PRINCE OF WALES'S STAKES | G1 | 1M2F | TURF | 4YO+ | SW | 1862 | JUN |
| ASCOT GOLD CUP | G1 | 2M4F | TURF | 4YO+ | SW | 1802 | JUN |
| CORONATION STAKES | G1 | 1M | TURF | 3YOF | SW | 1840 | JUN |
| DIAMOND JUBILEE STAKES | G1 | 6F | TURF | 3YO+ | SW | 1868 | JUN |
| KING GEORGE VI & QUEEN ELIZABETH STAKES | G1 | 1M4F | TURF | 3YO+ | SW | 1951 | JUL |
| CHAMPION STAKES | G1 | 1M2F | TURF | 3YO+ | SW | 1877 | OCT |
| QUEEN ELIZABETH II STAKES | G1 | 1M | TURF | 3YO+ | SW | 1955 | OCT |

## ROYAL MEETING

**DAY 1:**
QUEEN ANNE STAKES, KING'S STAND STAKES, ST JAMES'S PALACE STAKES

**DAY 2:**
PRINCE OF WALES'S STAKES

**DAY 3:**
ASCOT GOLD CUP

**DAY 4:**
CORONATION STAKES

**DAY 5:**
DIAMOND JUBILEE STAKES

Ascot

# FEATURE RACES

## QUEEN ANNE STAKES

The Queen Anne Stakes is always run as the first race of the Royal Ascot meeting, in honour of the course's founder. It was upgraded to a Group 1 race in 2003. Since then winners include **REFUSE TO BEND (2004)**, who won the National Stakes (2002), 2000 Guineas (2003) and the Eclipse Stakes (2004); Hong Kong Cup winner of the same year **RAMONTI (2007)**; **GOLDIKOVA (2010)**.

**FRANKEL (2012)** produced a devastating display to crush his rivals by 11 lengths. His undefeated 14-start career left even the most hardened racing cynics in awe. Frankel was barely challenged and dispensed with all opposition in effortless fashion. Winner of the Dewhurst Stakes (2010), 2000 Guineas, St James's Palace Stakes, Queen Elizabeth II Stakes (2011), Lockinge Stakes, Queen Anne Stakes, International Stakes, Champion Stakes (2012).

Earlier winners include **FLAMBEAU (1840, 41)** who won the first two runnings; **WORCESTER (1895, 96)** and **DEAN SWIFT (1906, 07)**,were also dual victors; **WHISK BROOM (1910)**, who later raced in America and became the first horse to win the New York Handicap Triple Crown (1912). Top 3yo **COMRADE (1920)** also won the Grand Prix de Paris and the Arc in 1920.

## KING'S STAND STAKES

Notable winners include **SPRINGFIELD (1877)**, **ABERNANT (1949)**, **RIGHT BOY (1957)**,

GODSWALK (1977) and **HABIBTI (1984)**. Several horses have won it twice: **WOOLTHORPE (1895, 97)**, **KILCOCK (1898, 99)**, **SUNDRIDGE (1903, 04)**, **FORESIGHT (1908, 09)**, **HORNET'S BEAUTY (1911, 13)**, **DIADEM (1919, 20)**, **GOLDEN BOSS (1923, 24)**, **GOLD BRIDGE (1933, 34)**, **ELBIO (1991, 93)** and **EQUIANO (2008, 10)**. **LAST TYCOON (1986)** would also win the Nunthorpe and the Breeders' Cup Mile that season and became a leading sire in Australia. **SHEIK ALBADOU (1992)** followed up his wins in the Nunthorpe and Breeders' Cup Sprint the previous year and would also win the Sprint Cup. **LOCH-SONG (1994)** was European Horse of the Year in 1993. Her 15 career wins included two wins in the Prix de l'Abbaye. **CHOISIR (2003)** led the Aussie invasion, taking the Ascot sprint double with victory in the Golden Jubilee four days later. He was followed by compatriots **TAKEOVER TARGET (2006)**, **MISS ANDRETTI (2007)** and **SCENIC BLAST (2009)**.

## ST JAMES'S PALACE STAKES

Great early winners included **ORMONDE (1886)**, **COMMON (1891)**, **SCEPTRE (1902)**, **ROCK SAND (1903)** and **BAHRAM (1935)**. **RAYON D'OR (1879)** won 17 races including the St Leger (1879) and the Prix du Cadran (1880).

Derby winners include **PLENIPOTENTIARY (1834)**; **DANIEL O'ROURKE (1852)**; **HERMIT (1867)**, who would be leading sire in Great Britain for seven consecutive years between 1880 and 1886; **BEND OR (1880)**; **IROQUOIS (1881)**, who was the first US-bred horse to win The Derby; **MINORU**

(1909); **LEMBERG (1910)**; **GRAND PARADE (1919)**; **CAPTAIN CUTTLE (1922)**; **CORONACH (1926)**; and **CAMERONIAN (1931)**.

2000 Guineas winners include **GANG FORWARD (1873)**, **SLIEVE GALLION (1907)**, **TUDOR MINSTREL (1947)**, **PALESTINE (1950)**, **RIGHT TACK (1969)** and **ROCK OF GIBRALTAR (2002)**.

Others notables include **BRIGADIER GERARD (1971)**, **KRIS (1979)**, **MARJU (1991)**, **GIANT'S CAUSEWAY (2000)**, **SHAMARDAL (2005)** and **FRANKEL (2011)**.

## PRINCE OF WALES'S STAKES

Those to also win The Derby include **IROQUOIS (1881)**, **DONOVAN (1889)**, **GALTEE MORE (1897)**, **JEDDAH (1898)**, **ARD PATRICK (1903)**, **SANSOVINO (1924)**, **HYPERION (1933)** and **ROYAL PALACE (1968)**.

Other notables include **PETRARCH (1876)**, **WHEEL OF FORTUNE (1879)**, **BAYARDO (1909)**; **HELIOPOLIS (1939)** would twice be leading sire in North America; and **BRIGADIER GERARD (1972)**.

Back-to-back winners include **CONNAUGHT (1969, 70)**, **MTOTO (1987, 88)**, who also won the Eclipse in both of those years, and **MUHTARRAM (1994, 95)**.

**BOSRA SHAM (1997)**; **DUBAI MILLENNIUM (2000)**; **FANTASTIC LIGHT (2001)** followed up a year in which he won the Dubai Sheema Classic, Man O'War Stakes at Belmont and the Hong Kong Cup by winning this race as well as the Tattersalls Gold

Cup, Irish Champion Stakes and the Breeders' Cup Turf; **GRANDERA (2002)** would win the Singapore International Cup (2002); **NAYEF (2003)** also won the Dubai Sheema Classic and International Stakes (2002); **OUIJA BOARD (2006)**; German star **MANDURO (2007)** would be the world's top-rated horse that year; Prix du Jockey Club winner **VISION D'ETAT (2009)** won the Hong Kong Cup and the Prix Ganay; and **SO YOU THINK (2012)** was a ten-time Group 1 winner, including two Cox Plates (2009, 10), the Eclipse Stakes (2011), Irish Champion Stakes (2011) and two Tattersalls Gold Cups (2011, 12).

## ASCOT GOLD CUP

Many of the greats of the turf have won the race, including **THE FLYING DUTCHMAN (1850)**, **WEST AUSTRALIAN (1854)**, **GLADIATEUR (1866)**, **APOLOGY (1876)**, **ST SIMON (1884)**, **LA FLECHE (1894)**, **ISINGLASS (1895)**, **BAYARDO (1910)**, **GAY CRUSADER (1917)** and **GAINSBOROUGH (1918)**.

Many Derby winners have been successful: **TEDDINGTON (1853)**, **THORMANBY (1861)**, **BLUE GOWN (1868)**, **CREMORNE (1873)**, **DONCASTER (1875)**, **ST GATIEN (1885)**, **PERSIMMON (1897)**, **SOLARIO (1926)**, **OWEN TUDOR (1942)** and **OCEAN SWELL (1944)**.

The 2000 Guineas winners include **GLENCOE (1835)** and **GREY MOMUS (1838)**.

**BEESWING (1842)** was one of the all-time great mares with 51 wins from 63 starts, including six Newcastle Gold Cups and four Doncaster Cups; **QUASHED (1936)** won the Oaks the previous year; **ALYCIDON (1949)**; **LEVMOSS (1969)** also won that year's Arc. **WESTERNER (2005)** scored consecutive wins in both the Prix du Cadran and the Prix Royal-Oak in 2003 and 2004.

Many have won it twice including **ANTICI-PATION (1816, 19)**, **BIZARRE (1824, 25)**, **TOUCHSTONE (1836, 37)**, **THE EMPEROR (1844, 45)**, **THE HERO (1847, 48)**, **FISHERMAN (1858, 59)**, **ISONOMY (1879, 80)**, **THE WHITE KNIGHT (1907, 08)**, **PRINCE PALATINE (1912, 13)**, **INVERSHIN (1928, 29)**, **TRIMDON (1931, 32)**, **FLYING CHARLIE (1965, 66)**, **LE MOSS (1979, 80)**, **ARDROSS (1981, 82)**, **GILDORAN (1984, 85)**, **SADEEM (1988, 89)**, **DRUM TAPS (1992, 93)**, **KAYF TARA (1998, 2000)** and **ROYAL REBEL (2001, 02)**.

The mighty **SAGARO (1975–77)** won it three times, but nothing can match the deeds of **YEATS (2006–09)**, who recorded four consecutive wins to eclipse all others in the 200-year-old race.

## CORONATION STAKES

The Coronation Stakes is a mile race for 3yo fillies.

Notables include 1000 Guineas winners

Royal procession at Ascot

**ACHIEVEMENT (1867)**, **FESTOON (1954)**, **HUMBLE DUTY (1970)**, **RUSSIAN RHYTHM (2003)**, **ATTRACTION (2004)** and **GHANATI (2009)**.

Great Triple Crown winners include **APOLOGY (1874)**, **PRETTY POLLY (1904)** and **MELD (1955)**; Oaks winner **SAUCY SUE (1925)**; Eclipse winner **KOOYONGA (1991)**; **RIDGEWOOD PEARL (1995)**, who won the Irish 1000 Guineas, Coronation Stakes, Prix de Moulin and the Breeders Cup Mile (1995) to claim European Horse of the Year honours. **BANKS HILL (2001)** also won the Breeders' Cup Filly and Mare Turf (2001) and the Prix Jacques Le Marois (2002).

## DIAMOND JUBILEE STAKES

The Diamond Jubilee has been known by a number other names over the years but has remained a time-honoured sprint race. It was elevated to Group 1 status in 2002 and always attracts a top-class field of international entrants.

Notable winners include **PRINCE CHARLIE (1872–74)**, who recorded the only hat-trick; back-to-back winners **LOWLANDER (1875, 76)**, **HORNET'S BEAUTY (1913, 14)**, **HAMLET (1923, 24)** and **RIGHT BOY (1958, 59)**.

Super sire **DANEHILL (1989)**, **ROYAL APPLAUSE (1997)**, **CHOISIR (2003)**; **CAPE OF GOOD HOPE (2005)** would provide the first winner in the race for Hong Kong on his way to being inaugural winner of the Global Sprint Challenge; **BLACK CAVIAR (2012)**.

A new feature at Ascot has been the establishment of

Champions Day. Partly modelled as England's answer to the Breeders' Cup, it was instituted in 2011 and centred around the Champion Stakes, with the intention to eventually build the meeting into an exclusively Group 1 race card.

On face value it would seem like an interesting choice to run such a card in October when inclement weather is generally the order of the day. Some purists consider it a triumph of marketing over horse sense but organisers were blessed for the inaugural meeting with fine conditions and the appearance of superstar Frankel.

As with any innovation, especially one that breaks with tradition, there are bound to be critics. But the elements aside, based on just the race card alone, there is more than enough fire power to ensure that it will immediately become a meeting of great prestige. And one would expect no less from Ascot.

## CHAMPION STAKES

Notable winners include **SPRINGFIELD (1877)**, **RAYON D'OR (1879)**, **ROBERT THE DEVIL (1880)**, **BEND OR (1881)**, three-time winner **TRISTAN (1882–84)**, **ORMONDE (1886)**, **LA FLECHE (1894)**, **SCEPTRE (1903)**, **PRETTY POLLY (1905)**, **BAYARDO (1909)**, **GAY CRUSADER (1917)**, **CAMERONIAN (1932)**, **PETITE ETOILE (1959)** and **PEBBLES (1985)**.

Dual winners include **VELASQUEZ (1897, 98)**, **LEMBERG (1910, 11)**, **ORPHEUS (1920, 21)**, **FAIRWAY (1928, 29)**, **WYCHWOOD ABBOT (1935, 36)**, **HIPPIUS (1940, 41)**, **DYNAMITER (1951, 52)**, **BRIGADIER GERARD (1971, 72)**,

Frankie Dettori performs his trademark leap from Mark of Esteem on his way to a perfect seven.

Yeats

Brown Jack

TRIPTYCH (1986, 87) and TWICE OVER (2009, 10).

FLARES (1937) won the Ascot Gold Cup (1938); NASRULLAH (1943) would be a five-time champion sire in the USA and sire of the legendary Northern Dancer; MIGOLI (1947) won the Arc.

Oaks winners include BELLA PAOLA (1958) and TIME CHARTER (1982). HULA DANCER (1963) and FLYING WATER (1977) were winners of the 1000 Guineas; PALACE MUSIC (1984), sire of Cigar; HATOOF (1993) won G1 races in four countries including the 1000 Guineas, EP Taylor Stakes, the Prix de l'Opera (1992) and the Beverly D Stakes (1994). PILSUDSKI (1997) won the Breeders' Cup Turf (1996) and the Japan Cup (1997); KALA-NISI (2000) also won the Breeders' Cup Turf (2000); NAYEF (2001) took out the Dubai Sheema Classic (2002); DAVID JUNIOR (2005) won the Dubai Duty Free (2006); PRIDE (2006) won the Hong Kong Cup the same year; and NEW APPROACH (2008) also won The Derby.

## QUEEN ELIZABETH II STAKES

First run in 1955, the race was upgraded to Group 1 status in 1987. Since then it has been won by DUBAI MILLENNIUM (1999) and FRANKEL (2011).

Dual winners include BRIGADIER GERARD (1971, 72) and ROSE BOWL (1975, 76).

The 2000 Guineas winners include KNOWN FACT (1980), SHADEED (1985), MARK OF ESTEEM (1996) and GEORGE WASHINGTON (2006); FALBRAV (2003) was a winner in five countries, taking out the Prix d'Ispahan, Eclipse Stakes, International Stakes, Japan Cup and Hong Kong Cup all in that year; STARCRAFT (2005) won the Australian Derby (2004) and the Prix du Moulin (2005); RAMONTI (2007) also won the Queen Anne Stakes and the Hong Kong Cup (2007); RAVEN'S PASS (2008) also took out the Breeders' Cup Classic Mile (2008).

Willie Carson rode the winner on eight occasions.

## KING GEORGE VI & QUEEN ELIZABETH STAKES

Run over the classic distance of a mile and a half, this is Britain's premier open weight-for-age contest. The history of the race is strewn with Derby winners including TULYAR (1952), PINZA (1953), ROYAL PALACE (1968), NIJINSKY (1970), MILL REEF (1971), THE MINSTREL (1977), TROY (1979), SHERGAR (1981), TEENOSO (1984), REFERENCE POINT (1987), NASHWAN (1989), GENEROUS (1991), LAMTARRA (1995) and GALILEO (2001).

Arc winners to have won the race include RIBOT (1956), BALLYMOSS (1958), MILL REEF (1971),

DANCING BRAVE (1986), noted sire MONTJEU (2000), HURRICANE RUN (2006), DYLAN THOMAS (2007) and DANEDREAM (2012).

Oaks winners include PAWNEESE (1976) and TIME CHARTER (1983).

RIGHT ROYAL (1961) was a five-time Group 1 winner in France; MATCH (1962) won the Washington DC International, RAGUSA (1963) was a winner of the Irish Derby, St Leger (1963) and the Eclipse (1964).

Star mare DAHLIA (1973, 74) was a back-to-back winner and is in the US Hall of Fame, having won the Prix Saint Alary, Irish Oaks (1973), Canadian International (1974), the International Stakes twice (1974, 75), Washington DC International (1975) and the Charles Whittingham Hcp (1976). SWAIN (1997, 98) also won it twice.

The battle virtually all of the way down the home straight between GRUNDY (1975) and Bustino is regarded as an all-time classic. Enhanced by the fact that Dahlia – winner of the previous two editions – was well beaten into third.

Other notable winners include BRIGADIER GERARD (1972); KALAGLOW (1982), who would sire 1994 Melbourne Cup winner Jeune; MTOTO (1988) was twice a winner of both the Eclipse and the Prince of Wales's Stakes (1987, 1988); DAYLAMI (1999); and CONDUIT (2009), who was a dual winner of the Breeders' Cup Turf (2008, 09).

While there have been many great riding achievements at Ascot, none can rival the feat of Frankie Dettori who rode every winner on the seven-race card on 28 September 1996. In doing so he established himself as one of the great riders of all time. His performance that day sent bookies to the wall and many £1 accumulator punters into early retirement.

Dettori's seventh winner, Fujiyama Crest, staved off all rivals for the entire length of the Ascot straight to cap off the remarkable performance. Dettori promptly purchased the horse as a pet to live out its days at his property.

# YORK

York, North Yorkshire, England, UK. www.yorkracecourse.co.uk

*Y*ork is one of the England's most historic racing centres. Events date back to Tudor times when racing was conducted near the city in the Forest of Galtres and evidence exists of a race for a silver bell as long ago as 1530.

Various courses were used in the area over the next two centuries before racing settled at its current home on Knavesmire in 1731, where it would thrive. Knavesmire gained notoriety as a venue for public hangings during this period including, most notably, that of infamous highwayman Dick Turpin in 1739.

During the 18th century the best horses in the surrounding area would gather for the Yorkshire meeting, establishing York as the northern equivalent of Newmarket in the south.

Highlight here is the four-day Ebor Festival in August, which features the International Stakes, Nunthorpe Stakes and Yorkshire Oaks. The Ebor, run on the final day, is the richest staying handicap race in Europe.

The Ebor meeting has an entirely different racing atmosphere to most across England. Yorkshire has a long and proud racing tradition and its inhabitants are knowledgeable racing people. Also a source of pride is the local hospitality with a hard-earned reputation for great food and drink at reasonable prices. The grandstand is an outstanding new facility.

## THE TRACK

York is a left-handed track on a flat piece of land on the Tadcaster Road. It was configured in a rough horseshoe shape until 2005 when it was remodelled to host the Royal Meeting that year while a new grandstand was built at Ascot. In order to stage the Ascot Gold Cup the course was modified and the ends of the track joined to form a circle so that the race could be run over the traditional distance of 2½ miles.

Races up to 6 furlongs are held on the straight course. The 7-furlong start is from a spur that joins the straight course.

The 2-mile start was formerly at the bottom of the course, with a long, straight run of just over 7 furlongs before a left turn and a run of 3 furlongs to the home bend.

The home straight is a run in of about 4 furlongs.

The alterations to the track in 2005 made it possible to run 2-mile races on the new round course.

Due to its proximity to the Ouse River the surrounding water table is very high, so just a small amount of rain can see the track affected quite badly.

| FEATURE RACES | | | | | | | |
|---|---|---|---|---|---|---|---|
| INTERNATIONAL STAKES | G1 | 1M2F88Y | TURF | 3YO+ | SW | 1972 | AUG |
| NUNTHORPE STAKES | G1 | 5F | TURF | 2YO+ | SW | 1922 | AUG |
| YORKSHIRE OAKS | G1 | 1M4F | TURF | 3YO+F&M | SW | 1849 | AUG |
| DANTE STAKES | G2 | 1M2F88Y | TURF | 3YO | SWP | 1958 | MAY |
| DUKE OF YORK STAKES | G2 | 6F | TURF | 3YO+ | SWP | 1968 | MAY |
| GIMCRACK STAKES | G2 | 6F | TURF | 2YO | SWP | 1846 | AUG |
| GREAT VOLTIGEUR STAKES | G2 | 1M4F | TURF | 3YO C&G | SWP | 1950 | AUG |
| LONSDALE CUP | G2 | 2M88Y | TURF | 3YO+ | SWP | 1980 | AUG |
| LOWTHER STAKES | G2 | 6F | TURF | 2YOF | SWP | 1946 | AUG |
| MIDDLETON STAKES | G2 | 1M2F88Y | TURF | 4YO+F&M | SWP | 1988 | MAY |
| YORKSHIRE CUP | G2 | 1M6F | TURF | 4YO+ | SWP | 1927 | MAY |
| YORK STAKES | G2 | 1M2F88Y | TURF | 3YO+ | SWP | 2006 | JULY |
| Ebor hcp | HCP | 14f | TURF | 3YO+ | HCP | 1843 | AUG |

## FEATURE RACES

### EBOR HANDICAP

First run in 1843 notable winners include **THE HERO (1849)** and **ISONOMY (1879)**, who both won dual Ascot Gold Cups; **LILY AGNES (1875)** won 21 races and was the dam of Ormonde; **FLINT JACK (1922, 23)** is the only dual winner.

Legendary **BROWN JACK (1931)** won a staggering six Queen Alexandra Stakes at Ascot (1929–34), the Goodwood Cup, Doncaster Cup (1930) and Chester Cup (1931) as well as a Champion Hurdle (1928).

The great hurdler **SEA PIGEON (1979)**, twice won the Fighting Fifth Hurdle (1978, 80) and the Champion Hurdle (1980, 81) as well as two Chester Cups (1977, 78); **JUPITER ISLAND (1983)** made it a record five wins for Lester Piggott and took out the Japan Cup (1986); **FURTHER FLIGHT (1990)**, five-time winner of the Jockey Club Cup, now the British Champions Long Distance Cup (Group 3, 2 miles) then run at Newmarket (1991–95); **SERGEANT CECIL (2005)**; and **ALL THE GOOD (2008)**, who provided the Godolphin stable with its first major Australian winner when it took out the Caulfield Cup (2008).

### INTERNATIONAL STAKES

First run in 1972 and also known as the Juddmonte International, the International Stakes quickly forged a history as a race for champions.

Three horses have won the race twice: **DAHLIA (1974, 75)**, **EZZOUD (1993, 94)** and **HALLING (1995, 96)**.

Other notable winners include **ROBERTO (1972)**; **WOLLOW (1976)**, who also won the 2000 Guineas and the Eclipse (1976); **TROY (1979)**; **ASSERT (1982)** won the Prix du Jockey Club, Irish Derby and Irish Champion Stakes that year; leading sire **CAER-LEON (1983)**; **TRIPTYCH (1987)**; **RODRIGO DE TRIANO (1992)**; **SINGSPIEL (1997)**; **ROYAL ANTHEM (1999)**, who won the Canadian International (1998) and Gulfstream Park Turf Hcp (2000); **GIANT'S CAUSEWAY (2000)**; **SAHKEE (2001)**; **NAYEF (2002)**; **FALBRAV (2003)**; **SULAMANI (2004)** also won the Prix du Jockey Club (2002), Dubai Sheema Classic, Arlington Million (2003) and the Canadian International (2004); **ELECTROCU-TIONIST (2005)**; **AUTHORIZED (2007)**; **SEA THE STARS (2009)** and **FRANKEL (2012)**.

### NUNTHORPE STAKES

One of Britain's top sprint races, staged on the straight 5-furlong course. Two horses have won the race three times: **TAG END (1928–30)** and **SHARPO (1980–82)**.

Dual winners include **HIGHBORN (1926, 27)**, **LINKLATER (1942, 43)**, **ABERNANT (1949, 50)**, **ROYAL SERENADE (1951, 52)**, **RIGHT BOY (1958, 59)** and **BORDERLESCOTT (2008, 09)**.

Other top sprinters include **MUMTAZ MAHAL (1924)**, grand dam of Nasrullah; **AHONOORA (1979)**; **HABIBTI (1983)**; **LAST TYCOON (1986)**, **DAYJUR (1990)**, winner of the King's Stand, Sprint Cup and Prix de l'Abbaye that season; **SHEIK ALBADOU (1991)**; **LOCHSONG (1993)**, **PIVOTAL (1993)** and **ORTENSIA (2012)**.

### YORKSHIRE OAKS

First run in 1849, early winners include **VIRAGO (1854)**, who won 10 of 11 starts as a 3yo filly, taking the 1000 Guineas, Goodwood Cup, Doncaster Cup, and the Nassau Stakes; **JANETTE (1878)**, who won 17 from 23 starts, with victory also in The Oaks, St Leger and Champion Stakes that season. Other Oaks

Frankel blitzes his rivals in the International Stakes

Frankel returns to scale

winners include **WHEEL OF FORTUNE (1879)**, **PETITE ETOILE (1959)**, **LUPE (1970)**, **MYSTERIOUS (1973)**, **SUN PRINCESS (1983)**, **USER FRIENDLY (1992)**, **RAMRUMA (1999)** and **ALEXANDROVA (2006)**. **DAR RE MI (2009)** won a Dubai Sheema Classic (2010); **MIDDAY (2010)** made it a record hat-trick of wins in the Nassau Stakes (2009–11) and also won the Breeders' Cup Filly and Mare Turf (2009) and the Prix Vermeille (2010).

## GIMCRACK STAKES

Named after the mighty Gimcrack, a tiny grey who won 27 of his 36 starts over a seven-year period beginning in the mid 1760s, and a very much beloved horse of the era. He also loans his name to the Gimcrack Club. Famous for its speeches, it is an ancient club of eminent Yorkshire racing men formed in 1767.

Established in 1846, the race is over 6 furlongs for 2yo colts and geldings. Currently rated at Group 2, it is a famous race and local authorities are lobbying strongly for an upgrade to the elite level.

Notable winners include **BLINK BONNY (1856)**, **SPRINGFIELD (1875)**, **BAHRAM (1934)**, **BLACK TARQUIN (1947)**, **MILL REEF (1970)**, **TURTLE ISLAND (1993)**, **ROYAL APPLAUSE (1995)** and **ROCK OF GIBRALTAR (2001)**.

History records that Gimcrack did not win a race at York.

## THE GREAT MATCH

Yorkshire-bred and trained The Flying Dutchman was the dominant horse of his era with an unbeaten record of 13 starts including the Derby and St Leger the previous year. When he went to post for the Doncaster Cup of 1850 there was only one rival in opposition. Three-year-old Voltigeur, also bred and trained in Yorkshire and a winner of the 1850 Derby and St Leger.

In a major upset, Voltigeur stalked his heavily favoured rival and proved too strong at the finish. A re-match between the two horses at their home track was promptly set down for 13 May 1851.

While matches were common during the time, it was rare for the two great champions of an era to clash head to head. Local fervour and national interest were inspired.

In a reverse of the tactics from Doncaster, Voltigeur was sent into the lead. The Flying Dutchman was able to wear him down for a victory of a 'short length' to avenge his only career loss. Voltigeur lost no admirers in defeat and the two are permanently linked in the folklore of racing.

# DONCASTER

Leger Way, Doncaster, South Yorkshire, England, UK. www.doncaster-racecourse.co.uk

*D*oncaster is one of the oldest venues for thoroughbred contests and evidence of racing can be traced back to at least 1595.

Local authorities threatened to close down racing in the early 17th century due to unruly crowd behaviour, but the will of the public prevailed to the extent that races proceeded with the backing of the same corporation that had attempted to curtail it.

Racing on the Town Moor began in 1710 and the first September meeting ran in 1751. It has been a permanent fixture on the racing calendar ever since.

## THE TRACK

The left-handed track is basically flat and shaped like an ice-cream cone, with a hairpin left turn out of the straight before a long straight run of about a mile. A sweeping bend of 5 furlongs then turns all of the way back onto the home straight. The run home is just under 5 furlongs.

Races up to a mile are conducted on the straight course. There is also a mile start from a chute on the round course.

## FEATURE RACES

### ST LEGER STAKES

Named after Lieutenant General Anthony St Leger, who conceived the race in 1776. At that time the racing of 3yos was not common practice and the idea was considered quite controversial. But the race was an obvious success and no doubt played a key role in the establishment of both The Oaks and The Derby within the next four years. The St Leger is the world's oldest Classic race.

The Triple Crown in the United Kingdom is not all consuming as it is in the United States and even attempts at the third leg have become rare due to the distance range and the fact that there are now so many more valuable races for the top 3yos to enter. Despite this, the St Leger is currently experiencing a renaissance after a period of stagnation. The race was under scrutiny

during the 1990s, but calls to shorten the distance were properly resisted and a revival has ensued.

The winner of the inaugural race was **ALLA-BACULIA (1776)**, owned by the then Prime Minister Lord Rockingham. Many horses have brought off the Derby–St Leger double including **CHAMPION (1800)**, **SURPLICE (1848)**, **THE FLYING DUTCHMAN (1849)**, **VOLTIGEUR (1850)**, **BLAIR ATHOL (1864)**, **SILVIO (1877)**, **IROQUOIS (1881)**, **MELTON (1885)**, **DONOVAN (1889)**, **SIR VISTO (1895)**, **SOLARIO (1925)**, **CORONACH (1926)**, **TRIGO (1929)**, **HYPERION (1933)**, **WINDSOR LAD (1934)**, **AIRBORNE (1946)**, **TULYAR (1952)**, **NEVER SAY DIE (1954)**, **ST PADDY (1960)** and **REFERENCE POINT (1987)**.

Oaks–St Leger winners include **QUEEN OF TRUMPS (1835)**, **JANNETTE (1878)**, Her Majesty's **DUNFERMLINE (1977)**, **SUN PRINCESS (1983)** and **USER FRIENDLY (1992)**.

Ascot Gold Cup winners include **MEMNON (1825)**, **TOUCHSTONE (1834)**, **ROBERT THE DEVIL (1880)**, **LA FLECHE (1892)**, **BAYARDO (1909)**, **PRINCE PALATINE (1911)** and **CLASSIC CLICHÉ (1995)**.

Winners of the Fillies' Triple Crown are **FORMOSA (1868)**, **HANNAH (1871)**, **APOLOGY (1874)**, **LA FLECHE (1892)**, **SCEPTRE (1902)**, **PRETTY POLLY (1904)**, **SUN CHARIOT (1942)**, **MELD (1955)** and **OH SO SHARP (1985)**.

**ELIS (1836)** was owned by leading racing man of the time Lord George Bentinck, who was renowned as a fearless gambler – especially when it came to his own horses, privately trained out of his stables at Goodwood.

Elis was long odds leading up to the St Leger and was not expected to run. In those times, it would take more than a fortnight to walk a horse from Goodwood to Doncaster, so bookmakers were surprised and suspicious when Lord George arrived in London only ten days before the race wanting to bet heavily on his horse at 40 to 1. Having been reliably informed that Elis was indeed still tucked away in his Goodwood stable, bookies accepted the wager. Meanwhile, Bentinck had commissioned the construction of a horse box – one of

## FEATURE RACES

| | | | | | | | |
|---|---|---|---|---|---|---|---|
| **ST LEGER STAKES** | G1 | 1M6F132Y | TURF | 3YOC&F | SW | 1776 | SEPT |
| **RACING POST TROPHY** | G1 | 8F | TURF | 2YOC&F | SW | 1961 | OCT |
| CHAMPAGNE STAKES | G2 | 7F | TURF | 2YOC&G | SWP | 1823 | SEPT |
| DONCASTER CUP | G2 | 2M2F | TURF | 3YO+ | SWP | 1766 | SEPT |
| FLYING CHILDERS STAKES | G2 | 5F | TURF | 2YO | SWP | 1967 | SEPT |
| MAY HILL STAKES | G2 | 1M | TURF | 2YOF | SWP | 1976 | SEPT |
| PARK HILL STAKES | G2 | 1M6F132Y | TURF | 3YO+F&M | SWP | 1839 | SEPT |
| PARK STAKES | G2 | 7F | TURF | 3YO+ | SWP | 1978 | SEPT |

the first ever. This box was large enough to carry two horses and padded with mattresses inside. Drawn by six horses, the box with Elis inside made the journey to Doncaster in just three days. Bentinck pulled off his plunge and in so doing started a revolution in horse transportation.

Other notables include 2000 Guineas winners **SIR TATTON SYKES (1846)**, **STOCKWELL (1852)** and **PETRARCH (1876)**; iron horse **CALLER OU (1861)** recorded 52 wins from 101 starts; **HURRY ON (1916)** would become a leading sire; the Aga Khan's **FIRDOUSSI (1932)** won in a year when he owned four of the first five past the post; **SNURGE (1990)** won a Canadian International (1992) as did **MUTAFAWEQ (1999)**; **MOONAX (1994)** also won the French version, the Prix Royal-Oak; **SCORPION (2005)** won the Grand Prix de Paris (2005) and the Coronation Cup (2007); **CONDUIT (2008)** would give Sir Michael Stoute a long overdue victory in the only English Classic to have previously eluded him; and **MASTERY (2009)**. Trainer John Scott had 16 wins in the race.

## RACING POST TROPHY

First run in 1961, this mile race for 2yos has been the launching pad for many top horses.

Notables include Derby winners **REFERENCE POINT (1986)**, **HIGH CHAPARRAL (2001)**, **MOTIVATOR (2004)**, **AUTHORIZED (2006)** and **CAMELOT (2011)**.

Oaks winner **NOBLESSE (1962)**; St Leger winner **RIBOCCO (1966)**; Arc winner **VAGUELY NOBLE (1967)**; **GREEN DANCER (1974)**, who would win the Poule d'Essai des Poulains; **KING'S THEATRE (1993)** also took out the King George VI & Queen Elizabeth Stakes (1994); **CELTIC SWING (1994)** won the Prix du Jockey Club; and **ST NICHOLAS ABBEY (2009)**.

## DONCASTER CUP

With a history dating back to 1766, the Doncaster Cup boasts a long list of champion winners. Great mare **BEESWING (1837, 40–42)** holds the benchmark with four wins in the race. **DOUBLE TRIGGER (1995, 96, 98)** won it three times; **HAMBLETO-NIAN (1795, 96)** won 18 of 19 starts including a St Leger (1795); **TOUCHSTONE (1835, 36)** won a St Leger (1834) and two Ascot Gold Cups (1836, 37).

Other great winners include **THE HERO (1846)**; **CANEZOU (1849)**; **VOLTIGEUR (1850)** upset The Flying Dutchman; **TEDDINGTON (1852)**; **KETTLEDRUM (1861)**; **ACHIEVEMENT (1867)**; **LILY AGNES (1874)**; **ISONOMY (1879)**; **THE BARD (1886)**; **LEMBERG (1911)**; **PRINCE PALATINE (1912)**; **BROWN JACK (1930)**; **MARSYAS (1946)**; **ALYCIDON (1949)**; dual Ascot Gold winner **LE MOSS (1979, 80)** won it twice; **ARDROSS (1982)**; **PERSIAN PUNCH (2003)**; and dual winner **MILLENARY (2004, 05)** also won the St Leger (2000).

Nijinksy wins the Triple Crown

Oh So Sharp

# SANDOWN PARK

Esher, Surrey, England, UK. www.sandown.co.uk

*S*andown Park was laid out for the first meeting by Sir Wilfred Brett,
General Owen Williams and his brother Hwfa Williams in 1875. The
latter was prominent in the court of King Edward VII and was chairman
and clerk of the course for nearly 50 years.

King Edward, then Prince of Wales, gave his support and attended the second meeting where he presented a cup. His Royal Highness won his first flat race with filly Counterpane at Sandown and would win the Eclipse Stakes twice, with his Derby winners Persimmon and Diamond Jubilee.

Royal patronage at Sandown Park has continued, and it was the Queen Mother's favourite course. She regularly attended meetings right up until her death at 102. There was no more popular winner than when her horse Special Cargo scored a thrilling last stride victory in the 1984 Whitbread Gold Cup. A statue erected in her honour now greets visitors to the course.

Sandown Park was the first enclosed or park course, which was a major break with tradition. Until 1875 the public could access every track for free, but fenced-in Sandown made it compulsory for race-goers there to pay admittance. Still, Sandown Park is a tremendously popular venue with good amenities making it very user friendly.

## THE TRACK

A right-handed rectangular-shaped course with a circumference of about 1m5f. From the winning post it is a very short run to an incline on the turn out of the back straight, then downhill to the turn into the long, flat back straight of 5 furlongs.

A short bend of about a hundred yards leads to the home straight. The 4½ furlong run in is uphill all the way and then kicks up again for the final furlong, providing the toughest run home on any course in Britain.

A unique feature is the separate 5-furlong straight track that runs parallel to the main straight across the centre of the course.

Hold on to all tickets as no race is over at Sandown until the winning post, as horses can tire quickly in the punishing final stages.

## FEATURE RACE

### ECLIPSE STAKES

Eclipse made his racetrack debut as a 5yo at his home track at Epsom on 2 May 1769 and famously won by so far that his three rivals were listed as unplaced. From that time his legend has continued to grow. Undefeated at every appearance in heat or race, he strung together a series of King's Plate wins and is reputed to have defeated his opposition with ease on all occasions. By the end of his 6yo season he had proved so superior to his contemporaries that none would oppose or put up a subscription to compete against him. After a string of walkover victories there was little option but to retire Eclipse to stud, where he met with quite some success.

Himself a great, great-grandson of the Darley Arabian, Eclipse would sire three of the first five Derby winners – over both distances. Largely through his sons Pot-8-os and King Fergus, Eclipse's influence can now be found in the bloodlines of nearly every thoroughbred in the world.

The race itself is a weight-for-age contest over a mile and a quarter for 3yos and up, and is one of Britain's premier open events.

Derby winners include **AYRSHIRE (1889)**, **PERSIMMON (1897)**, **FLYING FOX (1899)**, **DIAMOND JUBILEE (1900)**, **ARD PATRICK (1903)**, **LEMBERG (1910)**, **CORONACH (1926)**, **WINDSOR LAD (1935)**, **BLUE PETER (1939)**, **TULYAR (1952)**, **ST PADDY (1961)**, **ROYAL PALACE (1968)**, **MILL REEF (1971)** and **NASHWAN (1989)**.

Arc winners include **MIGOLI (1947)**, **BALLYMOSS (1958)**, **STAR APPEAL (1975)** and **DANCING BRAVE (1986)**.

Other greats on the honour roll include **BAYARDO (1909)**, **PRINCE PALATINE (1912)**, dual Champion Stakes winner **FAIRWAY (1928)**, **RAGUSA (1964)**, **BRIGADIER GERARD (1972)**, **SADLER'S WELLS (1984)**, **PEBBLES (1985)**,

| FEATURE RACES | | | | | | | |
|---|---|---|---|---|---|---|---|
| ECLIPSE STAKES | G1 | 1M2F7Y | TURF | 3YO+, | WFA | 1886 | JUL |
| SANDOWN MILE | G2 | 1M14Y | TURF | 4YO+, | SWP | 1985 | APR |
| BRIGADIER GERARD STAKES | G3 | 1M2F7Y | TURF | 4YO+ | SWP | 1953 | MAY |
| HENRY II STAKES | G3 | 2M78Y | TURF | 4YO+ | SWP | 1963 | MAY |
| SANDOWN CLASS TRIAL | G3 | 1M2F7Y | TURF | 3YO | SWP | 1953 | APR |

Eclipse

**PILSUDSKI (1997), DAYLAMI (1998), GIANT'S CAUSEWAY (2000), FALBRAV (2003), DAVID JUNIOR (2006), SEA THE STARS (2009)** and **SO YOU THINK (2011)**.

Sandown Park also stages four Grade 1 jumps events: Henry VII Novice Chase, Scilly Isles Novices' Chase, Tingle Creek Chase and the Tolworth Hurdle. The annual jumps highlight is the Bet365 Gold Cup Chase (Grade 3), formerly known as the Whitbread Gold Cup.

# GOODWOOD

Goodwood, Chichester, West Sussex, England, UK. www.goodwood.com

*L*ocated at beautiful Sussex Downs, on a sunny day there is no more picturesque track anywhere in England.

The course was laid out by the third Duke of Richmond on his own private land in April 1801 and a three-day meeting was held in April the following year.

The Glorious Goodwood meeting, now extended to five days, is held every July and still holds pride of place. Currently there is also a three-day meeting in May, a two-day meeting in August, and various other single-day fixtures. All feature races are run during the carnival in July–August.

## THE TRACK

Goodwood has a very unusual track design. The track is quite narrow and extremely tricky as it runs left- and right-handed. The course is basically a reverse L shape with a loop at the top.

Races over 2½ miles start in front of the stand. It is a flip start, no barrier stalls. It is a run up the straight of about 2½ furlongs, away from the stands and the winning post, before turning left. The riders then edge over to the opposite side of the course for a straight run of under half a mile before turning very sharply right at the mile and a half, onto the loop and sharp right again. It is then a straight run back to the right-hand home turn. Here it is mostly uphill from about the mile until the 3½ furlong mark.

There are two home bends. The bottom bend gives a run home of about 2½ furlongs whereas the top bend provides for a straight run home of 3½ furlongs.

With the twists and turns inherent in the course design, luck can be a major factor at Goodwood as riders can often find it difficult to negotiate a clear passage in running. A good draw is crucial here.

## FEATURE RACES

### SUSSEX STAKES

Notable winners include **RAYON D'OR (1879)**, **PARADOX (1885)**, **ORME (1892)**, **MINORU (1909)**, **PETITE ETOILE (1959)**, **HUMBLE DUTY (1970)**, **BRIGADIER GERARD (1971)**, **WOLLOW (1976)**, **KRIS (1979)**, **GIANT'S CAUSEWAY (2000)**, **ROCK OF GIBRALTAR (2002)**, **SOVIET SONG (2004)** and **RAMONTI (2007)**. **FRANKEL (2011, 12)** became the first to win it twice.

### NASSAU STAKES

Established in 1840, it was a race for 3yo fillies only until 1975 when the conditions were extended to include older fillies and mares. The race was granted Group 1 status in 1999. Many greats won in the early days including **LA FLECHE (1892)**, **SCEPTRE (1902)**, **PRETTY POLLY (1904)**, **CHERRY LASS (1905)** and **SAUCY SUE (1925)**. Each had also won the Oaks.

Since becoming a Group 1, notable winners include **ALEXANDER GOLDRUN (2005)**, winner of the Hong Kong Cup (2004); **OUIJA BOARD (2006)**; and **MIDDAY (2009–11)** who won it a record three times in succession and took out Breeders' Cup Filly & Mare (2009) and the Prix Vermeille (2010).

### GOODWOOD CUP

First run in 1812, notables include Derby winners **PRIAM (1831, 32)**, **FAVONIUS (1872)**, **DONCASTER (1874)** and **ISONOMY (1879)**; and Ascot Gold Cup winners **GLENCOE (1834)**, **THE**

| FEATURE RACES | | | | | | |
|---|---|---|---|---|---|---|
| SUSSEX STAKES | G1 | 1M | TURF | 3YO+ | WFA | 1841 |
| NASSAU STAKES | G1 | 1M1F192Y | TURF | 3YO+F&M | SW | 1840 |
| GOODWOOD CUP | G2 | 2M | TURF | 3YO+ | SWP | 1812 |
| CELEBRATION MILE | G2 | 1M | TURF | 3YO+ | SWP | 1967 |
| KING GEORGE STAKES | G2 | 5F | TURF | 3YO+ | SWP | 1911 |
| LENNOX STAKES | G2 | 7F | TURF | 3YO+ | SWP | 2000 |
| RICHMOND STAKES | G2 | 6F | TURF | 2YOC+G | SWP | 1877 |
| VINTAGE STAKES | G2 | 7F | TURF | 2YO | SWP | 1975 |
| Stewards' Cup | HCP | 6F | TURF | 3YO+ | HCP | 1840 |

a genuine phenomenon who was undefeated in all 54 starts. As a 3yo she swept the Hungarian classics, the Austrian Derby and scored the first of three wins in the Grosser Preis von Baden. After her Goodwood Cup win, she travelled the following year to France and won the Grand Prix de Deauville (G2). She was also a three-time winner of the Hungarian Autumn Oaks (1877–79) during her illustrious career. Her tally of wins still stands as an all-time record for an undefeated horse. Puerto Rican star Camarero registered 56 successive wins in the 1950s to eclipse Kincsem's consecutive wins record.

## THE STEWARDS' CUP

The Stewards' Cup is a time-honoured sprint race. Conceived at the suggestion of Lord George Bentinck, it has a history dating back to 1840. The race is always a spectacular sight as the 6-furlong start is not visible from the grandstands and the large field of up to 28 runners will suddenly come thundering over the hill like the Charge of the Light Brigade.

HERO (1847), ST SIMON (1884), ALYCIDON (1949), ZARATHUSTRA (1956), ARDROSS (1981) and KAYF TARA (1999).

Three-time winner DOUBLE TRIGGER (1995, 97, 98) also won three Doncaster Cups (1995, 96, 98) and an Ascot Gold Cup (1995).

Dual winners also include FLEUR DE LYS (1829, 30), HARKAWAY (1838, 39), CHARLES THE TWELFTH (1841, 42), CANEZOU (1849, 50), COUNT SCHOMBERG (1896, 97), PROVERB (1973, 74), LE MOSS (1979, 80), FURTHER FLIGHT (1991, 92), PERSIAN PUNCH (2001, 03) and YEATS (2006, 08). Other notables include THE BARD (1886), BROWN JACK (1930), MARSYAS (1946) and TENERANI (1948).

Hungarian national hero KINCSEM (1878) was

# NEWBURY

Newbury, Berkshire, England, UK. www.newbury-racecourse.co.uk

## FEATURE RACES

| LOCKINGE STAKES | G1 | 1M | TURF | 4YO+ | WFA | 1958 | MAY |
|---|---|---|---|---|---|---|---|
| HUNGERFORD STAKES | G2 | 7F | TURF | 3YO+ | SWP | 1949 | AUG |
| MILL REEF STAKES | G2 | 6F8Y | TURF | 2YO | SWP | 1972 | SEPT |
| ARC TRIAL | G3 | 1M3F | TURF | 3YO+ | SWP | 1975 | SEPT |
| GREENHAM STAKES | G3 | 7F | TURF | 3YOC&G | SW | 1906 | APR |

Mill Reef

## FEATURE RACE

### LOCKINGE STAKES

A mile race for 4yos and up, it was upgraded to Group 1 status in 1995. Since then winners include **SOVIET LINE (1995, 96)**, who won it twice.

**CAPE CROSS (1998)**, sire of Ouija Board and Sea The Stars; **HAWK WING (2003)** followed up his win in the Eclipse (2002) with a stunning 11-length win; 1000 Guineas winner **RUSSIAN RHYTHM (2004)**; **RAKTI (2005); CANFORD CLIFFS (2011)** and **FRANKEL (2012)**. Earlier winners included **BRIGADIER GERARD (1972)** and **KRIS (1980)**.

*N*ewbury is a charming course set in Berkshire and was one of the first dual-purpose tracks. The current course has been in operation since 1910 and is host to races at the elite level on the flat and over the jumps. Highlights include the Lockinge Stakes and the Challow Novices' Hurdle. The Hennessy Gold Cup is the showcase jumps event.

A recent addition has been the introduction of the Arc Trial. It is a Group 3 race over a mile and 3 furlongs, and while yet to produce Arc winners it has quickly become a good-quality race and a viable option for trainers with an eye to Longchamp just three weeks after.

## THE TRACK

Newbury is an elongated oval-shaped track. Left-handed and mostly flat, it has a long run in of 5 furlongs, which gives every horse an equal chance.

Events from the 1m5f start begin from a chute from the back straight. It is a long straight run of nearly 6 furlongs before a left-hand bend and a short run to the home turn.

Races of up to a mile are held on the straight course. There is also a 7-furlong chute and a mile chute start on the round course.

Newbury is a quality track that suits a 'galloper', and is considered one of the fairest in the country. Consequently many good young horses step out here.

# HAYDOCK PARK

Haydock Park, Merseyside, England, UK. www.haydock-park.co.uk

## FEATURE RACES

| | | | | | | |
|---|---|---|---|---|---|---|
| HAYDOCK SPRINT CUP | G1 | 6F | TURF | 3YO+ | WFA | 1966 | SEPT |
| LANCASHIRE OAKS | G2 | 1M4F | TURF | 3YO+F&M | SWP | 1939 | JUL |
| TEMPLE STAKES | G2 | 5F | TURF | 3YO+ | SWP | 1965 | MAY |

## FEATURE RACE

### HAYDOCK SPRINT CUP

First held in 1966, the Sprint Cup was awarded Group 1 status in 1998. It has been won by many top sprinters since its inception.

Early winners include **BE FRIENDLY (1966, 67)**, owned by legendary race caller Peter O'Sullevan, who called home his own horse on both occasions. The course considered the horse worthy of a statue. **HABIBTI (1983)** and **GREEN DESERT (1986)** are other notable early winners.

Since being promoted to Group 1 status, prominent winners include: **DANEHILL (1989)**; **DAYJUR (1990)**; **SHEIK ALBADOU (1992)**; **ROYAL APPLAUSE (1997)**; dual Group 1-winner in France, **SOMNUS (2003)**; **REVERENCE (2006)** won the Nunthorpe (2006) and **DREAM AHEAD (2011)** also took out the July Cup (2011).

*H*aydock Park is a high-class track and a good all-round, dual-purpose course. *It is well appointed in a lovely setting for a meeting, with the paddock and the parade ring well sheltered by the trees.*

Ideally situated between Liverpool and Manchester, race-goers flock in numbers from both directions. Convenient access via the M6 also serves to make Haydock a very popular racing venue.

Highlights on the calendar are the Haydock Sprint Cup and the 3-mile Betfair Chase, both run at the elite level.

## THE TRACK

Haydock Park is a quirky kidney-shaped left-handed track with tight turns. It has a circumference of approximately 1m7f.

The 1m3f start is from a chute at the end of the home straight. Runners quickly turn hard left before cutting the corner by edging over to the outside rail, then back again to the inside for the very tight turn into the home straight. The straight is about 4½ furlongs and slightly uphill throughout. Races up to 6 furlongs are held on the straight course.

# CHESTER

Chester, Cheshire, England, UK. www.chester-races.co.uk

**RULER OF THE WORLD (2013)**; St Leger winners **INDIANA (1963)**, **TOULON (1991)** and **MILLENERY (2000)** have also been successful. **BAYARDO (1910)**; **HELIOPOLIS (1939)**; **SKY HIGH (1946)**, who made it a record five wins for jockey Tommy Weston; **SUPREME COURT (1951)** won the King George VI & Queen Elizabeth Stakes, as did **ALCIDE (1958)** and **BELMEZ (1990)**; **PROVERB (1973)**; **OLD VIC (1989)** won the Prix du Jockey Club and the Irish Derby; **SOLDIER OF FORTUNE (2007)** won the Irish Derby and the Coronation Cup (2008) and **TREASURE BEACH (2011)** won an Irish Derby and the Secretariat Stakes (2011). Quest for Fame was runner-up in the race before taking out The Derby (1990).

## CHESTER CUP

First run as the Tradesmen's Cup in 1824 and won by **DOGE OF VENICE**. In those times the track was used for many sports on race days including the cock fighting event 'The Main of Cocks', which at 500 guineas was worth more than the horse race.

Early winners include St Leger and dual Ascot Gold Cup winner **TOUCHSTONE (1834)**; **ALICE HAWTHORN (1842)**, who won 52 races from 71 starts; **RED DEER (1844)** was the first 3yo to win and brought off a massive plunge for Lord George Bentinck; 3yo filly **NANCY (1851)**; **WILLONYX (1911)**, who also won the Ascot Gold Cup and the Cesarewitch (1911); and **BROWN JACK (1931)**.

Recent winners include champion hurdler **SEA PIGEON (1977, 78)**, who won the race twice, **HUGS DANCER (2003)** and **OVERTURN (2011)**.

*C*hester is an ancient walled city founded by the Romans in the year 79. For the most part, the walls and the aqueduct still remain to provide a historic setting, and fittingly the track has an amphitheatre-like quality that gives meetings here a great atmosphere. The Roman walls are also popular vantage points for spectators looking to obtain a view of the races at no charge.

Known as The Roodee, the top half of the track traces the natural course of the River Dee and it is one of the country's most popular and well-attended racing venues. Racing really is a social event in Chester and race fans always turn out no matter the quality of the card. It has been said that they could run a bullock race at Chester and 20,000 would still show up.

The first official races were held here in 1540 and are among the first races ever recorded in Britain.

## THE TRACK

The Roodee is a circular or saucer-shaped course and is the smallest, tightest circuit in the country. The 239yd straight is the shortest run in of any track in the UK. Apart from the straight, runners are on the tight circle for the entire race. Consequently low draws and on pace are cast-iron rules here.

## FEATURE RACES

### CHESTER VASE

Established in 1907, the conditions were changed in 1959 to make it a race for 3yos only.

Won by Derby winners **PAPYRUS (1923)**, **HYPERION (1933)**, **WINDSOR LAD (1934)**, **HENBIT (1980)**, **SHERGAR (1981)** and

# LINGFIELD PARK

Lingfield, Surrey, England, UK. www.lingfield-racecourse.co.uk

## FEATURE RACES

| CHARTWELL FILLIES' STAKES | G3 | 7F | TURF | 3YO+F&M | SWP | 1994 |
|---|---|---|---|---|---|---|
| LINGFIELD DERBY TRIAL | G3 | 1M3F106Y | TURF | 3YOC&G | SWP | 1932 |
| Lingfield Oaks Trial | L | 1M3F106Y | TURF | 3YOF | SWP | 1933 |

Runners travel for a furlong before linking up with the round course. Out of the straight the ground becomes steeper on the run to the second turn.

There is also a straight turf course of 7f140yds. The ground descends most of the way, particularly over the first 3 furlongs where it falls quite sharply.

The inner all-weather Polytrack has a circumference of 1m2f.

## FEATURE RACES

### LINGFIELD DERBY TRIAL

Due to its undulating nature, the Lingfield course is an appropriate test for Derby hopefuls on their way to Epsom. Instituted in 1932, the race was an instant success with the first winner, **APRIL THE FIFTH**, going on to win the Derby.

Since then the race has spawned Derby winners such as **MID-DAY SUN (1937)**, **PARTHIA (1959)**, **TEENOSO (1983)**, **SLIP ANCHOR (1985)**, **KAHYASI (1988)** and **HIGH-RISE (1998)**.

Those that went on to St Leger glory include **SAYAJIRAO (1947)**, **BLACK TARQUIN (1948)**, **ALCIDE (1958)**, **BUSTINO (1974)**, **BOB'S RETURN (1993)** and **SILVER PATRIARCH (1997)**. **TULYAR (1952)** won both The Derby and the St Leger.

### LINGFIELD OAKS TRIAL

Established a year after the Derby Trial, those to go on to win The Oaks include **USER FRIENDLY (1992)**, who also won the St Leger; **LADY CARLA (1996)** and **RAMRUMA (1999)**. **MIDDAY (2009)** was also a winner.

L*ingfield Park was first opened for jumps racing in 1890 and flat racing followed four years later. In 1989 Lingfield was the first English course to install an all-weather surface so that racing could continue through the winter months.*

The turf flat and jumps tracks remain and the character of Lingfield is unchanged despite the loss of many trees due to local development. While it may not be 'Leafy Lingfield' any more, the course still retains much of its charm.

## THE TRACK

Lingfield is a left-handed, triangular shaped track.

The turf track is quite undulating with a circumference of 1m4f and a straight of 3½ furlongs.

The 2-mile start is on the straight course.

# KEMPTON PARK

Sunbury-on-Thames, Middlesex, England, UK.
www.kempton.co.uk

## FEATURE RACES

| SEPTEMBER STAKES | G3 | 1M4F | AWT | 3YO+ | SWP | SEPT |
|---|---|---|---|---|---|---|
| SIRENIA STAKES | G3 | 6F | AWT | 2YO | SWP | SEPT |

Located in the outer London suburb of Sunbury, Kempton Park is a track with a great history dating back to 1878.

In 2006, the turf track for flat racing was demolished and a new all-weather surface installed, complete with floodlights to allow night racing. Originally constructed primarily with wet-weather racing in mind, the track now races year round and hosts up to 100 meetings per season.

While all-weather racing has not proved overly popular with race-goers, the track continues to be very well supported by the top trainers with strong entries. Many good horses are introduced here to build confidence.

The biggest meeting of the year is the traditional Boxing Day fixture, which features the Grade 1 King George VI Chase. The King George is one of the great races on the jumps calendar and such is its popularity that authorities were persuaded to save the turf jumps track so that the race would not be lost. A crowd of more than 20,000 people regularly attends the annual event.

## THE TRACK

The Kempton all-weather track is a right-handed oval Polytrack with very sharp turns. The course has two home bends. The first, used for the 5-furlong and the mile and a quarter races, provides a run in of 2 furlongs. The second or top bend allows a 3-furlong run home.

## FEATURE RACE

### SEPTEMBER STAKES

Inaugurated in 1979, the September Stakes has been won by 1994 Melbourne Cup winner **JEUNE (1992)**, dual winner **MUTAMA (2000, 01)** and two-time German Group 1 winner **MAMOOL (2004)**.

# NEWCASTLE

High Gosforth Park, Newcastle upon Tyne, Tyne, England, UK. www.newcastle-racecourse.co.uk

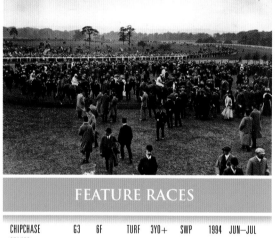

## FEATURE RACES

| CHIPCHASE STAKES | G3 | 6F | TURF | 3YO+ | SWP | 1994 | JUN–JUL |
|---|---|---|---|---|---|---|---|
| Northumberland Plate | HCP | 2M19Y | TURF | 3YO+ | HCP | 1833 | JUN–JUL |

Newcastle racecourse is located only 5 miles from the city centre of Newcastle-on-Tyne. Racing has been conducted at the current course since 1882 with the highlight summer meeting in late June or early July drawing large crowds. Racing is particularly well attended here all year round with the locals turning out in force.

Newcastle is a dual-purpose course with a separate jumps track. The Fighting Fifth Hurdle (Grade 1) is the premier jumping event.

## THE TRACK

Newcastle is a hugely expansive, left-handed course that is triangular in shape. It has a total length of 1m6f and is generally flat throughout. It is considered a very testing track.

Races up to a mile are held on the straight course.

There is also a mile start on the round course, which begins near the back of the course. Runners are on a bend from the start until straightening for the run in of 4 furlongs, which rises slightly.

From the 2-mile start, runners have a straight 2½-furlong run past the winning post, turn left for a slightly downhill run of more than 2 furlongs before the left turn at the mile and a quarter for the long sweeping bend to the home turn.

## FEATURE RACES

### NORTHUMBERLAND PLATE

A time-honoured staying handicap, still referred to as the 'Pitmen's Derby' as it was a public holiday for local mine workers until 1949. The race was originally staged on the Newcastle Town Moor from 1833 but transferred to the present course upon its opening.

**TOMBOY (1833)** won the first running on the Town Moor at Newcastle; **UNDERHAND (1857–59)** won it three times.

Dual winners include **ST BENNET (1838, 39)**, **CALLER OU (1863, 64)** and **TUG OF WAR (1977, 78)**. Other notables include **LILY AGNES (1874)**; **HAMPTON (1877)** won a Goodwood Cup; **BARCALDINE (1883)** was undefeated in 13 starts and a highly influential stallion; **CELERIC (1996)** would win the Ascot Gold Cup the following year; **SERGEANT CECIL (2005)**. **OVERTURN (2010)** won the Fighting Fifth Hurdle (Grade 1) the next season to become the first horse to win Newcastle's major flat and hurdle races.

### CHIPCHASE STAKES

Although only instituted in 1994, the Chipchase Stakes has already begun to accumulate an impressive list of winners including King's Stand victor **PICCOLO (1994)** and Golden Jubilee winners **SOLDIER'S TALE (2005)** and **FAYR JAG (2006)**. **TEDBURROW (2000, 02)** won it twice.

# SALISBURY

Northampton, Salisbury, England, UK.
www.salisburyracecourse.co.uk

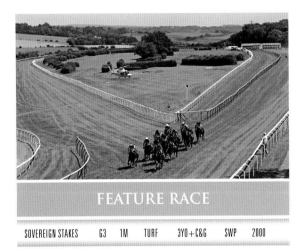

## FEATURE RACE

| SOVEREIGN STAKES | G3 | 1M | TURF | 3YO+C&G | SWP | 2000 |
|---|---|---|---|---|---|---|

Salisbury has been host to racing since before the times of Sir Francis Drake. Records show that Queen Elizabeth I attended the races here in 1588, almost three months before Drake was instructed to set sail from Plymouth to take on the Spanish Armada.

One can easily feel a sense of history when attending Salisbury. It is the quintessential English country track, and meetings have a delightful, distinctly rural atmosphere.

Local racing fans in the 1760s were treated to the spectacle of two all-time champions in consecutive years. Gimcrack was victorious here in 1768 and a year later Eclipse won the City Bowl.

While Salisbury is not laden with top-class races there is a long tradition of unveiling good horses here. Mill Reef won here on debut, Brigadier Gerard won here at his second start, as did Derby winner Sir Percy to name just a few. It was at Salisbury in 1948 that a 12-year-old Lester Piggott made his race debut.

## THE TRACK

The unusually designed track is located on a small strip of land high above the town and set against the picturesque backdrop of the medieval Salisbury Cathedral, which was completed in 1258.

It is basically a straight mile track with a tight right-handed loop. Races up to a mile are held on the straight course, which doglegs slightly right at about the 5-furlong mark.

For races longer than a mile, runners start on the home straight and race away from the winning post. Past the mile and a quarter it is a left turn onto the very sharp right-handed loop, which leads back onto the home straight. From there it is a 7-furlong run that rises steadily throughout, as competitors head back to the winning post in the opposite direction from which they came.

The long run in provides every horse with a fair chance, but the loop makes it a difficult track to ride, so local knowledge and experience are a huge asset.

# WINDSOR

Maidenhead Road, Windsor, Berkshire, England, UK.
www.windsor-racecourse.co.uk

## FEATURE RACE

| WINTER HILL STAKES | G3 | 1M2F7Y | TURF | 3YO+ | SWP | AUGUST |
|---|---|---|---|---|---|---|

Set on an island in the Thames, Windsor has hosted racing since 1866. The Windsor course is often used as a location for filming television shows, as the historic nature of the track and the lack of telegraph poles and overhead wires lends itself to any production that has a period setting.

The feature event is the Winter Hill Stakes. The race was granted Group 3 status in 1995 and became the first Group race to be run at Windsor.

## THE TRACK

The unusual course is a very difficult figure of 8. It is level throughout.

The mile start is from a chute set just back from the junction of the figure of 8. Competitors run in a straight line for about 2 furlongs before a tight right-handed loop brings the runners onto the home straight of approximately 5 furlongs. Low draws best here as the preferred position is the right-hand rail for the loop.

For mile-and-a-half events the start is on the back straight just after the turn out of the home straight. After a furlong and a half it is a left turn and runners continue along the left-hand rail for 3 furlongs before cutting the corner and drifting over to the right-hand rail ready for the loop back on to the run in.

There is also a straight 6-furlong course that has a slight dogleg at about the halfway point.

Despite the twisting, turning nature of the course, the 5-furlong run in does mean that the track races quite fairly.

# PONTEFRACT

The Park, Pontefract, West Yorkshire, England, UK.
www.pontefract-races.co.uk

## FEATURE RACES

| Castle Stakes | L | 1M4F | 4YO+ | JUN |
|---|---|---|---|---|
| Pipalong Stakes | L | 1M | 4YO+F&M | JUL |
| Pomfret Stakes | L | 1M | 3YO+ | JUL |
| Flying Fillies Stakes | L | 6F | 3YO+F&M | AUG |
| Silver Tankard Stakes | L | 8F | 2YO | OCT |

Pontefract is a course with tremendous history and character. Racing dates back to the 17th century when a meeting was held in the shadow of Pontefract Castle in March 1648, only a week or so before the final surrender of the castle by Colonel John Morris during the Civil War. With the garrison under siege, the races were still conducted.

In the era before train travel, its location between York and Doncaster meant that many of the North's top horses competed here, especially in the early 1800s, such as Oiseau and St Leger winners Matilda (1827), The Colonel (1828) and Rowton (1829).

The area was long the location for collieries and coking plants and up until recently the card would always commence at 2:45pm, allowing workers from the nearby mines and slag heaps to knock off in time for the first race.

## THE TRACK

Pontefract is a sharp turning, severely undulating left-handed course in a pear shape. It has a circumference of 2 miles and 125 yards was Europe's longest circuit until the reconfiguration of the York course to accommodate the Royal Meeting in 2005.

Pontefract is considered one of England's toughest and most demanding tracks as runners are required to travel downhill along the back where the course doglegs twice before a right-angle bend, then steeply uphill for 2 furlongs to the home turn. On straightening, the run in of 2 furlongs rises even more severely to the finish.

## FEATURE RACE

### SILVER TANKARD STAKES

Viva Pataca

A mile race for 2yos, its most notable winner is **COMIC STRIP (2004)**, who would race in Hong Kong as Viva Pataca, dominating the local staying ranks. Viva Pataca won the Hong Kong Derby (2006), Champions and Chater Cup three times (2006, 07, 09), the QE II Cup twice (2007, 10) and the Hong Kong Gold Cup twice (2008, 09) and collected more than HK$83M in prize money (US$10.7m).

# RIPON

Boroughbridge Road, Ripon, North Yorkshire, England, UK. www.ripon-races.co.uk

| FEATURE RACES | | | | | |
|---|---|---|---|---|---|
| Ripon Champion 2 Year Old Trophy | L | 6F | TURF | 2YO | AUG |
| Great St Wilfred Stakes | HCP | 6F | TURF | 3YO+ | AUG |

Dubbed the 'Garden Race Course of the North', Ripon is as beautiful as the name suggests. Situated on the meadowlands of the Yorkshire Dales between the River Ure and the Ripon Canal, it carries the distinct flavour that is characteristic of the Yorkshire tracks.

Ripon is one of England's oldest cities – St Wilfrid brought skilled tradesmen from Italy and France in 672AD to commence the building of the Ripon Cathedral – and racing has a long history.

The Bondgate Green course staged its first official meeting in 1664, with the current track at Boroughbridge Road in use since 1900.

## THE TRACK

This is a right-handed oval track with a circumference of 1m5f. There is also a straight 6-furlong course.

The home straight on the round course gives a run in of 5 furlongs with only slight undulations. The tight turns are well cambered and the long run home ensures that it is a very fair track. Consequently the Ripon track is also well supported by southern trainers.

# REDCAR

Redcar, Tees Valley, North Yorkshire, England, UK. www.redcarracing.co.uk

| FEATURE RACES | | | | | |
|---|---|---|---|---|---|
| Redcar 2 Year Old Trophy | L | 6F | TURF | 2YO | OCT |
| Guisborough Stakes | L | 7F | TURF | 3YO+ | OCT |

Redcar is a coastal town in the north-east of England. Before the opening of the current course in 1872 races were held on the sands of Redcar Beach. In the mid–20th century many improvements were made and Redcar became the first course in England to introduce closed circuit TV, furlong posts and a timing clock.

## THE TRACK

Redcar is a wide, left-handed track with a circumference of about 1m5f. Considered to be a very fair track, it is a classic oval shape with tight turns and is flat throughout. The home straight is 5 furlongs.

Races up to a mile are staged on the straight course. The expansive nature of the course lends itself to large fields.

# WARWICK

Hampton Street, Warwick, England, UK. www.warwickracecourse.co.uk

| FEATURE RACES | | | | | |
|---|---|---|---|---|---|
| WARWICKSHIRE OAKS | L | 1M3F | TURF | 4YO+F&M | JUN |
| ETERNAL STAKES | L | 7F | TURF | 3YOF | JUN |

Due to the threat of Danish invaders, the town of Warwick was founded as a defensive position on the banks of the River Avon in the year 914 by Ethelfeda, daughter of King Alfred the Great and sister of Edward the Elder.

Racing has a long history here and was well established by the turn of the 19th century, when it was far more prestigious than currently the case.

The dual-purpose course is well located close to the centre of town. Listed racing is the highlight with the showcase jumps race the Classic Chase run in January.

## THE TRACK

Warwick is a left-handed irregular rectangle track that extends for over 1m6f. As runners approach the 1m4f, steeply rising ground is encountered until a sharp left-hand bend. The track continues to rise as runners take the bend before descending for 2 furlongs into another very tight left-handed bend and a straight run of four furlongs to the home turn.

The run in is slightly more than 2 furlongs. There is a 6-furlong sprint course, which has a pronounced dogleg after 3½ furlongs as it links up with the straight on the round course.

The mile start is from a separate chute joining the back straight, providing only one bend. The 1m3f start is also from a chute.

# NOTTINGHAM

Colwick Park, Nottingham, England, UK.
www.nottinghamracecourse.co.uk

## FEATURE RACES

| Further Flight Stakes | L | 1M6F | TURF | 4YO+ | APR |
|---|---|---|---|---|---|
| Kilvington Fillies' Stakes | L | 6F | TURF | 3YO+F&M | MAY |

Famed Nottingham is the second most populous city in the East Midlands of England. Set within the 280 acres of Colwick Park, it staged its first meeting in 1892. The course is handily located less than 2 miles east of the city centre.

## THE TRACK

The track is a left-handed oval track with a circumference of almost a mile and a half.

It has a half-mile run home on the round course with a chute allowing a straight 6-furlong sprint course.

Large and mainly flat throughout, it is a popular and very fair racetrack. Britain's top trainers are regularly in attendance to provide good-quality race fields.

## FEATURE RACE

### FURTHER FLIGHT STAKES

Further Flight was a top horse who won the Ebor (1990), two Goodwood Cups (1991, 92) and five consecutive Jockey Club Gold Cups (1991–95). Run since 2001. Notables include dual winner **ALCAZAR (2003, 04)** and **OPINION POLL (2010)**.

# WOLVERHAMPTON

Dunstall Park, Goresbrook Road, Wolverhampton, England, UK. www.wolverhampton-racecourse.co.uk

## FEATURE RACE

| Lady Wulfruna Stakes | L | 7F | AWT | 4YO+ | MAR |
|---|---|---|---|---|---|

Dunstall Park, a mile north-west of the city, is the venue for racing here and in recent years the track has undergone a number of significant changes. In late 1993, a fibresand inner track was installed and subsequently replaced in 2004 when both the turf and fibresand tracks were ripped up and the course redesigned to install an all-weather Polytrack. Initially the intention was to stage racing uninterrupted throughout the winter but the course now hosts over a hundred fixtures year round.

Wolverhampton was Britain's first floodlit track, and while all-weather racing may lack the glamour of the turf, the course has become a real workhorse for English racing and is arguably the fairest of the artificial surface tracks. Plans are afoot to create Britain's first 'Racino' as part of another major redevelopment.

The feature event is named after Lady

Wulfruna who founded the town of Wolverhampton in the year 985.

## THE TRACK

A classic oval of about 1 mile in length and a run home of 1½ furlongs. It is a flat left-handed track.

Separate chutes are used for the 6-furlong start at the top of the back straight and the 7-furlong start at the end of the home straight.

# GREAT YARMOUTH

Jellicoe Road, Great Yarmouth, Norfolk, England .
www.greatyarmouth-racecourse.co.uk

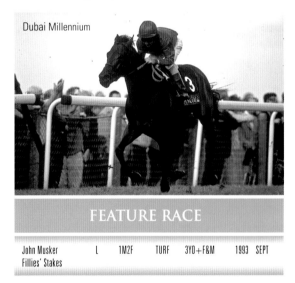
Dubai Millennium

## FEATURE RACE

| John Musker Fillies' Stakes | L | 1M2F | TURF | 3YO+F&M | 1993 | SEPT |
|---|---|---|---|---|---|---|

The port city of Great Yarmouth is situated 20 miles east of Norwich at the entrance to the River Yare. It is one of the largest and most popular seaside resorts in Britain, with the track located only minutes walk from the beach. Racing in the area can be traced back to the early 1700s with the current course in use since 1920.

While racing tends to be in the lower grades due to its fair nature and reasonably close proximity to Newmarket, many top trainers will unveil a promising young prospect at Yarmouth.

Dubai Millennium, Ouija Board and future Breeders' Cup winners Wilko (Breeders' Cup Juvenile, 2004), Raven's Pass (Breeders' Cup

Classic, 2008) and Donativum (Breeders' Cup Juvenile Turf, 2008) are just a few to have gained a confidence builder here early in their careers.

## THE TRACK

A left-handed, oval-shaped course with a circumference of 1m5f.

Mainly flat throughout, and the sandy soil provides excellent drainage.

Races up to a mile are run on the straight course. The home straight on the round course is a run in of just over 5 furlongs.

# BEVERLEY

York Road, Beverley, East Riding of Yorkshire, England, UK. www.beverley-racecourse.co.uk

| Beverley Bullet Stakes | L | 5F | TURF | 3YO+ | 2004 | AUG |
|---|---|---|---|---|---|---|

Located 8 miles north-west of Hull, racing has been conducted here for more than 300 years.

Nearby Kiplingscotes is renowned as host to the Kiplingscotes Derby, which is acknowledged as the oldest continuous horse race in the world. The 4-mile event across the farms and fields of the hamlet has been held annually since 1519.

## THE TRACK

The Beverley course is an irregular oval-shaped, right-handed course with a circumference of about 1m3f. It is a quirky, very undulating track that rises slightly in the back straight from the mile to the 7 furlongs then runs downhill until approaching the tight home turn where the ground starts to rise into the home straight.

The run in of 3 furlongs is a very stiff uphill test, rising steeply all the way to the post.

The straight course is 5 furlongs but actually starts on a slightly right-handed spur, giving a pronounced bias to runners

drawn low. Runners suspect at a trip are to be avoided at all costs at Beverley.

Good horses to have won this race include Prix de l'Abbaye winner **TANGERINE TREES (2011)** and dual Nunthorpe Stakes winner **BORDERLESCOTT (2012)**.

# BATH

Lansdown, Bath, England, UK.
www.bath-racecourse.co.uk

| Lansdown Fillies Stakes | L | 5F | TURF | 3YO+ | | APR |
|---|---|---|---|---|---|---|

The beautiful historic city of Bath is a World Heritage site, established by the Romans in around the year 60. It is renowned as one of England's premier tourist destinations.

Set on top of a hill, the course is situated 780ft above sea level, making it the highest altitude flat course in Britain. The location provides spectacular views over Bristol and beyond.

## THE TRACK

Bath is a very unusual, kidney-shaped course with a circumference of 1m4f. It is a left-handed track that twists, turns and undulates for the most part with only about a furlong of straight level ground.

Runners must negotiate a tight left-handed elbow approaching the home turn.

The half-mile straight is uphill and slightly curved for the most part. The sprint course is 5f161yds and starts from a spur that doglegs after 150yds before joining the course proper.

A chute that extends inside the main track brings them onto the course for races over a mile. The mile-and-a-quarter start is also from a chute that bends left then turns right at the mile point before a straight run to the elbow. Inside draws an advantage from all starting positions here.

It is the only British track without irrigation. Its hilltop setting leaves the course very exposed to the elements so the surface can become very firm during the warmer months. While racing at Bath tends to be a notch below top class, the location and spectacular setting make it a very popular course.

# LEICESTER

Oadby, Leicester, England.
www.leicester-racecourse.co.uk

| Leicestershire Stakes | L | 7F8Y | TURF | 4YO+ | (EXCL. G1 AND G2 WINNERS) | APR |
|---|---|---|---|---|---|---|

The city of Leicester in the East Midlands lies on the River Soar on the outskirts of the National Forest. The course is situated in Oadby, only 2 miles south-east of the town centre.

## THE TRACK

The course is a large, right-handed, slightly odd rectangular oval shape that extends for 1m6f. It has a 7-furlong straight course, which travels downhill for 2 furlongs until it joins the course proper where the 5-furlong run in is mainly uphill until it flattens out just before the winning post.

Out of the straight it is an uphill run that turns quickly twice into the long back straight of 5 furlongs before looping back on to the home straight.

It is a great course for the horse with its open expanses and lush racing surface. While undulating, it is a track where runners can still build momentum into a race without changing stride, unlike many of the up-and-down courses that Britain is famous for.

Leicester is a dual-purpose track and its enormous size ensures that it regularly accommodates large fields.

# CHELTENHAM

Prestbury Park, Cheltenham, Gloucestershire, England, UK. www.cheltenham.co.uk

Cheltenham is the headquarters of National Hunt racing. The four-day meeting in March is the biggest jumps festival in the world and continues to grow.

The Cheltenham Gold Cup is the highlight and run on the Friday, the final day.

The first organised meeting in Cheltenham was held on the flat at Nottingham Hill in 1815 and then at Cleve Hill from 1818. Racing moved to its current location at Prestbury Park in 1831 after the grandstand at the previous course was burnt down by local parishioners in an attempt to save its misguided residents from the evils of racing.

Jumps racing was transferred from Andoversford in 1898. More than 700,000 people attend the track annually, with the March festival worth an estimated £50m to the local economy. Runners compete for

prize money in excess of £3.6m over the four days.

Cheltenham is the ultimate destination for any jumper with the potential to make it to the top in National Hunt racing. It is considered the pinnacle for all jumps fans.

## THE TRACK

There are three courses: the Old Course, New Course and the Cross Country Steeplechase Course.

The Cheltenham Gold Cup is run on the New Course. The track is a test of stamina, jumping prowess, speed and agility under the intense pressure of competition. Of particular note is the steep downhill run onto the home turn, which makes not only jumping but cornering difficult to negotiate.

## FEATURE RACE

### CHELTENHAM GOLD CUP

First run in 1924, there can be no greater Cheltenham hero than **GOLDEN MILLER (1932–36)**, who won the race five times in succession and triumphed in the Grand National in 1934. Vincent O'Brien's champion **COTTAGE RAKE (1948–50)** was a three-time winner and **MILL HOUSE (1963)** also won the King George VI Chase that year before running second to three-time winner **ARKLE (1964–66)** the following year. The mighty Arkle was a winner of 27 races from 35 starts and rated by Timeform as the greatest ever steeplechaser.

Other notable winners include back-to-back winner **L'ESCARGOT (1970, 71)**, who went on to defeat Red Rum in the 1975 Grand National, having been placed in it the previous two years. **CAPTAIN CHRISTY (1974)** won the race as a novice and went on to win a total of six Grade 1 jumps events.

Jenny Pitman became the first female trainer to win

Arkle

with **BORROUGH HILL LAD (1984)** and would win it again with **GARRISON SAVANNAH (1991)**. **DAWN RUN (1986)** was a champion hurdler and winner of 21 races and seven Grade 1s, including two steeplechase victories at the elite level. She was ridden to victory at Cheltenham by Jonjo O'Neill, who later trained **SYNCHRONISED (2012)** to victory in this race.

The great **DESERT ORCHID (1989)** won 34 of 70 starts including four victories in the King George VI Chase (1986, 88–90) at Kempton Park, where there is a statue in his honour. In his Gold Cup win his enormous courage overcame his intense dislike for the course.

**THE FELLOW (1994)** was also a dual French G1 winner; **IMPERIAL CALL (1996)**; **SEE MORE BUSINESS (1999)** was the first of four winners for trainer Paul Nicholls; and champion **BEST MATE (2002–04)** made it a hat-trick for trainer Henrietta Knight. Having been sparingly raced, he never fell or finished out of the top two in 21 starts including 14 wins. His death after collapsing at Exeter sent the racing world into mourning. Mighty **KAUTO STAR (2007, 09)** also won the Grade 1 Betfair Chase four times and the King George VI Chase on five occasions among his 23 victories. His Gold Cup wins were remarkably separated by his constant companion in the very next stable box, **DENMAN (2008)**, who was also one of the modern-day greats.

# AINTREE

Ormskirk Road, Aintree, Liverpool, England, UK.
www.aintree.co.uk

Red Rum defeats Crisp

The Merseyside village of Aintree, 6 miles north of Liverpool, is the venue for England's iconic national obsession, the Grand National Steeplechase.

Waterloo Hotel innkeeper William Lynn initially leased the site from the second Lord Sefton in 1829, and it was Lynn who transformed Aintree from a flat course and instigated the first steeplechase races here, including the Grand National.

While the exact date of the inaugural running is a matter for conjecture, a race under similar conditions was struck in 1836. Three years later the race had been shortened and a selling clause deleted. This race in 1839, then known as the Grand Liverpool Steeplechase, is now considered to be the first running.

Steeped in history, the race is an institution and a phenomenon with once-a-year punters stepping up to the plate in droves. The Grand National is the ultimate equine test of skill, stamina, horsemanship, courage and out-and-out bravery as up to 40 runners take on the formidable course comprising 30 fences. To merely complete the race is considered a feat in itself for horse and rider. No doubt it is a nerve-wracking experience. It is often said that pre-race in the jockey's room the talkative go quiet and the quiet find a voice.

These days the race is watched by a worldwide television audience of more than 500 million viewers. At the track an unbelievable atmosphere prevails due in no small part to the fact that spectators know they are witnessing history in the making.

Undeniably the air is also charged because of the real danger the race presents. In recent years racing officials have become increasingly sensitive to the issues of animal rights and have modified the course to make it safer while still preserving the challenging nature of the race, which has made it an institution.

## THE TRACK

### GRAND NATIONAL COURSE

Aintree is a triangular course with an enormous circumference of 2¼ miles.

The gruelling Grand National of 4m3½f is twice around the track, taking in 30 obstacles. There are 16 fences on the circuit. On the second lap runners take an elbow, which cuts out The Chair and the water jump, leaving a further 14 fences to negotiate.

Many of the individual fences are famous in their own right. Fence 6 & 22, known as Becher's Brook, is named after celebrated horseman and cross-country rider Captain Martin Becher. Becher's presence at the early jumps races in Liverpool generated much interest and publicity and contributed significantly to the success of the races. In the first running of the Grand National, the fence was a man-made water ditch. Captain Becher and his horse Conrad were well clear in the lead when they tumbled here and both took a thorough drenching as they rolled over into the brook. Becher only narrowly managed to avoid the heels of the oncoming field as they thundered over.

Fence 7 & 23, Foinavon, is the smallest obstacle on the course. In the 1967 edition, it was at this fence that the leaders all fell. In the ensuing melee, every single horse in the field either fell, refused, dislodged its rider or became entangled – except for the 100 to 1 outsider Foinavon. Having been at back of the field Foinavon had lost sight of the leaders, but rider John Buckingham steered a path towards the outside wing of the fence and managed to avoid the carnage. Foinavon suddenly had the race to himself with seven fences left to negotiate. Many of the jockeys managed to remount but the despised outsider was off and gone with a furlong lead and was able to stay upright for the remainder of the course to record a stunning and remarkable victory. The drama, confusion and mayhem were perfectly captured by Irish commentator Michael O'Hehir whose race call is considered one of the all-time greats.

Fence 8 & 24, Canal Turn, requires horses to turn left at a 90-degree angle immediately upon landing. Fence 9 & 25, Valentine's, is named for the horse who, legend has it, leapt hindquarters first over this brook fence during the 1840 Grand National.

Fence 12 & 28, Melling Road, takes its name from the public road that runs through the course. A ditch fence is crossed twice after runners cross the road to rejoin the course proper. Fence 15, The Chair, is the most formidable obstacle on the course. As the name suggests, it requires a horse to jump high and long.

## FEATURE RACE

### GRAND NATIONAL

Notable winners include inaugural winner **LOTTERY (1839)**, who was the dominant jumper of his era. Such was his superiority that officials were known to change race conditions deliberately to exclude or impose enormous weight penalties upon him. **CHARITY (1841)** was the first of only 12 mares to have won; and **VANGUARD (1843)** was the first to win under handicap conditions. Rider Tom Oliver became the first to win consecutive Grand Nationals.

**ABD-EL-KADER (1850, 1851)** became the first dual winner. Others to win twice are **PETER SIMPLE (1849, 53)**, who at 15 was the oldest horse ever to win; **THE LAMB (1868, 71)** was the first of only three greys ever to win; **THE COLONEL (1869, 70)**; **MANIFESTO (1897, 99)** contested the event a record eight times; and **REYNOLDSTOWN (1935, 36)**, ridden by Fulke Walwyn in 1936, who would achieve a rare double by training **TEAM SPIRIT (1964)** to victory.

**FREETRADER (1856)** was the first of a record five wins for rider George Stevens; **FATHER O'FLYNN (1892)** ridden by Captain Roddy Owen; **AMBUSH (1900)** for the Prince of Wales, later King Edward VII, remains the only royal winner; **RUBIO (1908)** was the first US-bred horse to win; **TIPPERARY TIM (1928)** at 100 to 1 in a race where only two horses completed the course; **GREGALACH**

(1929), also at 100 to 1, defeated a record field of 66 runners; **GOLDEN MILLER (1934)** is the only horse to have won the Cheltenham Gold Cup in the same year; **BATTLESHIP (1938)** ridden by 17-year-old Bruce Hobbs, making him the youngest jockey ever to have won. A son of Man O'War, Battleship completed a unique double, having won the American Grand National in 1934. **NICKEL COIN (1951)** was the last mare to win; **EARLY MIST (1953)** provided Vincent O'Brien with the first of three consecutive winners. He would prove to be a master trainer of both jumps and flat horses.

E.S.B. **(1956)** won one of the most memorable editions. Devon Loch, owned by the Queen Mother and ridden by Dick Francis, had cleared the last and was approaching the post well ahead and with the race all parcelled up. There is no accepted explanation as to what happened next. For no accountable reason the horse leapt at an imaginary jump and belly flopped onto the track, presenting the race to E.S.B. The Queen Mother famously shrugged and declared, 'That's racing'. Francis later turned his hand to literature and became a celebrated writer of crime fiction. E.S.B.'s win was the first of a record four victories for trainer Fred Rimell, who also won with **NICOLAUS SILVER (1961)**, only the second grey to win; **GAY TRIP (1970)** and **RAG TRADE (1976)**.

**MERRYMAN (1960)** won the first televised event; **AYALA (1963)** was trained by Keith Piggott

and owned by celebrity hairstylist Pierre 'Teasy-Weasy' Raymond; and **RED RUM (1973, 74, 77)** scored a record three victories in the race. In all he would make five appearances in the Grand National for three wins and two seconds to stamp himself as the greatest Aintree horse of all time. His epic battle with dashing Australian champion Crisp in 1973 was a classic and Red Rum slashed 19 seconds off the course record, which had stood since 1934. Red Rum's subsequent deeds only served to enhance the reputation of the great Crisp who went down by half a length but conceded 23 pounds to the winner. History records this as one of the all-time great races – jumps or flat.

**MR FRISK (1990)** ridden by Marcus Armytage who remains the last amateur rider to be successful in the race; **BOBBYJO (1999)** won for Tommy and Paul Carberry; **PAPILLON (2000)** for Ted and Ruby Walsh; and **AMBERLEIGH HOUSE (2004)** was the record-equalling fourth winner for Red Rum's trainer Ginger McCain. The win underlined the skill of his trainer but McCain, a self-professed lucky mug, would have none of it, claiming that he wasn't fit to lace the boots of the legendary Fred Rimell, whose record he tied.

**DON'T PUSH IT (2010)** was ridden by champion jockey Tony McCoy, who had already won 14 riders' titles and finally managed to win the Grand National at his 15th attempt for a popular and well-deserved victory.

Becher's Brook

**NEPTUNE COLLONGES (2012)** carried 11st 6lb – the highest weight carried to victory since Red Rum carried 11st 8lb in 1977 – and was the first grey since 1961 to win and only the third ever.

## MILDMAY COURSE

Over the three-day Aintree meeting the National Course is used once each day for the Topham Chase, Foxhunters Chase and the Grand National. The other races are run on the smaller Mildmay Course.

The Mildmay Course is a tight, sharp, oval-shaped course with a circumference of approximately 1½ miles. It is a virtual inner track that joins up with the National Course at each end of the oval.

# AYR

Whitletts Road, Ayr, South Ayrshire, Scotland, UK www.ayr-racecourse.co.uk

## FEATURE RACES

| FIRTH OF CLYDE | G3 | 1M2F7Y | TURF | 2YOF | SWP | SEPT | 1976 |
|---|---|---|---|---|---|---|---|
| Ayr Gold Cup | Hcp | 6f | TURF | 3YO+ | HCP | Sept | 1804 |

Ayr Gold Cup

Situated 35 miles south-west of Glasgow, Ayr is the premier racetrack in Scotland and the only course there that stages Group racing. Its origins can be traced to 1576, but the first organised meeting was not conducted until 1771. In those times the Ayr course was located at Seafield on a tight 1 mile oval track. It was moved to its more spacious present location in 1901.

Ayr is the scene of the Scottish Grand National, run two or three weeks after Aintree, and the time-honoured Ayr Gold Cup which is the richest handicap sprint in Europe.

## THE TRACK

Ayr is an extremely wide, generally flat, left-handed oval track. It has a circumference of 1m4½f. It has a long sweeping bend into a home straight of half a mile.

Races of up to 6 furlongs are held on the straight course, which is slightly downhill for the first 2 furlongs until it meets the course proper, where it rises slightly near the winning post. There is a chute off the back straight for the 1m3f start.

The jumps course was established in 1950, and the Scottish Grand National (G3) transferred from the romantically named Bogside course in 1965. The Scottish Champion Hurdle (G2) is also run here.

## FEATURE RACES

Both feature races are run in September on the final day of the three-day Ayr Gold Cup fixture.

### FIRTH OF CLYDE

The Firth of Clyde takes its name from the body of water off the nearby coast that serves as the port to the town of Ayr. The race was promoted to Group 3 status in 2004 and is the only Group race held in Scotland.

In 1990 it was won by **IMPERFECT CIRCLE**, ridden by Tony Cruz, now leading Hong Kong trainer and famous for preparing world-champion sprinter Silent Witness.

### AYR GOLD CUP

The event was transferred to Ayr in 1907 after the closure of Belleisle racetrack, where the event was established in 1804. The distance was shortened from a mile to 6 furlongs.

The expansive course provides for huge fields, especially in races conducted down the straight course, and the Ayr Gold Cup always attracts a capacity field. **DAZZLE (1889–91)** won the Belleisle version a record three times. Since becoming a 6-furlong race at Ayr, it has been won twice by **RAEBERRY (1908, 10)**, **HERONSEA (1930, 31)** and **FUNFAIR WANE (2002, 04)**. Top sprinters **BE FRIENDLY (1967)** and **LOCHSONG (1992)** have won it, as have Queen Anne Stakes winner **ROYAL CHARGER (1946)** and **CONTINENT (2001)**, who also won the July Cup and Prix de l'Abbaye (2002).

# HAMILTON PARK

Bothwell Road, Hamilton, Lanarkshire, Scotland. www.hamilton-park.co.uk

| FEATURE RACES | | | | | |
|---|---|---|---|---|---|
| GLASGOW STAKES | L | 1M3F16Y | TURF | 3YO | JULY |
| BRAVEHEART STAKES | L | 1M4F17Y | TURF | 4YO+ | MAY |

*Hamilton Park is a lovely track on the outskirts of Glasgow on the south bank of the River Clyde. Racing has taken place in the region since 1746 with the current course first set out in 1888 on the grounds of the estate then owned by Lord Hamilton.*

Races are often conducted here on Saturday nights and the proactive marketing department has done a great job with innovations such as the regular Saints and Sinners nights, which have succeeded in drawing large crowds of younger race-goers. Patrons are encouraged to wear a carnation in their lapels – white for saints, red for sinners. From there, the possibilities are endless. In keeping with the party atmosphere, bars on course remain open for two hours after the last race.

## THE TRACK

The track is similar to Salisbury in that it is a straight course with a right-handed loop that brings runners back on to the course proper. The straight course is of 6 furlongs and dips for the first 2 furlongs, then uphill for the remainder, rising even more sharply approaching the post.

The mile-and-a-half races start in front of the winning post with runners heading down the home straight away from the finish line. It is a run of 4 furlongs before the left turn onto the right-handed loop, which rejoins the straight course just before the 6-furlong mark for the return run back down the straight towards home. The mile start begins right on the loop, so low draws are definitely an advantage.

## FEATURE RACES

### GLASGOW STAKES

The Glasgow Stakes was formerly run at York and given Listed status in 1999. In 2006 the race was transferred to Hamilton Park. Derby victor **COMMANDER IN CHIEF (1993)** is a former winner.

### BRAVEHEART STAKES

Run since 2003, the race was won by **RED CADEAUX (2011)** on the way to his narrow defeat by Dunaden in the Melbourne Cup of 2011 and a win in the Hong Kong Vase (2012).

# THE CURRAGH

Curragh Racecourse, County Kildare, Ireland. www.curragh.ie

*R*acing was first officially recorded at The Curragh in 1727. It is the headquarters of Irish racing and home to all of Ireland's Classic races.

Ireland has long been a nursery for great horses and riding talent. The training ranks boast some of the world's biggest names, including Aidan O'Brien, Dermot Weld, John Oxx and Jim Bolger.

The emergence in the 1950s of horsemen Paddy Prendergast and Vincent O'Brien raised local competition to a new level, targeting the English Classics and establishing Irish racing as world class. From there trace the origins of Ballydoyle and Coolmore Stud. Not surprisingly, Irish racing continues to flourish as a source of talent both equine and human.

The Curragh is known as a galloping track with vast, open expanses and a lot of undulations making it a demanding test suited to a horse who likes to wind up into a race. Definitely not a sit-and-sprint course.

## THE TRACK

The design is that of a misshapen horseshoe. It is a right-handed track 2 miles in length.

There are various layouts, but the main track – used for most feature races over 1½ miles or more – tests a horse's galloping prowess, with stamina and an ability to cope with a downhill run essential.

The mile start is on a course that is basically straight but doglegs right at the 6-furlong point.

## FEATURE RACES

| IRISH 1000 GUINEAS | G1 | 1M | TURF | 3YOF | MAY |
|---|---|---|---|---|---|
| IRISH 2000 GUINEAS | G1 | 1M | TURF | 3YOC&F | MAY |
| IRISH DERBY | G1 | 1½M | TURF | 3YOC&F | JUNE |
| IRISH OAKS | G1 | 1½M | TURF | 3YOF | JULY |
| IRISH ST LEGER | G1 | 1M6F | TURF | 3YO+ | SEPT |
| TATTERSALLS GOLD CUP | G1 | 1M2½F | TURF | 4YO+ | MAY |
| PRETTY POLLY STAKES | G1 | 1M2F | TURF | 3YO+F&M | JUNE |
| PHOENIX STAKES | G1 | 6F | TURF | 2YOC&F | AUG |
| MOYGLARE STUD STAKES | G1 | 7F | TURF | 2YOF | AUG |
| VINCENT O'BRIEN STAKES | G1 | 7F | TURF | 2YOC&F | SEPT |

## FEATURE RACES

### IRISH 2000 GUINEAS

The Irish 2000 Guineas was instituted in 1921 with **SOLDENNIS** the inaugural winner. Derby winners include **HARD RIDDEN (1958)**, **SANTA CLAUS (1964)** and **GRUNDY (1975)**.

Other notables include Irish Triple Crown winners **MUSEUM (1935)** and **WINDSOR SLIPPER (1942)**; **JACK KETCH (1957)**, who also won the International Stakes (1957) and Canadian International (1958); **RIGHT TACK (1969)**; and **SADLER'S WELLS (1984)**, who also won the Eclipse Stakes (1984) and Irish Champion Stakes (1984) but it was in retirement that he really made his mark. He became one of the Northern Hemisphere's most influential sires of the 20th century, winning 14 sires titles in Britain & Ireland as well as seven broodmare titles. He is now on the verge of a dynasty through the deeds of his sons such as Galileo and High Chaparral.

Filly **TRIPTYCH (1985)**; **RODRIGO DE TRIANO (1992)**; **BARATHEA (1993)** and **SPINNING WORLD (1996)** both won the Breeders' Cup Mile; **DESERT KING (1997)**, sire of three-time Melbourne Cup winner Makybe Diva; **DESERT PRINCE (1998)**; **ROCK OF GIBRALTAR (2002)**; **DUBAWI (2005)**; **COCKNEY REBEL (2007)**; **HENRYTHENAVIGATOR (2008)**; **MASTERCRAFTSMAN (2009)** and **CANFORD CLIFFS (2010)**.

### IRISH 1000 GUINEAS

Notables include **LADY VIOLETTE (1922)**, who won the first running; **SMOKELESS (1935)**; **VALORIS (1966)** and **IMAGINE (2001)** both won The Oaks; **PIDGET (1972)**; **L'ATTYRAYANTE (1983)**; **SONIC LADY (1986)**; **IN THE GROOVE (1990)**; **KOOYONGA (1991)** won the Coronation Stakes (1991) and Eclipse Stakes (1992); **MARLING (1992)**; **RIDGEWOOD PEARL (1995)**; **CRIMPLENE (2000)**; **ATTRACTION (2004)** won the Coronation Stakes, 1000 Guineas, Sun Chariot Stakes (2004) and Matron Stakes (2005); **FINSCAEL BEO**

(2007); and **MISTY FOR ME (2011)** won the Prix Marcel Boussac, Moyglare Stud Stakes (2010) and Pretty Polly Stakes (2011).

## IRISH DERBY

The Irish Derby has become a great race with an honour roll brimming with Derby winners and, in more recent times, winners of the Prix de l'Arc de Triomphe.

First won by **SELIM (1866)**. Derby winners include **ORBY (1907)**, **SANTA CLAUS (1964)**, **NIJINSKY (1970)**, **GRUNDY (1975)**, **THE MINSTREL (1977)**, **SHIRLEY HEIGHTS (1978)**, **TROY (1979)**, **SHERGAR (1981)**, **COMMANDER IN CHIEF (1993)**, **SINNDAR (2000)**, **GALILEO (2001)**, **HIGH CHAPARRAL (2002)** and **CAMELOT (2012)**.

Arc winners include **BALLYMOSS (1957)**, **MONTJEU (1999)**, **SINNDAR (2000)**, **HURRI-CANE RUN (2005)** and **DYLAN THOMAS (2006)**.

Other notables include St Leger winners **SAYA-JIRAO (1947)**, **RAGUSA (1963)**, **RIBOCCO (1967)**, **RIBERO (1968)**; Ascot Gold Cup winners **ZARATHUSTRA (1954)** and **FAME AND GLORY (2009)**; Prix du Jockey Club winners **ASSERT (1982)** and **DREAM WELL (1998)**; **ST JOVITE (1992)** and **ALAMSHAR (2003)** both won the King George VI & Queen Elizabeth Stakes; **BALANCHINE (1994)** won The Oaks; **DESERT KING (1997)**; **CAPE BLANCO (2010)** won the Irish Champion Stakes (2010), Man O'War Stakes, Arlington Million and the Joe Hirsch Invitational Stakes (2011); and **TREASURE BEACH (2011)** won the Secretariat Stakes (2011).

## IRISH OAKS

First won by **SAPLING (1895)**.

Notable winners include **ALTESSE ROYALE (1971)**, **USER FRIENDLY (1992)**, **RAMRUMA (1999)**, **OUIJA BOARD (2004)**, **ALEXANDROVA (2006)**, **SARISKA (2009)** and **SNOW FAIRY (2010)**. All triumphed at Epsom to take out the Anglo–Irish Oaks double.

Other notable winners include champion US-bred mare **DAHLIA (1973)**, who would beat the older males in the King George VI & Queen Elizabeth Stakes just seven days later; and **BLUE BUNTING (2011)**, who also took out the 1000 Guineas.

## IRISH ST LEGER

**VINNIE ROE (2001–04)** recorded an amazing four consecutive victories; **ROYAL LANCER (1922)** would become the first to also win the English St Leger; **TRIGO (1929)** won The Derby and the St Leger; **MUSEUM (1935)** was Ireland's first Triple Crown winner, having won the Irish 2000 Guineas and the Irish Derby – a feat also achieved by **WINDSOR SLIPPER (1942)**, **ZARATHUSTRA (1954)**; **MASHAALLAH (1992)**, who had earlier won the Gran Premio di Milano and the Grosser Preis von Baden.

Melbourne Cup winner **VINTAGE CROP (1993, 94)**, went back to back, as did **OSCAR SCHINDLER (1996, 97)** and **KAYF TARA (1998, 99)**.

Other notables include dual Group 3 Stockholm Cup winner **COLLIER HILL (2005)**, who later won the Canadian International Stakes, Hong Kong Vase (2006); and **YEATS (2007)**.

## TATTERSALLS GOLD CUP

Won twice by **YANKEE GOLD (1976, 77)** and **SO YOU THINK (2011, 12)**; **ERINS ISLE (1981)** won the Hollywood Invitational Stakes (1983); **GOLDEN FLEECE (1982)** won The Derby; **OPERA HOUSE (1992)** won a Coronation Cup, Eclipse Stakes and King George VI & Queen Elizabeth Stakes (1993); **DAYLAMI (1998)**; **MONTJEU (2000)**; **FANTASTIC LIGHT (2002)**; **HURRICANE RUN (2004)**; **DUKE OF MARMALADE (2008)**; and **FAME AND GLORY (2010)**.

## PRETTY POLLY STAKES

Pretty Polly

Pretty Polly was a champion filly who won 22 of her 24 starts, finishing second in the other two. Undefeated in 9 starts as a 2yo, including wins in the Cheveley Park Stakes and Middle Park Stakes, she won the fillies' Triple Crown (1904), Coronation Stakes (1904), Nassau Stakes (1904), Champion Stakes (1905) and two Coronation Cups (1905, 06). At stud she was also one of the all-time great broodmares, founding one of the most influential female dynasties.

Notable winners include **NASHUA (1952)** and **NORTHERN GLEAM (1953)**, both winners of the Irish 1000 Guineas; **DANCE DESIGN (1996, 97)** won two on end as did **ALEXANDER GOLDRUN (2003, 04)**, who also won the Hong Kong Cup (2004); **PEEPING FAWN (2007)** was an Irish Oaks winner; **DAR RE MI (2009)** won the Dubai Sheema Classic (2010); and **MISTY FOR ME (2011)**.

## PHOENIX STAKES

A 2yo contest instituted in 1907 at the former course at Phoenix Park. The event moved to The Curragh in 1992 after a short stint at Leopardstown.

The most notable early winner was **TRIGO (1928)**, who would win The Derby and the St Leger as well as the Irish Derby. Of recent times it has become a stallion-making race. Among those **DANE-HILL DANCER (1995)**, **FASLIYEV (1999)**, **JOHANNESBURG (2001)**, **SPARTACUS (2002)**, **ONE COOL CAT (2003)** and **HOLY ROMAN EMPEROR (2006)**.

## MOYGLARE STUD STAKES

A 7-furlong race for 2yo fillies, it has been won by **HABIBTI (1982)**; **SAYYEDATI (1992)** also won the 1000 Guineas; **RUMPLESTILTSKIN (2005)**, who also won the Prix Marcel Boussac; and **MISTY FOR ME (2010)**.

## VINCENT O'BRIEN STAKES

Formerly known as the National Stakes, it was first run in 1849. Elevated to Group 1 level in 1985, the

Shergar with Aga Khan after winning the Irish Derby, 1981

name was changed in 2012 to honour Vincent O'Brien, widely regarded as the greatest trainer of all time. He prepared the winner of this race on 15 occasions.

Among his achievements O'Brien won The Derby (6 times), 1000 Guineas (4), Dewhurst Stakes (7), Eclipse Stakes (5), Diamond Jubilee Stakes (5), July Cup (5), The Oaks (2), St Leger (3), Sussex Stakes (4), Irish 1000 Guineas (3), Irish 2000 Guineas (5), Irish Champion Stakes (5), Irish Derby (6), Irish Oaks (4), Irish St Leger (9), National Stakes (15), Pretty Polly Stakes (7), Tattersall's Gold Cup (5), Prix de l'Arc de Triomphe (3), Grand National Steeplechase (3), Cheltenham Gold Cup (4), Breeders' Cup Mile and many others.

Notable winners of this race include **CHAT-TERBOX (1849)** and the legendary **BARCALDINE**

**(1880)**, undefeated during his 13-start career.

The race has produced many winners of The Derby including **GRAND PARADE (1918)**, **SANTA CLAUS (1963)**, **SIR IVOR (1967)**, **ROBERTO (1971)**, **SINNDAR (1999)** and **NEW APPROACH (2007)**.

Also 2000 Guineas winners **EL GRAN SENOR (1983)**, **KING OF KINGS (1997)**, **REFUSE TO BEND (2002)** and **GEORGE WASHINGTON (2005)**; **DANEHILL DANCER (1995)**; **DESERT KING (1996)**; **HAWK WING (2001)** won the Eclipse Stakes (2002) and the Lockinge Stakes (2003).

# LEOPARDSTOWN

Leopardstown, Dublin, Ireland. www.leopardstown.com

Fantastic Light defeats Galileo

## FEATURE RACES

| | | | | | |
|---|---|---|---|---|---|
| IRISH CHAMPION STAKES | G1 | 1M2F | TURF | 3YO+ | SEPT |
| MATRON STAKES | G1 | 1M | TURF | 3YO+F&M | SEPT |
| DERRINSTOWN STUD DERBY TRIAL STAKES | G2 | 1M2F | TURF | 3YO | MAY |
| BALLYROAN STAKES | G3 | 1½M | TURF | 3YO+ | JULY–AUG |
| DESMOND STAKES | G3 | 1M | TURF | 3YO+ | AUG |
| KILTERNAN STAKES | G3 | 1M2F | TURF | 3YO+ | AUG–SEPT |
| KILLAVULLAN STAKES | G3 | 7F | TURF | 2YO | OCT–NOV |

**SUAVE DANCER (1991)**; **DR DEVIOUS (1992)**; **PENTIRE (1995)** won the King George VI & Queen Elizabeth Stakes (1996); **PILSUDSKI (1997)**; **SWAIN (1998)**; **DAYLAMI (1999)**; **GIANT'S CAUSEWAY (2000)**; **FANTASTIC LIGHT (2001)**; **HIGH CHAPARRAL (2003)**; **NEW APPROACH (2008)**; **SEA THE STARS (2009)** made it a record seven wins for Michael Kinane; **CAPE BLANCO (2010)**; **SO YOU THINK (2011)**; and **SNOW FAIRY (2012)**.

## MATRON STAKES

Upgraded to Group 1 status in 2004, the Matron Stakes has since been won by **SOVIET SONG (2004)**; **ATTRACTION (2005)**; **LUSH LASHES (2008)**, who followed up wins in the Coronation Stakes and the Yorkshire Oaks; and **RAINBOW VIEW (2009)** won the Fillies' Mile the previous year.

J ust 14 miles south of the Dublin city centre, Leopardstown has played host to racing since 1888. The course design is based on Sandown Park.

It is a dual-purpose track that hosts top-class racing on both the flat and over the jumps, with the highlight on the flat the prestigious Irish Champion Stakes. Many notable races are run here over the obstacles, including the important Irish Hennessy Gold Cup in February.

Great amenities make Leopardstown a very customer friendly and well-attended racetrack. The most popular annual event is the big five-day meeting that commences on Boxing Day.

In 1955, Leopardstown became the first Irish course to allow helicopters to land. It was also the first in Ireland to introduce Sunday racing.

## THE TRACK

Leopardstown is a left-handed oval course of 1m6f in length with long straights and sweeping bends. The run home is 3 furlongs.

Turning out of the home straight it is a downhill run to the back of the course, where a sharp left leads into a long straight run of 4 furlongs. Past the 6-furlong mark runners enter a sweeping bend for 3 furlongs until the home turn.

## FEATURE RACES

### IRISH CHAMPION STAKES

First won by **MALACATE (1976)**, ridden by Lester Piggott. Since then it has produced an impressive roster of winners in its relatively short history including **ASSERT (1982)**; **SADLER'S WELLS (1984)**; **COMMANCHE RUN (1985)**; **TRIPTYCH (1987)**; **INDIAN SKIMMER (1988)**;

# FAIRYHOUSE

Ratoath, County Meath, Ireland.
www.fairyhouse.ie

## FEATURE RACES

| | | | | |
|---|---|---|---|---|
| BROWNSTOWN STAKES | G3 | 7F | TURF | 3YO+F&M | JUN–JUL |
| Belgrave Stakes | L | 6F | TURF | 3YO+ | JUL |

Fairyhouse is one of Ireland's most famous racing venues. It is host to some high-class flat racing but is better known as the venue for the Irish Grand National, staged annually on Easter Monday during the popular Easter Festival.

## THE TRACK

Right-handed. A square-shaped track, undulating in places, with a circumference of 1m6f.

It is uphill to Ballybrack at the top of the track before turning sharply onto the back of the course. A run of more than 4 furlongs follows, taking runners to the home bend and the slightly uphill home straight of 2½ furlongs.

## FEATURE RACES

### BROWNSTOWN STAKES

Originally run at Leopardstown, the race was upgraded from Listed to Group 3 status in 2003. It was transferred to Fairyhouse in 2009.

Best winner has probably been **KOSTROMA (1992)**, who campaigned successfully in the USA winning the Beverly D Stakes.

### IRISH GRAND NATIONAL

First run in 1870, many great horses have won here including **ARKLE (1964)**, **FLYINGBOLT (1966)** and **DESERT ORCHID (1990)**. **BROWN LAD (1975, 76, 78)** holds the benchmark with three wins.

Other notables include **ASCETIC'S SILVER (1904)**, **RHYME 'N' REASON (1985)**, **BOBBYJO (1998)** and **NUMBERSIXVALVERDE (2005)**, who also won the Grand National at Aintree.

# CORK

Killarney Road, Mallow, County Cork, Ireland
www.corkracecourse.ie

## FEATURE RACES

| | | | | | |
|---|---|---|---|---|---|
| NOBLESSE STAKES | G3 | 1M4F | TURF | 3YO+F&M | JUN |
| GIVE THANKS STAKES | G3 | 1M4F | TURF | 3YO+F&M | JUL–AUG |
| Cork Stakes | L | 6F | TURF | 3YO+ | APR |
| Rochestown Stakes | L | 6F | TURF | 2YO | JUN |
| Midsummer Sprint Stakes | L | 5F | TURF | 3YO+ | JUN |
| Platinum Stakes | L | 1M | TURF | 3YO+ | JULY–AUG |
| Navigation Stakes | L | 8½F | TURF | 3YO+ | OCT |

Cork is located in south-west Ireland, in the province of Munster. Originally known as Mallow Racecourse, the venue opened in 1924 for both flat and jumps racing following the closure of the Cork Park track. The course is situated 35km north of the city.

An interesting part of the area's history revolves around nearby Buttevant – the site of what is considered to be the first ever steeplechase race. Legend has it that in 1752 neighbours Cornelius O'Callaghan and Edmund Blake challenged each other to a race across the natural terrain of stone walls, hedges and ditches, over a distance of about 4½ miles. By keeping the spire of the St Leger Church in sight, both riders were able to plot their course to the finish.

## THE TRACK

Cork is a flat, right-handed oval circuit about 1½ miles in length. The run home is about 4 furlongs. Straight 6-furlong sprint course.

# TIPPERARY

County Tipperary, Ireland. www.tipperaryraces.ie

## FEATURE RACES

| | | | | | | |
|---|---|---|---|---|---|---|
| FAIRY BRIDGE STAKES | G3 | 7F100Y | TURF | 3YO+F&M | SWP | 2003 AUGUST |
| CONCORDE STAKES | G3 | 7F100Y | TURF | 3YO+ | SWP | 1983 OCTOBER |

Tipperary is located 112 miles from Dublin, which is not as far away as perhaps it once seemed.

Racing was first officially recorded here in 1848. The current venue commenced operations in 1916. Formerly known as Limerick Junction, as it is situated adjacent to the railway station of the same name, the course was renamed in 1986.

The track hosts flat and jumps racing, including the G2 Tipperary Hurdle.

## THE TRACK

Tipperary is a flat, left-handed oval track with a slight bend shortly after the turn into the back straight. The circumference is 1m2f.

The run home is 2½ furlongs with the winning post positioned half way up the straight. Generally low draws are favoured on the round course.

There is a 5-furlong straight track. This can tend more to high drawn runners, especially in the event of a soft track.

## FEATURE RACES

### CONCORDE STAKES

First held in 1983 it has been won twice by **KINGS RIVER (1985, 86)** and **WIZARD KING (1996, 97)**. **MR BROOKS (1991)** went on to win the July Cup and the Prix de l'Abbaye. Michael Kinane has ridden the winner five times. Dermot Weld has so far trained nine winners.

Named after Fairy Bridge, dam of Sadler's Wells, this is a 7-furlong race for fillies and mares, established in 2003.

# NAAS

Tipper Road, Naas, County Kildare, Ireland
www.naasracecourse.com

## FEATURE RACES

| BLUE WIND STAKES | G3 | 1M2F | TURF | 3YO+F&M | MAY |
|---|---|---|---|---|---|
| Woodlands Stakes | L | 5F | TURF | 3YO+F&M | APR |
| Fillies' Sprint Stakes | L | 5F | TURF | 2YOF | JUN |
| Owenstown Stud Stakes | L | 7F | TURF | 3YO+ | JUN |
| Sweet Mimosa Stakes | L | 7F | TURF | 3YO+F&M | JUN |
| Garnet Stakes | L | 1M | TURF | 3YO+F&M | OCT |

Naas takes its name from the residence of the Kings of Leinster, who resided here until 989AD. It translates from the original Gaelic as 'assembly place of kings'.

Located about 24 miles from Dublin, the course at Naas staged its first meeting in 1924. Better known for quality jumps racing, Naas has built up its stocks on the flat with the Blue Wind Stakes having acquired Group 3 status in recent years.

## THE TRACK

This left-handed course is a squared circle in shape with a circumference of 1m4f. The home straight is 4 furlongs and features a long uphill finish.

Straight sprint course of 6 furlongs.

# DUNDALK

Mullgrove, Ballymascanlon, Dundalk, County Louth, Ireland. www.dundalkstadium.com

## FEATURE RACES

| DIAMOND STAKES | G3 | 1M2½F | AWT | 3YO+ | SEPT—OCT |
|---|---|---|---|---|---|
| Star Appeal Stakes | L | 7F | AWT | 2YO | OCT |
| Mercury Stakes | L | 7F | AWT | 2YO+ | OCT |
| Carlingford Stakes | L | 1M2½F | AWT | 3YO+ | NOV |
| EBF Cooley Fillies' Stakes | L | 1M | AWT | 3YO+F&M | NOV |

Dundalk is situated approximately half way between Belfast and Dublin on Dundalk Bay, at the mouth of the Castletown River.

The track is set in a beautiful location in the shadow of the Carlingford mountains and against the backdrop of the mountain of Mourne.

## THE TRACK

Dundalk is Ireland's only all-weather track, installed in 2007. Floodlit for night racing, it is a left-handed oval Polytrack with a circumference of 10 furlongs.

The home straight is a run in of 2½ furlongs. Five furlong races start from a chute that joins the track at the top of the home bend. Inside draws are a plus from this position.

## FEATURE RACE

### DIAMOND STAKES

Run on turf since 1988, the race was transferred to Dundalk in 2008. It was Ireland's first Group race that was not run on turf. In 2009, the race was upgraded to Group 3 status and won by Aidan O'Brien's four-time Group 1 winner **MASTERCRAFTSMAN**.

# GOWRAN PARK

Mill Road, Gowran, County Kilkenny, Ireland
www.gowranpark.ie

## FEATURE RACES

| DENNY CORDELL EBF FILLIES' STAKES | G3 | 9F | TURF | 3YO+F&M | SEPT |
|---|---|---|---|---|---|
| Victor McCalmont Memorial Stakes | L | 9½F | TURF | 3YO+F&M | MAY |
| Hurry Harriet Fillies' Stakes | L | 9½F | TURF | 3YO+F&M | AUG |

The village of Gowran is situated 6 miles east of Kilkenny. The course at Gowran Park first opened its gates for a race meeting in 1914. Much investment has been made in the course in recent years, with an upgrade to the stable yard and parade ring and the opening of a new grandstand in 2003.

The Denny Cordell EBF Fillies' Stakes was upgraded to Group 3 status in 2006 to make Gowran Park officially a Group racing track for the first time. High-class jumps racing is also held here.

In 1952, the course held the distinction of being the first track in Ireland to feature race commentary.

Some of the great horses successful at Gowran Park include Refuse To Bend, Arkle, Flyingbolt, Brown Lad and Numbersixvalverde.

## THE TRACK

Gowran Park is an undulating, right-handed track of 1m4f in length.

# NAVAN

Proudstown, Navan, County Meath, Ireland
www.navanracecourse.ie

## FEATURE RACES

| Vintage Crop Stakes | L | 1M3F | TURF | 4YO+ | MAY |
|---|---|---|---|---|---|
| Salsabil Stakes | L | 1M2F | TURF | 3YO+F&M | APR—MAY |

Navan is located on the Boyne River, 30 miles north-west of Dublin. It is the centre of local government in County Meath.

## THE TRACK

Navan is a left-handed, rectangular track with a circumference of 1m4f.

The track is large with wide sweeping bends and is considered a true test of stamina, especially during the winter months when the ground is typically very heavy.

The home straight is 3½ furlongs in length and rises steadily for the final 2 furlongs.

Races of up to 6 furlongs are run on the straight course. Jumps racing is also conducted here.

## FEATURE RACE

| VINTAGE CROP STAKES |
|---|

Dermot Weld's Vintage Crop became the first European trained winner of the Melbourne Cup in 1993, and was also a winner of the Cesarewitch (1992) and a dual winner of the Irish St Leger (1993, 94). Weld famously charmed his way into the hearts of the Australian public with his reverence toward the Melbourne Cup and his intimate knowledge of the works of legendary bush poet Banjo Patterson.

Vintage Crop, a gelding, was retired to the Irish National Stud where he is a popular attraction for public visits, especially among Australian tourists who flock in numbers to pay their respects.

# GALWAY

Ballybrit, Galway, County Galway, Ireland
www.galwayraces.com

## FEATURE RACE

| Oyster Stakes | L | 1½M | TURF | 3YO+ | AUG |
|---|---|---|---|---|---|

Galway is located in western Ireland on the River Corrib. The first racing festival in Ballybrit took place in 1869 with a two-day meet. These days it is an extremely popular week-long affair that begins on the last Monday of July and draws crowds of more than 150,000 people over the seven days.

The annual Galway Festival runs concurrently with Glorious Goodwood in England but attracts a very different audience. It is a mixed meeting that caters to many types of horses, with both flat and jumps racing as well as events for amateur riders.

It also attracts big punting interest and the huge crowds really do join in the holiday spirit with plenty of craic and lines six deep at the bar. The party then spills into the town where it continues well into the night. Galway is an absolute must for the Irish racing fan.

For those wishing to invest, it is a meeting that is always a prime target for Dermot Weld, who regularly unveils some of his most promising gallopers, especially 2yos. It is not unusual for Weld to claim up to a dozen winners or more for the week, producing horses such as Go And Go – the first and only Irish horse to win the Belmont Stakes.

## THE TRACK

Galway is a right-handed, squarish track with sharp turns. The circumference is a mile and a quarter with a steep dip along the side approaching the home turn. The ground then rises sharply up the home straight of more than 2 furlongs. The feature jumps races are the Galway Plate and the Galway Hurdle.

# LIMERICK

Greenmount Park, Patrickswell, County Limerick, Ireland. www.limerickraces.ie

## FEATURE RACE

| Martin Molony Stakes | L | 1M3F | TURF | 3YO+ | JUN |
|---|---|---|---|---|---|

Located in Ireland's mid-west, racing here dates back to 1790. The current site at Greenmount Park began operations in 2001.

Situated amid rich farming and breeding country, the location provides panoramic views of the surrounding countryside.

## THE TRACK

The right-handed track is oval shaped with a circumference of 1 mile 3 furlongs. In

the back straight the ground rises 65ft over a section of only 3 furlongs then starts to descend approaching the turn out of the back straight until just after the home bend. From there the straight climbs slightly to the finish.

The course has a width of 76yds, catering for very large fields. When racing is conducted on consecutive days the expansive nature of the course allows riders to find fresh ground when the track is soft.

It is a dual-purpose course and the feature jumps race, the Greenmount Park Novice Chase (G2), is run on Boxing Day, the first day of the four-day Christmas Festival.

Triple Cheltenham Gold Cup winner Cottage Rake scored his maiden victory here at Limerick.

# KILLARNEY

Muckross Road, Killarney, County Kerry, Ireland.
www.killarneyraces.ie

## FEATURE RACE

| Vincent O'Brien Ruby Stakes | L | 8½F | TURF | 3YO+C | H&G | AUG |
|---|---|---|---|---|---|---|

Killarney is situated in the Ring of Kerry in the south-west of Ireland and is one of the country's most popular and exquisite tourist destinations. While Ireland has many beautiful racetrack settings, there is none more so than this breathtaking locale set against the heather-clad sandstone mountains and the lakes of Killarney.

The summer meetings in July and August draw huge holiday crowds and a party atmosphere prevails throughout the area, with the course only a short stroll from the centre of town with its vibrant bars and restaurants.

Racing in Killarney dates back to 1822 with the current course opened in 1936.

## THE TRACK

A dual-purpose track, it is a flat, left-handed oval course with a circumference of 1 mile 100yds.

The home straight is 3 furlongs.

# ROSCOMMON

Lenabane Racecourse Road, Roscommon, County Roscommon, Ireland. www.roscommonracecourse.ie

| FEATURE RACE | | | | | |
| --- | --- | --- | --- | --- | --- |
| Lenabane Stakes | L | 1½M | TURF | 3YO+ | JUL |

Roscommon County is the geographical heart of Ireland, with the course set in an area of lush pastoral land. While racing tends to cater for the lower grades, Roscommon is considered a good course to introduce a promising horse, and the leading Irish stables regularly take quality young horses there. Many good broodmares have also experienced success here early in their careers.

## THE TRACK

An oval-shaped, right-handed track 10 furlongs in circumference. The home straight is an uphill run of 3 furlongs. The track is fairly tight and can play to front runners on occasions; however, the uphill run home does require a horse with the necessary stamina to run the distance.

# PUNCHESTOWN

Punchestown, Naas, County Kildare, Ireland. www.punchestown.com

The course at Punchestown staged its first meeting in 1824 and it is the home of jumps racing in Ireland.

The annual Punchestown Festival is a five-day meeting in the last week of April and the major festival of the Irish National Hunt season. Eleven Grade 1 jumps events are staged during the week including the Champion Chase, Champion Hurdle and the Punchestown Gold Cup.

Great jumpers Arkle, Viking Flagship, Moscow Flyer, Neptune Collonges and Hurricane Flyer have all made their mark during the festival.

The La Touche Cup is a cross-country race that is the most traditional, prestigious and longest of its kind. Trainer Enda Bolger has dominated the race. RISK OF THUNDER, owned by Sean Connery, won the La Touche Cup seven times in a row from 1995 to 2002, the race having been abandoned in 2001. Bolger trained Risk Of Thunder to five of those victories. He also trained the winners of five of the next six renewals.

# LAYTOWN

Laytown Beach, Ireland. www.laytownstrandraces.ie

Laytown is situated 30 miles north of Dublin on the coast of County Meath.

The annual meeting is one with a difference in that it is conducted on the beach, as it has been since 1876. Thousands converge to enjoy the unique spectacle of racing in this casual environment.

While it all sounds like a hit and giggle, races are run under official rules and the faces of the competitors are always familiar. Most of the top local trainers like to support the meeting and its tradition, and many of the great jockeys have ridden here, including Michael Kinane and Johnny Murtagh. All come to enjoy the atmosphere but once legged up it's on for keeps.

There is no fixed date for the meeting as it depends on the cycle of the moon and movement of the tides. No running rail is in effect, with the track marked out using poles driven into the sand. It is not unknown for a rider to go for an impromptu dip. While the racing is serious, it is all about fun and everyone gets into the spirit.

Television stations join in the frivolity and will cross live on the morning of the race meeting for the track report. Typically a presenter is standing waist-deep in the ocean and will cheerfully report that the track is a little bit damp at the moment but otherwise conditions are ideal. The beach has excellent drainage since the installation of tides quite some years previous, and on it goes.

This type of strand course was not unusual around the coast of Ireland in days past but Laytown is the last remaining course of its kind.

# LONGCHAMP

Route des Tribunes, Bois de Boulogne, France. www.france-galop.com

*T*he Hippodrome de Longchamp opened to much fanfare in 1857 with many royals in attendance, including Prince Jerome Bonaparte and his son, Prince Napoleon.

The course is set on 57 hectares of park land in the Bois de Boulogne district alongside the River Seine, west of Paris.

Racing at Longchamp is top class with rich prizes on offer throughout the spring and autumn. Most of France's Group 1 racing is conducted here.

The obvious highlight is the Prix de l'Arc de Triomphe, one of the greatest races in the world and the undisputed weight-for-age championship of Europe.

Struck in 1920 to commemorate the famous monument on the Champs Elysees, the Prix de l'Arc de Triomphe has become one of the world's benchmark races with the winner among the top-rated horses internationally for that year. As the Arc is run on the first Sunday in October, the weather always has a large influence on the result, with the threat of soft ground ever present.

Attending the races in Paris is not exactly considered *de rigeur*, with crowds generally small, but Arc Day – with an all Group 1 card of seven races – draws 40,000 people. The French accent can still be discerned among the thousands of English and Irish who flock to witness an assembly of quality horse flesh rivalled only by the Dubai World Cup and Royal Ascot meetings. But the French do love their thoroughbreds, which was clearly demonstrated when racing continued unabated throughout World War II and the occupation.

While on-track attendances in France may be relatively low, off-track betting has boomed since the introduction of the Tierce, with pools taking on large proportions giving the prospect of a big collect for a small outlay. Run on a nominated race once a week, the Tierce is the showcase bet here and is very popular among punters as well as those who have no real interest in racing.

## THE TRACK

Longchamp has a multi-layout design comprising four intertwining courses. The main or long track – known as the Grande Piste – has a circumference of 2750m. The average length track has a circumference of 2500m. The new track is 1400m in length. The small track has a circumference of 2150m.

| FEATURE RACES | | | | | | | |
|---|---|---|---|---|---|---|---|
| PRIX GANAY | G1 | 2100M | TURF | 4YO+ | SW | 1889 | APR–MAY |
| PRIX D'ISPAHAN | G1 | 1850M | TURF | 4YO+ | SW | 1873 | MAY |
| PRIX SAINT-ALARY | G1 | 2000M | TURF | 3YOF | SW | 1960 | MAY |
| POULE D'ESSAI DES POULAINS | G1 | 1600M | TURF | 3YOC | SW | 1883 | MAY |
| POULE D'ESSAI DES POULICHES | G1 | 1600M | TURF | 3YOF | SW | 1883 | MAY |
| GRAND PRIX DE PARIS | G1 | 2400M | TURF | 3YOC&F | SW | 1863 | JULY |
| PRIX VERMEILLE | G1 | 2400M | TURF | 3YO+F&M | SW | 1897 | SEPT |
| PRIX DU MOULIN DE LONGCHAMP | G1 | 1600M | TURF | 3YOC&F | SW | 1957 | SEPT |
| PRIX DE L'ARC DE TRIOMPHE | G1 | 2400M | TURF | 3YO+ | WFA | 1920 | OCT |
| PRIX ROYAL-OAK | G1 | 3100M | TURF | 3YO+ | WFA | 1861 | OCT |
| PRIX DE L'ABBAYE DE LONGCHAMP | G1 | 1000M | TURF | 2YO+ | SW | 1957 | OCT |
| PRIX DE L'OPERA | G1 | 2000M | TURF | 3YO+F&M | SW | 1974 | OCT |
| PRIX DE LA FORET | G1 | 1400M | TURF | 3YO+ | SW | 1858 | OCT |
| PRIX DU CADRAN | G1 | 4000M | TURF | 4YO+ | SW | 1837 | OCT |
| PRIX JEAN-LUC LAGARDERE | G1 | 1400M | TURF | 2YOC&F | SW | 1853 | OCT |
| PRIX MARCEL BOUSSAC | G1 | 1600M | TURF | 2YOF | SW | 1969 | OCT |

The course can accommodate up to 46 different starting points between distances of 1000m and 4000m. While on the face of it, anywhere on a racecourse can be a starting point, the interwoven nature of the track allows for multiple starting points for most distances. For instance, a 1600m event can start from a number of different locations.

There is also a 5-furlong straight track that runs across the infield towards the back of the course.

## FEATURE RACES

### PRIX DE L'ARC DE TRIOMPHE

The inaugural winner was **COMRADE (1920)**, who also won the Grand Prix de Paris (1920). **KSAR (1921, 22)** was the first of the dual winners, and also won 11 of 15 starts including the Prix du Jockey Club (1921), Prix Ganay, Grand Prix de Saint-Cloud and the Prix du Cadran (1922).

Other dual winners are **MOTRICO (1930, 32)**; Hardwicke Stakes winner **CORRIDO (1936, 37)** became the first mare to win twice; **TANTIEME (1950, 51)**, who had 15 starts for 12 wins including the Poule d'Essai des Poulains (1950), Prix Ganay, Coronation Cup (1951).

Undefeated Italian champion **RIBOT (1955, 56)** was Italy's Horse of the Century and also voted that country's fourth greatest athlete of the 20th century. Of his 16 wins, Ribot only ventured outside Italy on three occasions for a 3-length win in The Arc (1955), a 5-length romp in the King George VI & Queen Elizabeth Stakes (1956) and then when trotting up by 6 lengths in The Arc the following year. He achieved the unique distinction in 1956 of being named Horse of the Year in three separate jurisdictions – the UK, France and Italy.

**ALLEGED (1977, 78)** won 9 of 10 starts; **MASSINE (1924)** achieved a rare double after taking the Ascot Gold Cup (1924), a feat only repeated by **LEVMOSS (1969)**; **PEARL CAP (1931)** was the first filly to win; and **BRANTOME (1934)** won 12 of 14 starts including the Poule d'Eassai des Poulains and Prix Royal-Oak (1934). He had the speed to win the 1100m Prix Robert Papin (Group 2) at 2, and won the Prix du Cadran over 4000m two years later.

**LE PACHA (1941)** having swept the Prix du Jockey Club, Grand Prix de Paris and the Prix Royal-Oak; **DJEBEL (1942)** won 15 of 22 starts including the Gimcrack Stakes, Middle Park Stakes (1939), 2000 Guineas (1940) and the Grand Prix de Saint-Cloud (1942); **ARDAN (1944)** won 16 of 23 including the Prix du Jockey Club (1944), Grand Prix de Saint-Cloud (1945), the Prix Kergolay twice (1945,46) and the Coronation Cup (1946); **MIGOLI**

**(1948)** was a winner of the Dewhurst Stakes (1946), Eclipse Stakes and the Champion Stakes (1947); Irish hero **BALLYMOSS (1958)** won the Irish Derby, St Leger (1957), Eclipse Stakes, King George VI & Queen Elizabeth Stakes and the Coronation Cup (1958); **EXBURY (1963)** also won the Prix Ganay, Coronation Cup and the Grand Prix de Saint-Cloud that year.

**SEA BIRD (1965)** destroyed his rivals following his win in The Derby. Others to do the Derby–Arc double include **MILL REEF (1971)**, **LAMMTARRA (1995)**, **SINNDAR (2000)**, **SEA THE STARS (2009)** and **WORKFORCE (2010)**.

**VAGUELY NOBLE (1968)** was the sire of Dahlia and Exceller; **SASSAFRAS (1970)** famously inflicted the first defeat of Nijinsky in this race; **RHEINGOLD (1973)** won the Grand Prix de Saint-Cloud (1972, 73) twice and also took out the Prix Ganay, Hardwicke Stakes (1973) and ran second to Roberto in The Derby; **ALLEZ FRANCE (1974)** was a seven-time Group 1 winner in France including the Poule d'Essai des Pouliches, Prix de Diane (1973) and the Prix Ganay twice (1974, 75); German-trained **STAR APPEAL (1975)** won the Eclipse Stakes and the Gran Premio di Milano (1975); and **IVANJICA (1976)** won the Poule d'Essai des Pouliches, as did **THREE TROIKAS (1979)**.

**DETROIT (1980)** became the first Arc-winning mare to also produce an Arc winner when **CARNEGIE (1994)** was successful, and **URBAN SEA (1993)** did the same as dam of **SEA THE STARS (2009)**.

**GOLD RIVER (1981)** won the Prix Royal-Oak (1980) and the Prix du Cadran (1981); **ALL ALONG (1983)** would go on to success in the Joe Hirsh Turf Invitational, Canadian International and the Washington DC International (1983); **SAGACE (1984)** also won the Prix Ganay, Prix d'Ispahan (1985); **RAINBOW QUEST (1985)** also won the Coronation Cup (1985), having gained the day from Sagace in the stewards' room.

**DANCING BRAVE (1986)** produced a stunning display to give his rivals a start and a beating as he trounced a field that included seven Group 1 winners. Widely regarded as one of the best winners of the great race.

Italian star **TONY BIN (1988)**; **SUAVE DANCER (1991)** after victories in the Prix du Jockey Club and Irish Champion Stakes; **HELISSIO (1996)** was a dual winner of the Grand Prix de Saint-Cloud (1996, 97); **PEINTRE CELEBRE (1997)** after taking out the Prix du Jockey Club and Grand Prix de Paris; **MONTJEU (1999)** also won the Prix du Jockey Club, Irish Derby (1999), Tattersalls Gold Cup, Grand Prix de Saint-Cloud and the King George VI & Queen Elizabeth Stakes (2000); **HURRICANE RUN (2005)** followed in the footsteps of his sire

Montjeu by winning the Irish Derby (2005), Tattersalls Gold Cup, King George VI & Queen Elizabeth Stakes (2006); **RAIL LINK (2006)** defeated a top field that contained Pride, Deep Impact, Shirocco and Hurricane Run; **DYLAN THOMAS (2007)** won the Irish Derby (2006), Prix Ganay, King George & Queen Elizabeth Stakes (2007) and twice won the Irish Champion Stakes (2006, 07).

Top filly **ZARKAVA (2008)** had an undefeated 7-start career that included 5 Group 1 wins with victories in the Prix Marcel Boussac (2007), Poule d'Essai des Pouliches, Prix de Diane and the Prix Vermeille (2008); and German mare **DANEDREAM (2011)** won the King George VI & Queen Elizabeth Stakes (2012) and was a dual winner of the Grosser Preis von Baden (2011, 12).

## PRIX ROYAL-OAK

Named after influential French stallion Royal Oak, who was foaled in 1823, the race was called the Grand Prix du Prince Imperial when inaugurated in 1861. The current name was adopted in 1869. Considered the French equivalent of the St Leger.

Since its inception in 1861 when won by **PALESTRO** the Prix Royal-Oak has been won by some great horses including **GLADIATEUR**

(1865), **STOCKHOLM (1883)**, **MAINTENON (1906)**, **KSAR (1921)**, **BRANTOME (1934)**, **LE PACHA (1941)**, **RELKO (1963)**, **RELIANCE (1965)**, **SASSAFRAS (1970)**, **EXCELLER (1976)**, **GOLD RIVER (1980)**, **ARDROSS (1981)** and **VINNIE ROE (2001)**. **MATCH (1961)** took out the King George VI & Queen Elizabeth Stakes, Grand Prix de Saint-Cloud, Washington DC International (1962); dead-heater **INDIAN QUEEN (1990)** won the Ascot Gold Cup (1991); **TURGEON (1991)** was also a winner of the Irish St Leger and the Prix Kergolay (1991); **RAINTRAP (1993)** won the Prix Kergolay (1993) Canadian International Stakes (1994); **MOONAX (1994)** also won the St Leger; **AMILYNX (1999, 2000)** won it twice; and so did **WESTERNER (2003, 04)**, who also won the Prix du Cadran twice (2003, 04) and the Ascot Gold Cup (2005).

## PRIX DE L'ABBAYE DE LONGCHAMP

Notable winners include **TEXANA (1957)**, who won the inaugural edition; dual winners **TEXANITA (1963, 64)**, **GENTILHOMBRE (1976, 77)**, **COMMITTED (1984, 85)** and **LOCHSONG (1993, 94)**; **BE FRIENDLY (1968)**; **SHARPO (1982)**; **HABIBTI (1983)**; **DAYJUR (1990)** followed up wins in the King's Stand Stakes, Nunthorpe Stakes and the Sprint Cup.

**MR BROOKS (1992)** also won the July Cup, as did **CONTINENT (2002)** and **MARCHAND D'OR (2008)**.

## PRIX DE L'OPERA

Notable winners include **CHERYL (1974)**; **WAYA (1977)** won 14 of 29 starts, including the Flower Bowl Invitational Stakes, Man O' War Stakes, Joe Hirsch Turf Classic (1978), Beldame Stakes (1979); **ROYAL HEROINE (1983)** won the Breeders' Cup Mile (1984); **ATHYKA (1988, 89)** remains the only horse to have won twice; **HATOOF (1992)** won the 1000 Guineas, EP Taylor Stakes (1992), Champion Stakes (1993), Beverley D Stakes and the Prix Rothschild (1994); **PETRUSHKA (2000)** had won the Irish Oaks and the Yorkshire Oaks; **ALEXANDER GOLDRUN (2004)**; and **MANDESHA (2006)** won the Prix Rothschild and Prix Vermeille (2006).

## PRIX DE LA FORET

Inaugurated in 1858, notable winners include **TOUR-MALET (1864)**; dual winners **AZUR (1883, 84)**, **CARAVELLE (1943, 44)**, **FINE TOP (1953, 54)**, **SANEDTKI (1977, 78)** and **MOORESTYLE (1980, 81)**; **OMNIUM (1894)**; **EPINARD (1922)** won 12 of 20 including the Prix d'Ispahan and Stewards' Cup (1923); **TANTIEME (1949)**; **LYPHARD (1972)** was

the sire of 115 stakes winners including Dancing Brave; **NORTHERN TASTE (1974)** would become arguably the most influential sire in the history of Japanese racing, producing a record number of winners and taking victory in the sires' title on ten occasions; **PRODUCER (1979)** also won the Prix de l'Opera (1979); **SOVIET STAR (1987)**; **DOLPHIN STREET (1993)**; **SOMNUS (2004)** won the Haydock Sprint Cup (2003); **PACO BOY (2008)** was a winner of the Queen Anne Stakes (2009), Lockinge Stakes (2010); **GOLDIKOVA (2010)**; and **DREAM AHEAD (2011)**.

## PRIX DU CADRAN

Prominent winners include four-time winner **MARSYAS (1944–47)**, who won 17 of 27 starts, including the Prix Kergolay (1944), Goodwood Cup and Doncaster Cup (1946); **MISS ANNETTE (1837)**; **FRANCK (1838)**, first winner of the Prix du Jockey Club (1836).

Three-time winner **NAUTILUS (1839, 40, 42)**; and dual winners **TAINE (1962, 63)**, **BUCKSKIN (1977, 78)** and **WESTERNER (2003, 04)**.

Other notables include **NATIVA (1844)**, who won the first edition of the French Oaks (1843); **RAYON D'OR (1880)** won 17 of 23 starts including the St Leger, Champion Stakes and the St James's Palace Stakes (1879); **OMNIUM (1896)**; **KSAR (1922)**; **BRANTOME (1935)**; **LEVMOSS (1969)**; **SAGARO (1976)**; **GOLD RIVER (1981)** and **SERGEANT CECIL (2006)**.

## PRIX JEAN-LUC LAGARDERE

Formerly known as the Grand Criterium, the name was changed in 2003 to recognise the contribution of Jean-Luc Lagardere, who was a leading owner and breeder, and foundation president of France Galop. It is France's oldest and most prestigious race for juveniles.

Notable winners include **CELEBRITY (1853)**; **JONGLEUR (1876)**, winner of the Prix d'Ispahan (1878); **HERO (1895)**, winner of the Prix de la Foret (1895); **ODOL (1919)** also took out the Prix du Cadran (1921); **EPINARD (1922)**; **BRANTOME (1933)**; **CARAVELLE (1942)**; **TANTIEME (1949)**; **SICAMBRE (1950)**; **BELLA PAOLA (1957)** went on to victory in the 1000 Guineas, The Oaks, Champion Stakes (1958); **RIGHT ROYAL (1960)**; **HULA DANCER (1962)**, who also won the 1000 Guineas and Champion Stakes (1963); **GREY DAWN (1964)** famously inflicted the only defeat of the great Sea Bird; **SIR IVOR (1967)**.

**BLUSHING GROOM (1976)**; **IRISH RIVER (1978)** won 10 of 12 starts including the Poule d'Essai des Poulains (1979) and was sire of 87 stakes winners including Hatoof; **HECTOR PROTECTOR (1990)**.

**ARAZI (1991)** was a four-time Group 1 winner including a brilliant victory in the Breeders' Cup

Juvenile (1991); **ROCK OF GIBRALTAR (2001)**; and **HOLY ROMAN EMPEROR (2006)** who won the Phoenix Stakes (2006).

## PRIX MARCEL BOUSSAC

Marcel Boussac dominated French racing for 30 years from the 1930s. He was 14-time leading owner and leading breeder on 17 occasions. Among his many great horses were Arc winners Corrida, Djebel, Ardan, Coronation and Caracalla. He also owned Derby winner Galcador.

Formerly known as the Criterium des Pouliches, the name was changed to commemorate Boussac, who died in 1980.

Notable winners include **VELA (1969)**, the inaugural winner; **ALLEZ FRANCE (1972)**; **TRIP-TYCH (1984)**; **MIDWAY LADY (1985)** won the 1000 Guineas and The Oaks (1986); **MIESQUE (1986)**; **SALSABIL (1989)**; **SHADAYID (1990)** also won the 1000 Guineas (1991); **CULTURE VULTURE (1991)**; **RYAFAN (1996)** won the Falmouth Stakes, Nassau Stakes (1996) and the Queen Elizabeth Challenge Cup (1997) at Keeneland.

**SIX PERFECTIONS (2002)** went on to success in the Breeders' Cup Mile (2003); **DIVINE PROPORTIONS (2004)**; **RUMPLESTILTSKIN (2005)**; **FINSCAEL BEO (2006)** also won the 1000 Guineas (2007); **ZARKAVA (2007)**; and **MISTY FOR ME (2010)**.

## POULE D'ESSAI DES POULAINS

Sometimes referred to as the French 2000 Guineas. Notable winners include **REGAIN (1883)**; **SIR GALLAHAD (1923)** would be four-time leading sire in the USA and a staggering 12-time leading broodmare sire there.

**BRANTOME (1934)** won the Arc, as did **DJEBEL (1940)** and **TANTIEME (1950)**; **RIGHT ROYAL (1961)** won the Prix du Jockey Club, as did **SHAMARDAL (2005)** and **LOPE DE VEGA (2010)**. **RELKO (1963)** went on to claim The Derby; **CARO (1970)** was a winner of the Prix d'Ispahan (1970) and Prix Ganay (1971) and would sire 78 stakes winners; **RIVERMAN (1972)** was twice leading French sire; **GREEN DANCER (1975)** followed up his victories in the Racing Post Trophy (1974) and Prix Lupin (1975); **BLUSHING GROOM (1977)** would be leading sire in Britain; and **IRISH RIVER (1979)** won 10 of 12 with seven of those at Group 1. He would sire 87 stakes winners. **BLUSHING JOHN (1988)** won the Hollywood Gold Cup (1989); **HECTOR PROTECTOR (1991)** was a winner of the Prix Morny, Prix de la Salamandre (1990) and Prix Jacques Le Marois (1991); **KINGMAMBO (1993)** won the St James's Palace Stakes and would sire Lemon Drop Kid, King's Best and Henrythenavigator; **DAYLAMI (1997)**; and **LANDSEER (2002)**, who also won the Shadwell Turf Mile (2002).

## GRAND PRIX DE PARIS

In the earlier history of the race it was not uncommon for winners of The Derby to target this race. They include Triple Crown champion **GLADIATEUR (1865)**, **CREMORNE (1872)**, **KISBER (1876)**, **SPEARMINT (1906)**, **MY LOVE (1948)** and **PHIL DRAKE (1955)**. In latter times winners of The Arc have become more prominent including inaugural Arc winner **COMRADE (1920)**, **LE PACHA (1941)**, **SAUMAREZ (1990)**, **SUBOTICA (1991)**, **PEINTRE CELEBRE (1997)**, **BAGO (2004)** and **RAIL LINK (2006)**.

Other notable winners include **THE RANGER (1863)**; **NEARCO (1938)** arrived undefeated from Italy and made it a perfect 14 from 14. Off the track, Nearco's influence could not have been greater. As sire of Nasrullah and grandsire of Northern Dancer he stands as patriarch to one of the greatest sire lines in the history of the thoroughbred.

**RELIANCE (1965)** won the Prix du Jockey Club and the Prix Royal-Oak (1965); **SAGARO (1974)** won three Ascot Gold Cups; **EXCELLER (1976)**; **AT TALAQ (1984)** won the Melbourne Cup (1986); **BEAT HOLLOW (2000)** went to take the Manhattan Hcp, Turf Classic Stakes and Arlington Million (2002); and **SCORPION (2005)** won the St Leger (2005) and Coronation Cup (2007).

## POULE D'ESSAI DES POULICHES

Considered France's equivalent of the 1000 Guineas. **STOCKHOLM (1883)** won the first running. Fillies to claim the Prix de Diane double include **PRIM-ROSE (1891)**, **ROXELANE (1897)**, **CARAVELLE (1943)**, **APOLLONIA (1956)**, **LA SEGA (1962)**, **GAZALA (1967)**, **MADELIA (1977)**, **EAST OF THE MOON (1994)**, **DIVINE PROPORTIONS (2005)** and **GOLDEN LILAC (2011)**.

Those to have won the English 1000 Guineas as well are **IMPRUDENCE (1947)**, **MIESQUE (1987)**, **RAVINELLA (1988)** and **SPECIAL DUTY (2010)**, who had the rare distinction of taking out the double despite not being first past the post in either race. American-bred Miesque is in the US Hall of Fame having won 12 of 16 starts, with ten wins at the elite level including two Breeders' Cup Turf Miles (1987, 88). She was the dam of Kingmambo.

The exclusive club of Arc winners includes **PEARL CAP (1931)**, **ALLEZ FRANCE (1973)**, **IVANJICA (1975)**, **THREE TROIKAS (1979)** and **ZARKAVA (2008)**. **CULTURE VULTURE (1992)** followed up wins in the Fillies' Mile and Prix Marcel Boussac (1991).

## PRIX GANAY

Established as the Prix des Sablons, the name was changed in 1949 in memory of former Societe d'Encouragement president Jean de Ganay, who passed away the previous year.

Five horses have been successful twice. **CAIUS (1904, 05)**, **GOYA (1939, 40)**, **TANERKO (1957, 58)**, **ALLEZ FRANCE (1974, 75)** and **SAINT ANDREWS (1988, 89)**. Arc winners to also win the Prix Ganay include **KSAR (1922)**, **TANTIEME (1951)**, **EXBURY (1963)**, **RHEINGOLD (1973)**, **SAGACE (1985)**, **SUBOTICA (1992)**, **HELISSIO (1996)**, **BAGO (2005)** and **DYLAN THOMAS (2007)**. **MILL REEF (1972)** won the Arc and the Derby **(1971)**; and **RELKO (1964)** won the Derby (1963).

Other notables include **ACHERON (1889)**; **MAIN-TENON (1907)**; **NIMBUS (1914)** won a Prix du Cadran (1914); **DIATOME (1966)** won the Washington DC International the previous year; **CARO (1971)** was a winner of the Prix D'Ispahan and Poule d'Essai des Poulains (1970); **TRIPTYCH (1987)**; **AQUAREL-LISTE (2002)** followed up victories in the Prix de Diane and Prix Vermeille (2001); **DUKE OF MARMALADE (2008)**; **VISION D'ETAT (2009)** and **CIRRUS DES AIGLES (2012)**, who won the Champion Stakes (2011) and Dubai Sheema Classic (2012).

## PRIX D'ISPAHAN

Inaugurated in 1873 to honour the visiting Shah of Persia. Several have won the race twice including **CHAMPAUBERT (1897, 98)**, **LE CAMARGO (1903, 04)**, **MOULINS LE MARCHE (1908, 09)**, **RENETTE (1935, 36)**, **HIEROCLES (1942, 43)**, **COARAZE (1946, 47)**, **FRIC (1955, 56)**, **CRYSTAL GLITTERS (1983, 84)** and **GOLDIKOVA (2010, 11)**.

Other notables include **CAMPECHE (1873)**; **JONGLEUR (1878)** won the Prix Jean-Luc Lagardare (1876); **CAIUS (1905)**; **EPINARD (1923)**; Poule d'Essai des Poulains winners **CARO (1970)** and **RIVERMAN (1972)**; Arc winners **ALLEZ FRANCE (1974)** and **SAGACE (1985)**; **IRISH RIVER (1979)**; **MIESQUE (1988)**; **INDIAN SKIMMER (1989)**; **ARCANGUES (1993)** was victorious in the Breeders' Cup Classic (1993); **HALLING (1996)**; **FALBRAV (2003)**; German star **MANDURO (2007)** was the world's top-rated horse that year after also winning the Prince of Wales's Stakes and the Prix Jacques Le Marois; and **GOLDEN LILAC (2012)** followed up her win in the Prix de Diane (2011).

## PRIX VERMEILLE

One of France's premier contests for fillies and mares. Fillies to take out the race after winning the Poule d'Essai des Pouliches and the Prix de Diane include **SEMENDRIA (1900)**; **LA CAMARGO (1901)**; **PEARL CAP (1931)**, **NICKELLORA (1945)**, **ALLEZ FRANCE (1973)** and **ZARKAVA (2008)** all won the Arc.

Other Arc winners successful include **SAN SAN (1972)**, **IVANJICA (1975)**, **THREE TROIKAS (1979)** and **ALL ALONG (1982)**. Other notables include **ORTIE BLANCHE (1897)**; Oaks winners **BELLA PAOLA (1958)**, **SALSABIL (1990)** and **INTREPIDITY (1993)**; Prix de Diane winners **NORTHERN TRICK (1984)**, **AQUARELLISTE (2001)** and **STACELITA (2009)**.

Poule d'Essai des Pouliches winners **SESARA (1899)**, **RONDE DE NUIT (1909)** and **DANCING MAID (1978)**; **CORTEIRA (1948)**; **AUNT EDITH (1965)** won the Nassau Stakes (1965), Yorkshire Cup, King George VI & Queen Elizabeth Stakes (1966); **APRIL RUN (1981)** won the Joe Hirsch Turf Classic twice (1981, 82) and the Washington DC International (1982); **MANDESHA (2006)** won the Prix Roth-schild. Prix de l'Opera (2006); and **MIDDAY (2010)**.

## PRIX SAINT-ALARY

Evremond de Saint-Alary was a successful owner and breeder. Among his many winners was Comrade, inaugural winner of the Arc.

Notable winners include **LA MOTTE (1960)**, **MADELIA (1977)** also won the Poule d'Essai des Pouliches and Prix de Diane that year, **THREE TROIKAS (1979)**; **INDIAN SKIMMER (1987)**, **INTREPIDITY (1993)** and **STACELITA (2009)**.

## PRIX DU MOULIN DE LONGCHAMP

Notable winners include **ROSE ROYALE (1957)**; **HULA DANCER (1963)**; **GREAT NEPHEW (1967)**, sire of Derby winners Shergar and Grundy; **IRISH RIVER (1979)**; **MIESQUE (1987)**; **KING-MAMBO (1993)**; **RIDGEWOOD PEARL (1995)**; **SPINNING WORLD (1997)**; **ROCK OF GIBRALTAR (2003)**; **STARCRAFT (2005)**; **GOLDIKOVA (2008)**; **EXCELEBRATION (2011)** won the Prix Jacques Le Marois, and the Queen Elizabeth II Stakes (2012); and **MOONLIGHT CLOUD (2012)** is a dual winner of the Prix Maurice de Gheest (2011, 12) and was a narrow second to Black Caviar in the Diamond Jubilee Stakes (2012).

# CHANTILLY

Chantilly, Ouise, France. www.france-galop.com

*C*hantilly *racecourse is situated about 50km from Paris in the district of Oise, surrounded by picturesque forests and opulent chateaux.*

The first meeting here was held in May 1834.

Dominating the landscape is le chateau et Les Grandes Ecuries, or the Grand Stables, which were built in 1719 by the Prince de Conde. The story goes that the prince was of the firm belief that he would be reincarnated as a horse. Not one to sit idly by his convictions, he conceived the most lavish accommodation imaginable for a horse and had constructed the type of stables befitting royalty – a horse palace. These Grand Stables accommodate 250 horses.

While it would be easy to label the prince an eccentric for his beliefs, his great legacy remains in the form of this magnificent structure. The course here at Chantilly was designed and built using the chateau as its centerpiece and, in fairness to the prince, it could be equally said that his theory on the next life has never been disproven.

While Longchamp is the scene for most French Group 1 racing, Chantilly stages two of the French Classic races: the Prix du Jockey Club and the Prix de Diane – France's equivalent of The Derby and The Oaks.

The Prix de Diane is one of the most prestigious days on the French racing calendar, and the Parisian social set all turn out in their finery for the occasion.

Shortly after the establishment of the Prix du Jockey Club in 1836 and the Prix de Diane in 1843, wealthy owner the Duc d'Orleans transferred all of his horses to Chantilly to be trained. This move began a trend that quickly saw Chantilly take over the mantle as the nation's major training centre.

It is a position that it still holds with as fine a roster of trainers as one would find anywhere in the world. Among the residents here are Andre Fabre, Freddie and Criquette Head, Alain Royer-Dupre, Mikael Dezangles, John Hammond and much of the Aga Khan's racing stock.

Add the gorgeous forest setting where many of the gallops take place and Chantilly is horse paradise for the 3000 thoroughbreds housed here.

## THE TRACK

Chantilly is a right-handed track with a circumference of 2600m. Races up to 1400m can be held on the straight course using the third of the three winning post positions.

There is a chute for a 1400m start on the round course, and another chute that accommodates starts for races at 1600m and 1800m. Races from 2000 to 2400m start from a diagonal chute that cuts across the round course before linking up with it near the 1400m mark, just before runners start to swing onto the home bend.

With three finish line positions, the home straight on the round course can be up to 900m, depending on which winning post is used.

## FEATURE RACES

### PRIX DU JOCKEY CLUB – FRENCH DERBY

The distance of the race was shortened in 2005 from 2400m to 2100m. First won by **FRANCK (1836)**. Many winners of the Prix du Jockey Club have won the Arc, including dual winner **KSAR (1921, 22)**, **LE PACHA (1941)**, **ARDAN (1944)**, **SASSAFRAS (1970)**, **SUAVE DANCER (1991)**, **PEINTRE CELEBRE (1997)**, **MONTJEU (1999)** and **DALAKHANI (2003)**.

Those to also claim the Poule d'Essai des Poulains include **RIGHT ROYAL (1961)**, who also won a King George VI & Queen Elizabeth Stakes (1961); **SHAMARDAL (2005)** and **LOPE DE VEGA (2010)**. Those to also win the Grand Prix de Paris include **AJAX (1904)**, **FINASSEUR (1905)**, **PHARIS (1939)**, **SICAMBRE (1951)** and **RELIANCE (1965)**, who also claimed the Prix Royal-Oak.

**OMNIUM (1895)** was a winner of 17 races

| FEATURE RACES | | | | | | | |
|---|---|---|---|---|---|---|---|
| PRIX DU JOCKEY CLUB | G1 | 2100M | TURF | 3YOC&F | SW | 1836 | JUN |
| PRIX DE DIANE | G1 | 2100M | TURF | 3YOF | SW | 1842 | JUN |
| PRIX JEAN PRAT | G1 | 1600M | TURF | 3YOC&F | SW | 1858 | JUN–JUL |
| GRAND PRIX DE CHANTILLY | G2 | 2400M | TURF | 4YO+ | SWP | 1973 | MAY–JUN |
| PRIX DE SANDRINGHAM | G2 | 1600M | TURF | 3YOF | SWP | 1967 | MAY–JUN |
| PRIX DU GROS-CHENE | G2 | 1000M | TURF | 3YO+ | SWP | 1857 | MAY–JUN |

including the Prix du Cadran (1896); **MAINTENON (1906)** won 13 of 19 with six wins at Group 1 including the Grand Prix de Saint-Cloud and the Prix Kergolay (1906); **TEDDY (1916)** would sire 65 stakes winners; **TOURBILLON (1931)** was three-time leading sire in France, as was **VAL DE LOIR (1962)**; **HERBAGER (1959)** sired 64 stakes winners, mainly in the USA; **YOUTH (1976)** took out the Canadian International Stakes, Washington DC International Stakes (1976).

ASSERT (1982) went on to win the Irish Derby, International Stakes at York, Irish Champion Stakes (1982); **CAERLEON (1983)** was also a winner of the International Stakes (1983) and topped the sires' list in the UK; **DARSHAAN (1984)**; Chester Vase winner **OLD VIC (1989)** went on to win the Irish Derby, as did **DREAM WELL (1998)**; **CELTIC ARMS (1994)** won the Breeders' Cup Turf (1996); **CELTIC SWING (1995)** sire of champion sprinter Takeover Target; Globetrotting **SULAMANI (2002)** won the Dubai Sheema Classic, Arlington Million, Joe Hirsch

Turf Classic (2003), International Stakes, Canadian International Stakes (2004); **SHAMARDAL (2005)** won the first edition at the shortened distance; and **VISION D'ETAT (2008)** also won the Hong Kong Cup (2009).

Yves St Martin rode the winner on nine occassions, and Tom Jennings Snr trained ten winners of the race.

## PRIX DE DIANE

The French equivalent of The Oaks. Notable winners include **NATIVA (1843)**; Arc winners **PEARL CAP (1931), ALLEZ FRANCE (1973)** and **ZARKAVA (2008)**; **HIGHCLERE (1974)** won the 1000 Guineas; **PAWNEESE (1976)** won by 11½ lengths after winning The Oaks by 5 lengths. Later that season she was victorious in the King George VI & Queen Elizabeth Stakes. **INDIAN SKIMMER (1987)** defeated Miesque in a much-awaited clash between the two outstanding fillies of their generation. She also won

the Pretty Polly Stakes (1987), Sun Chariot Stakes, Champion Stakes, Irish Champion Stakes (1988), Prix d'Ispahan (1989). **AQUARELLISTE (2001)** won the Prix Vermeille (2001) and Prix Ganay (2002); and **STACELITA (2009)** won the Prix Vermeille (2009), Prix Jean Romanet (2010), Beverly D Stakes and the Flower Bowl Invitational Hcp (2011).

## PRIX JEAN PRAT

Notable winners include **CAIUS (1903)**; **DUNBAR (1914)** won The Derby (1914); **ODOL (1920)**; **RIVERMAN (1972)**; **PRIOLO (1990)** also won the Prix Jacques Le Marois (1990), Prix du Moulin de Longchamp (1991); **TORRENTIAL (1995)**; **ALMUTAWAKEL (1998)** won the Dubai World Cup (1999); **GOLDEN SNAKE (1999)**; and Arc winner **BAGO (2004)**.

# DEAUVILLE

Avenue Hocquart de Turtot, Deauville, France. www.france-galop.com

*Every August, France packs up and converges on the various seaside locations to the south and the north. Deauville in the north is a tourist hot spot with absolutely stunning architecture. The course has been designed in keeping with its surroundings to enhance the beautiful setting for the top-class racing that Deauville provides.*

And it is a racing feast, with up to 24 meetings staged here throughout the month. Consequently the installation of an all-weather inner track has been a welcome addition, as it has successfully relieved some of the obvious stress on the turf track.

The course – the Hippodrome Deauville-La Touques – was opened in 1834. Racing in previous years had been conducted on the beach.

With the course located only a short stroll from the centre of town, which is in full party mode, the atmosphere is very relaxed but still maintains an air of class.

Three hundred horses are stabled here and the annual yearling sale at Deauville is one of the world's premier thoroughbred sales.

## THE TRACK

Right-handed. The track is a classic oval with a circumference of 2000m. Races up to 1600m are held on the straight course. Start positions for races between 2600m and 3200m are also located on the straight course.

Start positions for races over 1400m and 1600m are located on the back straight of the round course.

The 2000m races are run on the round course. The start is from a chute that links up with the bend out of the home straight. Runners are on the bend from virtually the time they jump so inside draws are a definite advantage.

## FEATURE RACES

### PRIX JACQUES LE MAROIS

Named after the former president of the course's ruling body, le Societe des courses de Deauville. Notable winners include **SIR GALLAHAD (1923)**, **PEARL CAP (1931)**, **HULA DANCER (1963)**, **IRISH RIVER (1979)**, **LEAR FAN (1984)**, **HECTOR PROTECTOR (1991)**, **DUBAI MILLENNIUM (1999)**, **SIX PERFECTIONS (2003)**, **MANDURO (2007)**, **GOLDIKOVA (2009)** and **EXCELEBRATION (2012)**.

Other notables include top sires **LUTHIER (1968)** and **LYPHARD (1972)**; 2000 Guineas winners **NONOALCO (1974)** and **MAKFI (2010)**; 1000 Guineas winners **FLYING WATER (1977)** and **SAYYEDATI (1993)**; **TAIKI SHUTTLE (1998)** was a top Japanese horse who won 11 of 13 starts including the Sprinters Stakes (1997), Yasuda Kinen (1998) and twice won the Mile Championship (1997, 98).

**BANKS HILL (2002)** followed up her win in the Breeders' Cup Filly & Mare Turf (2001); **DUBAWI (2005)** won the National Stakes (2004), Irish 2000 Guineas (2005) and sired star Hong Kong sprinter Lucky Nine; **MIESQUE (1987, 88)** and **SPINNING WORLD (1996, 97)** both won the race twice. Miesque was also the dam of **EAST OF THE MOON (1994)**, who won the Poule d'Essai des Pouliches and Prix de Diane that year. **WHIPPER (2004)** also won the Prix Morny (2004) and Prix Maurice de Gheest (2005) to give him the distinction of winning three of the five Group 1 races run at the Deauville course.

| FEATURE RACES | | | | | | |
|---|---|---|---|---|---|---|
| PRIX JACQUES LE MAROIS | G1 | 1600M | 3YO+(EXCL. G) | SW | 1921 | AUG |
| PRIX JEAN ROMANET | G1 | 2000M | 4YO+F&M | SW | 2004 | AUG |
| PRIX MAURICE DE GHEEST | G1 | 1300M | 3YO+ | SW | 1922 | AUG |
| PRIX MORNY | G1 | 1200M | 2YOC&F | SW | 1865 | AUG |
| PRIX ROTHSCHILD | G1 | 1600M | 3YO+F&M | SW | 1929 | AUG |
| GRAND PRIX DE DEAUVILLE | G2 | 2500M | 3YO+ | SWP | 1866 | AUG |
| PRIX GUILLAUME D'OMANO | G2 | 2000M | 3YO | SW | 1952 | AUG |
| PRIX KERGOLAY | G2 | 3000M | 3YO+ | SWP | 1864 | AUG |
| PRIX DE POMONE | G2 | 2500M | 3YO+F&M | SWP | 1920 | AUG |

## PRIX JEAN ROMANET

Established in 2004 to honour the former president of the Societe d'Encouragement, previous ruling body of French racing, notable winners include **PRIDE (2005)**, who went on to claim the Grand Prix de Saint-Cloud, Champion Stakes and Hong Kong Cup the following year; back-to-back winner **SATWA QUEEN (2006, 07)**; **STACELITA (2010)** and **SNOW FAIRY (2012)**.

## PRIX MAURICE DE GHEEST

Named in memory of Maurice de Gheest who was a prominent member of the Societe des course de Deauville. Run over the unusual Group 1 distance of 1300m.

First won by **ZARIBA (1922)**. There have been a number of dual winners including **AZIYADE (1936, 37)**, **VAMARIE (1953, 54)**, **NICE GUY (1961, 62)**, **BOITRON (1979, 80)** and **MOONLIGHT CLOUD (2011, 12)**. **MARCHAND D'OR (2006–08)** made it a hat-trick. Other interesting winners include **FLYING WATER (1977)**, **DOLPHIN STREET (1994)**, July Cup winner **ANABAA (1996)**, and **SOMNUS (2004)**, who won the Haydock Sprint Cup (2003).

## PRIX MORNY

Named in honour of the course founder, Auguste de Morny, who passed away in 1920. Notable winners include **PEARL CAP (1930)**; **BRANTOME (1933)**; **CORRIDA (1934)**; **GREY DAWN (1964)**; **NONOALCO (1973)**; **BLUSHING GROOM (1976)**; **IRISH RIVER (1978)**; **MACHIA-VELLIAN (1989)**, sire of Street Cry; **HECTOR PRTECTOR (1990)**; **ARAZI (1991)**; **ZAFONIC (1992)**, who won the 2000 Guineas (1993); **ELUSIVE CITY (2002)**; **DIVINE PROPORTIONS (2004)**; **DREAM AHEAD (2010)**; and Middle Park Stakes winner **RECKLESS ABANDON (2012)**.

## PRIX ROTHSCHILD

Formerly known as the Prix d'Astarte, the race was upgraded to Group 1 status in 2004. Since its elevation, **GOLDIKOVA (2008–11)** has dominated, winning on four consecutive occasions. A winner of 17 of her 27 starts and unplaced only once, Goldikova was a three-time winner of the Breeders' Cup Mile (2008–10) and winner of the Prix du Moulin de Longchamp (2008), Falmouth Stakes, Prix Jacques Le Marois (2009), Queen Anne Stakes, Prix de la Foret (2010) and took out the Prix d'Ispahan twice (2010, 11).

Other notables include **DIVINE PROPOR-TIONS (2005)** and **MANDESHA (2006)**. **HATOOF (1994)** was also a previous winner.

# SAINT-CLOUD

Rue du Camp Canadien, Saint Cloud, France.
www.france-galop.com

## FEATURE RACES

| | | | | | | | |
|---|---|---|---|---|---|---|---|
| GRAND PRIX DE SAINT-CLOUD | G1 | 2400M | TURF | 4YO+ | SW | 1904 | MAY |
| CRITERIUM DE SAINT-CLOUD | G1 | 2000M | TURF | 2YOC&F | SW | 1901 | NOV |
| CRITERIUM INTERNATIONAL | G1 | 1600M | TURF | 2YOC&F | SW | 2001 | NOV |
| PRIX GREFFULHE | G2 | 2000M | TURF | 3YOC&F | SW | 1882 | MAY |

Saint Cloud is a fashionable and affluent suburb of Paris, less than 10km from the city's heart. Its hillside location offers wonderful panoramic views over the west side of Paris. The course has been one of France's premier tracks since opening in 1901 and is host to very high-quality racing.

Saint-Cloud is the most heavily used racetrack in Paris, but the turf here handles the workload well and is always turned out in good condition.

Feature races include the Grand Prix de Saint-Cloud, a race won by many great horses during its history dating back more than a century. The course was declared a Monument Historique in 1992.

## THE TRACK

Left-handed, the track is triangular shaped and 2300m in length. Home straight of 600m. A diagonal chute runs inside the track from the home turn to about the 1900m point in the straight out of the turn. From the turn out of the straight it is a tight left turn, then a straight run of 500m to the top of the course and another quite tight left-handed bend. It is then a run of 600m to the sweeping home bend, which leads to a run home of 600m. There is also a straight sprint course.

## FEATURE RACES

### GRAND PRIX DE SAINT-CLOUD

First run at Maisons-Laffitte in 1904. The impressive honour roll includes **MAINTENON (1906)**, CORRIDA (1936), DJEBEL (1942), HERBAGER (1959), MATCH (1962), EXBURY (1963), RELKO (1964), SEA BIRD (1965), EXCELLER (1977), USER FRIENDLY (1993), MONTJEU (2000) and PRIDE (2006).

Dual winners include **NINO (1926, 27), TAMERKO (1957, 58), RHEINGOLD (1972, 73), HELISSIO (1996, 97)** and **ANGE GABRIEL (2002, 03)**. Other notables include **PRINCE ROSE (1932)**, who won 16 from 20 and sired Princequillo; **STRAWBERRY ROAD (1985)** was a top Australian horse who won 17 races including the ATC Derby, Cox Plate (1983), Grosser Preis von Baden (1984) and the Arcadia Hcp (1986); German star **ACATENANGO (1986)**; **MOON MADNESS (1987)**, who won the St Leger (1986), Yorkshire Cup (1988); Breeders' Cup Turf winner **IN THE WINGS (1990)**; **EL CONDOR PASA (1999)** won the Japan Cup (1998), as did **ALKAASED (2005)**.

### CRITERIUM DE SAINT-CLOUD

Established in 1901, the race was promoted to Group 1 level in 1987. Since then the race has been won by **BALLINGARRY (2001)**, who was also victorious in the Canadian International Stakes (2002), and **FAME AND GLORY (2008)**. Earlier notables include dual Arc winner **MOTRICO (1927)**; **PROVIDENTIAL (1979)**, who won a Washington DC International, Hollywood Turf Club Stakes (1981); and **DARSHAAN (1983)**.

### CRITERIUM INTERNATIONAL

A 1600m race for 2yos established in 2001. Winners include **DALAKHANI (2002)** and **BAGO (2004)**, who would both capture the Arc as 3yos; and **RODERIC O'CONNOR (2010)**, who went on to take the Irish 2000 Guineas (2011).

# MAISONS-LAFFITTE

1 Avenue de la Pelouse, Maisons-Laffitte, France.
www.france-galop.com

**Maisons-Laffitte is a suburb of Paris, 18km north-west of the city centre.**

Located on the banks of the River Seine, the course opened in 1878 as part of a property development constructed by Jacques Lafitte. The course was initially leased then bought outright by the Societe Sportive d'Encouragement.

A delightful feature on the perimeter of the track is a beautifully quaint French restaurant that offers excellent food and wine in the best local tradition. At the main meetings it is certainly the place to be and be seen.

Maisissons-Lafitte is the largest racecourse in the Paris region and stages high-quality racing. Trainers of both codes, jumps and flat, are based here with facilities catering for the preparation of over 700 horses.

Wet weather can be a problem as the water table is high due to its proximity to the River Seine, and the ground often becomes very heavy during the winter months.

## FEATURE RACES

| | | | | | | |
|---|---|---|---|---|---|---|
| PRIX ROBERT PAPIN | G2 | 1100M | TURF | 2YOC&F | 1892 | JUL |
| PRIX EUGENE ADAM | G2 | 2000M | TURF | 3YO | 1893 | JUL |
| CRITERIUM DE MAISONS-LAFFITTE | G2 | 1200M | TURF | 2YO | 1891 | NOV |
| PRIX IMPRUDENCE | G3 | 1400M | TURF | 3YOF | 1949 | APR |
| PRIX DJEBEL | G3 | 1400M | TURF | 3YOC&G | 1949 | APR |
| PRIX MESSIDOR | G3 | 1600M | TURF | 3YO+ | 1949 | JUL |
| PRIX DE RIS-ORANGIS | G3 | 1200M | TURF | 3YO+ | 1970 | JUL |
| LA COUPE DE MAISONS-LAFFITTE | G3 | 2000M | TURF | 3YO+ | 1906 | SEPT |
| PRIX MIESQUE | G3 | 1400M | TURF | 2YOF | 2001 | NOV |
| PRIX SEINE-ET-OISE | G3 | 1200M | TURF | 3YO+ | 1906 | NOV |

## THE TRACK

The track has a unique layout.

The design is similar to Salisbury with its long straight course, in this case 2000m, with a loop back onto the course proper. It is the longest straight course in Europe.

Where it differs is that there is also a length of track almost parallel to the straight that swings left at the end of the course to form a triangle. This provides the option of joining the inner figure-of-8 track that links up with the straight courses on both sides, making the track both left- and right-handed.

Consequently there are dual start points on the course for most distances of 1600m and beyond with the option of running either down the straight course or using the figure of 8. Depending on the distance of the race, there are three separate positions for the winning post.

## FEATURE RACES

### PRIX ROBERT PAPIN

Time-honoured 2yo race run since 1892. Notable winners include **PEARL CAP (1930)**, **BRANTOME (1933)**, **ARDAN (1943)**, Mill Reef suffered his first defeat at the hands of **MY SWALLOW (1970)**, **BLUSHING GROOM (1976)**, **ARAZI (1991)**, **DIVINE PROPORTIONS (2004)**, **NATAGORA (2007)** also won the 1000 Guineas (2008), **SPECIAL DUTY (2009)** and **RECKLESS ABANDON (2012)**.

### PRIX EUGENE ADAM

This race for 3yo over 2000m has a long history dating back to 1893. Notable winners include **MAINTENON (1906)**, **TRICTRAC (1965)**, **ARCANGUES (1991)**, **CARNEGIE (1994)**, **DUBAI MILLENNIUM (1999)**, **TWICE OVER (2008)** won the Champion Stakes twice (2009, 10), and **DEBUSSY (2009)** also won the Arlington Million (2010).

### CRITERIUM DE MAISONS-LAFFITTE

Notable winners include **EPINARD (1922)**, **BELLA PAOLA (1957)**, **SEA BIRD (1964)**, **ZINO (1981)** won the 2000 Guineas (1982), and **CAPTAIN RIO (2001)**.

# TOULOUSE

Hippodrome de la Cepiere, 1 Chemin des Courses, Toulouse, France. www.hippodrome-toulouse.com

### FEATURE RACES

| PRIX FILLE DE L'AIR | G3 | 2100M | TURF | 3YO+F8M | NOV |
|---|---|---|---|---|---|
| Prix Caravelle | L | 2100M | TURF | 3YOF | APR |
| Prix Aymeri de Mauleon | L | 1800M | TURF | 3YO | APR |
| Le Vase d'Argent | L | 2000M | TURF | 4YO+ | APR |
| Derby du Languedoc | L | 2400M | TURF | 3YO | JUN |
| Prix Occitanie | L | 1900M | TURF | 3YOF | SEPT |
| Prix Panacee | L | 2400M | TURF | 3YO+F&M | SEPT |
| Criterium du Languedoc | L | 1600M | TURF | 2YO | NOV |
| Prix Max Sicard | L | 2400M | TURF | 3YO+ | DEC |

Located in the Haute-Garonne in south-western France, the Hippodrome Cepiere is set on 34 hectares of park land just 4km from the city centre of Toulouse. The Toulouse course is one of France's oldest with a history dating back to 1866.

## THE TRACK

Right-handed oval. The track has a circumference of 1875m. The straight run home is 430m.

## FEATURE RACE

### PRIX FILLE DE L'AIR

Established in 1902, the race is usually staged on the Armistice Day public holiday.

Won by **LA CAMARGO (1903)**, **DETROIT (1980)**; **PUNTA GORDA (1906, 07)** and **AHOHONEY (1984, 85)** won it twice.

# VICHY

Rue Alquie, Vichy, France.
www.courses-de-vichy.fr

### FEATURE RACES

| Grand Prix de Vichy | G3 | 2000M | TURF | 3YO+ | JUL |
|---|---|---|---|---|---|
| Prix des Jouvenceaux et des Jouvencelles | L | 1400M | TURF | 2YO | JUL |
| Prix Madame Jean Couturie | L | 2000M | TURF | 3YOF | JUL |
| Prix Jacques de Bremond | L | 1600M | TURF | 4YO+ | JUL |
| Prix Frederic de lagrange | L | 2400M | TURF | 3YO | JUL |
| Prix des Reves d'Or | L | 1000M | TURF | 2YO | JUL |

The spa and resort town of Vichy is located in Auvergne, central France. It was at the instigation of the young Baron de Veauce that the first race meeting at Vichy took place on the Bellerive grounds by the banks of the River Allier in 1875.

Racing at the Hippodrome de Vichy-Bellerive takes place from May through to September but the undoubted highlight of the calendar is the week-long Festival of the Gallop, which begins in mid July. Most of the high-class racing in Vichy occurs during this week.

The course also accommodates jumps, harness and cross-country events. It is the only course in France to stage night racing.

## THE TRACK

Right-handed. Classic oval with long straights and narrow turns. The circumference is 2000m with a home straight of 800m.

## FEATURE RACE

### GRAND PRIX DE VICHY

Inaugurated at the same time as the track in 1875, the race was elevated to Group 3 status in 1976. Since then three horses have been successful twice: **PEROUGES (1979, 80)**, **MARILDO (1993, 95)** and **TOUCH OF LAND (2005, 06)**. Most notable winner is **CIRRUS DES AIGLES (2011)**.

# LYON-PARILLY

Avenue de Bohlen, Vaux en Velin, Lyon, France.
www.leshippodromesdelyon.fr

### FEATURE RACES

| Prix Rene Et Jacquel Bedel | L | 2400M | TURF | 4YO+ | MAY |
|---|---|---|---|---|---|
| Coupe des Trois Ans | L | 2400M | TURF | 3YO | MAY |
| Grand Prix de Lyon | L | 2400M | TURF | 4YO+ | JUN |
| Criterium de Lyon | L | 1600M | TURF | 2YO | SEPT |
| Prix du Grand Camp | L | 2400M | TURF | 3YO+ | NOV |

Lyon is situated in the Rhone-Alpes region in east-central France, between Paris and Marseille.

The 178-hectare Parilly Park is the location for racing and the venue is the Hippodrome Parilly. The first meeting here was staged in 1965.

## THE TRACK

Left-handed. The course is 1800m in length with a home straight of 500m. It is a dual-purpose track. The Hippodrome complex also contains a cross-country course and a track for harness racing.

# MARSEILLES-BORELY

16 Avenue de Bonneveine, Marseilles, France.
www.lescourseshippiquesregionales.com

## FEATURE RACES

| | | | | | |
|---|---|---|---|---|---|
| Prix Georges Trabaud | L | 2000M | TURF | 3YO | MAY |
| La Coupe de Marseilles | L | 2000M | TURF | 3YO | SEPT |
| Prix Delahante | L | 1800M | TURF | 2YO | NOV |
| Grand Prix de Marseilles | L | 2000M | TURF | 3YO+ | NOVR |

Historic Marseilles is one of the oldest cities in France and the second most-populous after Paris. The Parc Borely and the seaside location combine to form a beautiful setting for the Hippodrome Marseilles-Borely, which held its first meeting in 1860. Major renovations in 1999 transformed the facilities to make it a very user-friendly track. Harness racing is also conducted here.

## THE TRACK

Left-handed. Classic oval of 1600m. The straight is 400m.

# NANTES

Boulevard des Tribunes, Nantes, France.
www.hipponantes-courses.com

## FEATURE RACES

| | | | | | |
|---|---|---|---|---|---|
| Grand Prix Anjou Bretagne | L | 1600M | TURF | 4YO+ | JUN |
| Derby de l'Ouest | L | 2400M | TURF | 3YO | JUL |
| Prix des Sablonnets | L | 1600M | TURF | 2YO | OCT |
| Grand Prix de Nantes | L | 2400M | TURF | 3YO+ | OCT |

Located on the Loire River in western France, Nantes has hosted racing since 1834, but at that time it was strictly for the gentry only. Legislation was passed to allow racing for the public and the first organised meeting was staged here in 1875. The complex at the Hippodrome de Nantes at Petit Port hosts flat, jumps and harness racing.

## THE TRACK

Left-handed. The course is almost skull-shaped, with a circumference of 2068m. The run in is 400m. Out of the straight it is a hairpin bend left into a straight run of about 400m. From there it is left onto a round, sweeping bend for around 1000m, which takes runners all of the way to the home straight.

# BORDEAUX

Avenue d'Eysines, Le Bouscat, Bordeaux, France.
www.hippodromebordeauxlebouscat.com

## FEATURE RACES

| | | | | | |
|---|---|---|---|---|---|
| Grand Prix de Bordeaux | L | 1900M | TURF | 4YO+ | MAY–JUN |
| Derby du Midi | L | 2400M | TURF | 3YO | MAY–JUN |
| Prix Millkom | L | 1600M | TURF | 3YO+ | SEPT |
| Grand Criterium de Bordeaux | L | 1600M | TURF | 2YO | OCT |

The port city of Bordeaux on the Garonne River is best known as the world capital of the wine industry but racing also has a long history in the area. The inaugural race meeting in Bordeaux was conducted in 1836, following the merger of the Societe des Steeple-Chases de Bordeaux and the Societe d'Encouragement de Bordeaux.

The Hippodrome Bordeaux Le Bouscat is located less than 6km from the centre of Bordeaux and the complex hosts flat and jumps racing with a separate harness racing track.

## THE TRACK

Right-handed. The track is an irregular oval of 2000m in length. The run home is about 600m.

# LA TESTE-DE-BUCH

785 Route de Canaux, La Teste-de-Buch, France.
www.hippodrome-lateste.com

## FEATURE RACES

| | | | | | |
|---|---|---|---|---|---|
| Prix La Sorellina | L | 1600M | TURF | 3YOF | JUN |
| Criterium du Bequet | L | 1200M | TURF | 2YO | JUL–AUG |
| Prix Occitanie | L | 1800M | TURF | 3YOF | SEPT |
| Prix Millkom | L | 1600M | TURF | 3YO | SEPT |

La Teste-de-Buch is situated on the Acheron coast of south-western France and is known as home to the world's largest sand dune. The Hippodrome du Becquet was constructed on 80 hectares of park land and the first meeting was staged in 1903. Facilities have received a major upgrade in the past decade. La Teste is also a training centre with over 300 horses prepared here.

## THE TRACK

Right-handed. Classic oval with a circum-ference of 2050m. It is a track with narrow bends and long straights. The run home is approximately 900m. Steeplechase races are also held here.

# CAGNES-SUR-MER

Hippodrome de la Cote d'Azur, Cagnes-Sur-Mer .
www.hippodrome-cotedazur.fr

## FEATURE RACES

| | | | | | |
|---|---|---|---|---|---|
| Prix de la Californie | L | 1600M | TURF | 3YO | FEB |
| Grand Prix de la Riviera Cote d'Azur | L | 2000M | TURF | 4YO | FEB |
| Prix Policeman | L | 2500M | TURF | 3YO | FEB |
| Grand Prix du Conseil General des Alpes Mairitimes | L | 2500M | TURF | 4YO+ | FEB |

Cagnes-Sur-Mer in the south-east of France is a suburb of Nice and a beautiful seaside setting for racing at the Hippodrome de la Cote d'Azur. As with many French courses, the complex at Cagnes-Sur-Mer also caters for jumps racing and harness racing.

## THE TRACK

Left-handed. The oval turf course features a multi-layout design.

A fibresand Polytrack circuit of 2100m in length was installed in 2008.

# CRAON

Hippodrome de la Touche, Craon, France.
www.hippodrome-course-cheveax-53-craon.courses-craon.com

## FEATURE RACES

| | | | | | |
|---|---|---|---|---|---|
| Grand Prix de la Ville de Craon-Meyenne | L | 2400M | TURF | 3YO+ | SEPT |
| Criterium de l'Ouest | L | 1650M | TURF | 2YO | SEPT |
| Prix du Point du Jour | L | 1650M | TURF | 3YO+ | SEPT |

Craon is situated on the Oudon River in the north-west of France, providing a delightful and picturesque location for equine sports of all varieties. The Hippodrome de la Touche in Craon is a massive equestrian centre known as the Temple of the Horse.

First opened in 1848, it is a very popular destination for racing with crowds in excess of 20,000 regularly in attendance to soak up the unique French rural ambience. The 65-hectare complex provides for flat racing, jumps racing, has a separate track for harness racing, and cross–country courses, including one of 6000m in length.

## THE TRACK

The track is a right-handed classic oval of 1850m in length. The straight run in is 400m.

# CLAIREFONTAINE

Route de Clairefontaine, Tougeville, France.
www.hippodrome-deauville-clairefontaine.com

## FEATURE RACES

| | | | | | |
|---|---|---|---|---|---|
| Prix Luth Enchantee | L | 1800M | TURF | 4YO+ | AUG |
| Grand Prix de Clairefontaine | L | 2400M | TURF | 3YO | AUG |

Clairefontaine is one of the most ornate tracks on the Normandy coast, with the summer meetings a highlight. The Hippodrome de Clairefontaine staged its first meeting in 1928 and consists of four courses with separate tracks for flat racing, hurdles, steeplechases and also harness racing. It is a gorgeous setting for racing and the quality of the race card often benefits from its proximity to neighbouring Deauville. The course was constructed so that the season could be extended in the area.

## THE TRACK

Right-handed. The course is oval shaped with a sweeping bend into the home straight and a narrow bend out of the home straight. The track circumference is 2000m. The home straight is approximately 400m.

# COMPIEGNE

Avenue Baron de Soultrait, Compiegne, France.
www.hippodrome-compiegne.fr

## FEATURE RACES

| | | | | | |
|---|---|---|---|---|---|
| Grand Prix de Compiegne | L | 2000M | TURF | 4YO+ | JUN–JUL |
| Prix Pelleas | L | 2000M | TURF | 3YOC&G | JUL |

Compiegne is situated on the Oise River in the north of France. Nestled in an enclave of the Compiegne Forest, the Hippodrome du Putois is located near the

Imperial Palace of Compiegne. Racing in the area dates back to 1875.

Recently renovated, Compiegne is a great horse centre with courses for flat racing, jumps and cross-country. In 1992 an equine complex was constructed adjacent to the racetrack to accommodate showjumping and dressage.

## THE TRACK

The course is a left-handed, classic oval of 2200m in circumference. The straight run home is 600m long.

# FONTAINEBLEAU

Hippodrome de la Solle, Fountainebleau, France.
www.hippodrome-fontainebleau.com

### FEATURE RACE

| Prix Cor de Chasse | L | 1100M | TURF | 3YO+ | MARCH–APRIL |
|---|---|---|---|---|---|

Renowned for its forest, Fontainebleau is situated in metropolitan Paris, 55km south-east of the capital's centre. The first races were run at Fontainebleau in 1776 during the reign of Louis XVI. The King's brother, the Count d'Artois, along with the Duc de Chartres organised a race meeting to be held as a prelude to the royal hunt. The first official events were conducted at the Hippodrome de la Solle in 1862.

In recent times the course has renovated the existing facilities.

It is a dual-purpose course.

Vision d'Etat

## THE TRACK

Left-handed. The track is a broken or incomplete oval of 2400m in length. The run home is 750m. There is a 1200m straight sprint course.

The straight at Fontainebleau does not link up with the remainder of the round course after passing the winning post. For races over the longer distances, the start is from an inner diagonal chute, which has a tight left-handed loop that returns runners onto the course proper as it joins the back straight.

# STRASBOURG

Rue de Cheval Noir, Hoerdt, Strasbourg, France>
www.hippodromes-est.fr

### FEATURE RACE

| Grand Prix de la Region Alsace | L | 2100M | TURF | 3YO+ | SEPT |
|---|---|---|---|---|---|

Strasbourg in eastern France is the seat of the European Parliament and capital of the Alsace region. The Hippodrome Strasbourg Hoerdt is on the Lower Rhine, 15km north of Strasbourg. The recently renovated course was opened in 1970.

## THE TRACK

Right-handed. Classic oval of 1800m in circumference. Home straight of 400m.

# AUTEUIL

Route des Lacs, Paris, France.
www.france-galop.com

The Auteuil course is purpose built for jumps racing, with France's feature events over the obstacles conducted at the track.

The Societe anonyme des courses des d'obstacles was established and the course opened in 1873 on the 33-hectare site. The society would then become the Societe des Steeple-Chases de France in 1878. In 1893, it became the first racing body ever to offer breeding bonuses, with the owner of the dam of all winners receiving 10% of the prize money.

The outer track was constructed in 1924, the same year that the course hosted the equestrian events at the Olympic Games. In 1966, Auteuil was the first French racecourse to introduce an electronic betting system that displayed the odds on television screens.

Feature races include the Grand Steeple-Chase de Paris run in May, the Prix du President de la Republique run in April, Grande Course de Haies in June and the Prix La Haye Jousselin in November.

Only three horses have won both the Grand Steeple-Chase de Paris and the Grand Course de Haies: Blageur in the early 1900s, Loreto in the 1960s and Ubu in the 1990s. The double has never been taken out in the same year.

Le Paillon won the Grand Course de Haies (1947) then went on to win the Grand Prix de Deauville and the Arc that year.

Al Capone achieved the remarkable feat of winning the Prix La Haye Jousselin on seven consecutive occasions from 1993 to 1999 and ran second in the race in 2000. A life-sized statue of the champion was unveiled in 2000 with the horse in attendance.

Few horses in history have won the same race seven times. These include Doctor Syntax who won the Preston Gold Cup from 1815–21; Franc Picard won the Grand Steeple-Chase de Dieppe seven times between 1853 and 1861; Belgian horse Redpath won the Steeple-Chase des Flandres at Waereghem on seven occasions between 1887 and 1896; and Sean Connery's horse Risk of Thunder took out the La Touche Cup at Punchestown seven times between 1995 and 2002.

Notable riding achievements at Auteuil include those of Pierre de Delfarguiel, who set a record 6 wins from 6 rides here in 1955, and Beatrice Marie who became the first female jockey to win the Grand Course de Haies in 1988.

# CAPANNELLE

Via Appia Nuova, Rome, Italy. www.capannelleippodromo.it

*The Ippodromo Capannelle is located south-west of Rome. The course was opened in 1881 and reconstructed in 1926.*

Capannelle is one of the two major racing venues in Italy and home of the Derby Italiano, which remains the richest and most prestigious race on the Italian calendar despite being downgraded to Group 2 status in 2009. Floodlights were installed in 2006 with night racing mainly conducted on the all-weather track.

## THE TRACK

Right-handed. The track features three courses. The main turf course has a circumference of 2600m with a home straight of 1000m.

Straight sprint course of 1200m joins the home straight. The inner turf course is 2200m in length.

All-weather track 2000m in circumference.

## FEATURE RACES

### PREMIO PRESIDENTE DELLA REPUBLICA

The race has seen many dual winners including **ADREINA (1884, 85)**, **SANSONETTO (1895, 98)**, **MARCANTONIO (1900, 01)**, **TARANTELLA (1902, 03)**, **MANISTEE (1925, 26)**, **ALBERIGO (1953, 55)**, **SURDI (1960, 61)**, **MANNSFIELD (1974, 75)**, Arc winner and top sire in Japan **TONY BIN (1987, 88)**, **SIKESTON (1991, 92)**, **ALTIERI (2004, 05)** and **DISTANT WAY (2006, 07)**.

Other notables include **MAKUFA (1912)**; **PILADE (1934)**; **BELLINI (1941)**; **TENERANI (1948)**, who won the Gran Premio del Jockey Club, Derby Italiano (1947), Goodwood Cup (1948); **NUCCIO (1951)** won the Arc, Coronation Cup (1952); **SEDAN (1959)**; **VERONESE (1964)**; **MOULTON (1973)** won the International Stakes at York that year; **BOB BACK (1985)**; **ALWUHUSH (1989)**; **MUHTARRAM (1994)** won the Irish Champion Stakes (1993), Prince of Wales's Stakes (1995); **FLAGBIRD (1995)**; **CENTRAL PARK (1999)**; **TIMBAROA (2000)** won the Joe Hirsch Turf Classic (2001); and **PAOLINI (2001)** won the Dubai Duty Free (2004).

### PREMIO ROMA

Dual winners include **PAMPINO (1933, 34)**, **GRIFONE (1947, 49)**, **SURDI (1961, 62)**, **BACUCO (1969, 70)**, **DUKE OF MARMALADE (1975, 76)**, **TAIPAN (1997, 98)**, **ELLE DANZIG (1999, 2000)** and **SOLDIER HOLLOW (2004, 05)**.

Other notable winners include **WORDEN (1952)**, who won the Washington DC International (1953); **BEWITCHED (1955)** won the Prix du Cadran (1956); **TISSOT (1956)**; **VERONESE (1963)**; **CHICAGO (1968)**; top filly **ORSA MAGGIORE (1974)**; **NOBLE SAINT (1979)**; **CAMPERO (1982)**; **YAWA (1984)** won the Grand Prix de Paris (1983); **OLD COUNTRY (1985)** won the Prix Royal-Oak (1983); **LEGAL CASE (1990)** won the Champion Stakes (1989); **SIKESTON (1991)**; **MISIL (1992)**; **CHERRY MIX (2006)**; and **RIO DE LA PLATA (2010)**.

### PREMIO LYDIA TESIO

Named in honour of Lydia Tesio, wife of Frederico Tesio, who single-handedly transformed racing in Italy before his passing in 1954.

Tesio has an unparalleled record as an owner, breeder and trainer. He bred many champions, including legendary horses Nearco and Ribot – both undefeated on the racetrack and enormously influential stallions. He was a master trainer who, among his many great successes, prepared the winner of the Derby Italiano on 21 occasions.

The Premio Lydia Tesio was inaugurated in 1936 and rated at Group 1 level between 1977 and 1987 and then again since 2004.

### DERBY ITALIANO

Notable winners include **ANDREINA (1884)**; **SANSONETTO (1894)**; **FAUSTA (1914)**, who also won the Italian Oaks and was dam of three winners of this race – all by Signorino. Others to win the Italian Derby–Oaks double include **GIANPIETRINA**

| FEATURE RACES | | | | | | |
|---|---|---|---|---|---|---|
| PREMIO PRESIDENTE DELLA REPUBLICA | G1 | 2000M | TURF | 4YO+ | 1879 | MAY |
| PREMIO LYDIA TESIO | G1 | 2000M | TURF | 3YO+F&M | 1968 | OCT |
| PREMIO ROMA | G1 | 2000M | TURF | 3YO+ | 1911 | NOV |
| DERBY ITALIANO | G2 | 2200M | TURF | 3YOC&F | 1884 | MAY |

**(1917); JACOPA DEL SELLAIO (1932)**, who also won the Italian 1000 and 2000 Guineas; **ARCHI-DAMIA (1936)**, the last filly to win; **MANISTEE (1924); APELLE (1926)** won the Coronation Cup (1926) and is considered Italy's greatest broodmare sire; **ORTELLO (1929)** won the Arc that year and was six times leading sire in Italy; **PILADE (1933); DONA-TELLO (1937)**.

Legend **NEARCO (1938)** was undefeated in his 14-start career including the Gran Criterium (1937), Premio Parioli, Gran Premio di Milano and Grand Prix de Paris (1938). Enormously influential sire of Nearctic, Nasrullah and Royal Charger.

**BELLINI (1940); NICCOLO DELL'ARCA (1941); ORSENIGO (1943); GLADIOLO (1946); TENERANI (1947)**, sire of Ribot; **DAUMIER (1951); BOTICELLI (1954)** won the Ascot Gold Cup (1955); **SEDAN (1958); RIO MARIN (1959); APPIANI (1966)** sired Star Appeal; **ORTIS (1970); ORANGE BAY (1975); SIRLAD (1977); GLINT OF GOLD (1981)** won the Gran Criterium (1980), Grand Prix de Paris, Preis von Europa (1981), Grosser Preis von Baden Grand Prix de Saint-Cloud (1982);

**OLD COUNTRY (1982); LUSO (1995); SINGLE EMPIRE (1997); CENTRAL PARK (1998); RAKTI (2002);** and **MASTERY (2009)**, who also won the St Leger (2009) and the Hong Kong Vase (2010).

# SAN SIRO

Via Ippodromo, Milan, Italy. www.ippodromimilano.it

## FEATURE RACES

| | | | | | | |
|---|---|---|---|---|---|---|
| GRAN PREMIO DI MILANO | G1 | 2400M | TURF | 3YO+ | 1889 | JUN |
| GRAN CRITERIUM | G1 | 1600M | TURF | 2YOC&F | 1925 | OCT |
| PREMIO VITTORIO DI CAPUA | G1 | 1600M | TURF | 3YO+ | 1958 | SEPT |
| GRAN PREMIO DEL JOCKEY CLUB | G1 | 2400M | TURF | 3YO+ | 1920 | OCT |
| OAKS D'ITALIA | G2 | 2400M | TURF | 3YOF | 1910 | MAY |

*M*ilan is the second-largest city in Italy and home to one of the country's premier racing venues, the San Siro Ippodromo.

The original course at San Siro was laid out in 1889. The course was redesigned by famed architect Vietti Violli and completely reconstructed in 1926.

The stables of Frederico Tesio were located north of Milan and Tesio used the San Siro course to prepare many of his star gallopers. His great rivalry with trainer Giuseppe de Montel during the 1920s and 1930s set Italian racing on fire, with supporters of the two major stables often evoking scenes more reminiscent of a football match than a racetrack.

The San Siro complex was redeveloped in 1975. The course now features a botanical garden, a racing museum and exhibition centre dedicated to the history of thoroughbred and harness racing, and is also home to the imposing statue Leonardo's Horse, which is intended to replicate the original design by Leonardo da Vinci. The track is also equipped for night racing and contains a harness-racing course.

## THE TRACK

Right-handed track that has a number of layouts within the course. The main turf track is 3200m in circumference. The home straight is an uphill run of 900m.

## FEATURE RACES

### GRAN PREMIO DI MILANO

Dual winners include **SANSONETTO (1895, 96)**, **KEEPSAKE (1903, 05)**, **BURNIE JONES (1918, 19)**, **MANISTEE (1924, 25)**, **CRANACH (1927, 28)**, **MEXICO (1961, 62)**, **MARCO VISCONTI (1966, 67)**, **TONY BIN (1987, 88)** and **QUIJANO (2008, 09)**.

Other notable winners include filly **HIRA (1897)**, who won the Derby Italiano; **MARCAN-TONIO (1901)**; **SCOPAS (1923)**; **APELLE (1926)**; **ORTELLO (1929)**; **CAVALIERE D'ARPINO (1930)**, the horse who Tesio claimed was the best he had ever bred; **CRAPOM (1933)** won the Arc (1933); **ARCHIDAMIA (1936)**; **DONATELLO (1937)**; **NEARCO (1938)**; **NICCOLO DELL'ARCA (1941)**; **ORSENIGO (1943)**; **MACHERIO (1944)**; **GLADIOLO (1946)**; **TENERANI (1947)**; **ASTOLFINA (1948)**; and **BOTICELLI (1954)**;

Undefeated legend **RIBOT (1956)** won the Gran Criterium (1954), Gran Premio del Jockey Club (1955), King George VI & Queen Elizabeth Stakes (1956) and twice won the Arc (1954, 55).

**BRAQUE (1957)**; **SEDAN (1958)**; **EXAR (1959)** won the Doncaster and Goodwood Cups (1960); **VERONESE (1963)**; **PRINCE ROYAL (1964)** won the Arc that year; **ORSA MAGGIORE (1975)**; **STAR APPEAL (1975)** also won the Arc (1975); **SIRLAD (1977)**; **DIAMOND SHOAL (1983)**; **ESPRIT DU NORD (1984)**; **ALWUHUSH (1989)**; **SNURGE (1991)**; **MASHAALLAH (1992)** and **STRATEGIC CHOICE (1996)** both won the Irish St Leger; **LANDO (1995)**; **SHANTOU (1997)** won the St Leger (1996); **UNGARO (1998)**; **DARK MOONDANCE (1999)** won the Prix Ganay (1999); **ENDLESS HALL (2000)** won the Singapore International Cup (2001); **PAOLINI (2001)**; **FALBRAV (2002)**; and **ELECTROCUTIONIST (2005)**.

### GRAN CRITERIUM

Premier 2yo contest on the Italian racing calendar. Notable winners include top filly **ERBA (1927)**, **ORTELLO (1928)**, **EMANUELE FILIBERTO (1929)**, **JACOPA DEL SELLAIO (1931)**, **DOSSA DOSSI (1932)**, **ARCHIDAMIA (1935)**, **DONATELLO (1936)**, **NEARCO (1937)**, **NICCOLO DELL'ARCA (1940)**, **ORSENIGO (1942)**, **TREVISANA (1947)**, **STIGLIANO (1949)**, **DAUMIER (1950)**, **RIBOT (1954)** and **RIO MARIN (1958)**.

**MARGUERITE VERNAUT (1959)** won the Champion Stakes and was dual winner of the Premio Lydia Tesio (1959, 60); **MOLVEDO (1960)** won the Arc (1961); **TADOLINA (1964)**; **SIRLAD (1976)**; **GLINT OF GOLD (1980)**; **SIKESTON (1988)**; **ALHIJAZ (1991)**; **PELDER (1992)** won the Prix Ganay (1993); and **SPARTACUS (2002)**.

### PREMIO VITTORIO DI CAPUA

The race has had many dual winners including **PHARYLLIS (1958, 59)**, **MOLVEDO (1961, 62)**, **PRETENDRE (1964, 65)**, **MARCO VISCONTI**

(1967, 68), **BACUCO (1970, 71)**, **TIERCERON (1972, 73)**, **RIBECOURT (1975, 76)**, **ISOPACH (1979, 80)**, **SIKESTON (1990, 91)**, **ALHIJAZ (1992, 93)** and **SLICKLY (2001, 02)**.

Other prominent winners include **ORSA MAGGIORE (1974)**; **INFRA GREEN (1977)** won the Prix Ganay **(1976)**; **MAHTATHIR (1999)** won the Prix Jacques Le Marois (2000); **RAMONTI (2006)** won the Sussex Stakes, Queen Anne Stakes, Queen Elizabeth II Stakes at Ascot, Hong Kong Cup (2007); **GLADIATORUS (2009)** won the Dubai Duty Free (2009); **RIO DE LA PLATA (2010)**; **DICK TURPIN (2011)** won the Prix Jean Prat (2010).

## GRAN PREMIO DEL JOCKEY CLUB

Dual winners include **SCOPAS (1920, 22)**, **ERBA (1928, 29)**, **NORMAN (1953, 54)** and **SCHI-APARELLI (2007, 08)**.

Other notable winners include **PILADE (1935)**; **BELLINI (1940)**; **TENERANI (1947)**; **ASTOL-FINA (1948)**; **GRIFONE (1949)**; **DAUMIER (1951)**; **RIBOT (1955)**; **TISSOT (1956)**; **NAGAMI (1958)** won the Coronation Cup **(1959)**; **SEDAN (1959)**; **RIO MARIN (1960)**; **MOLVEDO (1961)**; **MISTI (1962)** won the Prix Ganay (1962); **SOLT-IKOFF (1963)** won the Arc (1962); **VERONESE (1964)**; **MARCO VISCONTI (1966)**; **CHICAGO (1968)**; **GLANEUSE (1969)**, dam of Gold River; **BACUCO (1970)**; **TIERCERON (1972)**; **INFRA GREEN (1976)**.

**KONIGSSTUHL (1981)** remains the only ever winner of the German Triple Crown; **AWAASIF (1983)** won the Yorkshire Oaks (1982); **TONY BIN (1987)**; **MISIL (1993)**; **LANDO (1994)**; **SHANTOU (1996)**; **SILVER PATRIARCH (1998)** won the St Leger (1997) after a narrow defeat in The Derby, and won the Coronation Cup (1998); **GOLDEN SNAKE (2000)** won the Prix Jean Prat (1999), Preis von Europa (2000) and Prix Ganay (2001); **KUTUB (2001)** won the Preis von Europa, Bayerisches Zuchtrennen, Singapore Gold Cup (2001); **SHIROCCO (2004)**; **CHERRY MIX (2005)**; and **CAMPANOLOGIST (2011)**.

# PISA

Viale delle Cascine, Pisa, Italy.
www.sanrossore.it

| FEATURE RACES | | | | | |
|---|---|---|---|---|---|
| Criterium di Pisa | L | 1500M | TURF | 2YO | DEC |
| Premio Andred | L | 2200M | TURF | 3YO+F&M | DEC |
| Premio Enrico Camici | L | 1200M | TURF | 4YO+ | FEB |
| Premio Reione Toscana | L | 2200M | TURF | 4YO+ | MAR |
| Premio Pisa | L | 1500M | TURF | 3YO | MAR |

Pisa is situated on the central north coast of Tuscany.

The venue for racing is the Ippodromo San Rossore, which lies only 2km from the heart of Pisa within the Migliarino National Park. Its breathtaking setting makes it a stunning location for racing.

The first meeting was staged here in 1854, and the highlight on the calendar is the Premio Pisa, run in March. The historic race for 3yos was established in 1885 and was formerly one of the main precursors for horses bound for the Derby Italiano, with many winners of the country's most prestigious race successful here at Pisa.

Great names of the Italian turf adorn the winners list of the Premio Pisa – Ribot, Cranach, Ortello, Crapom, Manistee and Archimadia are just a few of the legendary horses to grace the San Rossore track.

The course still plays host to a number of Listed races and in 2010 unveiled a new extension to the track to allow races up to 1750m to be run around only a single bend. San Rossore is also used as a training track and the area is prime breeding country with many of Italy's top stud farms located in the region.

## THE TRACK

Right-handed. The original turf track has a circumference of 1610m with a home straight of 530m. The new track extension runs diagonally parallel with the back straight before linking up with the home bend on the course proper to give the course a length of 1750m. An inner steeplechase track is a figure-of-8 course of 1474m.

# SIRACUSA

C. da Spinagallo n. 50, Siracusa, Cicily, Italy.
www.ippomed.it

| FEATURE RACES | | | | | |
|---|---|---|---|---|---|
| Criterium del Mediterraneo | L | 1600M | TURF | 2YO | DEC |
| Premio Memorial Francesco Faraci | L | 2200M | TURF | 3YO+ | DEC |
| Criterium Aretusio | L | 1600M | TURF | 2YOF | DEC |

Siracusa is situated in the south-east of the island of Sicily.

The Ippodromo di Mediterraneo is located on the eastern outskirts of Plateau Ibleo, 20km from the heart of Siracusa. The course is a modern facility having opened in 1995 amid much excitement with Lester Piggott, Willie Carson and John Riddle all engaged to ride at the inaugural meeting. Harness racing was introduced in 2000 and state-of-the-art lighting installed in 2002 to enable night racing.

## THE TRACK

The main turf course is 2200m in circumference.
Inner turf course of 1800m.

# PALIO DI SIENA

Piazza del Campio, Siena, Italy. www.ilpalio.org

*I*l Palio is the famous ancient bareback race around the Piazza del Campio in the heart of Siena. For the residents of Siena, the palio is not a matter of life and death. It is far more important.

Its origins date back to the 16th century when buffalo were raced around the square. After a period as a race for donkeys, the palio became a horse race in 1656 and is still referred to as the *modern palio*.

The city of Siena is divided into 17 formal zones, or *contrade*, and for the winning *contrada* victory brings bragging rights over its neighbours and a great blessing to its people. The cobblestones of the piazza are covered with a layer of clay, which is rolled and watered at regular intervals to prevent it baking under the Tuscan sun.

Horses are brought in from outside of Siena at the beginning of the week leading up to the race and trials are run in the mornings and the afternoons so that the organisers can view the horses in action and select a field of ten runners who are as evenly matched as possible. Once the composition of the field is decided, the residents gather en masse outside the municipal hall in the piazza to witness the drawing of lots to assign each horse to a *contrada*. As the draw is announced the people of each *contrada* then take charge of their runner until the big race.

Trials continue for the next two days so that the jockey, chosen by each competing *contrada*, and the horse can familiarise themselves with each other and the tricky, treacherous course. Twice daily the streets are filled with locals sporting their individual colours as they march behind their horses to and from the course, chanting and singing as they go.

One the eve of the race each area stages a sit-down dinner for its residents and guests. It is a wonderfully festive occasion that also raises money. Part of the fund is allocated to the jockey to use on the starting line to pay a friendly *contrada* for a better position behind the start rope. On the day of the palio, horses are taken to church to be blessed.

Tickets can be purchased for seats around the course but it is free for the public to stand on the inside of the piazza, where an enormous crowd packs in.

The race is preceded by the Corteo Storico – a magnificent and colourful pageant conducted as it was in medieval times, with traditional costumes, charges of sword-brandishing cavalry, armour-clad warriors on horseback, flag-wavers with spectacular choreographed routines and the entrance of the runners. The parade culminates with the arrival of an ox-drawn wooden coach bearing

the winner's prize – a banner known as the *palio*, from which the race takes its name. The banner is placed high upon a wall until the race is complete.

The course is three laps around the piazza, which is a circuit of only 334m with four sharp corners, two of which are right-angled bends. Consequently the draw for starting positions is vital and only takes place once all runners are behind the start rope. Riders can then jostle for better position, and jostle they do. Fists, elbows and whips fly, and bribes are exchanged with fellow riders, urged on by a vocal crowd.

Officials endeavour to ensure a fair release for all competitors, so there are often a number of false starts. Riders will be called up again for a fresh round of fisticuffs and it can take an hour or two from the time the horses initially line up before the race gets underway.

The rules of the race are simple, in that there are none to speak of, other than the winner is the first horse past the post – with or without its rider. The race on in earnest, crowd noise rises to a deafening fever pitch, and a mixture of carnage and chaos reigns on the track.

The official guidebook states that the winner must be formally ratified by the committee before the prize is awarded. But in the same instant that the first horse passes the finish line, a cannon sounds and spectators pile onto the course with some entrants still running and riderless horses loose on the track. In the blink of an eye, followers from the winning *contrada* have scaled the wall and wrested the prize from its lofty perch with no correspondence entered into. Along with the triumphant horse and rider, the *palio* is whisked back to home base for wild celebrations to begin.

Il Palio is the most amazing, unbelievable and thrilling spectacle imaginable in the world of horse racing. And it's in Siena! An absolute must on the bucket list for every fan of the sport.

Run twice annually on 2 July and 16 August.

# HAMBURG

Rennbahnstrasse 96, Hamburg, Germany. www.galopp-hamburg.de

## FEATURE RACES

| DEUTSCHES DERBY | G1 | 2400M | TURF | 3YOC&F | 1869 | JUL |
|---|---|---|---|---|---|---|
| HANSA-PREIS | G2 | 2400M | TURF | 3YO+ | 1892 | JUL |

## FEATURE RACE

### DEUTSCHES DERBY

Shirocco

*H*amburg is situated on the River Elbe in the northern region of Germany and is the second-largest city in the nation. The Hamburg Racing Club staged its inaugural meeting here at the Horner Rennbahn in 1869 and the course is famous as the venue for Germany's richest race, the Deutsches Derby, which was established the same year as the course.

Conducted in July, the Deutsches Derby remains the most well-attended day on the racing calendar. The track, located only 8km from the heart of town, can accommodate crowds of up to 50,000, which exceeds any other course in Germany. Facilities have recently been upgraded and the historic grandstand was restored in 2011. Hamburg currently conducts one race meeting annually, over six days in late June and early July.

While it is for all intents and purposes a racetrack, the course doubles as a public park, so it is a common sight to find people enjoying their picnics right on the actual course only hours before a Classic race is to be staged. Rubbish and empty wine bottles often have to be cleared away so that the races can be run.

## THE TRACK

Right-handed. Oval-shaped turf course of approximately 2000m in circumference. The run home is 500m.

Chute start for 1200m races, which joins the top of the home bend.

Inner track for jumps races.

Notable winners of the Deutsches Derby include **DALBERG (1890)**; **AUGIAS (1923)** was a dual winner of the Grosser Preis von Berlin (1923, 24); **ALBA (1930)**; **ALCHIMIST (1933)**; **MAGNAT (1941)**; **NORDLICHT (1944)**; **MANGON (1952)** won the Grosser Preis von Baden (1952) and twice won the Grosser Preis von Berlin (1952, 54); **ORSINI (1957)**; **LUCIANO (1967)**; **ALPENKONIG (1970)**; **ATHENAGORAS (1973)**; **MARDUK (1974)**; **SURUMU (1977)**; **KONIGSSTUHL (1979)** is the only ever winner of the German Triple Crown; **OROFINO (1981)**; **MONDRIAN (1989)**.

**LANDO (1993)** was a dual winner of the Grosser Preis von Baden (1993, 94) and won the Gran Premio del Jockey Club Italiano (1994), Gran Premio di Milano, Grosser Preis von Berlin and Japan Cup (1995); **BORGIA (1997)**; **BOREAL (2001)** won the Coronation Cup (2002); **SHIROCCO (2004)**; **SCHIAPARELLI (2006)**; **KAMSIN (2008)**. Those to win the German Oaks–Derby double include **NEREIDE (1936)**, top broodmare **SCHWARZGOLD (1940)**, **ASTERBLUTE (1949)** and **LUSTIGE (1955)**.

# BADEN-BADEN

Rennbahnstrasse 16, Iffezheim, Germany. www.baden-racing.com

| GROSSER PREIS VON BADEN | G1 | 2400M | TURF | 3YO+ | SEPT |
|---|---|---|---|---|---|
| OETTINGEN-RENNEN | G2 | 1600M | TURF | 3YO+ | AUG |
| GOLDENE PEITSCHE | G2 | 1200M | TURF | 3YO+ | AUG |
| GROSSER PREIS DER BARDISCHEN | G2 | 2200M | TURF | 4YO+ | MAY |

*T*he spa town of Baden-Baden is situated near the French border on the banks of the Oos River in the northern foothills of the Black Forest. The Iffezheim racecourse is arguably the most prestigious in Germany. Located 12km from the centre of town, it staged its first meeting in 1858.

Construction of the track was instigated by Frenchman Edouard Benazet, who at that time owned the casino in Baden-Baden. The course was originally operated by the French racing authority but following the Franco–Prussian War of 1870–71 ownership was transferred to the Internationaler Club, which ran the course until 2010.

Iffezheim is now managed by Baden Racing and it is a stunning location with its forest setting and lovely architecture reminiscent of the Deauville course.

A feature is the Gontard Garden, which offers quality food and beverages in a relaxed atmosphere.

Racing occurs three times a year with the spring meeting in May, the Grand Festival meeting in August and September, and the Sales & Racing Festival conducted in October.

The highlight event is the Grosser Preis von Baden in September.

Iffezheim is also host to fairs and open-air concerts and the public can enjoy breakfast overlooking the course while the gallopers go through their early morning paces on the training track.

## THE TRACK

Left-handed. The course has a circumference of about 2000m. Home straight of 600m.

Straight sprint course of 1200m doglegs left at the halfway point.

## FEATURE RACE

### GROSSER PREIS VON BADEN

Historic race inaugurated in 1858 with a very impressive honour roll.

Undefeated all-time great mare **KINCSEM (1877–79)** scored a hat-trick of wins in the race, as did **OLEANDER (1927–29)**.

Dual winners include **ESPRESSO (1963, 64)**, **ACATENANGO (1986, 87)**, **MONDRIAN (1989, 90)**, **LANDO (1993, 94)**, **TIGER HILL (1998, 99)**, **WARRSAN (2004, 05)** and **DANEDREAM (2011, 12)**, who also won the Oaks D'Italia, Grosser Preis von Berlin, the Arc (2011) and King George VI & Queen Elizabeth Stakes (2012).

Other notable winners include **GEOLOGIE (1859)**, who won the Prix de Diane (1859), Prix du Cadran (1860); **STRADELLA (1862)** won the Prix Jean-Luc

Lagardere (1861), Poule d'Essai des Poulains, Prix de Diane (1862); **LA TOUCQUES (1863)** won the Prix Royal-Oak, Grand Prix de Paris, Prix du Jockey Club (1863); **VERMOUTH (1864)** won the Grand Prix de Paris (1864); **ETOILE FILANTE (1866)** won the Prix Jean Prat, Prix Royal-Oak (1866); **PLAISANTERIE (1885)** took out the Cambridgeshire–Cesarewitch double (1885); **YELLOW (1890)** won the Prix d'Ispahan and Prix Jean Prat (1890).

Champion French filly **SEMENDRIA (1901)** won the Prix de la Foret (1899), the fillies' Triple Crown in France, Prix Vermeille, Grand Prix de Paris (1900); **LA CAMARGO (1902)** won 24 of 34 starts including the Prix de la Foret (1900), Prix de Diane, Poule d'Essai des Pouliches, Prix Vermeille (1901), Prix du Cadaran (1902), Prix Ganay (1903) and was a dual winner of the Prix d'Ispahan (1902, 03); **VINICIUS (1903)** won the Prix Morny, Prix Jean-Luc Lagardere (1902), Poule d'Essai des Poulains (1903); **EXEMA (1904)**.

**GOUVERNANT (1905)** won the Poule d'Essai des Poulains, Grand Prix de Saint-Cloud (1904), Prix du Cadran (1905); **FAUST (1908)**; **SCOPAS (1924)**; **ALBA (1930)**; top filly **SICHEL (1931)**; **MAGNAT (1941)**; **MANGON (1952)**; **MASETTO (1956)**; **DUSHKA (1958)** won the Prix de Diane (1958).

**SHESHOON (1960)** won the Grand Prix de Saint-Cloud, Ascot Gold Cup (1960) and was sire of Sassafras; **RIO MARIN (1961)**; **LUCIANO (1968)** was twice German Horse of the Year; **ALPENKONIG (1970)**; **ATHENAGORIS (1973)** was a dual winner of the Rheinland-Pokal (1973, 74) and won the Deutsches Derby (1973), Grosser Preis von Berlin (1975); **WINDWURF (1977)**; **M-LOL-SHAN (1979)** won the Irish St Leger (1978); **NEBOS (1980)**; **GLINT OF GOLD (1982)**; **DIAMOND SHOAL (1983)**; **STRAWBERRY ROAD (1984)**; **GOLD AND IVORY (1985)**; **CARROLL HOUSE (1988)** won the Arc (1989); **LOMITAS (1991)**; **MASHAALLAH (1992)**; **PILSUDSKI (1996)**; **BORGIA (1997)** won the Hong Kong Vase (1999); **MARIENBARD (2002)** won the Arc (2002); and **QUIJANO (2007)**.

# COLOGNE

Rennbahnstrasse 152, Koln, Germany.
www.koeln-galopp.de

## FEATURE RACES

| PREIS VON EUROPA | G1 | 2400M | TURF | 3YO+ | SEPT |
|---|---|---|---|---|---|
| GERLING-PREIS | G2 | 2400M | TURF | 4YO+ | APR |
| MEHL-MUHLENS RENNEN | G2 | 1600M | TURF | 3YOC&F | MAY |
| OPPENHEIM UNION-RENNEN | G2 | 2200M | TURF | 3YO | JUN |

Cologne is situated in the Rhineland in the mid-west region of Germany. Originally constructed on pastoral land on the northern outskirts of the city, the Cologne-Weidenpesch racecourse is located on a 33-hectare site in the Weidenpascher Park in Nippes.

The Koln Racing Club was formed in 1897 and held its inaugural meeting the following year. Hoppegarten was the main training venue in Germany but following the division of Germany after World War II many of the country's leading trainers relocated to Cologne.

With the permanent arrival of top horsemen and the increased quality and size of the local horse population, the Cologne course quickly established itself as one of the premier racing venues in Germany.

The course has comfortable facilities while still retaining its old-world charm and, as one would expect in this part of the world, offers an array of great food, wine and beer.

The racing highlight is the Preis von Europa, which is run in September and one of the most prestigious events on the German calendar. Cologne is also the venue for the Mehl-Muhlens Rennen – the German 2000 Guineas. The season generally comprises ten race dates scheduled between April and October.

## THE TRACK

Right-handed. Oval-shaped track of almost 2000m in circumference. Home straight – 600m.

Out of the straight, runners are on a bend until the 1500m. It is then a straight run of over 600m to the home turn. Races up to 1000m are conducted on the straight course.

## FEATURE RACE

### PREIS VON EUROPA

Preis von Europa winner Schiaparelli

Russian champion **ANILIN (1965–67)** won three times in succession. Dual winners include **WINDWURF (1975, 76)**, **MONSUN (1993, 94)** and **TAIPAN (1997, 98)**.

Other notable winners include **LOMBARD (1971)**; **NEBOS (1979)** was a dual winner of the Grosser Preis von Berlin (1979, 80), won the Grosser Preis von Baden (1980) and was leading sire in Germany; **GLINT OF GOLD (1981)**; **ESPRIT DU NORD (1983)**; **GOLD AND IVORY (1984)**; **SUMAYR (1985)** won the Grand Prix de Paris (1985); **ALLEZ MILORD (1986)** won the John Henry Turf Championship (1987); **IBN REY (1989)** won the Grosser Preis von Berlin, Irish St Leger (1990); **MONDRIAN (1990)** was a dual winner of both the Grosser Preis von Bayern and Grosser Preis von Baden (1989, 90), and won the Deutsches Derby, Grosser Preis von Berlin (1989); **LOMITAS (1991)**; **APPLE TREE (1992)** won the Joe Hirsch Turf Classic (1993), Grand Prix de Saint-Cloud, Coronation Cup (1994); **GOLDEN SNAKE (2000)**; **KUTUB (2001)**; **ALBANOVA (2004)** was the first mare to win; **YOUMZAIN (2007)** won the Gran Prix de Saint-Cloud (2008); **SCHIAPARELLI (2007)** won the Deutsches Derby (2006), Grosser Preis von Berlin (2007) and twice won the Gran Premio del Jockey Club Italiano (2007, 09); **JUKEBOX JURY (2009)**; and **CAMPANOLOGIST (2011)**.

# MUNICH

Graff-Lehndorff-Strasse 36, Munich, Germany.
www.galoppmuenchen.de

## FEATURE RACES

| BAYERISCHES ZUCHTRENNEN | G1 | 2000M | TURF | 3YO+ | 1940 | JUL |
|---|---|---|---|---|---|---|
| GROSSER PREIS VON BAYERN | G1 | 2400M | TURF | 3YO+ | 1957 | AUG |
| GROSSER EUROPA-MEILE | G2 | 1600M | TURF | 3YO+ | 1951 | SEPT |

The Munich Racing Association was founded in 1895 with the course, located east of the city, completed for its inaugural meeting in 1897. The track is very spacious and considered a very fair test of a horse. Situated on a 100-hectare site, the complex is also a training base with 350 horses stabled at the track, and contains a 12-hole golf course. Racing season in Munich is from April until November with Group 1 races staged in July and August.

## THE TRACK

The course has a circumference of 1830m. The home straight is 560m. Straight sprint course of 1000m.

## FEATURE RACES

### GROSSER PREIS VON BAYERN (RHEINLAND-POKAL)

Formerly the Aral-Pokal and the Rheinland-Pokal, the name was changed again in 2012 when transferred to the Munich course. The race has held Group 1 status since 1973.

Notable winners since include dual victors **ATHENAGORAS (1973, 74)**, **WLADIMIR (1977, 78)**, **WAUTHI (1980, 81)**, **ACATENANGO (1985, 86)**, **MONDRIAN (1989, 90)** and **LUSO (1996, 98)**. Other prominent winners include **KONIGSSTUHL (1979)**, **OROFINO (1982)**, **ALMAARAD (1988)** won the Cox Plate (1989), **TEL QUEL (1992)** won the Champion Stakes (1991), **MONSUN (1993)**, **WIND IN HER HAIR (1995)** is the dam of Deep Impact, **UNGARO (1999)**, **SABIANGO (2001)** won the Charles Whittingham Memorial (2004) and twice won the Grosser Preis von Berlin (2001, 2003), **ALBANOVA (2004)**, **CHERRY MIX (2006)**, **KAMSIN (2008)** and **CAMPANOLOGIST (2010)**.

### GROSSER DALLMAYR-PREIS BAYERISCHES ZUCHTRENNEN

First run in 1866, the race was upgraded to Group 1 in 1990. Notable winners since include dual winner **TURFKONIG (1989, 90)**; **KURTAJANA (1991)** won the Prix Ganay (1991); **KOOYONGA (1992)**, who won the Irish 1000 Guineas, Coronation Stakes (1991) and Eclipse Stakes (1992).

Globetrotting **TIMARIDA (1996)** registered G1 wins in five countries, having won the EP Taylor Stakes, Prix de l'Opera (1995), Irish Champion Stakes, Beverly D Stakes (1996); **ELLE DANZIG (1998)**; **TIGER HILL (1999)**; **KUTUB (2001)** won the Singapore Gold Cup, Grosser Preis von Europa, Gran Premio del

Jockey Club Italiano (2001); **LINNGARI (2008)**; and **SOLDIER HOLLOW (2005, 07)** won twice.

# HOPPEGARTEN

Goetheallee 1, Hoppegarten, Germany.
www.hoppegarten.com

| FEATURE RACES | | | | | |
|---|---|---|---|---|---|
| GROSSER PREIS VON BERLIN | G1 | 2400M | TURF | 3YO+ | JUL |
| DIANA TRIAL | G2 | 2000M | TURF | 3YOF | MAY |

Hoppegarten is located near the eastern suburbs of Berlin. The course originally opened to much fanfare in 1868 with Kaiser Wilhelm and Otto von Bismarck in attendance to launch proceedings.

Following the separation of Germany after World War II, the course was cut off from the West and lay dormant or under-used for long periods and, despite some successes, struggled to regain momentum even after the Reunification. Hoppegarten has recently been acquired by Gerhard Schoningh, who has undertaken the task of restoring the track to its former glory, including an upgrade to the training track and stable complex.

The Grosser Preis von Berlin is the feature race on the fixture. First run at Hoppegarten in 1888, the Group 1 race was run at Dusseldorf from 1947 until 2009. After just one edition at the Hamburg course, the event returned to its original home in July 2011. Meetings at Hoppegarten racecourse are scheduled between April and October.

## THE TRACK

Right-handed. Oval-shaped turf course with a circumference of approximately 2350m. The home straight is 700m. Races over 1800m start from a chute that gives a straight run of almost 500m before a dogleg onto the back straight.

## FEATURE RACE

### GROSSER PREIS VON BERLIN

The race has had many multiple winners. **TICINO (1942–44)** and **MERCURIUS (1963–65)** both brought up hat-tricks. Dual winners include **AUGIAS (1923, 24)**, **OLEANDER (1928, 29)**, **STURMVOGEL (1935, 36)**, **MANGON (1952, 54)**, **LOMBARD (1971, 72)**, **WINDWURF (1976, 77)**, **NEBOS (1979, 80)**, **ABARY (1983, 84)** and **UNGARO (1998)**.

Other prominent winners include **FELS (1907)**, **ALBA (1930)**, **SICHEL (1931)**, **ALCHIMIST (1933)**, dual Arc-winner **CORRIDA (1937)**, **SCHWARZ-GOLD (1940)**, **NICCOLO DELL'ARCA (1941)**, **MASETTO (1955)**, **LUCIANO (1968)**, **ALPEN-KONIG (1970)**, **ARRATOS (1973)**, **ATHENAG-ORAS (1975)**, **OROFINO (1982)**, **ACATENANGO (1986)**, **LE GLORIEUX (1987)** won the Washington DC International and Japan Cup (1987), **MONDRIAN (1989)**, **IBN REY (1990)**, **LOMITAS (1991)**, **PLATINI (1992)**, **LANDO (1995)**, **LUSO (1997)**, **MUTAFAWEQ (2000)**, **MARIENBARD (2002)**, **SABIANGO (2003)**, **ALBANOVA (2004)**, **SCHI-APARELLI (2007)**, **CAMPANOLOGIST (2010)**, **DANEDREAM (2011)** and **MEANDRE (2012)** won the Grand Prix de Paris (2011) and Grand Prix de Saint-Cloud (2012).

# DUSSELDORF

Rennbehnstrasse 20, Dusseldorf, Germany.
www.duesseldorf-galopp.de

Racing at Dusseldorf, in Germany's central west, dates back to 1836. The Dusseldorf Riding and Racing Club, established in 1844, was the first in Germany to conduct events under the British rules of racing. The current site, nestled in the Grafenberg Forest, held its first meeting in 1909.

The Grafenberg racecourse is one of the most attractive courses in Germany and is noted as a very severe test of horse and rider. Set in the hills, it is a very undulating course that rises 15m from about the 800m to the end of the home straight and features an incredibly steep, uphill run to the home bend. The course dips slightly upon straightening for home, then climbs up again for the entire run to the finishing post.

Racing dates are scheduled from late March until mid October, and two of the German classics are run here – the 1000 Guineas and the German Oaks, officially known as the Preis der Diana, which is one of the major social highlights on the racing calendar in Germany.

## THE TRACK

Right-handed. Hilly, very undulating, triangular oval course of about 1900m in circumference. The home straight is 500m.

## FEATURE RACE

### PREIS DER DIANA

The German Oaks has been run at many venues, before settling at Mulheim and then briefly in Munich. The race achieved Group 1 status in 2001 and was transferred to Dusseldorf in 2006.

Winners since 2001 include **NIGHT MAGIC (2009)**, who won the Grosser Preis von Baden (2010); and English Oaks winner **DANCING RAIN (2011)**.

# DORTMUND

Rennweg 70, Dortmund, Germany.
www.dortmunder-rennverein.de

| FEATURE RACES | | | | | |
|---|---|---|---|---|---|
| GROSSER PREIS DER DORTMUNDER WIRTSCHAFT | G3 | 2000M | TURF | 3YO+ | JUNE |
| DEUTSCHES ST LEGER | G3 | 2800M | TURF | 3YO+ | SEPT |

Dortmund is situated in western Germany. The Dortmund-Wambel racecourse conducted its first meeting in 1886, and racing here is staged year round with the turf course in operation from April to October and night racing on the all-weather track from November to March.

While racing is generally in the restricted grades, Dortmund is the venue for the German St Leger, run annually in September. Rated at Group 3 level, the Classic race has been won by many greats since 1881.

## THE TRACK

Right-handed. The main turf course is a classic oval of 2100m in circumference. The home straight is 700m. Races over 2000m start from a chute that jumps onto the turn out of the back straight.

Straight sprint course of 1000m.

Inner all-weather track of 1600m with a run home of 400m.

## TABY

Taby Galopp, Taby, Stockholm, Sweden. www.tabygalopp.se

| FEATURE RACES | | | | | |
|---|---|---|---|---|---|
| STORA PRIS | G3 | 1950M | TURF | 4YO+ | JUNE |
| TABY OPEN SPRING CHAMPIONSHIP | G3 | 1160M | TURF | | SEPT |
| STOCKHOLM CUP INTERNATIONAL | G3 | 2400M | TURF | 3YO+ | SEPT |

Racing in the Swedish capital of Stockholm is conducted at the Taby racecourse, which has forged a reputation as the premier racing venue for thoroughbreds in Scandinavia.

Located 15km north of Stockholm, the course held its first meeting in 1960. In 1993 it became the first in the region to stage a Group race with the upgrading of the Stockholm Cup to Group 3 status. Run in September, the Cup has been won by some good horses, most notably Collier Hill who took it out in 2004 and 2006.

Racing is conducted year round with the dirt course used for night meetings during winter and spring, and the turf course in operation for the summer and autumn months. Jumps racing is also staged here as well as selected events for Arabians.

### THE TRACK

Left-handed classic dirt oval of 1600m. Major races are all staged on the inner turf course.

There is a figure-of-8 jumps course on the inside of the track.

## JAGERSRO

Jagersrovagen, Malmo, Sweden. www.jagersro.se

| FEATURE RACES | | | | | |
|---|---|---|---|---|---|
| Pramms Memorial | L | 1730M | DIRT | 4YO+ | MAY |
| Svenskt Derby | L | 2400M | DIRT | 3YO | AUG |

Malmo is situated in Scania, the southernmost province of Sweden.

The venue for racing is the Jagersro racecourse, which is home to the Swedish Derby. First run in 1918, the Derby is a Listed event run on the dirt in mid August.

### THE TRACK

Left-handed. Classic dirt oval of 1600m in circumference.

## OVREVOLL

Ovrevoll Court, Vollsveien 132, Jar, Norway. www.ovrevoll.no

| FEATURE RACES | | | | | |
|---|---|---|---|---|---|
| POLAR CUP | G3 | 1350M | TURF | 3YO+ | JUL |
| MARIT SVEASS MINNELOP | G3 | 1800M | TURF | 3YO+ | AUG |
| Norsk Derby | L | 2400M | TURF | 3YO | AUG |

The Ovrevoll course is located on the outskirts of Oslo in the semi-rural setting of Jar in Baerum. It is one of the prime venues for racing in Scandinavia.

King Haarkon VII was in attendance for the inaugural meeting in 1932. The racing and social highlight is the Norwegian Derby, which is staged on the last Sunday in August. The locals take the opportunity to dress in their finery as they turn out in force for Norway's most prestigious and traditional event. While the Derby is a Listed race, Ovrevoll currently hosts two Group 3 races.

Racing season at the Ovrevoll Galoppbane is from mid April until early December with all main races staged on the turf track. The dirt course was installed in 1984.

### THE TRACK

Left-handed. The main turf course is 2000m in length. The home straight is approximately 800m.

Straight sprint course for races up to 1200m.

Inner dirt course of 1375m.

## COPENHAGEN

Klampenborgvej 52, Klampenborg, Denamrk. www.galopbane.dk

| FEATURE RACES | | | | | |
|---|---|---|---|---|---|
| SCANDINAVIAN OPEN CHAMPIONSHIP | G3 | 2400M | TURF | 3YO+ | AUG |
| Danish Jockey Club Cup | L | 1800M | TURF | 4YO+ | APR |
| Danish Pokallob | L | 1880M | TURF | 3YO+ | JUN |

Racing in Denmark dates back to 1770. The first organised meeting was held in 1820.

The Copenhagen course is located in a lovely natural setting and is very picturesque. Situated in the northern suburb of Klampenborg, the first meeting was staged here in 1910. Accordingly it is also referred to as the Klampenborg racecourse.

The feature race on the calendar is the Scandinavian Open Championship, which was awarded Group 3 status in 2000 to become the first Group race run in Denmark. As the only track that hosts thoroughbred racing in Denmark it is naturally the home to all of its Classic races, including the Dansk Derby.

### THE TRACK

Right-handed. Pear-shaped oval turf track with a circumference of about 1800m. The home straight is 500m. The course has a tight bend leaving the home straight, is quite undulating along the back straight, and has a wide home bend.

# ST MORITZ

Via Mulin 4, 7500 St Moritz, Switzerland.
www.whiteturf.ch

The Engadin Valley of Switzerland is home to a truly wonderful and unique racing festival – the legendary White Turf meeting. With the imposing Swiss Alps as a backdrop, runners negotiate a tight 6-furlong course on the ice and snow around the frozen lake of St Moritz.

Competition takes in three disciplines with events on horseback, trotting races using sleds and skijoring races. Skijoring requires jockeys to be towed behind their charges on skis. In the past, jumps races have also been conducted on the track.

Horses wear special shoes equipped with steel spikes to help maintain their footing in the snow. While this helps them stay upright, it adds an extra element of danger for a fallen rider caught up in the trample.

Early speed is an enormous advantage on the snow-covered track, with leaders able to avoid the kickback – which is both unpleasant and considerable.

The meeting takes place over three Sundays in February – conditions permitting – with the feature race the Grand Prix of St Moritz rated at Group 2.

International trainers often chance their arm and the Grand Prix is a regular target for Classic-winning English trainer Mark Johnson, who numbers Swiss owner Marcus Graf among his clients.

While not exactly a meeting for the rank and file, the location ensures thrilling and spectacular viewing with the horses and riders in their silks in starkly beautiful contrast to the surroundings.

## THE TRACK

Right-handed. Six-furlong snow track.

## FEATURE RACES

| GROSSER PRIES VON ST MORITZ | G2 | 2000M | SNOW | 3YO+ | FEB |
|---|---|---|---|---|---|
| Sheik Zayed Bin Sultan Al Wahyan Listed Cup | L | 1800M | SNOW | 3YO+ | FEB |

# CZECH REPUBLIC

## PARDUBICE

Prazska 607, Pardubice, Czech Republic.
www.pardubice-racecourse.cz

Situated on the River Elbe 96km east of Prague, Pardubice is the capital city of the Pardubice region of the Czech Republic. Synthesia Park racecourse is the venue for the world-famous Velka Pardubicka steeplechase.

The Pardubicka is a race across 30 obstacles over 7200m. It is known as the most fearsome test of horse and rider in the entire field of equestrian sports. The race is run annually on the second Sunday in October and has a long and esteemed tradition beginning in 1874.

Crowds of up to 50,000 take up various vantage points around the track and beyond, as runners leave the course to cross over roads, ploughed fields and massive hedges.

The course features the most ferocious jump anywhere in the world, known as the Taxis, which is enormously high and wide, requiring a prodigious leap. There is also a huge water jump referred to as The Moat.

To compete in the event, horses must complete the course in one of four qualifying races. It is considered a feat just to ride in the race, and local rider Josef Vana is a celebrity in the Czech Republic having won the race on eight occasions as a rider and eight times as trainer.

**ZELEZNICK** won the race 1987–89 and then again in 1991 to hold the record of four wins. Vana rode him to victory each time.

In 1909 only three runners faced the starter and none made it home.

# FLEMINGTON

Racecourse Road, Flemington, Victoria, Australia. www.flemington.com.au

*F*lemington is the home of the fabled Melbourne Cup, the richest handicap race in the world, and is Australia's premier racetrack.

The first race meeting in Melbourne was at a course on Batman's Hill near Spencer Street railway station in 1838. In 1840 a meeting was held on the rough flats alongside the Maribyrnong River, and racing has been staged here ever since, making it the oldest continuously used course in Australia.

The site permanently set aside for a racecourse in 1848. The Victoria Turf Club was formed in 1852 and the Victoria Jockey Club in 1857, with both conducting meetings at Flemington.

It was the VTC that ran spring meetings and conceived the Melbourne Cup, first run in 1861. A new controlling body was established three years later with the merger of the clubs to form the Victoria Racing Club.

Robert C Bagot, the first VRC chairman, was instrumental in making improvements with extensive work to the track surface and then construction of a grandstand for members in 1873. His successor, Henry B Moore, continued to transform the course and instigated the building of four new stands.

The Flemington Spring Carnival has long been the largest racing and social event on the Australian calendar.

Derby Day on the Saturday, three days before the Melbourne Cup, is considered the premier race day on the Australian calendar, featuring all Group racing including four at Group 1 level, with the Victoria Derby the highlight.

Thursday is Ladies' Day for the VRC Oaks and the carnival concludes the following Saturday with the feature race a Group 1 over 1600 metres.

Flemington is also the autumn venue for Australia's two premier Group 1 sprint races – the Lightning Stakes (1000m) and the Newmarket Handicap (1200m).

The course has had much redevelopment in recent times with a new grandstand completed in 2000. Due to its proximity to the river, the course had always been prone to flooding, so in 2006 major works were carried out to build retaining walls, new drainage systems and completely re-lay the course proper.

Flemington has had its own railway station since 1861 and special express trains make only a short journey to deposit patrons right at the Hill Stand entrance.

## THE TRACK

Left-handed. Flemington is a spacious, flat track with a circumference of 2312m.

The course is shaped like an ice-cream cone. From the turn out of the home straight it is a hairpin bend left and then a straight run of 800m to the 1400m point. Runners are then on a sweeping bend for 950m until straightening for the run home.

| FEATURE RACES | | | | | | | |
|---|---|---|---|---|---|---|---|
| LIGHTNING STAKES | G1 | 1000M | TURF | 2YO+ | WFA | 1955 | FEB |
| AUSTRALIAN CUP | G1 | 2000M | TURF | 3YO+ | WFA | 1861 | MAR |
| NEWMARKET HCP | G1 | 1200M | TURF | OPEN | HCP | 1874 | MAR |
| AUSTRALIAN GUINEAS | G1 | 1600M | TURF | 3YO | SW | 1986 | MAR |
| TURNBULL STAKES | G1 | 2000M | TURF | SWP | SWP | 1948 | OCT |
| VICTORIA DERBY | G1 | 2500M | TURF | 3YO | SW | 1855 | OCT–NOV |
| ASCOT VALE STAKES | G1 | 1200M | TURF | 3YO | SW | 1933 | OCT–NOV |
| LKS MACKINNON STAKES | G1 | 2000M | TURF | 3YO+ | WFA | 1869 | OCT–NOV |
| EMPIRE ROSE STAKES | G1 | 1600M | TURF | 3YO+F&M | WFA | 1988 | OCT–NOV |
| MELBOURNE CUP | G1 | 3200M | TURF | 3YO+ | HCP | 1861 | NOV |
| VRC OAKS | G1 | 2500M | TURF | 3YOF | SW | 1861 | NOV |
| CANTALA STAKES | G1 | 1600M | TURF | 3YO+ | HCP | 1919 | NOV |
| VRC STAKES | G1 | 1200M | TURF | 3YO+ | WFA | 1868 | NOV |

Black Caviar

It is a run of 450m from the home turn to the winning post.

Races of up to 1200m are conducted on the straight course.

The 1400m start is from a chute virtually at the top of the long home bend. Inside draws and on-pace always an advantage.

The 1600m and 2000m starts are situated on the back of the course. The 1600m start gives a run of just 200m before the circle on to the run in, but the straight 600m run from the 2000m start gives riders plenty of time to take up positions. It is considered the fairest starting point on the round course.

The Victoria Derby start at the 2500m is just before the turn out of the home straight, providing only a very short run to the first turn.

The Melbourne Cup start at 3200m begins on the straight course providing a run of 880m to the first turn.

## FEATURE RACES

### MELBOURNE CUP

First run in 1861, it was the early dominance of trainers and horses from neighbour colony New South Wales that set the Sydney–Melbourne rivalry in stone and the race quickly became a national obsession. Every office and workplace runs a sweep and the race is a once-a-year must for even the non-punter to chance their arm, as would seem their civic duty.

Held on the first Tuesday in November since 1875, the day was declared a public holiday in 1877 and soon became known as 'the race that stops a nation'.

Fervour was so pronounced that by 1880 attendance at Flemington on Cup Day reached 100,000 – in a city with a population of 290,000.

The Melbourne Cup is now one of richest races in the world and the most valuable handicap race run anywhere. In recent years it has become an international race, attracting top-class entries from around the world.

The four-day Spring Carnival attracts over 400,000 people annually.

It is not just about the racing. As Australia's biggest party and social event, the carnival is also a massive boost for the local economy, attracting many tourists and ensuring that Melbourne's hotels, bars and restaurants are bursting at the seams. The department stores do a roaring trade in frocks, hats, shoes and accessories.

The honour roll of the Melbourne Cup is a history of Australian racing in itself.

**ARCHER (1861, 62)** won the first two editions for Etienne de Mestre, who would train the winner on five occasions. His record stood for 99 years until surpassed by Bart Cummings.

And while the fable of Archer's 1000km walk from Sydney to Melbourne has long since been disproved, it demonstrates that the folklore of the Melbourne Cup dates back to the very first running.

Mighty mare **MAKYBE DIVA (2003–05)** holds the benchmark as the only horse to win three times. She also won the Sydney Cup (2004), Australian Cup, Tancred Stakes, Turnbull Stakes and the Cox Plate (2005), and record Australian earnings of $14.5m.

Other multiple winners include **PETER PAN (1932, 34)**, **RAIN LOVER (1968, 69)** and **THINK BIG (1974, 75)**.

Horses to have won the Caulfield Cup–Melbourne Cup double in the same year include **POSEIDON (1906)**, **THE TRUMP (1937)**, **RIVETTE (1939)**, **RISING FAST (1954)**, **EVEN STEVENS (1962)**, **GALILEE (1966)**, **GURNER'S LANE (1982)**, **LET'S ELOPE (1991)**, **DORIEMUS (1995)**, **MIGHT AND POWER (1997)** and **ETHEREAL (2001)**.

Rising Fast is the only horse to ever achieve the feat of winning the Caulfield Cup–Cox Plate–Melbourne Cup treble in a single season.

Filly **BRISEIS (1875)** won the Doncaster Hcp and All Aged Stakes as a 2yo then won the Victoria Derby, Melbourne Cup and the VRC Oaks in the space of six days. Unbelievable! Ridden in the Cup by 12-year-old jockey Peter St Albans – the youngest jockey ever to win.

**GRAND FLANEUR (1880)** won the Australian Derby and Victoria Derby that year. He was sire of 1900 Ascot Gold Cup winner Merman. Unbeaten in nine starts, he is the only undefeated winner of the Melbourne Cup.

Incredible **MALUA (1884)** won the Oakleigh Plate and Newmarket Hcp (1884), Australian Cup (1886) and a Grand National Hurdle (1889).

All-time great **CARBINE (1890)** arrived in Australia following an unbeaten 5-start 2yo career in New Zealand and went on to win 33 of 43 starts including two Sydney Cups (1889, 90), two All Aged Stakes (1889, 90), the Mackinnon Stakes (1890) and a hat-trick of AJC Plates (1889–91) – now known as the Queen Elizabeth Stakes. Carbine's Melbourne Cup win was one for the history books. He set a weight-carrying record of 10st 5lb (66.5kg) to defeat a record field of 39 runners, and in race record time.

After his racing career Carbine stood four seasons at stud in Australia where he sired influential stallion Wallace, winner of the Australian Derby, Caulfield Guineas and Sydney Cup. A crowd of 10,000 people lined the docks at Port Melbourne to farewell Carbine when he was purchased to stand at Welbeck Stud in England, alongside the dominant St Simon. There he sired influential 1906 Derby winner Spearmint, sire of Catnip – grand dam of Nearco – and Plucky Leige, dam of both Bois Roussel (1938 Derby and sire) and French star, Sir Gallahad, who left his mark as four-time leading stallion in North America and leading brood-mare sire on 12 occasions.

More than 50 Melbourne Cup winners, including Makybe Diva, have Carbine in their pedigree and any horse with Nearco, Nasrullah or Northern Dancer in their bloodlines can be traced back to Carbine. Phar Lap was a grandson of his, with Carbine on both sides of his pedigree.

**COMEDY KING (1910)** was the first imported European horse to win.

**POITREL (1920)** has a unique record. Until the recent deeds of Black Caviar, it was Desert Gold and Gloaming who jointly held the record of 19 consecutive wins in Australasia. Poitrel was the last horse to defeat Gloaming before his winning streak began, and he defeated Desert Gold to end her record run. Carried 10st (63kg) to win this race.

**NIGHTMARCH (1929)** won the New Zealand

Phar Lap

Derby (1928), Epsom Hcp and the Cox Plate (1929).

New Zealand–bred **PHAR LAP (1930)** is the all-time hero of Australian racing. After an undistinguished beginning to his career in which he netted only a maiden win from his first ten starts, Phar Lap then won 36 of his next 41 starts including the Australian Derby (1929), Victoria Derby (1929) and two Cox Plates (1930, 1931).

At one stage he won 23 out of 24 including 14 straight wins. At 10 furlongs or more he won 24 of 26 starts with his only defeats in the Melbourne Cups of 1929 and 1931 – in the latter he carried 10st 10lbs (68.5kg) while the winner, **WHITE NOSE (1931)**, carried just 43.5kg.

Phar Lap's performance to win on all four days of the Flemington carnival in 1930, including the Melbourne Cup, stands as one of the all-time great feats of Australian racing.

After the Melbourne Cup of 1931, he travelled to Mexico to take on the best horses in the USA in the rich Agua Caliente of 1932. Fearing opposition riding tactics, his jockey had him sitting back and wide before rounding up the field to win easily. His subsequent death by arsenic poisoning was a cause for national mourning in Australia and New Zealand, and remains a mystery.

In 1993 he was the subject of the movie *Phar Lap – Heart of a Nation*, his statue stands at the entrance gates at Flemington and his hide is on display at Museum Victoria, where he has always been the most popular of the permanent exhibits. His skeleton can be seen at the New Zealand National Museum in Wellington, and his enormous 6.2kg heart is retained at Canberra's National Museum of Australia.

In 1999, US *Blood-Horse Magazine* assembled a panel of experts to rate the USA's 100 greatest racehorses of the 20th century. On the strength of his lone start, in the Agua Caliente, Phar Lap was rated at #22 – three places higher than Seabiscuit.

Few winners are known primarily for their strapper or groom, especially a horse who wins 28 races including the Victoria Derby (1948), Caulfield Stakes (1950), William Reid Stakes, CF Orr Stakes, Chipping Norton Stakes (1951) and was a dual winner of the Turnbull Stakes (1949, 50), Mackinnon Stakes (1949, 50) and the St George Stakes (1950, 51).

Trained by Jim Cummings, **COMIC COURT (1950)** was led in by his son, Bart, who would train an awesome record of 12 Melbourne Cup winners in his own right.

**TOPAROA (1955)** gave legendary Sydney trainer TJ Smith the first of his two wins; **LIGHT FINGERS (1965)** won the VRC Oaks (1964), ATC Australian Oaks (1965) and was the first winner of this race for Bart Cummings; **KIWI (1983)** produced an amazing last to first finish; **AT TALAQ (1986)** won the Grand Prix de Paris (1984).

Dermot Weld's **VINTAGE CROP (1993)** was the first European-trained winner; **JEUNE (1994)** won the Hardwicke Stakes (1993); **SAINTLY (1996)** won the Australian Cup, Cox Plate (1996).

**MEDIA PUZZLE (2002)** was the second winner of the race for Dermot Weld in an unforgettable renewal, and was ridden by champion jockey Damien Oliver whose brother, Jason, had been killed in a track fall only days earlier. Wearing his brother's riding breeches, Oliver's salute to the heavens on crossing the winning post ensured that there was not a dry eye in the house and provided one of the great moments in Australian sporting history. The race was the subject of the 2011 movie, *The Cup*.

**DELTA BLUES (2006)** was the first Japanese-trained winner; **VIEWED (2008)** made it a dozen Cup wins for Bart Cummings and won the Caulfield Cup the following year; **AMERICAIN (2010)** became the first French-trained horse to win, quickly followed by **DUNADEN (2011)**, winner of the Hong Kong Vase (2011) and also won the Caulfield Cup the following year.

## VICTORIA DERBY

Many Derby winners have gone on to success in the Melbourne Cup including **LANTERN (1864)**, **BRISEIS (1876)**, **CHESTER (1877)**, **GRAND FLANEUR (1880)**, **NEWHAVEN (1896)**, **MERRIWEE (1899)**, **POSEIDON (1906)** won 19 races including the AJC Derby and two Caulfield Cups (1906, 07), **PRINCE FOOTE (1909)**, **PATROBAS (1915)**, **TRIVALVE (1927)**, **PHAR LAP (1929)**, **HALL MARK (1933)**, **SKIPTON (1941)**, **COMIC COURT (1948)**, **DELTA (1949)** and **EFFICIENT (2006)**.

Other notable winners include filly **ROSE OF MAY (1855)**, who won the first running.

Due to a change in the programming date **FIRE-WORKS (1867, 68)** created a record unlikely to be matched by winning the Victoria Derby twice.

Also doubtful to be equalled is New Zealander **MARTINI-HENRY (1883)**, who won the Victoria Derby on debut and the Melbourne Cup at his second start three days later.

**WALLACE (1895)** was the best-performed Australian son of Carbine and a leading stallion; **FRANCES TRESSADY (1923)** took out the Victoria Derby–VRC Oaks double; **HYDROGEN (1951)**; **SAILOR'S GUIDE (1955)** had 18 wins including the Sydney Cup (1956) and the Washington DC International, where he defeated Arc winner Ballymoss; **TULLOCH (1957)**; **SKY HIGH (1960)**; and **CRAFTSMAN (1963)**.

**TOBIN BRONZE (1965)** was a dual Cox Plate winner (1966, 67) and also won the CF Orr Stakes, Doncaster Hcp, All Aged Stakes, Toorak Hcp and the Caulfield Cup in 1967 among his 28 race wins; **DULCIFY (1978)**; **BIG PRINT (1979)** caused a boil over when he defeated Kingston Town; **SOVEREIGN RED (1980)**; **GROSVENOR (1982)**; **RED ANCHOR (1984)** swept the Caulfield Guineas, Cox Plate and the Derby; **MAHOGANY (1993)**; **ELVSTROEM (2003)** won the Caulfield Cup (2004) and the Dubai Duty Free (2005); and Clare Lindop became the first female rider to win on **REBEL RAIDER (2008)**.

## VRC OAKS

First won by **PALESTINE (1861)**.

**FLORENCE (1870)** also won the Victoria Derby, as did **LADY WALLACE (1905)**, **CARLITA (1914)**, **FURIOUS (1921)** and **FRANCES TRESSADY (1923)**.

Melbourne Cup winners include **BRISEIS (1877)**, **EVENING PEAL (1955)** and **LIGHT FINGERS (1964)**. **SWEET NELL (1903)** also took out the Caulfield Guineas and the Caulfield Cup that year.

Chiquita Lodge, the famous stables along the side of the Flemington course, was named after **CHIQUITA (1949)**, who also won the 1000 Guineas and was a dual winner of the Craiglee Stakes (1950, 51).

**TRUE COURSE (1950)** won the ATC Sires' Produce, Champagne Stakes and the Thousand Guineas (1950); **DENISE'S JOY (1975)** won the Queensland Oaks, Turnbull Stakes, Underwood Stakes in 1976; **SURROUND (1976)**; **ROSE OF KINGSTON (1981)** won the Ascot Vale Stakes (1981), ATC Australian Derby (1982).

**RESEARCH (1988)** won the Flight Stakes Thousand Guineas (1988); **TRISTANAGH (1989)** won the ATC Sires' Produce, Thousand Guineas (1989); **SLIGHT CHANCE (1992)** won the QTC Sires' Produce, Flight Stakes (1992), Queensland Oaks, Storm Queen Stakes (1993); **GRAND ARCHWAY (1988)** won the ATC Australian Oaks, CF Orr Stakes, Australia Stakes (1999); **SERENADE ROSE (2005)** won the Storm Queen Stakes, Australasian Oaks; **MISS FINLAND (2006)**; **SAMANTHA MISS (2008)** won the Champagne Stakes, Flight Stakes (2008); and **MOSHEEN (2011)** took out the Storm Queen Stakes, Randwick Guineas and Australian Guineas (2012).

## AUSTRALIAN CUP

Instituted in 1861, the race has been run over a variety of longer distances. In 1964 it was shortened to 2000m.

Notable winners since then include **CRAFTSMAN (1964, 65)**, who won the first two editions at the new distance; **BORE HEAD (1966)** won the Caulfield Cup (1965); and star mare **LEILANI (1975)** had won the ATC Australian Oaks, Turnbull Stakes, Toorak Hcp, Caulfield Cup and Mackinnon Stakes the previous year.

**MING DYNASTY (1978, 80)** won it twice, and was also a dual winner of the Caulfield Cup (1977, 80); **DULCIFY (1979)** won the Victoria Derby (1978), ATC Australian Derby, Turnbull Stakes and the Cox Plate (1979) by a record 7 lengths; **HYPERNO (1981)** won 20 races including the Melbourne Cup (1979); **BONECRUSHER (1987)**; dashing Queensland frontrunner **VO ROGUE (1989, 90)** went back to back. His 26 wins included two Turnbull Stakes (1987, 88), three CF Orr Stakes (1988–90), the Futurity Stakes (1988) and the Kingston Town Classic (1988).

**BETTER LOOSEN UP (1991)** won the Cantala Stakes, Railway Stakes (1989), Mackinnon Stakes (1990), Cox Plate (1990) and is Australia's only ever winner of the Japan Cup (1990); **LET'S ELOPE (1992)** followed up her double in the Caulfield Cup and Melbourne Cup (1991); **SAINTLY (1996)** went on to victory in the Cox Plate and Melbourne Cup that year; **OCTAGONAL (1997)** won ten Group 1 races including the ATC Sires Produce, Cox Plate (1995), ATC Australian Derby (1996) and two Tancred Stakes (1996, 97).

**DANE RIPPER (1998)** won the Cox Plate (1997) and **NORTHERLY (2001, 03)** won it twice. His 19 wins included the Underwood Stakes (2001, 02) twice, Railway Stakes (2000), Caulfield Cup (2001) and successive wins in the Cox Plate (2001, 02).

**LONHRO (2004)** won the Caulfield Guineas (2001), Chipping Norton Stakes, George Main Stakes (2003) and was a dual winner of the George Ryder Stakes (2003, 04) and Caulfield Stakes (2002, 03); **MAKYBE DIVA (2005)**; **ZIPPING (2010)**; **SHOCKING (2011)** won the Melbourne Cup (2009).

## BLACK CAVIAR LIGHTNING STAKES

**BLACK CAVIAR (2011–13)** brought up a hat-trick of victories, the most recent in track-record time. Undefeated in all 25 starts, the flying mare thrilled crowds and packed grandstands as she reeled off displays of raw speed and awesome power, gracefully disposing of all opposition with absolute ease. She often recorded 200m sectionals in less than 10 seconds with seemingly no effort.

Black Caviar broke the record of consecutive wins in Australasia and holds the benchmark of 15 wins at Group 1 – nine of those in succession. She was a phenomenon in our time and probably the greatest sprinter that the world has ever seen.

There have been a number of dual winners including **SKY HIGH (1961, 62)**, a winner of 26 stakes races from 1000m to 2500m including the Golden Slipper, Champagne Stakes, Victoria Derby (1960), Epsom Hcp, All Aged Stakes, Futurity Stakes, Caulfield Stakes, Mackinnon Stakes (1961), Chipping Norton Stakes, Linlithgow Stakes (1962) and two Ranvet Stakes (1962, 63).

**WENONA GIRL (1963, 64)** won 27 races including the ATC Sires' Produce, Rosehill Guineas, Thousand Guineas, Flight Stakes (1960), ATC Australian Oaks (1961), two Ranvet Stakes (1961, 64), CF Orr Stakes (1962), Cantala Stakes, George Main Stakes (1963) and All Aged Stakes (1964).

**MAYBE MAHAL (1977, 78)** won the Cantala Stakes (1976), Doomben 10,000 (1977), Newmarket Hcp and Doncaster Hcp (1978).

**RIVER ROUGH (1984, 85)**; **SCHILLACI (1992, 93)** also won the Oakleigh Plate, Newmarket Hcp, The Galaxy (1992), George Ryder Stakes (1993) and two Futurity Stakes (1993, 95); and **MAHOGANY (1995, 97)**.

**TODMAN (1960)** won 10 of 12 including the Golden Slipper and Champagne Stakes (1957); **STORM QUEEN (1967)** won the Golden Slipper, Champagne Stakes, Caulfield Guineas and the Cantala Stakes the previous year; **DUAL CHOICE (1971)**;

CENTURY (1974); **THE JUDGE (1979)**; **ZEDITAVE (1989)**; **CHOISIR (2003)**; and **FASTNET ROCK (2005)**.

**TAKEOVER TARGET (2006)** was famously bought for $1250 by former Queanbeyan cab driver Joe Janiak. The affable Janiak never could have guessed when he shook hands on his purchase that he was destined to also shake the hand of the Queen of England. Janiak trained the horse to 21 wins across the globe including the Newmarket Hcp, King's Stand Stakes, Sprinters Stakes (2006), Doomben 10,000 (2007), Singapore International Sprint (2008), TJ Smith Stakes, and the Goodwood Stakes (2009) to rack up over $6m in prize money.

**MISS ANDRETTI (2007)**, **APACHE CAT (2008)**, and **SCENIC BLAST (2009)**, who won the Newmarket Hcp and the King's Stand Stakes that year.

## NEWMARKET HANDICAP

Dual winners include **ASPEN (1880, 81)**; **GOTHIC (1927, 28)** won the Caulfield Stakes, Futurity Stakes, Mackinnon Stakes, Linlithgow Stakes (1928), CF Orr Stakes, William Reid Stakes (1929); **AURIE'S STAR (1937, 39)** also won the Lightning Stakes twice (1937, 39); **CORRECT (1960, 61)**; and **RAZOR SHARP (1982, 83)**.

Other notables include **MALUA (1884)**; **LOCHIEL (1887)** won the Auckland Cup (1888), Australian Cup (1889); **WAKEFUL (1901)**; and notorious rogue beginner **HEROIC (1926)**, who could win at any distance when he got away within sight of the field. His 21 victories included the ATC Australian Derby, Caulfield Guineas, Champagne Stakes, Ascot Vale Stakes (1924), Caulfield Stakes (1925), Underwood Stakes, Cox Plate (1926), William Reid Stakes (1927). He also sired champion **AJAX (1938)**.

**WALTZING LILY (1933)** won the William Reid Stakes (1933), Futurity Stakes (1934); **BERNBOROUGH (1946)**; **ROYAL GEM (1948)** won 23 of 51 including the Caulfield Guineas, Cantala Stakes (1945), Goodwood Hcp, Toorak Hcp and Caulfield Cup (1946); **MANIHI (1968)** sire of Manikato; **BAGUETTE (1971)** followed his triumph in the 2yo Triple Crown the previous year; **CENTURY (1973)** won the Lightning Stakes (1974); and **TOY SHOW (1976)** also won the Golden Slipper, ATC Sires' Produce, Thousand Guineas (1975) and William Reid Stakes (1977).

**MAYBE MAHAL (1978)**, **PLACID ARK (1987)**, **SPECIAL (1988)** followed up her win in the Lightning Stakes, **SHAFTESBURY AVENUE (1991)**, **SCHILLACI (1992)**, **GENERAL NEDIYM (1998)** won the Lightning Stakes, **BELLE DE JOUR (2003)** won the Golden Slipper, **EXCEED AND EXCEL (2004)**, **ALINGHI (2005)**, **TAKEOVER TARGET (2006)**, **MISS ANDRETTI (2007)**, **WEEKEND HUSSLER (2008)**, **SCENIC BLAST**

(2009), **BLACK CAVIAR (2011)** and **HAY LIST (2012)** earlier won the Manikato Stakes (2010) and the All Aged Stakes (2011).

## AUSTRALIAN GUINEAS

Notable winners include **ZABEEL (1990)**, outstanding sire of Melbourne Cup winners Might And Power, Jezabeel and Efficient.

**TRISCAY (1991)** won the Champagne Stakes, Flight Stakes (1990), ATC Oaks and Queensland Oaks (1991); **MAHOGANY (1994)** won eight Group 1 races including the Victoria Derby (1993), ATC Australian Derby (1994), Linlithgow Stakes (1996) and the Lightning Stakes twice (1995, 97); **FLYING SPUR (1996)** won the Golden Slipper (1995); **PINS (2000)** sired 2007 Cox Plate winner El Segundo and Hong Kong star Ambitious Dragon.

**APACHE CAT (2006)** won the Lightning Stakes (2008), Australia Stakes twice (2008, 09), TJ Smith Stakes, BTC Cup (2008) and was a dual winner of the Doomben 10,000 (2008, 09); **MISS FINLAND (2007)** won the Golden Slipper Stakes, Thousand Guineas and VRC Oaks (2006); and **MOSHEEN (2012)** followed up her win in the VRC Oaks (2011).

## TURNBULL STAKES

The Turnbull Stakes has been a good race for Melbourne Cup horses. Cup winners include **COMIC COURT (1949, 50)**, **RISING FAST (1954)**, **GALILEE (1968)**, **LET'S ELOPE (1991)**, **DORIEMUS (1996)**, **MAKYBE DIVA (2005)**, **EFFICIENT (2009)** and **GREEN MOON (2012)**.

**REDCRAZE (1955)** won 32 races including the Brisbane Cup, Metropolitan Hcp, Caulfield Stakes, Caulfield Cup (1956) and Cox Plate (1957).

**PANDIE SUN (1958)** is famous for his part in Australia's first-ever triple dead heat recorded by a photo-finish camera, when the judge could not separate Ark Royal, Pandie Sun and Fighting Force in the Hotham Hcp in 1956.

**AQUANITA (1962)** won the Railway Stakes (1959), Cantala Stakes twice (1960, 61), Doomben 10,000 (1961), Underwood Stakes twice (1961, 62), Futurity Stakes, Mackinnon Stakes, Cox Plate (1962); **CRAFTSMAN (1965)**; **TOBIN BRONZE (1966)**; **LEILANI (1974)**; **DENISE'S JOY (1976)**; **DULCIFY (1979)**; dual winner **VO ROGUE (1987, 88)**; **SUPER IMPOSE (1989)**; **BETTER LOOSEN UP (1990)**; **NATURALISM (1992)**, who won the ATC Australian Derby, Rosehill Guineas and Caulfield Stakes (1992); **THE PHANTOM CHANCE (1993)** won the New Zealand Derby (1992) and Cox Plate (1993); **SUNLINE (2001)**; **NORTHERLY (2002)**; **ELVSTROEM (2004)**; and **ZIPPING (2010)**.

## LKS MACKINNON STAKES

Instituted in 1869 as the Melbourne Stakes, the race name was changed in 1936 to honour the former Chairman of the VRC.

Run on Derby Day, the race is often used as a final prep race for the Melbourne Cup but is a genuine Group 1 in its own right.

Two horses – both of them legendary fillies – have won the race three times: **WAKEFUL (1901–03)** and **TRANQUIL STAR (1942, 44, 45)**, who won 23 races including the St George Stakes three times (1941, 44, 45), Chipping Norton Stakes (1941), Caulfield Cup (1942) and two Cox Plates (1942, 44).

Dual winners include **DAGWORTH (1873, 74)**, **BATTALION (1897, 98)**, **CETIGNE (1917, 19)**, **EURYTHMIC (1920, 21)**, **PHAR LAP (1930, 31)**, **PETER PAN (1933, 34)**, **BEAU VITE (1954, 55)**, **COMIC COURT (1949, 50)**, **RISING FAST (1954, 55)** and **BELMURA LAD (1980, 81)**.

Many winners have also taken out the Melbourne Cup including **GLENCOE (1869)**, **TIM WHIFFLER (1870)**, **CHESTER (1878)**, **MALUA (1884)**, **CARBINE (1890)**, **POSEIDON (1907)**, **THE TRUMP (1937)**, **DELTA (1951)**, **DALRAY (1952)**, **RAIN LOVER (1968)**, **GOLD AND BLACK (1976)**, **AT TALAQ (1986)**, **EMPIRE ROSE (1988)**, **LET'S ELOPE (1991)** and **ROGAN JOSH (1999)**.

Other notables include **ROBINSON CRUSOE (1877)**, so named because he was one of only two horses to survive a storm that claimed the lives of nine horses, including Cup favourite Robin Hood, when aboard the ship *City of Melbourne*. The ATC Australian Derby winner would go on to sire **TRENTON (1885)**, who in turn was sire of Wakeful.

**MANFRED** (1926) won the Victoria Derby, ATC Australian Derby, Cox Plate (1925) and Caulfield Cup (1926); **ROGILLA** (1933) won 26 races including the Caulfield Cup (1932), Sydney Cup and Cox Plate (1933); **FAMILY OF MAN** (1978) won the WATC Australian Derby (1976), Cox Plate (1977), William Reid Stakes, Cantala Stakes (1978) and was a dual winner of the Kingston Town Classic (1976, 78).

**PARIS LANE (1994)** won the Caulfield Cup (1994); **SIRMIONE (2007)** won the Australian Cup (2008).

Other greats to win include **GLOAMING (1924)**, **GOTHIC (1928)**, **AJAX (1938)**, **FLIGHT (1946)**, **HYDROGEN (1953)**, **SAILOR'S GUIDE (1957)**, **TULLOCH (1960)**, **SKY HIGH (1961)**, **AQUANITA (1962)**, **TOBIN BRONZE (1967)**, **LEILANI (1974)**, **DULCIFY (1979)**, **RUBITON (1987)**, **HORLICKS (1989)**, **BETTER LOOSEN UP (1990)**, **VEANDERCROSS (1992)**, **LONHRO (2002)**, **GRAND ARMEE (2004)**, **DESERT WAR (2006)** and **SO YOU THINK (2010)**.

## ASCOT VALE STAKES

Conditions of the race were altered in 1969 to make it a race for 3yos. Since then notable winners include **VAIN (1969)**, one of the all-time great sprinters who won 12 of 14 including hollow victories in the Golden Slipper and Caulfield Guineas (1969). He ran three times during the Flemington carnival as a 3yo – winning the Group 1 open sprint by 12 lengths and the Linlithgow Stakes by 6 lengths before carrying 4.5kg over weight for age to win the Cantala Stakes.

**CENTURY (1972)** and **ENCOSTA DE LAGO (1996)** were top sires; **SURROUND (1976)**; **MANIKATO (1978)**; **ROSE OF KINGSTON (1981)** won the VRC Oaks (1981), Australasian Oaks and ATC Australian Derby (1982); Blue Diamond Stakes winners **RANCHER (1982)**, **ZEDITAVE (1988)** and **ALINGHI (2004)**, who also won the Thousand Guineas (2004) and Newmarket Hcp (2005); and **WEEKEND HUSSLER (2007)** won the Caulfield Guineas (2007), Oakleigh Plate, Newmarket Hcp and George Ryder Stakes (2008).

## EMPIRE ROSE STAKES

Registered as the Empire Rose Stakes, the race has had a range of sponsors over its short journey. It is currently called the Myer Classic.

The most prominent winners have been **DIVINE MADONNA (2007)**, who won the Cantala Stakes, Queen of the Turf Stakes and Toorak Hcp (2007); and **TYPHOON TRACY (2009)**, who won the Coolmore Classic (2009), Futurity Stakes, Queen of the Turf Stakes (2010) and twice won the CF Orr Stakes (2010, 11).

## VICTORIA RACING CLUB STAKES

Formerly the Linlithgow Stakes, the race has had a number of sponsors.

Five horses have been successful three times in the race: **BARBELLE (1870–72)**; **SCAMANDA (1876–78)**; and **AMOUNIS (1926, 27, 29)**, who had 33 wins including the Epsom (1925, 28) and Cantala Stakes (1926, 29) twice, Rosehill Guineas (1925), Chipping Norton Stakes, Cox Plate (1927), Futurity Stakes, St George Stakes, All Aged Stakes, Caulfield Stakes and Caulfield Cup (1930). Amounis defeated Phar Lap by a short head in the Group 2 Warwick Stakes of 1930.

**CHATHAM (1931–33)** was a dual winner of the Cox Plate (1932, 34) and Epsom Hcp (1932, 33), and also won the Caulfield Stakes (1933), All Aged Stakes and Doncaster Hcp (1934) carrying 10st 4lb (65.5kg); and **HIGH CASTE (1939–41)** dead heated in 1939 then won the next two editions.

Dual winners include **CARBINE (1888, 89)**, **WOLAROI (1916, 18)**, **THE NIGHT PATROL (1924, 25)**, **AJAX (1937, 38)**, **MATRICE (1956, 57)**, **ALL SHOT (1972, 73)**, **REDELVA (1988, 90)** and **BLACK CAVIAR (2010, 11)**.

Other notable winners include **COLUMNIST (1947)**, who won the Caulfield Cup; **WIGGLE (1958)** won the Caulfield Guineas, Stradbroke Hcp (1958); **NOHOLME (1959)** also won the Champagne Stakes, Epsom Hcp, All Aged Stakes and Cox Plate that year; **SKY HIGH (1962)**; **STAR AFFAIR (1965)** won the Ascot Vale Stakes, Caulfield Guineas and Cox Plate in 1965; **ROYAL GEM (1945)**; **WENONA GIRL (1963)**; **VAIN (1969)**; **PLACID ARK (1987)**; **MAHOGANY (1996)**; **CHOISIR (2002)**; **FASTNET ROCK (2004)**; and **MISS ANDRETTI (2007)**.

## CANTALA STAKES

Currently known as the Emirates Stakes, dual winners include **AMOUNIS (1926, 29)**, **AQUANITA (1960, 61)** and **SEASCAY (1994, 95)**.

Other notables include **THE NIGHT PATROL (1924)**; **ROYAL GEM (1945)**; **MATRICE (1956)**; **WENONA GIRL (1963)**; **STORM QUEEN (1966)**; **VAIN (1969)**; **GUNSYND (1971)**; **MAYBE MAHAL (1976)**; **FAMILY OF MAN (1978)**; **BETTER LOOSEN UP (1989)**; **SHAFTESBURY AVENUE (1990)**; **TESTA ROSSA (2000)**; **DIVINE MADONNA (2006)**; **SILVER BOUNTY (1980)** won the Caulfield Cup (1981); **MAGARI (1982)** won the Sir Rupert Clark Stakes, Toorak Hcp (1982); and **DESERT EAGLE (2001)** raced as Grand Delight in Hong Kong where he won the sprint Triple Crown.

# CAULFIELD

Station Street, Caulfield, Victoria, Australia. www.melbourneracingclub.net.au

*C*aulfield held its first meeting in 1859 and at that time races were conducted across rough bush, heath and sand hills. The course is still referred to as 'The Heath'.

Located 8km east of the centre of Melbourne, it is host to some of Australia's oldest and most famous races – the Caulfield Guineas, Oakleigh Plate, Blue Diamond Stakes and the Caulfield Cup.

The Caulfield Cup is second only to the Melbourne Cup as Australia's premier staying contest, and the two races, held 17 days apart, make up the big spring double.

The course has been thoroughly renovated in recent times with the construction of the Sir Rupert Clarke Stand providing outstanding facilities to view the top-class racing that Caulfield provides.

Caulfield is also one of Victoria's major training bases, accommodating 500 horses. While it has long been so, a recent changing of the guard currently sees Melbourne's top trainers all based here.

## THE TRACK

Left-handed. The course is almost triangular in shape and has a circumference 2080m. The straight is 367m.

The Caulfield Cup start at the 2400m begins at the top of the home straight.

From the winning post runners turn left out of the straight and are on a straightish bend to the 1800m point. The track then rises along the straight run until about the 1300m and keeps rising around the left turn on to the side of the track at the 1000m.

From there it is a straight downhill run of 600m to the graduated home bend into the straight.

The 1400m start is from a chute that starts virtually on a bend, so inside draws are a definite advantage.

Races up to 1200m start from a chute that joins the side of the track, giving a straight downhill run all the way to the turn.

## FEATURE RACES

### CAULFIELD CUP

**NEWMINSTER (1879)** won the first running. Dual winners include **PARIS (1892, 94), POSEIDON (1906, 07), UNCLE SAM (1912, 14), WHITTIER (1922, 25), RISING FAST (1954, 55)** and **MING DYNASTY (1977, 80)**.

Other notables include **SWEET NELL (1903), MANFRED (1926), AMOUNIS (1930), ROGILLA (1932), THE TRUMP (1937), TRANQUIL STAR (1942), ROYAL GEM (1946), REDCRAZE (1956), TULLOCH (1957), GALILEE (1966), TOBIN BRONZE (1967), BIG PHILOU (1969), LEILANI (1974), NORTHERLY (2002)** and **DUNADEN (2012)**.

**EURYTHMIC (1920)** won the WATC Derby, Perth Cup (1919), Mackinnon Stakes twice (1920, 21), Caulfield Stakes three times (1920–22) and the Sydney Cup (1921); **MIGHTY KINGDOM (1979)** also won the Spring Champion Stakes, Sir Rupert Clark Stakes, Caulfield Stakes and WATC Australian Derby that year. He remains the last 3yo to win.

**MIGHT AND POWER (1997)** made all to street his rivals by 7 lengths in track-record time. He won 15 races including the Melbourne Cup (1997), Tancred

| FEATURE RACES | | | | | | | |
|---|---|---|---|---|---|---|---|
| BLUE DIAMOND STAKES | G1 | 1200M | TURF | 2YO | SW | 1971 | FEB |
| OAKLEIGH PLATE | G1 | 1100M | TURF | OPEN | HCP | 1884 | FEB |
| CF ORR STAKES | G1 | 1400M | TURF | 3YO+ | WFA | 1925 | FEB |
| FUTURITY STAKES | G1 | 1400M | TURF | 3YO+ | WFA | 1897 | FEB |
| UNDERWOOD STAKES | G1 | 1800M | TURF | 3YO+ | WFA | 1924 | SEPT |
| SIR RUPERT CLARKE STAKES | G1 | 1400M | TURF | 3YO+ | HCP | 1951 | SEPT |
| CAULFIELD CUP | G1 | 2400M | TURF | 3YO+ | HCP | 1879 | OCT |
| CAULFIELD GUINEAS | G1 | 1600M | TURF | 3YO | SW | 1881 | OCT |
| THOUSAND GUINEAS | G1 | 1600M | TURF | 3YOF | SW | 1946 | OCT |
| TOORAK HCP | G1 | 1600M | TURF | 3YO+ | HCP | 1881 | OCT |
| CAULFIELD STAKES | G1 | 2000M | TURF | 3YO+ | WFA | 1886 | OCT |

Fields of Omagh

Stakes, Doomben Cup, Caulfield Stakes and also broke the course record in the Cox Plate (1998); **TAUFAN'S MELODY (1998)** controversially survived a protest to be the first European-trained winner; **MUMMIFY (2003)** won the SA Derby, Underwood Stakes (2003), Caulfield Stakes (2004) and the Singapore International Cup (2005); and **ALL THE GOOD (2008)** gave Godolphin its first major win in Australia.

## CAULFIELD GUINEAS

Acknowledged as a sire-making race, it is one of the country's top contests for 3yos.

First won by **WHEATEAR (1881)**, prominent winners include **WALLACE (1895)**; **SWEET NELL (1903)**; **PATROBAS (1915)** won the Melbourne Cup, as did **ARTILLERYMAN (1919)**; **HEROIC (1924)**;

**AJAX (1937)**; **HIGH CASTE (1939)**; **HYDROGEN (1951)**; **TULLOCH (1957)**; **WIGGLE (1958)**; **STAR AFFAIR (1965)**; **VAIN (1969)**; **SURROUND (1976)**; **MANIKATO (1978)**; **RED ANCHOR (1984)**; **MAHOGANY (1993)**; **LONHRO (2001)**; and **WEEKEND HUSSLER (2007)**.

**AUTONOMY (1892)** won the ATC Sires' Produce, Champagne Stakes and Mackinnon Stakes (1892); **DUAL CHOICE (1970)** won the Lightning Stakes (1971), was dual winner of the Oakleigh Plate (1971, 72) and took out the William Reid Stakes (1972); **LUSKIN STAR (1977)** won 13 of 17 including the 2yo Triple Crown, QTC Sires' Produce (1977) and The Galaxy (1978).

**SOVEREIGN RED (1980)** took out the Victoria Derby, WATC Australian Derby, Kingston Town Classic (1980) and Doomben 10,000 (1981); **REDOUTE'S CHOICE (1999)** won the Blue Diamond Stakes, Manikato Stakes (1999) and CF Orr Stakes (2000), and was leading sire in Australia; and **STARSPANGLED BANNER (2009)** won the Oakleigh Plate, Diamond Jubilee Stakes and July Cup (2010).

## THOUSAND GUINEAS

Notable winners include **CHICQUITA (1949)**; **TRUE COURSE (1950)**; **WENONA GIRL (1960)**; **BEGONIA BELLE (1967)** won the Lightning Stakes (1968) and Newmarket Hcp (1969); **TOY SHOW (1975)**; **RIVERINA CHARM (1988)**; **WHISKED (1990)**, dam of Tie The Knot; **ALINGHI (2004)**; **MISS FINLAND (2006)**; and **ATLANTIC JEWEL (2011)**.

## BLUE DIAMOND STAKES

This race is Victoria's major 2yo event, second only to the Golden Slipper Stakes as Australia's premier contest for 2yos.

First won by **TOLERANCE (1971)**, other notable winners include **MANIKATO (1978)**; **REDOUTE'S CHOICE (1999)**; **ALINGHI (2004)**; **BOUNDING AWAY (1986)** won the 2yo Triple Crown, Flight Stakes (1986), Coolmore Classic (1987) and ATC Oaks (1987); **ZEDITAVE (1988)** won the TJ Smith Stakes (1988), Lightning Stakes, Futurity Stakes, William Reid Stakes (1989); and **SEPOY (2011)** won the Golden Slipper, Manikato Stakes and Coolmore Stud Stakes (2011).

Dwayne Dunn rode four consecutive winners from 2005 to 2008.

## OAKLEIGH PLATE

Time-honoured sprint race over 1100m. The saying 'He went like an Oakleigh Plater' has long been part of the Australian sporting vernacular.

First won by **MALUA (1884)**. Dual winners include **AURIE'S STAR (1937, 39)** and **DUAL CHOICE (1971, 72)**.

Other prominent winners include **WAKEFUL (1901)**; **TIME AND TIDE (1965)**, who won the ATC Sires' Produce, Champagne Stakes, Caulfield Guineas (1963), Ranvet Stakes, Doncaster Hcp (1965) and the George Ryder Stakes twice (1964, 67); **CITIUS (1966)** won the Lightning Stakes and Doncaster Hcp (1966); **TONTONAN (1973)** won the Golden Slipper, ATC Sires' Produce (1973), Doncaster Hcp and All Aged Stakes (1973); **PLACID ARK (1987)**; **SNIPPETS (1988)** won the inaugural Magic Millions 2yo Classic, ATC Sires' Produce (1987), The Galaxy (1988); **SCHILLACI (1992)**; **FASTNET ROCK (2005)**; **WEEKEND HUSSLER (2008)** and **STARSPANGLEDBANNER (2010)**.

## TOORAK HCP

The Toorak is a 1600m handicap race with an esteemed history.

Dual winners include **SAXONY (1948, 49)**, **DESERT BREEZE (1952, 53)**, **NICOPOLIS (1963, 64)** and **UMRUM (1999, 2000)**.

Notable winners include **UNCLE SAM (1912)**; **THE TRUMP (1937)**; **ROYAL GEM (1946)**; **TOBIN BRONZE (1967)**; **GUNSYND (1971)**; **LEILANI (1974)**; **MORE JOYOUS (2010)**; **KING MUFHASA (2011)**.

**HIGHLAND (1929)** dual winner of the Stradbroke Hcp (1925, 26) and the Underwood Stakes (1928, 29), and won the the Cantala Stakes and Cox Plate (1928); **COUNSEL (1943)** won when the race was run in two divisions, and also won the Futurity Stakes, Caulfield

Might and Power

Cup, Mackinnon Stakes (1944); **TAUTO (1970)** won the Cox Plate (1971).

**ALL SHOT (1972)** twice won the Linlithgow Stakes (1972, 73) and William Reid Stakes (1973, 74) and won the Cantala Stakes (1972), George Main Stakes, George Ryder Stakes (1973) and CF Orr Stakes (1974); and **PLUSH (1975)** won the Ascot Vale Stakes, Moonee Valley Stakes (1974), CF Orr Stakes (1976).

## UNDERWOOD STAKES

Champion **AJAX (1938–40)** was a winner of 36 of 46 starts. In addition to his record three consecutive wins in this race he also won the Futurity Stakes and All Aged Stakes three times (1938–40), twice won the Linlithgow Stakes (1937, 38) and took out the ATC

Sires' Produce, Champagne Stakes, Rosehill Guineas, Caulfield Guineas (1937), Newmarket Hcp carrying 8lb over weight for age, Caulfield Stakes, Cox Plate, Mackinnon Stakes (1938) and St George Stakes (1939).

Ajax won 18 races in succession, but in his attempt to equal the standing record of 19 consecutive victories, jointly held by Desert Gold and Gloaming, suffered the dubious distinction of being one of the shortest-priced beaten favourites in Australian racing history, when second in the Rawson Stakes of 1939 at odds of 1/40.

Several horses have won the race twice including **WHITTIER (1924, 25)**, **HIGHLAND (1928, 29)**, **HALL MARK (1933, 34)**, **YOUNG IDEA (1935, 37)**, **ATTLEY (1946, 47)**, **BEAU GEM (1949, 50)**, **FLYING HALO (1953, 54)**, **LORD (1958, 60)**, **AQUANITA (1961, 62)** and **NORTHERLY (2001, 02)**.

Other prominent winners include **HEROIC (1926)**; **PHAR LAP (1931)**; **ROYAL GEM (1948)**; **TOBIN BRONZE (1966)**; **RAIN LOVER (1969)**; **BIG PHILOU (1970)**; **HOW NOW (1976)** won the ATC Oaks, Caulfield Stakes and Caulfield Cup (1976); **DENISE'S JOY (1977)**; **SOVEREIGN RED (1981)**; **TRISTARC (1985)** took out the ATC Australian Derby, Caulfield Stakes and Caulfield Cup (1985).

**BONECRUSHER (1986)**; **RUBITON (1987)** won the Futurity Stakes, Cox Plate and Mackinnon Stakes (1987); **ALMAARAD (1989)** won the Grand Prix de Deauville (G2) and Prix Kergolay (G2) in 1987, Rheinland-Pokel and Hardwicke Stakes (1988), and the Cox Plate (1989); **JEUNE (1994)**; **OCTAGONAL (1996)**; **TIE THE KNOT (1998)**; **ELVSTROEM (2004)**; **EL SEGUNDO (2006)** won the Caulfield Stakes (2005), CF Orr Stakes and Cox Plate (2007); **WEEKEND HUSSLER (2008)**; and **SO YOU THINK (2010)**.

## CAULFIELD STAKES

**LORD (1958–60)** won three times including a dead heat in 1960. He was a dominant weight-for-age horse in his era and loved the Caulfield track. He was dual winner of the Underwood Stakes (1958, 60), CF Orr Stakes (1959, 60) and St George Stakes (1959, 60), winner of the Futurity Stakes (1959) and also scored four consecutive victories in the G2 Memsie Stakes (1958–61).

**EURYTHMIC (1920–22)** and **WINFREUX (1965–67)** both scored three successive victories.

Dual winners include **WAKEFUL (1901, 02)**, **ARTILLERIE (1909, 10)**, **HIGH CASTE (1939, 40)**, **LAWRENCE (1944, 45)**, **SKY HIGH (1961, 62)**, **KINGSTON TOWN (1981, 82)** and **LONHRO (2002, 03)**.

Other notables include **THE ADMIRAL (1890)**, who won the Victoria Derby (1890); **HEROIC (1925)**; **MANFRED (1926)**; **AMOUNIS (1930)**; **YOUNG IDEA (1936)**; **AJAX (1938)**; **TRANQUIL STAR (1942)**; **BERNBOROUGH (1946)**; **COMIC COURT (1950)**; **GREY BOOTS (1951)** won the Doncaster Hcp, Toorak Hcp, Caulfield Cup (1950), Ranvet Stakes (1951) and CF Orr Stakes (1952); **FLYING HALO (1953)**; **RISING FAST (1954)**; **REDCRAZE (1956)**; **GUNSYND (1972)**; **HOW NOW (1976)**; **FAMILY OF MAN (1977)**; **HYPERNO (1980)**; **TRISTARC (1985)**; **BONECRUSHER (1986)**; **ALMAARAD (1989)**; **SHAFTESBURY AVENUE (1991)**; **NATURALISM (1993)**; **ROUGH HABIT (1994)**; **MIGHT AND POWER (1998)**; **SKY HEIGHTS (2000)** won the Rosehill Guineas, ATC Australian Derby, Caulfield Cup (1999); **NORTHERLY (2001)**; **EL SEGUNDO (2005)**; **MALDIVIAN (2007)**; **SO YOU THINK (2010)**; and **OCEAN PARK (2012)**.

## CF ORR STAKES

**THE NIGHT PATROL (1925)** won the inaugural running, **MANIKATO (1979–81)** and **VO ROGUE (1988–90)** scored hat-tricks. **LORD (1959, 60)** and **TYPHOON TRACY (2010, 11)** both won it twice.

Other notables include **WHITTIER (1926)**; **HEROIC (1927)**; **GOTHIC (1929)**; **HIGH CASTE (1940)**; **FLIGHT (1946)**; **ATTLEY (1947)**; **COMIC COURT (1951)**; **FLYING HALO (1954)**; **RISING FAST (1956)**; **WENONA GIRL (1962)**; **AQUANITA (1963)**; **WINFREUX (1968)** won three successive Caulfield Stakes (1965–67), Doomben 10,000, Stradbroke Hcp (1965), Doomben Cup (1966), Mackinnon Stakes (1967) and William Reid Stakes (1968); **TOBIN BRONZE (1967)**; **CREWMAN (1970)** was a winner of the Australian Cup, Futurity Stakes and William Reid Stakes that year.

**ALL SHOT (1974)**; **LEILANI (1975)**; **SURROUND (1977)**; **HYPERNO (1978)**; **AT TALAQ (1987)**; **LET'S ELOPE (1992)**; **JEUNE (1995)**; **SAINTLY (1997)**; **GRAND ARCHWAY (1999)**; **REDOUTE'S CHOICE (2000)**; **LONHRO (2004)**; **ELVSTROEM (2005)**; **EL SEGUNDO (2007)**; **MALDIVIAN (2009)** followed up his win in the Cox Plate (2008); and **BLACK CAVIAR (2012)**.

## FUTURITY STAKES

Mighty **MANIKATO (1979–81, 83)** holds the record of four wins in the race.

**AJAX (1938–40)** made it three in succession.

Dual winners include **GLADSOME (1904, 05)**, **ST RAZZLE (1949, 50)**, **IDOLOU (1973, 74)**, **SCHILLACI (1993, 95)** and Australian Cup winner **NICONERO (2008, 09)**.

Other notables include **COMEDY KING (1909)**; **EURYTHMIC (1921)**; **AMOUNIS (1929)**; **PHAR LAP (1930)**; **WALTZING LILY (1933)**; **HIGH CASTE (1941)**; **COUNSEL (1944)**; **BERNBOROUGH (1946)**; **ATTLEY (1947)**; **ROYAL GEM (1948)**; **SAN DOMENICO (1952)**; **LORD (1959)**; **TODMAN (1960)**; **SKY HIGH (1961)**; **AQUANITA (1962)**; **WENONA GIRL (1963)**; **STAR AFFAIR (1966)**; **CREWMAN (1970)**; **VITE CHEVAL (1985)** won the Doncaster Hcp (1984), All Aged Stakes (1985); **CAMPAIGN KING (1986)** won the George Main Stakes (1987), Doomben 10,000, Stradbroke Hcp (1988) and twice won both the All Aged Stakes and George Ryder Stakes (1987, 88); **RUBITON (1987)**; **VO ROGUE (1988)**; **ZEDITAVE (1989)**; and **REDELVA (1991)**.

**MANNERISM (1992)** took out the Australasian Oaks (1991), Caulfield Cup (1992); **ENCOUNTER (1998)** won the ATC Sires' Produce, Champagne Stakes, George Main Stakes, Caulfield Guineas (1997) and Chipping Norton Stakes (1998); **TESTA ROSSA (2000)**; dual Cox Plate winner **FIELDS OF OMAGH (2006)**; **TYPHOON TRACY (2010)**; **MORE JOYOUS (2011)**; and **KING MUFHASA (2012)**.

## INVITATION / SIR RUPERT CLARKE STAKES

**JOVIAL LAD (1951)** won the inaugural race, **ANONYME (1961, 62)**, **TAUTO (1970, 71)** and **TESTA ROSSA (1999, 2000)** each scored successive victories.

Other notable winners include **MATRICE (1955)**; **SAMSON (1963)**; **NICOPOLIS (1965)**; **CAP D'ANTIBES (1975)** won the Flight Stakes (1974), Lightning Stakes, Newmarket Hcp (1975) and ran second in the VRC Oaks (1974); **MANIKATO (1978)**; **MANNERISM (1992)**; **ENCOSTA DE LAGO (1996)**; and **EXCEED AND EXCEL (2003)**.

# MOONEE VALLEY

McPherson St, Moonee Ponds, Victoria, Australia. www.mvrc.net.au

*Moonee Valley racecourse is located in the inner Melbourne suburb of Moonee Ponds.*

William S Cox purchased farmland from John F Feehan in 1883 and it was his vision to set out the course. It is one of four metropolitan tracks in Victoria, and the only privately owned racing club in Melbourne.

The race that bears the name of the course's founder, the WS Cox Plate, is considered the weight-for-age championship of Australia, and the race has been won by so many of the nation's greatest horses.

Moonee Valley is a great racecourse for the spectator with modern facilities and the close proximity of the grandstands to the track provides a real amphitheatre-like quality, which generates genuine excitement and atmosphere for the race-goer. Many leading riders have said that nothing compares to the roar of the crowd for the start and finish of the Cox Plate.

Moonee Valley is the only metropolitan course in Victoria that stages night racing, with meetings held most Friday nights between September and March. The most prominent of these is the Manikato Stakes meeting in September.

## THE TRACK

Left-handed. It is a small rectangular course with a circumference of 1805m.

The very short home straight is only 173m, making it the shortest run home of any track in Australia.

Out of the home straight runners are on a bend until the 1600m. Then it is a run of 400m to the bend to the top of the track, followed by another straight run of 250m until the next bend takes runners to the side of the course at the 700m. A straight run of 300m leads to the home turn at the 400m.

Races over 1000m start from a diagonal chute that joins the course proper at the 600m.

The 1200m chute joins the back of the course, proving a run of 200m to the first of two bends.

The 1600m start is on the course proper, giving a run of 400m until the first turn.

The Cox Plate start at the 2040m is at the top of the straight, with a short run of just over 200m until the first turn.

A chute for the 2600m start joins the side of the course and the 3000m chute links up with the back of the track.

Inside draws are a big advantage from the 1200m and 2040m start positions.

While it is a tight course, the track rises 5.05m from the 800m to the winning post, so it does provide a truly searching test and back markers can be well suited, particularly when the rail is in the true position.

On pace runners are advantaged when the rail is out.

| FEATURE RACES | | | | | |
|---|---|---|---|---|---|
| WILLIAM REID STAKES | G1 | 1200M | OPEN | WFA | MAR |
| MANIKATO STAKES | G1 | 1200M | OPEN | WFA | SEPT |
| WS COX PLATE | G1 | 2040M | 3YO+ | WFA | OCT |
| NORMAN CARLYON STAKES | G2 | 1200M | 3YO+ | WFA | JAN |
| SUNLINE STAKES | G2 | 1600M | 3YO+ F&M | WFA | MAR |
| ALISTAIR CLARK STAKES | G2 | 2040M | 3YO | SW | MAR |
| DATO TAN CHIM NAN STAKES | G2 | 1600M | OPEN | WFA | SEPT |
| BILL STUTT STAKES | G2 | 1600M | 3YO+ | SW | SEPT |
| WH STOCKS STAKES | G2 | 1600M | 4YO+M | WFA | SEPT |
| AJ MOIR STAKES | G2 | 1200M | OPEN | WFA | OCT |
| CRYSTAL MILE | G2 | 1600M | OPEN | HCP | OCT |
| MOONEE VALLEY GOLD CUP | G2 | 2500M | 3YO+ | SWP | OCT |
| AAMI VASE | G2 | 2040M | 3YO | SW | OCT |

# FEATURE RACES

## WS COX PLATE

The Cox Plate is held in late October, a week before the Flemington Carnival.

With a history dating back to 1922, the 2040m race is the highest quality event on the Australian racing calendar. The list of winners is a virtual honour roll of the legends of the Australasian turf.

All-time great **KINGSTON TOWN (1980–82)** holds the record with three consecutive victories. A winner of 30 of his 41 starts, he was virtually unbeatable on right-handed tracks, at one stage bringing up 21 consecutive victories on Sydney and Brisbane tracks over a three-year period.

In Melbourne his record was not as impressive because he was never as comfortable racing left-handed, but it was his Cox Plate victories that wrote his name into Australian racing folklore. Kingston Town did not really handle the tight Moonee Valley circuit but despite this, showed his determination and absolute class to win Australia's finest race three times.

He also won the Spring Champion Stakes (1979), Rosehill Guineas, ATC Australian Derby, Tancred Stakes, the Sydney Cup as a 3yo by 7 lengths, Queensland Derby (1980), the George Main Stakes (1981, 82) and the Caulfield Stakes (1981, 82) twice. At his final appearance he won the Western Mail Classic (1982), which is now known as the Kingston Town Classic. He claimed 14 wins at Group 1 level, which stood as an Australian record until 2013.

Dual winners include **PHAR LAP (1930, 31)**; **CHATHAM (1932, 33)** after being denied only by Phar Lap when second in 1931; **YOUNG IDEA (1936, 37)**; **BEAU VITE (1940, 41)**; **TRANQUIL STAR (1942, 44)**; **FLIGHT (1945, 46)** dead heated for first in 1946; **HYDROGEN (1952, 53)**; **TOBIN BRONZE (1966, 67)**; **SUNLINE (1999, 2000)**; **NORTHERLY (2001, 02)**; **FIELDS OF OMAGH (2003, 06)**; and **SO YOU THINK (2009, 10)**.

Other notables include **THE NIGHT PATROL (1924)**, **MANFRED (1925)**, **HEROIC (1926)**, **AMOUNIS (1927)**, **HIGHLAND (1928)**, **NIGHTMARCH (1929)**, **ROGILLA (1933)**, **AJAX (1938)**.

**CARBON COPY (1948)** won the Victoria Derby, ATC Derby (1948), two Chipping Norton Stakes (1949, 1950) and a Sydney Cup (1949); **DELTA (1949)**; **RISING FAST (1954)**; **REDCRAZE (1957)**; **NOHOLME (1959)**; **TULLOCH (1960)**; **AQUANITA (1962)**; **STAR AFFAIR (1965)**; **TAUTO (1971)**; **GUNSYND (1972)**; and **TAJ ROSSI (1973)** won the Ascot Vale Stakes, Victoria Derby, and Cantala Stakes (1973).

**SURROUND (1976)** won 12 of 16 in her 3yo season, racking up ten successive wins. She is the only 3yo filly ever to win, and set a track record that stood for 22 years in doing so. She also won the Caulfield Guineas, VRC Oaks (1976), CF Orr Stakes, ATC Oaks

So You Think

and Queensland Oaks (1977).

Ill-fated **DULCIFY (1979)** won by a record 7 lengths. He won the Victoria Derby (1978), ATC Australian Derby, Rosehill Guineas, Australian Cup, Turnbull Stakes and Mackinnon Stakes (1979). He fatally broke down during the running of the 1979 Melbourne Cup.

**FAMILY OF MAN (1977)**; **STRAWBERRY ROAD (1983)**; **RED ANCHOR (1984)**; **RUBITON (1987)**, sire of **FIELDS OF OMAGH**; **ALMAARAD (1989)**; **BETTER LOOSEN UP (1990)**, winner of the Cantala Stakes, Railway Stakes, Kingston Town Classic (1989), Ranvet Stakes, Turnbull Stakes, Mackinnon Stakes (1990), Australian Cup (1991) and is the only Australian horse to win the Japan Cup (1990).

**BONECRUSHER (1986)** produced a legendary victory; **SUPER IMPOSE (1992)**; **OCTAGONAL (1995)**; **SAINTLY (1996)**; 1997 Caulfield Cup and Melbourne Cup winner **MIGHT AND POWER (1998)** broke Surround's long-standing track record;

and **MAKYBE DIVA (2005)** scored a famous triumph en route to her third Melbourne Cup.

## THE MANIKATO STAKES

The Manikato Stakes was formerly known as the Freeway Stakes until 1984 when the name was changed to honour the deeds of the mighty Manikato, one of the greatest sprinters in Australia's history. Manikato won the big double for 2yos – the Blue Diamond Stakes and the Golden Slipper – and went on to achieve the remarkable feat of winning the Group 1 William Reid Stakes on five consecutive occasions from 1979 to 1983. He won a total of 29 races including 11 at Group 1 level and became the first sprinter in Australia to earn $1m in prize money.

Other wins include the Caulfield Guineas (1978), Doomben 10,000 (1979), George Ryder Stakes (1980) and four Futurity Stakes (1979–81, 83).

Manikato dominated the Australian sprinting ranks for six years but possibly his greatest run came in defeat

Kingston Town

as a 3yo, when attempting to stretch his brilliance to 2000m in the Group 1 Australian Cup. He led until the shadows of the post only to be collared near the line by Dulcify, who would go on to be a champion in his own right. Manikato died in 1984 and is buried at the Moonee Valley racecourse.

The race has been run at Group 1 level since 1989. Notable winners include **DANE RIPPER (1998)**, who also won the Cox Plate (1997); **REDOUTE'S CHOICE (1999); SUNLINE (2000); SPINNING HILL (2002, 03)** and **SPARK OF LIFE (2004, 05)** scored consecutive victories; **MISS ANDRETTI (2006); GOLD EDITION (2007); HAY LIST (2010); SEPOY (2011)** won the Blue Diamond and the Golden Slipper (2011); **SEA SIREN (2012)** won the BTC Cup and Doomben 10,000 (2012) as a 3yo filly.

Earlier notables include **WINFREUX (1968); VAIN (1969)**; back-to-back winner **DUAL CHOICE (1970, 71); CENTURY (1972); TAUTO (1973, 74)** also won it twice; **SCAMANDA (1976);**

**MANIKATO (1979, 82)** made it a double three years apart; Caulfield Cup winner **SILVER BOUNTY (1981); STRAWBERRY ROAD (1983)** and **RUBITON (1987)**.

Named after prominent owner William Reid, the race was established in 1925.

Also a 1200m race, it is held in the autumn and became a Group 1 race in 1989. Winners since include **REDELVA (1991), HAREEBA (1995), GRAND ARCHWAY (1999)**, Hong Kong-trained **CAPE OF GOOD HOPE (2005)** was the first international horse to win, **MISS ANDRETTI (2007), APACHE CAT (2008, 09)** notched up consecutive victories and **BLACK CAVIAR (2011, 13)**.

Earlier notables include Cox Plate winners **THE NIGHT PATROL (1925, 26); TRANQUIL STAR (1946); CHANAK (1948); STAR AFFAIR (1966) FAMILY OF MAN (1978); HEROIC**

**(1927); GOTHIC (1929); WALTZING LILY (1933); COMIC COURT (1951)**, who followed up his win in the Melbourne Cup the previous year; three-time winner **FLYING HALO (1952, 53, 55); WINFREUX (1968); CREWMAN (1970); DUAL CHOICE (1972)**; dual winner **ALL SHOT (1973, 74); LEICA SHOW (1975); TOY SHOW (1977); CAMPAIGN KING (1986)** and **VO ROGUE (1988)**.

# SANDOWN PARK

Princes Hwy, Springvale, Victoria, Australia. www.melbourneracingclub.net.au

| FEATURE RACES | | | | | | |
|---|---|---|---|---|---|---|
| ZIPPING CLASSIC | G2 | 2400M | TURF | 3YO+ | WFA | NOV |
| SANDOWN GUINEAS | G2 | 1600M | TURF | 3YO | SW | NOV |
| SANDOWN STAKES | G3 | 1500M | TURF | 3YO+ | HCP | NOV |
| ECLIPSE STAKES | G3 | 1800M | TURF | 3YO+ | HCP | NOV |
| Sandown Cup | L | 3200M | TURF | 3YO+ | HCP | NOV |

## FEATURE RACE

### ZIPPING CLASSIC

Zipping

*L*ocated 25km south-east of the city, Sandown Park racecourse is the fourth of the metropolitan courses in Melbourne and the city's most recently constructed.

Built in 1965, a crowd in excess of 50,000 people turned out for the first meeting.

In 2001 the track was remodelled to construct an additional inner turf course. Using the traditional home straight, the inner layout bypasses the hill at the back of the course to form what is known as the Lakeside course.

The original layout is now known as the Hillside course, on which all feature racing is run.

Racing here generally caters for the restricted city grades and the course hosts much of the metropolitan racing during the winter months, particularly mid-week.

With its long uphill run home, Sandown is considered the fairest of the Melbourne tracks and a good track for the progressive horse.

Highlight is Sandown Classic day, which is held on the Saturday after the Flemington carnival and features Group and Listed races exclusively on the card. Sandown also stages the Grand National Steeplechase and the Grand National Hurdle.

Sandown is also well known as a major motor racing venue for V8 touring cars and was formerly the home of the Australian Grand Prix in the days of the elite open wheel classes of the 1960s and 70s.

Facilities here are good for the spectator and the atmosphere more relaxed than its inner-city counterparts.

## THE TRACK

### HILLSIDE COURSE

Left-handed. The Hillside track is an undulating course with a circumference of 2087m.

The home straight is 491m.

On leaving the straight a wide sweeping bend takes runners on to the back of the course at the 1600m. It is an uphill run to the 1000m mark where the track turns sharp left for the downhill run to the home straight.

The straight dips slightly just upon entering before an uphill run of 400m to the winning post.

The start for the feature Zipping Classic at the 2400m is located at the top of the home straight.

Races at 1000m start from a chute at the top of the home bend. The downhill run to the turn ensures that it is one of the fastest short courses in the country.

### LAKESIDE COURSE

The Lakeside course circumvents the hill and is therefore much flatter than the Hillside layout.

The circumference is 1857m and the track joins the home straight on the course proper allowing an uphill run in of 407m.

Races at 1700m and 1800m start from a chute at the end of the back straight.

The Zipping Classic is one of the very few weight-for-age races in Australia run over 2400m.

The conditions of the race have regularly changed. It was originally run as the Williamstown Cup at that now defunct course, then as the Sandown Cup from 1964. The race was made a weight-for-age contest in 1999 and re-named the Sandown Classic. All seemed settled until Zipping won four in a row, prompting another name change.

A 3200m Listed race has recently been added to the calendar, and it is now known as the Sandown Cup.

Multiple winners include four-time victor **ZIPPING (2007–10)** and dual winner **SECOND WIND (1930, 31)**.

**LIGHT FINGERS (1966)**; **BAGHDAD NOTE (1973)** and **ARWON (1980)** won the Melbourne Cup.

Other notables include **MERMAN (1896)**, who won the Ascot Gold Cup (1900); **BATTALION (1897)** won the Brisbane Cup (1897) and two Mackinnon Stakes (1897, 98); **CARLITA (1915)** had swept the Victoria Derby and VRC Oaks (1914); **RICHMOND MAIN (1919)** won the Victoria Derby (1919); **WYNETTE (1923)** won the Caulfield Cup (1923), Adelaide Cup (1924); **AMOUNIS (1928)**; **COUNSEL (1945)**; **COLUMNIST (1946)**; **SAXONY (1949)** won consecutive Toorak Hcps (1948, 49); **FIGHTING FORCE (1956)**; and **SAILOR'S GUIDE (1957)**.

**GUNSYND (1971)**; **SYDESTON (1989)** took out the Caulfield Cup (1990); **STYLISH CENTURY (1991)** was a winner of the Victoria Derby (1989); and **SKY HEIGHTS (2001)**.

# GEELONG

Breakwater Road, Breakwater, Victoria, Australia.
www.grc.com.au

| FEATURE RACES | | | | | |
|---|---|---|---|---|---|
| GEELONG CUP | G3 | 2400M | TURF | 3YO+ | OCT |
| Geelong Classic | L | 2200M | TURF | 3YO | OCT |

Situated on Corio Bay, 75km south-west of Melbourne, Geelong is Victoria's second–most populated city.

Racing in the area dates back to 1841 with a number of courses used. The Geelong Racing Club was formed in 1866 with the first Geelong Cup run six years hence at the old Marshalltown course.

The track at Marshalltown was located on the flats alongside the Barwon River and consequently prone to flooding, so the racecourse and Geelong Showgrounds were relocated to the current site in 1908.

## THE TRACK

Left-handed. Classic oval of 2040m in circumference. The home straight is 380m and slightly uphill.

Out of the home straight a long sweeping bend takes runners to the 1400m. It is a straight run of about 500m to the sweeping home bend, which falls slightly to the home straight.

The 1500m start is from a chute on the back of the course, providing a long run to the home bend.

The 1700m chute only gives a short run before linking up with the turn out of the home straight.

Otherwise, all starting positions give ample distance for riders to take up positions.

An inner synthetic Thoroughtrack was added in 2000, and races are scheduled up to twice a week during the winter months. The venue has become a handy fall-back for Victorian racing during this time, with many potentially washed-out fixtures from other tracks transferred to the Geelong synthetic course in order for the meetings to proceed.

## FEATURE RACE

### GEELONG CUP

The Geelong Cup is a quality race. Run only 13 days before the Melbourne Cup, making it a target for horses looking to earn a weight penalty to qualify for a start in the race that stops the nation. In recent years much depth has been added to the field with international raiders such as Irish-trained **MEDIA PUZZLE (2002)** and French horses **AMERICAIN (2010)** and **DUNADEN (2011)** going on to victory in the Melbourne Cup, having earned a start by winning this race.

Many top horses have figured in the long history of the race, including **MELBOURNE (1875)**, who won the Victoria Derby the previous year; **NEWMINSTER (1878)** won the Caulfield Cup (1879); **MALUA (1889)**; **CRAFTSMAN (1966)**; **DOUBLE STEEL (1969)** won the VRC Oaks (1968); **AUSTRALASIA (1973)** won the Turnbull Stakes and Mackinnon Stakes that year; **ALLEZ BIJOU (1981)** won the Ranvet Stakes (1982); and **KARASI (2001)** went on to win the Nakayama Grand Jump on a record three consecutive occasions (2005–07).

# BENDIGO

Heinz Street, White Hills, Victoria, Australia.
www.countryracing.com.au/bendigo-jockey-club

| FEATURE RACE | | | | | |
|---|---|---|---|---|---|
| Bendigo Cup | L | 2400M | TURF | OPEN | HCP | OCT |

Bendigo is located 150km north-west of Melbourne.

Gold was discovered at The Rocks on Bendigo Creek in 1851 and soon after Bendigo became a boom-town in the Victorian Gold Rush. Today it is Victoria's fourth–most populated city.

The Bendigo Jockey Club was formed in 1858 and the first Bendigo Cup – then known as the Sandhurst Cup – was run in 1868. In its infancy the course was right-handed, but converted to left-handed in 1873.

Bendigo is Victoria's premier country track from a pure racing perspective, and the Bendigo Cup is currently a race of $250,000 – the richest country Cup in Victoria.

A wide, expansive course, it is one of the fairest tracks in the state and consequently well supported by the major trainers as a preferred venue for promising horses. Dubbed the Nursery of Champions, it can take a city class horse to win a maiden here. The standard of racing is always high, even in the lower grades.

## THE TRACK

Left-handed. Classic oval with a circumference of 1995m and a home straight of 400m. Flat throughout.

Races up to 1100m start from a chute that links up with the side of the course.

The 1600m start is from a chute that joins the back of the course.

## FEATURE RACE

### BENDIGO CUP

Notable winners of the Bendigo Cup include dual victor **MOST REGAL (1952, 53)**, who placed in both the Caulfield and Melbourne Cups of 1953; two-time Perth cup winner **MAGISTRATE (1981)**; New Zealand Cup winner **DOUBLE TAKE (1995)** and **GALLIC** who won twice **(2004, 06)** and went on to victory in the Adelaide Cup and Sydney Cup of 2007.

# CRANBOURNE

Grant Street, Cranbourne, Victoria, Australia.
www.cranbourneturfclub.com.au

| FEATURE RACE | | | | | |
|---|---|---|---|---|---|
| CRANBOURNE CUP | L | 2025M | TURF | 3YO+ | HCP | OCT |

Located 42km from Melbourne, the once rural centre of Cranbourne is now an outer suburb due to Melbourne's urban sprawl to the south-east of the city.

Racing at Cranbourne dates back to 1847 and the complex today is the largest training centre in the Southern Hemisphere. Up to 800 horses gallop daily on the array of training courses. More than 100 trainers make their base here – many of them well-known names.

The course generates an estimated $100m each year for the local economy.

It is the main Victorian venue for official race trials with around 500 trials run annually.

An inner synthetic course was recently added for racing and floodlights installed to allow night meetings. Cranbourne is one of only two Victorian racecourses to offer night racing.

Many top horses have progressed through here, most notably Manikato, who won his 2yo maiden on debut. Cox Plate winner El Segundo (2007) broke the track record for 1200m in 2005, and much-loved Apache Cat was trained on the track.

Feature event is the Cranbourne Cup in October.

## THE TRACK

Left-handed. The course is an irregular oval in shape.

The turf track has a circumference of 1700m with a straight run home of 300m.

Out of the straight a long bend takes runners to the 1000m. It is a straight run to the tight home bend at the 600m, with the ground rising gradually from the 600m to the winning post.

Races from 1200m to 1600m start from a chute that joins the round course at the top of the back straight, allowing long straight runs to the first bend from all starting positions.

The Cranbourne Cup start at the 2025m is on the course proper at the top of the home straight.

# BALLARAT

Kennedys Drive, Miners Rest, Victoria, Australia.
www.countryracing.com.au/ballarat-turf-club

### FEATURE RACE

| Ballarat Cup | L | 2200M | TURF | 3YO+ | HCP | NOV |
|---|---|---|---|---|---|---|

Historic Ballarat is situated on the lower western plains of the Great Dividing Range, 105km west-north-west of Melbourne.

The discovery of gold at nearby Poverty Point in 1851 transformed a sheep station into a major regional centre. It is now Victoria's third–most populated city.

In 1854, Ballarat was the scene of the Battle of Eureka Stockade, the only armed rebellion in Australia's history.

The Ballarat Turf Club was formed in the same year, and in 1972 racing settled at the current venue at Dowling Forest, 15km north of the city centre.

Ballarat has long been a major training facility and has recently been upgraded to add an uphill, straight 1400m synthetic training track. This track has automatic electronic timing and all sectional times for the gallops are digitally displayed on a screen in the trainer's tower.

The highlight is the Ballarat Cup. Held in November, it is the final feature race of the Melbourne Spring Racing Carnival.

## THE TRACK

Ballarat has two turf tracks. The New Track was added to reduce wear during the wet winter months. Often no distinction is made in the press to specify whether racing is being conducted on the inner or outer course, so obviously it is sensible to check before making an investment.

### OLD TRACK

Left-handed. The course has a circumference of 1900m. The home straight is 450m in length.

Out of the straight the bend takes runners to the 1500m mark. It is an uphill climb along the back of the track until the turn at the 900m. The home straight dips towards the 300m before rising slightly to the winning post.

### NEW TRACK

Inner track utilises the home straight on the Old Track. Circumference of about 1650m.

Inside draws are absolutely crucial from the 1400m and 1500m starts on the inner.

# WERRIBEE

Bulban Road, Werribee, Victoria, Australia.
www.countryracing.com.au/werribee-racing-club

### FEATURE RACE

| Werribee Cup | L | 2630M | TURF | OPEN | HCP | DEC |
|---|---|---|---|---|---|---|

Werribee is conveniently located just off the Princes Highway, less than 30 minutes drive south-west of Melbourne.

Racing at Werribee commenced in 1874.

In recent times the Werribee course has gained much exposure as the quarantine centre and training facility for international visitors preparing for the Caulfield and Melbourne Cups. Recent Melbourne Cup winners Americain and Dunaden – both from France – completed their preparations here.

The racing highlight is the Werribee Cup. A Listed race over 2630m, the race currently is worth $150,000 in prize money. In recent years the date of the race has varied but is now run in late December, with the race day adopting a Christmas theme.

## THE TRACK

Left-handed. Small triangular-shaped track with a circumference of 1737m. The home straight is 275m.

Out of the straight a tight bend takes runners to the 1600m. It a run of about 500m to another tight bend that takes runners to the 900m mark. It is then a straight run to the 600m and the home bend on to the short home straight.

Races up to 1100m begin from a chute at the back of the course, providing only one turn into the straight.

The 1200m start provides only a very short run before the first bend. Inside draws are definitely a plus.

The 1600m start is from a chute near the turn out of the home straight.

The Werribee Cup begins just back from the 800m point on the course proper, giving only a run of 200m to the first bend.

Mikel Delzangles and Luca Cumani

## FEATURE RACE

Past winners of the Werribee Cup include Melbourne Cup winners **EVEN STEVENS (1962)** and **MAKYBE DIVA (2002)**.
**MAGISTRATE (1980)**; **SAVAGE TOSS (1990)** was a three-time Group 1 winner in Argentina; **DOUBLE TAKE (1995)**; **ROMAN ARCH (2005)** won the Toorak Hcp (2003), Australian Cup (2006); and **UNUSUAL SUSPECT (2012)** was a winner of the Hollywood Turf Cup (2010).

# SEYMOUR

Kobyboyn Road, Seymour, Victoria.
www.seymourracing.com.au

### FEATURE RACE

| | | | | | | |
|---|---|---|---|---|---|---|
| Seymour Cup | L | 1600M | TURF | OPEN | HCP | OCT |

**Seymour is situated on the Goulburn River, about 100km north of Melbourne.**

Racing in the area dates back to the 1840s with the first officially recorded meeting held in 1853. The Seymour Racing Club was formed in 1882.

Feature event is the Seymour Cup, a 1600m race with a current purse of $150,000. Run in October, it is one of the country highlights of the Melbourne Spring Racing Carnival.

## THE TRACK

Left-handed. The course is an irregular oval shape of 1800m in length. The home straight is 380m.

Out of the home straight a left bend takes runners to the 1500m point, where it is a straight run to just past the 1000m. A left turn leads to the side of the track for a straight run of 400m to the home bend at the 600m.

Races up to 1300m begin from a chute that joins the side of the track, providing a long straight run to the home turn.

The 1600m start is from a chute on the back straight. The maximum distance is 2200m, which begins at the top of the home straight.

# KILMORE

Kilmore East Road, Kilmore, Victoria, Australia.
www.countryracing.com.au/kilmore-racing-club

### FEATURE RACE

| | | | | | | |
|---|---|---|---|---|---|---|
| Kilmore Cup | L | 1600M | TURF | OPEN | HCP | FEB |

Situated 60km north of Melbourne, Kilmore is one of Victoria's oldest inland settlements, featuring many historic bluestone buildings and structures.

Racing began at the current site in 1865. It is an undulating course that boasts one of the toughest layouts anywhere in Australia, with a substantial uphill climb to the winning post.

Run over 1600m, the Kilmore Cup in February is the highlight event.

The Kilmore course also contains an inner trotting track and has long been one of Victoria's major harness racing venues.

## THE TRACK

Left-handed. The course is 1735m in length with a straight run home of 320m.

From the 1700m, runners turn out of the straight and are on a bend until the 1100m. It is a straight run to the 800m, where a sweeping bend leads back to the home straight. From the start of the turn to the winning post the ground rises 4m, providing a testing run in.

The 1200m start is from a chute that joins the back straight.

Another chute is used for the 1600m start, which provides only a very short run before it links up with the bend out of the home straight. Inside barriers are a big advantage from this starting position.

# WARRNAMBOOL

Grafton Road, Warrnambool, Victoria, Australia.
www.countryracing.com.au/warrnambool-racing-club

**The regional city of Warrnambool is situated on the south-west coast of Victoria, 263km from Melbourne.**

The Warrnambool course is located on the eastern outskirts of the town and the first meeting was staged here in 1858.

The great three-day meeting held annually during the first week of May is the last bastion of the traditional racing carnival in Victoria.

Every year racing people make the pilgrimage en masse to 'The 'bool' to eat,

sleep, breathe, talk and watch racing. The local economy receives a huge shot in the arm with the hotels and pubs throughout the town and its surrounding areas all bursting at the seams.

Jumps racing is the highlight and the meeting is well supported by city trainers. Betting is always spirited as every local owner and trainer has his or her horses set for a race over the carnival. It is often said that it takes a city-class horse to win a maiden at this meeting.

There are no graded stakes events but the races are legendary, including the Grand Annual Steeplechase, Brierly Steeple, Galleywood Hurdle, and on the flat the Warrnambool Cup and the Wangoom Handicap – affectionately dubbed 'the Newmarket of the bush'.

First run in 1872, The Grand Annual is a marvellous spectacle with 33 obstacles to negotiate over a distance of 5500m. Set in a valley, the Warrnambool course provides great natural viewing platforms all around the track and the public pack every vantage point. Runners leave the left-handed course and turn right into adjoining paddocks and across roads before rejoining the course proper for the run home.

There are many great stories associated with the Grand Annual but none surpasses that of Galleywood. Prepared by veteran local trainer Jocka Baillie, Galleywood had won the Brierly in 1983 and the popular horse lined up for the 1984 Grand Annual. Unfortunately he came to grief at the last fence and lay motionless on the track, in full view of the crowd.

When screens were erected around the horse, only the worst could be assumed. But just as the vet was about to perform his most unpleasant duty, the old boy opened his eyes, rose to his feet and re-emerged from behind the curtain to rapturous applause from the stunned crowd. That applause was echoed two years later when **GALLEYWOOD** returned to take out the Grand Annual of 1986 amid scenes of great joy. There has never been a more popular winner.

Other notable winners include **ARION (1913)**, **EL PROGRESSO (1916)**, **WASSECA (1931)**, **MONT ARGIS (1938)**, **HIGH FLASH (1948)**, dual winner **McKENNA (1958, 59)**, **BUXTON (1963)**, **GYPSY GREY (1975)**, **SO AND SO (1978)**, dual winner **THACKERAY (1979, 80)**, **VENITE (1983)**, **FOXBOY (1997)** and **SIR PENTIRE (2009)**.

Warrnamboool is also one of Victoria's strongest provincial training bases and locals take advantage of the beach to complement the course's training facilities. The icy cold waters of the bay have legendary recuperative powers for horses, and many considered crocks have had their careers totally reinvigorated after relocation to 'The 'bool'.

## THE TRACK

Left-handed. The course has a circumference of 2035m. The home straight is 350m.

# RANDWICK

Alison Road, Randwick, New South Wales, Australia. www.ajc.org.au

*L*ocated only 6km from the Sydney CBD, Randwick is the headquarters of racing in New South Wales and the premier racetrack in Australia's most populous state.

Land was designated to establish a racecourse by Governor Bourke in 1833, with the course laid out and the first meeting held that year. Originally known as the Sandy Course, racing was abandoned in 1840 due to the deterioration of the track.

The Australian Jockey Club was formed in early 1842 with its base at the old Homebush Course. The AJC moved to Randwick in 1860 and racing resumed shortly after, quickly gaining in popularity.

Within a decade many of the course's famous races had already been struck, with the inauguration of the Derby in 1861,

Sydney Cup in 1862, Epsom Hcp in 1863, Champagne Stakes in 1864, Doncaster Hcp in 1865, All Aged Stakes in 1866 and Sires' Produce Stakes in 1867. The Queen's Plate, established in 1851, was transferred from Homebush and the race became the Queen Elizabeth Stakes in 1954.

The AJC merged with the Sydney Turf Club in 2011 to form the Australian Turf Club. Shortly after, a $150m redevelopment of the Randwick course was undertaken. Developments included the rebuilding and complete refurbishment of the members' grandstand and the construction of a covered parade ring, and an international standard hotel with balconies overlooking the racecourse.

Randwick is a major training centre with over 600 horses trained on the track. It is home to some of Australia's biggest name trainers.

## FEATURE RACES

| | | | | | | |
|---|---|---|---|---|---|---|
| RANDWICK GUINEAS | G1 | 1600M | TURF | 3YO | SW | MAR |
| TJ SMITH STAKES | G1 | 1200M | TURF | 3YO+ | WFA | APR |
| AJC AUSTRALIAN DERBY | G1 | 2400M | TURF | 3YO | SW | APR |
| AJC SIRES' PRODUCE | G1 | 1400M | TURF | 2YO | SW | APR |
| THE GALAXY STAKES | G1 | 1100M | TURF | 3YO+ | HCP | APR |
| DONCASTER HCP | G1 | 1600M | TURF | 3YO+ | HCP | APR |
| SYDNEY CUP | G1 | 3200M | TURF | 3YO+ | HCP | APR |
| AJC AUSTRALIAN OAKS | G1 | 2400M | TURF | 3YOF | SW | APR |
| QUEEN ELIZABETH STAKES | G1 | 2000M | TURF | 3YO+ | WFA | APR |
| CHAMPAGNE STAKES | G1 | 1600M | TURF | 2YO | SW | APR |
| ALL AGED STAKES | G1 | 1600M | TURF | 3YO+ | WFA | APR |
| GEORGE MAIN STAKES | G1 | 1600M | TURF | 3YO+ | WFA | SEPT |
| METROPOLITAN HCP | G1 | 2400M | TURF | 3YO+ | HCP | SEPT–OCT |
| SPRING CHAMPION STAKES | G1 | 2000M | TURF | 3YO | SW | SEPT–OCT |
| FLIGHT STAKES | G1 | 1600M | TURF | 3YOF | SW | SEPT–OCT |
| EPSOM HCP | G1 | 1600M | TURF | 3YO+ | HCP | SEPT–OCT |

## THE TRACK

Right-handed. The course is rectangular with a circumference of 2223m and a home straight of 410m.

Out of the straight, runners are on a bend from the 2200m to about the 1550m. It is a straight run along the back of the course until the bend approaching the 1000m. It is then a straight run from the 900m until the home turn.

Randwick has many chute starts. An angled chute for 1000m races gives a run of 50m before joining the side of the course for a long straight run to the home turn. The 3200m start is also from this chute.

A spur for the 1200m start gives a run of

250m before it doglegs right onto the side of the course.

The 1400m start is from a diagonal chute, providing a run of 450m before a right-hand turn links up with the side of the course.

A chute from the back of the course provides the starting position for the 1600m races. It is a straight run of over 600m until the first turn.

A chute for the 2000m races jumps straight onto the bend out of the home straight. Runners are on the bend for the first 450m of the race. Inside draws are a definite advantage.

Races over 2400m start in front of the stands with a run of 200m before they leave the home straight for the long bend to the 1550m.

Apart from the 1600m start, inside draws are preferable from most barrier positions, particularly the 2000m and 2400m starts.

The home straight rises slightly approaching the 300m. While rather insignificant as an undulation, 'the rise' has become an integral part of the theatre of the course. The oft-heard caller's cry of 'and as they top the rise' is the signal that the race is on in earnest and lifts the crowd to its feet.

The inner Kensington Track is also a turf course with a circumference of 2100m and a run in of 401m.

## FEATURE RACES

### ATC AUSTRALIAN DERBY

Notable winners include Melbourne Cup victors **THE BARB (1866)**, **GRAND FLANEUR (1880)**, **POSEIDON (1906)**, **PRINCE FOOTE (1909)**, **ARTILLERYMAN (1919)**, **TRIVALVE (1927)**, **PHAR LAP (1929)**, **PETER PAN (1932)** and **HALL MARK (1933)**.

Cox Plate winners include **CARBON COPY (1948)**, **DULCIFY (1979)**, **KINGSTON TOWN (1980)**, **STRAWBERRY ROAD (1983)** and **BONECRUSHER (1986)**.

Other prominent winners include **YATTENDON (1864)**, who won the Champagne Stakes (1864), Sydney Cup (1866), All Aged Stakes (1867) and was an influential stallion; **FLORENCE (1870)** won the Victoria Derby, VRC Oaks (1870) and Queensland Derby (1871); **ROBINSON CRUSOE (1879)**;

**TRIDENT (1886)** won the ATC Sires' Produce, Victoria Derby (1886) and Australian Cup (1887).

**CETIGNE (1915)** won the ATC Sires' Produce, Victoria Derby (1915), Ranvet Stakes (1916), Newmarket (1918) and twice won the Mackinnon Stakes (1917, 19); **GLOAMING (1918)**; **HEROIC (1924)**; **MANFRED (1925)**; **NUFFIELD (1938)** won the ATC Sires' Produce, Caulfield Guineas and Victoria Derby (1938); **SKYLINE (1958)** won the Golden Slipper (1958); **SUMMER FAIR (1961)** won the Caulfield Cup (1961) as did **TRISTARC (1985)**; and **ROYAL SOVEREIGN (1964)** also won the Victoria Derby and Queensland Derby that year.

**BELMURA LAD (1977)** won the Doncaster, All Aged Stakes (1979), two Mackinnon Stakes (1980, 81) and the Metropolitan (1981); **ROSE OF KINGSTON (1982)**; **NATURALISM (1992)**; **MAHOGANY (1994)**; **OCTAGONAL (1996)**; **STARCRAFT (2004)** and **EREMEIN (2005)** also won the Rosehill Guineas (2005), Ranvet Stakes, Tancred Stakes and Queen Elizabeth Stakes (2006).

TJ Smith and Tulloch (ATC Heritage Trust)

**TULLOCH (1957)** is one of the all-time greats of the Australian turf. Regarded by his legendary trainer Tommy Smith as the best horse whom he ever prepared, the New Zealand-bred Tulloch started 13 times as a 2yo for seven wins and six seconds. He burst into prominence as a 3yo, winning 12 of 14 starts including the ATC Sires' Produce, Rosehill Guineas, broke Phar Lap's track record that had stood since 1929 in the ATC Australian Derby, the Queensland Derby, and also ran a world-record time on turf for a mile and a half against the older horses in the Caulfield Cup before taking out the Victoria Derby.

Against the wishes of his trainer, he was a controversial non-runner in the Melbourne Cup, as his owner considered the Cup too demanding a test for a 3yo, especially only three days after the Victoria Derby. It remains one of the great maybes of the Australian turf as Prince Darius, whom Tulloch defeated by 8 lengths in the Victoria Derby, was to finish a neck second to Straight Draw in that Melbourne Cup.

In the autumn Tulloch was victorious in the Ranvet Stakes, All Aged Stakes, Chipping Norton Stakes and Queen Elizabeth Stakes.

A mystery stomach ailment almost killed the champ after his 3yo season and his racing career appeared over. But after a lay-off of almost two years Tulloch returned as a 5yo and while TJ Smith considered he was not quite the horse he was, Tulloch won all 5 starts including repeat successes in the Chipping Norton and Queen Elizabeth Stakes.

In his final campaign as a 6yo Tulloch had 19 starts for ten wins, five seconds and three thirds. Along the way he claimed the Cox Plate, Mackinnon Stakes and a third Queen Elizabeth Stakes. The only unplaced run in his career was in the Melbourne Cup that year (1960), under 10st 1lb (64kg). Tulloch claimed victory in the Brisbane Cup carrying 9st 12lb (63kg) at the end of his 6yo campaign, in what was to be a fitting swansong for a great champion. In the end his record stood at 53 starts for 36–12–4.

## ATC AUSTRALIAN OAKS

Notable winners include great mare **FLIGHT (1944)**, who won 24 races including the Champagne Stakes (1943), CF Orr Stakes, St George Stakes, Queen Elizabeth Stakes, Mackinnon Stakes (1946) and two Cox Plates (1945, 46). Grand dam of Skyline and Sky High.

Those to take out the VRC Oaks – ATC Australian Oaks double include **TRUE COURSE (1951)**; Melbourne Cup winners **EVENING PEAL (1956)** and **LIGHT FINGERS (1965)**; **CHICOLA (1959)**; **INDIAN SUMMER (1962)**; Cox Plate winner **SURROUND (1977)**; **RESEARCH (1989)**, who is also the only filly ever to take out the ATC Australian Derby–ATC Australian Oaks double; **GRAND ARCHWAY (1999)** and **SERENADE ROSE (2006)**.

Other notable winners include **WENONA GIRL (1961)**; **ANALIE (1973)** won the Queensland Oaks, Queensland Derby, Doncaster Hcp and Metropolitan Hcp (1973); **LEILANI (1974)**; **HOW NOW (1976)**; **BOUNDING AWAY (1987)**; **TRISCAY (1991)**; **CIRCLES OF GOLD (1995)**, dam of Elvstroem and Haradasun; and **SUNDAY JOY (2003)**, dam of More Joyous.

## SYDNEY CUP

First run 1862. Dual winners include **THE BARB (1868, 69)**, **CARBINE (1889, 90)**, 1939 Cox Plate winner **MOSAIC (1939, 40)**, **VEILED THREAT (1942, 44)** and **TIE THE KNOT (1988, 89)**.

Other notables include **YATTENDON (1866)**; **WALLACE (1896)**; **LORD CARDIGAN (1904)** followed up his win in the Melbourne Cup (1903), as did **STRAIGHT DRAW (1958)**; **EURYTHMIC (1921)**; **ROGILLA (1933)** won the Caulfield Cup (1932) and Cox Plate (1933); **CARBON COPY (1949)**; **SAILOR'S GUIDE (1956)**; **GALILEE (1967)**; 1968 ATC Australian Oaks winner **LOWLAND (1969)**; **APOLLO ELEVEN (1973)**; **BATTLE HEIGHTS (1974)**.

Sentimental favourite **RECKLESS (1977)** was trained by Phar Lap's former strapper and constant companion, Tommy Woodcock, by this time in his 70s. In one of the great fairytales of the turf, Woodcock transformed the 33-start maiden into a winner of the Adelaide Cup, Brisbane Cup and Sydney Cup in 1977. In his tilt at the Melbourne Cup that year, he was attempting to become the first horse to win the four major Cup races in Australia in the same year. He was denied only by Bart Cummings' Gold And Black. The reception of the crowd as the place-getters returned to scale was one of the greatest in memory for a beaten horse.

**KINGSTON TOWN (1980)** demolished his rivals by 7 lengths as a 3yo; mighty mare **MAKYBE DIVA (2004)**.

## ATC SIRES' PRODUCE

The ATC Sires' Produce makes up the second leg of Sydney's coveted 2yo Triple Crown, with the Golden Slipper and Champagne Stakes the other races.

Those to have won the Triple Crown include **BAGUETTE (1970)**, **LUSKIN STAR (1977)**, **TIERCE (1991)**, filly **BURST (1992)**, **DANCE HERO (2004)** and **PIERRO (2012)**.

Winners of the Golden Slipper–Sires' Produce double include dual Doncaster Hcp winner **FINE AND DANDY (1959)**, **ESKIMO PRINCE (1964)**, **TONTONAN (1973)**, **TOY SHOW (1975)**, **FULL ON ACES (1981)**, **MERLENE (1996)** and **SEBRING (2008)**.

Winners to take out the Melbourne Cup include **GLENCOE (1867)**, **CHESTER (1877)**, **PRINCE FOOTE (1909)** and **HALL MARK (1933)**.

Other prominent winners include **KINGSBOROUGH (1874)**, who won the Champagne Stakes, ATC Australian Derby (1874), Mackinnon Stakes (1875); **ROBINSON CRUSOE (1876)**; **URALLA (1885)** won the Champagne Stakes, Ascot Vale Stakes, ATC Australian Oaks and VRC Oaks (1885); **TRIDENT (1886)**; **CETIGNE (1915)**; **FURIOUS (1921)** won the Champagne Stakes, Rosehill Guineas and the Victoria Derby–VRC Oaks double (1921); **YOUNG IDEA (1935)**; **AJAX (1947)**; **NUFFIELD (1938)**.

**SHANNON (1944)** won the Epsom Hcp (1945), twice won the George Main Stakes (1946, 47) and campaigned in the USA in 1948 winning five stakes races including the Hollywood Gold Cup. He was named American Champion Older Male Horse in 1948.

**TULLOCH (1957)**; **TIME AND TIDE (1963)**; **BLACK ONYX (1968)** won the Lightning Stakes, Newmarket Hcp (1970) and was a dual winner of the Doomben 10,000 (1969, 70); **DESIRABLE (1976)** won the Lightning Stakes (1976), Newmarket Hcp (1977); **DIAMOND SHOWER (1986)** won the VRC Oaks (1976); **ST COVET (1994)**; **OCTAGONAL (1995)**; **ENCOUNTER (1997)**; and

**VISCOUNT (2001)** won the Champagne Stakes and George Main Stakes (2001).

## CHAMPAGNE STAKES

The third leg of the 2yo Triple Crown was first run in 1864. Notable winners include **YATTENDON (1864)**; **FLORENCE (1870)**; **KINGSBOROUGH (1874)**; **ROBINSON CRUSOE (1876)**; **CHESTER (1877)**; **HIS LORDSHIP (1878)**, who won the Ascot Vale Stakes, ATC Sires' Produce and ATC Australian Derby (1878); **NAVIGATOR (1882)** was a winner of the Ascot Vale Stakes, Victoria Derby, ATC Australian Derby (1882), Australian Cup (1883); **URALLA (1885)**; **AUTONOMY (1892)** won the ATC Sires' Produce, Caulfield Guineas, Mackinnon Stakes (1892); **CARNAGE (1893)** won the Victoria Derby that year; **FURIOUS (1921)**; **HEROIC (1924)**; **MANFRED (1925)**.

**MOLLISON (1928)** won the Ascot Vale Stakes, ATC Sires' Produce, Rosehill Guineas (1928), All Aged Stakes, Futurity Stakes and defeated Phar Lap in the G2 Chelmsford Stakes (1929); **HALL MARK (1933)**; **YOUNG IDEA (1935)**; **AJAX (1937)**; **HIGH CASTE (1939)**; **FLIGHT (1943)**; **TRUE COURSE (1950)**; **TODMAN (1957)**; **WIGGLE (1958)**; **NOHOLME (1959)**; **SKY HIGH (1960)**; **TIME AND TIDE (1963)**; **EYE LINER (1965)** won the Doomben Cup (1967); **STORM QUEEN (1966)**; **VAIN (1969)**; **ROSE OF KINGSTON (1981)**; **RED ANCHOR (1984)**; **BOUNDING AWAY (1986)**; **TRISCAY (1990)**; **MARCH HARE (1993)** won the George Main Stakes (1994) and George Ryder Stakes (1995); **INTERGAZE (1996)**; and **SAMANTHA MISS (2008)** won the Flight Stakes and VRC Oaks (2008).

## DONCASTER HANDICAP

Randwick hosts Australia's two biggest 1600m handicap races – the Doncaster Handicap in autumn and the Epsom handicap in spring.

Dual winners of the Doncaster Hcp include **MILDURA (1940, 41)**, **BLUE LEGEND (1946, 47)**, **SLOGAN (1956, 57)**, **TUDOR HILL (1959, 60)**, **FINE AND DANDY (1961, 63)**, **PHARAOH (1994, 95)** and **SUNLINE (1999, 2002)**.

Versatile champion **SUPER IMPOSE (1990, 91)** lays claim as Australia's greatest handicap miler, scoring unprecedented back-to-back wins in both the Doncaster Hcp and Epsom Hcp in 1990 and 1991. Super Impose won 20 races including the Turnbull Stakes (1989), Ranvet Stakes (1991), two Chipping Norton stakes (1991, 92), the Cox Plate (1992) and also ran second in the 1989 Melbourne Cup.

Other notable winners include **BRISEIS (1876)**; **WAKEFUL (1901)**; **SIR FOOTE (1902)** won the Newmarket Hcp, Futurity Stakes (1902); **WHITTIER (1924)**; **CHATHAM (1934)**; **HALL MARK (1933)**;

**CUDDLE (1936)**; **GREY BOOTS (1950)**; **TIME AND TIDE (1965)**; **CITIUS (1966)**; **TOBIN BRONZE (1967)**.

Legendary **GUNSYND (1972)** put the tiny country town of Goondiwindi on the map. The 'Goondiwindi Grey' won 29 of 54 starts, including 20 stakes races. Winner of the Epsom Hcp, Toorak Hcp, Cantala Stakes (1971), Futurity Stakes, Caulfield Stakes, Cox Plate (1972) and two Ranvet Stakes (1971, 73); **ANALIE (1973)**; **TONTONAN (1974)**; **DALRELLO (1975)** won the George Ryder Stakes (1975) and two All Aged Stakes (1976, 77); **MAYBE MAHAL (1978)**; **BELMURA LAD (1979)**; **LAWMAN (1981)**.

Top mare **EMANCIPATION (1983)** won 19 races, 16 at stakes level – including the All Aged Stakes, George Main Stakes, Coolmore Classic (1984) and successive George Ryder Stakes (1983, 84); **GRAND ARMEE (2003)** won seven Group 1 races including the George Main Stakes, Mackinnon Stakes (2004), Chipping Norton Stakes, Ranvet Stakes (2005) and consecutive ATC Queen Elizabeth Stakes (2004, 05); **HARADASUN (2007)** won the George Ryder Stakes (2007) and the Queen Anne Stakes at Ascot (2008); and **MORE JOYOUS (2012)**.

## EPSOM HANDICAP

Dual winners include **MASQUERADE (1881, 82)**, **MELODRAMA (1906, 07)**, **AMOUNIS (1926, 28)**, **CHATHAM (1932, 33)**, **TOI PORT (1963, 64)**, **SUPER IMPOSE (1990, 91)** and **DESERT WAR (2003, 04)**.

Other notable winners include **WOORAK (1915)**, who won the Ascot Vale Stakes, Champagne Stakes (1914), All Aged Stakes (1916), Oakleigh Plate (1917); **WOLAROI (1919)** won the Champagne Stakes, Rosehill Guineas, Victoria Derby (1916), two Linlithgow Stakes (1916, 18) and the Ranvet Stakes (1919); **NIGHTMARCH (1929)**; **SHANNON (1945)**; **NOHOLME (1959)**; **SKY HIGH (1961)**; **GUNSYND (1971)**; **IMPOSING (1979)**, sire of Super Impose; and **SHOGUN LODGE (2000)**.

## ALL AGED STAKES

First run in 1866. **AJAX (1938–40)** is the only horse to win the race three times.

Dual winners include **TIM WHIFFLER (1870, 71)**, **CARBINE (1889, 90)**; **GLADSOME (1904, 05)**, **MALT KING (1911, 12)**, **YARALLA (1942, 43)**, **DALRELLO (1976, 77)**, **ROUGH HABIT (1992, 93)** and **SUNLINE (2000, 02)**.

Other notables include **YATTENDON (1867)**, **GLENCOE (1869)**, **BRISEIS (1876)**, **WAKEFUL (1902)**, **WOORAK (1916)**, **DESERT GOLD (1918)**, **THE HAWK (1925)**, **MOLLISON (1929)**, **AMOUNIS (1930)**, **WINOOKA (1933)** won the Doncaster Hcp and Futurity Stakes (1933),

**CHATHAM (1934)**, **PETER PAN (1935)**, **CUDDLE (1936)**, **BERNBOROUGH (1946)**, **TULLOCH (1958)**, **LORD (1959)**, **NOHOLME (1960)**, **SKY HIGH (1961)**, **WENONA GIRL (1964) TOBIN BRONZE (1967)**.

**TRITON (1972)** won the Epsom Hcp, George Ryder Stakes, Stradbroke Hcp (1972), Doomben Cup (1973); **ALL SHOT (1973)**; **TONTONAN (1974)**; **BELMURA LAD (1979)**; **WATNEY (1981)** won the Toorak Hcp (1980), Stradbroke Hcp (1981); **EMANCIPATION (1984)**; **VITE CHEVAL (1985)**; **CAMPAIGN KING (1987)**; **SHAFTESBURY AVENUE (1991)**; **HURRICANE SKY (1995)** won the Blue Diamond Stakes (1994); **FLYING SPUR (1996)**; **INTERGAZE (1999)**; **HOT DANISH (2010)**; **HAY LIST (2011)**; and **ATLANTIC JEWEL (2012)**.

## FLIGHT STAKES

First run in 1947 the race is named after legendary mare Flight, who had 65 starts for 24–19–9 including wins in the Champagne Stakes, (1943), ATC Oaks (1944), CF Orr Stakes, St George Stakes, ATC Queen Elizabeth Stakes, Mackinnon Stakes (1946) and twice won the Cox Plate (1945, 46).

Notable winners include **WENONA GIRL (1960)**; **CAP D'ANTIBES (1974)**; **BOUNDING AWAY (1986)**; **RESEARCH (1988)**; **TRISCAY (1990)**; **SLIGHT CHANCE (1992)**, who won the VRC Oaks, TJ Smith Classic (1992), Queensland Oaks and Storm Queen Stakes (1993); **SUNLINE (1998)**; Golden Slipper winner **HA HA (2001)**; and **SAMANTHA MISS (2008)**.

**MORE JOYOUS (2009)** won 21 races including the George Main Stakes, Toorak Hcp (2010), Futurity Stakes (2011), Doncaster Hcp, ATC Queen Elizabeth Stakes (2012) and twice won the Queen of the Turf Stakes (2011, 12).

## GEORGE MAIN STAKES

First run 1945 and named after a former chairman of the AJC.

Dual winners include **SHANNON (1946, 47)**, **COUNT RADIANT (1964, 65)**, **REGAL RHYTHM (1967, 68)** and **KINGSTON TOWN (1981, 82)**.

Prominent winners include **SAN DOMENICO (1950)**, **WENONA GIRL (1963)**, **BAGUETTE (1971)**, **ALL SHOT (1973)**, **IMPOSING (1979)**, **EMANCIPATION (1983)**, Golden Slipper winner **INSPIRED (1984)**, **CAMPAIGN KING (1987)**, **VO ROGUE (1989)**, **SHAFTESBURY AVENUE (1990) MARCH HARE (1993)**.

**DURBRIDGE (1994)** won 17 stakes races including the ATC Australian Derby (1991), CF Orr Stakes (1993), Australian Cup, Doomben Cup and ATC Queen Elizabeth Stakes (1994); **JUGGLER (1996)**;

ENCOUNTER (1997); SHOGUN LODGE (1999); LONHRO (2003); GRAND ARMEE (2004); and MORE JOYOUS (2010).

Theatre of the Horse

## THE GALAXY STAKES

First run in 1972 this is one of Sydney's premier sprint races. GREY RECEIVER (1981, 82) won it twice.

Other notable winners include BLETCHINGLY (1975) who sired 61 individual stakes winners including Kingston Town; LUSKIN STAR (1978); SNIPPETS (1988); MR TIZ (1991); SCHILLACI (1993) and dual Manikato Stakes winner SPARK OF LIFE (2004).

## QUEEN ELIZABETH STAKES

First run in 1851, the Queen Elizabeth Stakes has an honour roll to rival any race in Australia.

Those to win three times include TIM WHIF-FLER (1868, 70, 71), CARBINE (1889–91), TRAFALGAR (1909–11), DAVID (1921–23) and TULLOCH (1958, 60, 61).

Dual winners include COSSACK (1851, 52), SPORTSMAN (1853, 54), TARRAGON (1863, 64), DAGWORTH (1873, 74), CHESTER (1878, 79), LA CARABINE (1900, 01), WINDBAG (1925, 26), LIMERICK (1927, 28), RUSSIA (1947, 48), INTERGAZE (1997, 99) and GRAND ARMEE (2004, 05).

Other great names include ARCHER (1862), THE BARB (1969), ROBINSON CRUSOE (1877), TRIDENT (1887), NEWHAVEN (1897), LORD CARDIGAN (1904), POSEIDON (1908), PRINCE FOOTE (1910), POITREL (1919), PHAR LAP (1930), PETER PAN (1933), ROGILLA (1934), BEAU VITE (1941), FLIGHT (1946), CARBON COPY (1949), LOWLAND (1969), TAILS (1972), APOLLO ELEVEN (1973), BATTLE HEIGHTS (1974), MING DYNASTY (1978), SYDESTON (1990), STYLISH CENTURY (1991), ROUGH HABIT (1992), VEANDERCROSS (1993), DURBRIDGE (1994), JEUNE (1995), DORIEMUS (1996), MIGHT AND POWER (1998), SHOGUN LODGE (2001), LONHRO (2003), EREMEIN (2006), DESERT WAR (2007) and MORE JOYOUS (2012).

## METROPOLITAN HANDICAP

First run 1867, those to win the Metropolitan Hcp and Melbourne Cup in the same year include TIM WHIF-FLER (1867), DELTA (1951), DALRAY (1952), STRAIGHT DRAW (1957) and MACDOUGAL (1959).

Dual winners include MURRAY STREAM (1945, 47), TAILS (1969, 70) and 1983 Caulfield Cup winner HAYAI (1983, 84).

Other prominent winners include BEAU VITE (1940); CARIOCA (1953) won the Sydney Cup (1953), George Ryder Stakes (1954) and two Chipping Norton Stakes (1953, 55); REDCRAZE (1956); ANALIE (1973); BATTLE HEIGHTS (1976); MING DYNASTY (1978); BELMURA LAD (1981); and more recently Caulfield Cup winners RAILINGS (2005) and TAWQEET (2006) followed up their wins in this race.

## SPRING CHAMPION STAKES

First run 1971, notable winners include GAY ICARUS (1971), whose 1971 campaign also netted the Underwood Stakes, ATC Queen Elizabeth Stakes, Chipping Norton Stakes, Caulfield Stakes, Australian Cup and Caulfield Cup; TARAS BULBA (1975); KINGSTON TOWN (1979); Golden Slipper winner SIR DAPPER (1983); BEAU ZAM (1987) went on to win the ATC Australian Derby, Tancred Stakes (1988) and two George Ryder Stakes (1988, 89); STYLISH CENTURY (1989); DANEWIN (1994).

TIE THE KNOT (1997) won 13 Group 1 races. His victories included the Rosehill Guineas, Underwood Stakes (1998), successive wins in the Sydney Cup (1988, 89), Tancred Stakes (1999, 2000) and Ranvet Stakes (2000, 01), and four consecutive wins in the Chipping Norton Stakes (1999–2002).

SAVABEEL (2004) also took out the 2004 Cox Plate.

It's a Dundeel

## RANDWICK GUINEAS

A new race established in 2006 to replace the discontinued Canterbury Guineas.

It has been won by WEEKEND HUSSLER (2008); METAL BENDER (2009) won the Rosehill Guineas (2009), Doomben Cup (2010) and George Ryder Stakes (2012); 2011 VRC Oaks winner MOSHEEN (2012); and IT'S A DUNDEEL (2013).

## TJ SMITH STAKES

Tommy Smith was born in 1916, the son of a drover and horse breaker. From the age of seven young Tommy worked alongside his father. With his knowledge and experience with horses from a young age, Smith had visions of becoming a jockey.

Weight and injury forced him to abandon his ambitions, but Smith took out a trainer's licence in 1941 and rented two stable boxes at Kensington – one to live in, the other for a horse called Bragger. In one of the Australian turf's great rags-to-riches stories, Bragger won 13 races and quickly established Smith's reputation as a trainer.

He would go on to be champion trainer in Sydney for the first time in 1952–53, and would not relinquish the title until 1984–85. He won again in 1987–88 at the age of 72, to compile a staggering 34 Sydney metropolitan championships – 33 of those in succession.

In all he trained a record 279 Group 1 winners, netting two Melbourne Cups, four Caulfield Cups, seven Cox Plates, six Golden Slippers and 35 Derby winners across Australia. He trained two of the all-time greats in Australian turf history – Tulloch and Kingston Town.

Before his passing in 1998, he handed over the reins of his establishment, Tulloch Lodge, to his daughter, Gai Waterhouse, now a multiple champion trainer in her own right.

The race named in his honour, on the track where he trained, was upgraded to Group 1 status in 2005.

Since then notable winners include APACHE CAT (2008), TAKEOVER TARGET (2009) and BLACK CAVIAR (2011, 13).

# ROSEHILL GARDENS

James Ruse Drive, Rosehill, New South Wales, Australia. www.ajc.org.au

Governor Arthur Phillip established Rose Hill, on the banks of the Parramatta River west of Sydney, as Australia's first inland settlement in 1788. It was renamed Parramatta in 1791.

Lieutenant John Macarthur, posted to the NSW Corps in Sydney in 1790, was granted land in Parramatta in 1794. Here he established Elizabeth Farm, which he and his wife used to pioneer the wool industry. Wool soon became the backbone of the Australian economy, but Macarthur found himself in constant dispute with Governor William Bligh. It was the trial of Macarthur in 1808 that triggered the Rum Rebellion, which overthrew Bligh.

After a period of exile in England, Macarthur returned to Australia in 1817 having received a much larger grant of land, which he operated until his death in 1834. In 1883, 850 acres (344ha) of this land was subdivided as an industrial zone with a portion of the estate set aside for a racecourse. The first meeting was conducted on the course in 1885. The Sydney Turf Club was founded in 1943.

The majority of New South Wales' feature races are split between Rosehill and Randwick, and held during spring and autumn. Rosehill is the home of the Golden Slipper Stakes – the richest 2yo race in the world and the highlight event on the Sydney racing calendar.

Facilities here are excellent with a fully covered betting ring and three-tiered grandstands providing spectacular views overlooking the track and the city skyline. The merger of the AJC and STC in 2011 has seen $24 million directed to Rosehill to further upgrade facilities.

## THE TRACK

Right-handed. A square track with a circumference of 2048m.

The home straight is 408m.

Out of the straight a right-hand bend takes runners to the 1900m for a straight run of 400m to the 1500m point, where the track bends sharply right again. Along the top of the course it is a straight run from the 1400m until passing the 1200m, then another turn takes runners to the 800m and another run of 200m to the home bend.

The Golden Slipper start at 1200m is from a diagonal chute inside the track, which gives a straight run of 400m before a bend at the 800m takes runners onto the course proper. It is then a very short run before the home turn. The 1100m start is also from this chute.

1500m races start from a chute from the back straight, giving a run of 450m to the first bend.

The 2000m chute provides a run of 500m to the first bend.

Races over 2400m start in the home straight with a run of 400m until the turn.

While the track generally races quite fairly, inside draws are preferable from all starting positions, particularly over the sprint distances.

## FEATURE RACES

### GOLDEN SLIPPER STAKES

First run in 1957, the Golden Slipper is the world's richest 2yo race and one of Australia's premier sire-making races, with many winners having a substantial influence in the breeding barn including **TODMAN (1957)**, **VAIN (1969)**, **BAGUETTE (1970)**, **LUSKIN STAR (1977)**, **RORY'S JESTER (1985)**,

| FEATURE RACES | | | | | | |
|---|---|---|---|---|---|---|
| GOLDEN SLIPPER STAKES | G1 | 1200M | TURF | 2YO | SW | APR |
| COOLMORE CLASSIC | G1 | 1500M | TURF | 3YO+F&M | HCP | MAR |
| RANVET STAKES | G1 | 2000M | TURF | 3YO+ | WFA | MAR |
| ROSEHILL GUINEAS | G1 | 2000M | TURF | 3YO | SW | MAR–APR |
| TANCRED STAKES | G1 | 2400M | TURF | 3YO+ | WFA | APR |
| GEORGE RYDER STAKES | G1 | 1500M | TURF | 3YO+ | WFA | APR |
| QUEEN OF THE TURF STAKES | G1 | 1500M | TURF | 3YO+F&M | SW | APR |
| STORM QUEEN STAKES | G1 | 2000M | TURF | 3YOF | SW | APR |
| GOLDEN ROSE STAKES | G1 | 1400M | TURF | 3YO | SW | SEPT |

MARAUDING (1987), CANNY LAD (1990), DANZERO (1994), FLYING SPUR (1995), CATBIRD (1999) and SEBRING (2008).

Winners of the Blue Diamond–Golden Slipper double include JOHN'S HOPE (1972), MANI-KATO (1978), COURTZA (1989) and SEPOY (2011).

Other notable winners include SKYLINE (1958); FINE AND DANDY (1959); SKY HIGH (1960); STORM QUEEN (1966); TONTONAN (1973); TOY SHOW (1975); BOUNDING AWAY (1986); TIERCE (1991); BURST (1992); BELLE DU JOUR (2000) put up a remarkable performance to win after missing the start; DANCE HERO (2004); MISS FINLAND (2006) won the Thousand Guineas, VRC Oaks (2006), Australian Guineas and Storm Queen Stakes (2007); and PIERRO (2012).

## COOLMORE CLASSIC

First run in 1973, the race was upgraded to Group 1 status in 1984.

Since then notables include EMANCIPATION (1984); BOUNDING AWAY (1987); SKATING (1993) won the Doncaster Hcp (1993); FLITTER (1995) won the Doomben 10,000 (1994); SUNLINE (2000, 02) scored twice; TUESDAY JOY (2007) won the Ranvet Stakes, Tancred Stakes (2008), Chipping Norton Stakes (2009); and TYPHOON TRACY (2009).

## RANVET STAKES

First run in 1903, the race was formerly known as the Rawson Stakes. There have been many dual winners including MALT KING (1911, 12), LIMERICK (1927, 28), LOUGH NEAGH (1936, 37), COLUMNIST (1947, 48), WENONA GIRL (1961, 64), SKY HIGH (1962, 63), REGAL RHYTHM (1968, 72), GUNSYND (1971, 73), MARCEAU (1978, 79), BEAU ZAM (1988, 89), TIE THE KNOT (2000, 01) and THESEO (2009, 10).

Those to also win the Melbourne Cup include POSEIDON (1908), WESTCOURT (1918), POITREL (1921), NIGHTMARCH (1930), PETER PAN (1935) and HYPERNO (1981).

Other prominent winners include CETIGNE (1916), WOLAROI (1919), FURIOUS (1923), WHITTIER (1924), THE HAWK (1925), ROGILLA (1934), BEAU VITE (1941), VEILED THREAT (1945), BERNBOROUGH (1946), REDCRAZE (1957), TULLOCH (1958), TIME AND TIDE (1965), BALMERINO (1976), BETTER LOOSEN UP (1990), SUPER IMPOSE (1991), VEANDERCROSS (1993), GRAND ARMEE (2005), EREMEIN (2006), DESERT WAR (2007), TUESDAY JOY (2008) and MANIGHAR (2012), won the Tancred Stakes and Australian Cup (2012).

Lonhro

Piero

## GEORGE RYDER STAKES

First run in 1973, dual winners include **MANI-KATO (1979, 80)**, **EMANCIPATION (1983, 84)**, **CAMPAIGN KING (1987, 88)** and **LONHRO (2003, 04)**.

Other notables include **ALL SHOT (1973)**; **DALRELLO (1975)**; **BUREAUCRACY (1991)**, dam sire of Silent Witness; **HARADASUN (2007)**; **WEEKEND HUSSLER (2008)**; **DANLEIGH (2010)** won the All Aged Stakes, Manikato Stakes (2009), Chipping Norton Stakes (2010); and **PIERRO (2013)**.

## ROSEHILL GUINEAS

First run in 1910, notables include **CARLITA (1914)**, who took out the Victoria Derby–VRC Oaks double (1914); **WOLAROI (1916)**; **FURIOUS (1921)**; **AMOUNIS (1925)**; **MOLLISON (1928)**; **PHAR LAP (1929)** recorded his second win at start 11; **AJAX (1937)**; **HIGH CASTE (1939)**; **HYDROGEN (1951)**; **TULLOCH (1957)**; **WENONA GIRL (1960)**; **ESKIMO PRINCE (1964)** won the Golden Slipper and ATC Sires' Produce Stakes (1964); **TARAS BULBA (1974)**; **DULCIFY (1979)**; **KINGSTON TOWN (1980)**; and **STRAWBERRY ROAD (1983)**.

**RIVERINA CHARM (1989)** won the Thousand Guineas, VRC Oaks (1988), Canterbury Guineas (1989), New Zealand Stakes (1990); **SURFERS**

**PARADISE (1991)**; **NATURALISM (1992)**; **DANEWIN (1995)**; **OCTAGONAL (1996)**; **TIE THE KNOT (1998)**; **SKY HEIGHTS (1999)**; **DIATRIBE (2000)** won the Caulfield Cup that year, ending a string of near misses in that race for astute veteran trainer George Hanlon; **HELENUS (2003)** won the Caulfield Guineas, Victoria Derby (2002); **EREMEIN (2005)**; and **JIMMY CHOUX (2011)**.

## TANCRED STAKES

First run as the HE Tancred Cup in 1963, then the Tancred Stakes, it is currently sponsored by BMW.

First won by **MAIDENHEAD (1963)**, who won the Sydney Cup (1963); **TAILS (1972)**; **APOLLO ELEVEN (1973)**; **HYPERNO (1978)**; **KINGSTON TOWN (1980)**; **BLUE DENIM (1981)**; **HAYAI (1984)**; **BONECRUSHER (1986)**; **BEAU ZAM (1988)**; **OUR POETIC PRINCE (1989)**; **SYDESTON (1990)**; **DR GRACE (1991)** won the ATC Australian Derby, Chipping Norton Stakes (1990) and Underwood Stakes (1991); **MIGHT AND POWER (1998)**; **ETHEREAL (2002)** following her Caulfield–Melbourne Cup double (2001); **FREE-MASON (2003)** made all to upset Northerly and also won the TJ Smith Classic (1999), Queensland Derby (2000); **MAKYBE DIVA (2005)**; **EREMEIN (2006)**; **TUESDAY JOY (2008)**; and **MANIGHAR (2012)**.

Dual winners include **OCTAGONAL (1996, 97)** and **TIE THE KNOT (1999, 2000)**.

## QUEEN OF THE TURF STAKES

First run in 1972, the race was elevated to Group 1 level in 2005. Since then winners include **DIVINE MADONNA (2007)**, **FORENSICS (2008)** won the Golden Slipper (2007), **TYPHOON TRACY (2010)**, and **MORE JOYOUS (2011, 12)** went back to back.

## STORM QUEEN STAKES

Storm Queen was a winner of ten stakes races including the Golden Slipper, Champagne Stakes, Caulfield Guineas, Cantala Stakes (1966) and Lightning Stakes (1967).

First run in 1979, it has been a Group 1 race since 1992. Notables since include VRC Oaks winners **SLIGHT CHANCE (1993)**, **NORTHWOOD PLUME (1995)**, **SALEOUS (1996)**, **SPECIAL HARMONY (2004)**, **HOLLOW BULLET (2005)**, **SERENADE ROSE (2006)** also won the ATC Australian Oaks, **MISS FINLAND (2007)**, **FAINT PERFUME (2010)** and **MOSHEEN (2012)**.

**ALCOVE (1994)** and **DANENDRI (1997)** won the ATC Australian Oaks; **SAVANNAH SUCCESS (1999)** won the New Zealand Oaks (1999).

## GOLDEN ROSE STAKES

Inaugurated in 2004, the race was quickly raised to Group 1 status in 2009. Its million-dollar purse has already made it one of the highlight races of the Sydney spring carnival and one of Australia's premier 3yo races.

# WARWICK FARM

Hume Highway, Warwick Farm, New South Wales, Australia. www.ajc.org.au

Tie the Knot

*Warwick Farm is located in the City of Liverpool, 30km south-west of Sydney, on the shore of the Georges River.*

Prominent owner, breeder and trainer William 'Black Bill' Forrester purchased the Warwick Park estate in 1882 and constructed a racetrack, stables and a stud farm on the property. He renamed the property Warwick Farm to match his initials. From there he trained the Melbourne Cup quinella in 1897 with Gaulus and The Grafter, and then won the race again with The Grafter in 1898.

The following year Forrester teamed up with Edwin Oatley to establish the Warwick Farm Racing Club and the first race meeting at the course was conducted.

The Australian Jockey Club purchased the track in 1922 and made many improvements to facilities. Racing resumed in 1925.

Warwick Farm motorway was opened on the site in 1960 and gained much fame with Jack Brabham, Jim Clark, Jackie Stewart and Peter Brock among the legendary names of motorsport who tasted success on the track before it closed in 1973.

While a metropolitan course, Warwick Farm is known for its relaxed, family-friendly picnic atmosphere. The feature is the Chipping Norton Stakes, which is run in March.

Warwick Farm is also a major training centre with many of Sydney's top trainers based there, including Peter Snowden who is the trainer for Darley's massive Australian operation.

## THE TRACK

Right-handed. A triangular course of 1937m in length. The home straight is 326m.

Out of the straight runners are on a bend until about the 1500m. It is a straight run of 300m until a sharp right-hand bend, then another straight run of about 600m to the tight home turn.

Races from 1000m to 1400m begin from a chute joining the side of the course, providing a long run to the home turn.

The 1600m chute joins the back straight with a run of 400m to the first bend.

The 2400m start is from a chute at the top of the home straight.

The tight turns can disadvantage horses attempting to make a wide run from the back of the field.

## FEATURE RACE

### CHIPPING NORTON STAKES

William Long, who originally sold the estate to William Forrester, developed training tracks and famous racing stables across the river at Chipping Norton.

First run in 1925, the race has a rich history and has been won by many of the greats of the Australian turf.

There have been many multiple winners including **TIE THE KNOT**, who won the race four times in succession **(1999–2002)**; **LOUGH NEAGH** scored three wins **(1933, 36, 37)** and **KATANGA (1944, 45)**, **CARBON COPY (1949, 50)**, **TULLOCH (1958, 60)**, **APOLLO ELEVEN (1973, 75)**, **SUPER IMPOSE (1991, 92)** and **SHOOT OUT (2012, 13)** all won it twice.

Other notable winners include **WINDBAG (1926)**, **AMOUNIS (1927)**, **LIMERICK (1928)**, **PHAR LAP (1930)**, **TRANQUIL STAR (1941)**, **VEILED THREAT (1943)**, **BERNBOROUGH (1946)**, **COMIC COURT (1951)**, **DELTA (1952)**, **CARIOCA (1953)**, **SKY HIGH (1962)**, **MAIDENHEAD (1964)**, **RAIN LOVER (1969)**, **GAY ICARUS (1971)**, **IGLOO (1974)**, **EMANCIPATION (1984)**, **RISING PRINCE (1985)** won the Cox Plate (1985), **OUR WAVERLEY STAR (1987)**, **DR GRACE (1990)** and **PHARAOH (1995)**.

Champion **OCTAGONAL (1997)** was trained on the track by John Hawkes. He won 14 of 28 starts including ten wins at Group 1 level. Winner of the ATC Sires' Produce, Cox Plate (1995), Canterbury Guineas, Rosehill Guineas, ATC Australian Derby, Underwood Stakes (1996), Australian Cup (1997) and two Tancred Stakes (1996, 97).

Octagonal's finest son **LONHRO (2003)** was also trained here by Hawkes. He was a winner of 11 Group 1s including the Caulfield Guineas (2001), Mackinnon Stakes (2002), George Main Stakes, ATC Queen Elizabeth Stakes (2003), CF Orr Stakes, Australian Cup (2004), two Caulfield Stakes (2002, 03) and two George Ryder Stakes (2003, 04);

**ENCOUNTER (1998)**, **STARCRAFT (2004)**, **GRAND ARMEE (2005)**, **DESERT WAR (2006)**, **TUESDAY JOY (2009)**, and **THESEO (2010)**.

# CANTERBURY

King Street, Canterbury, New South Wales, Australia.
www.ajc.org.au

The Sydney suburb of Canterbury, 11km south-west of the CBD, is the site of the fourth of Sydney's metropolitan tracks, Canterbury Park.

Rescheduling of the Sydney Autumn Racing Carnival in the past decade has seen most of Canterbury's feature races transferred to Rosehill.

While the course still conducts two Listed events, racing here is primarily in the restricted city grades, running many mid-week fixtures. It is the only Sydney course to stage night racing under lights. Night meetings are usually scheduled on Thursday or Friday nights.

While lacking the glamour of its metropolitan counterparts, Canterbury Park does a power of work for Sydney racing right throughout the year, especially during the winter months.

Due to its small size, the track is ideally suited to on-pace runners and it is a good venue for spectators to get a close-up view of all the action.

## THE TRACK

Right-handed. Oval-shaped course with a circumference of 1579m and a run in of 317m.

Out of the straight, runners are on a bend to the 1100m. It is a straight, slightly uphill run of 500m until the home bend.

Races over 1200m and 1290m start from a chute from the back straight.

The 1590m start chute jumps straight onto the bend out of the home straight.

The 1900m start is at the top of the home straight.

Inside draws and gate speed are a decided advantage from all start positions.

# NEWCASTLE

Chatmam Road, Broadmeadow, New South Wales, Australia. www.njc.com.au

The large industrial port city of Newcastle is situated 162km north-east of Sydney at the mouth of the Hunter River. It is the second-largest city in the state of New South Wales.

The discovery of massive coal reserves in the Hunter region shortly after European settlement transformed the area into a major mining centre with its associated heavy industries, and coal became the colony's first export commodity.

Broadmeadow Racecourse is the venue here with the Newcastle Jockey Club established in 1901, although racing in the area can be traced back to 1848 when bushland was cleared at Wallaby Flat to conduct race meetings.

Newcastle is one of the premier tracks outside the metropolitan areas of Australia, and it is a major training centre with many top trainers resident here. Champions such as Luskin Star, Choisir and Fastnet Rock were trained on the track, to mention but a few.

With the strength of the local training ranks, the proximity of the major racing and breeding operations in the nearby Hunter Valley, and strong support from city trainers due to the fairness of the track, the standard at Newcastle is always high for a provincial course.

The Broadmeadow track is the social nerve centre of the city of Newcastle. Feature days are in March for the Spring Stakes and the traditional two-day Newcastle Gold Cup meeting in September. Also worthy of mention is the annual Boxing Day fixture, which always sees a large crowd in attendance.

## THE TRACK

Right-handed. Classic oval turf track of 2000m in length and a home straight of 415m.

From the home straight, runners are on a sweeping bend to about the 1450m. It is a straight run until approaching the 900m. A sweeping bend leads to the home straight.

The 900m starting position is from a chute that gives a short run then joins the top of the home bend.

A chute for races over 1500m and 1600m links up with the back straight.

Races over 1850m start from a chute that joins the turn out of the straight.

While the chute starts all provide only a short run before the first turn, the long runs down the back and home straights give horses an equal chance from most starting positions.

## FEATURE RACE

The Newcastle Gold Cup was first run in 1898. With its excellent prize money and the programming of the race in early September, it is a race that is often a target of spring hopefuls attempting to progress to the major staying races later in their campaigns.

Notable winners include the Kiwi great **GLAD-SOME (1906)**, winner of 18 stakes races including the New Zealand 1000 Guineas (1903), New Zealand Derby, Wellington Cup, Caulfield Stakes (1904), successive Turnbull Stakes (1904, 05), Mackinnon Stakes (1904, 05) and Futurity Stakes (1905, 06) and three consecutive All Aged Stakes (1904–06).

Melbourne Cup winners successful include **RUSSIA (1944), HYPERNO (1977), GURNER'S LANE (1982)**, who took out the Caulfield–Melbourne Cup double that year; and **GREEN MOON (2011)**.

**BUZALONG (1940)** won the Caulfield Cup (1938); **CONDUCTOR (1950)** won the Metropolitan Hcp (1950); as did **HUNTER (1989)** and **GLENCADAM GOLD (2012)**.

**MANSINGH (1976)** was a winner of the New Zealand Derby (1974); **CHIAMARE (1983)** won the Brisbane Cup (1984); **EYE OF THE SKY (1988)** won the Doomben Cup (1990); and **AZZAAM (1993)** won the Sydney Cup (1994).

# HAWKESBURY

Racecourse Road, Clarendon, New South Wales, Australia. www.hawkesburyraceclub.com.au

The city of Hawkesbury, located on the Hawkesbury River, 50km north-west of Sydney, was first settled by Europeans in 1794 when 22 families were granted farmland in the area. In the 1800s the Hawkesbury River was a major transport route into Sydney.

The first meeting here was conducted in 1871 after a course was constructed on 80ha of formerly thick scrubland.

Set against the splendid backdrop of the Blue Mountains, the grandstands offer panoramic views of the mountains across the beautiful and rugged Grose Valley, making it a very picturesque course.

The Richmond Air Force Base is located directly opposite.

Race meetings are held twice a month with highlight days in May for the Hawkesbury Guineas meeting and the traditional November fixture for the Hawkesbury Gold Cup, run to coincide with VRC Oaks Day.

Prominent winners of the Gold Cup include **REGAL NATIVE (1988)**, who won the Epsom Hcp (1988), and George Ryder Stakes winners **QUICK FLICK (1997)** and **REFERRAL (1998)**.

## THE TRACK

Right-handed. Rectangular track with a circumference of 2067m. Home straight of 282m.

Out of the straight, runners are on a bend for about 700m until a sharp right turn at the 1300m. It is a straight run until just past the 900m. The bend straightens past the 700m for a run of approximately 350m to the tight home bend.

A chute for the 900m and 1000m starts joins the side of the course allowing for only one bend into the home straight.

Races from 1400m to 2000m start from a long chute that links up with the back of the course. The chute doglegs right at about the 1650m point.

# KEMBLA GRANGE

Princes Highway, Kembla Grange, New South Wales. www.kemblagrangeracing.com.au

Located 95km south of Sydney, the Wollongong suburb of Port Kembla is the major industrial city in the region. Kembla Grange racecourse is situated 8km from the heart of Wollongong in the foothills of the Illawarra Escarpment.

Racing in this port city has been under the auspices of the Illawarra Turf Club since 1976, and Kembla is considered the state's main provincial track south of Sydney.

The biggest day on the calendar is Sensational Saturday in late March, when the Keith Nolan Classic always attracts a top-class field. In recent years the race has been won by **HOT DANISH (2007)**, who won twelve stakes races including the Doomben 10,000 (2010); **ALLEZ WONDER (2009)** won the Toorak Hcp that year; and VRC Oaks winner **BRAZILIAN PULSE (2010)** won in 2011. The race was elevated to Group 3 status in 2010.

## THE TRACK

Right-handed. A very roomy classic oval of 2200m in circumference. Home straight – 420m.

Out of the turn, runners are on a long bend until the 1400m. It is a run of over 400m to the wide home bend.

The 1000m start is from a chute that gives a short run before linking up with the middle of the home bend.

The 1200m chute joins the top of the home bend. Runners jump virtually straight on to the long turn, so inside draws are an advantage from the sprint starts, but for all other distances the track is considered to race very fairly.

# SCONE

Bunnan Road, Scone, New South Wales, Australia. www.sconeraceclub.com.au

Ortensia wins the Nunthorpe

The Hunter Valley in New South Wales, with its lush pastoral land and limestone rivers, is Australia's prime thoroughbred breeding country.

Most of Australia's major stud farms are concentrated in the area, in particular at Scone, 270km north of Sydney.

The Scone Racing Club was formed in 1944 with the current course constructed in 1994.

The carnival in May boasts some of the

richest prize money on offer in country New South Wales. In 2011 the track was granted the first-ever provincial stand-alone Saturday meeting – in that it is the main Saturday fixture with no Sydney metropolitan meeting scheduled against it.

With its uncomplicated design, 400m home straight and one of the country's most beautiful racing surfaces, it is a good place to find a promising young horse stepping through the grades early in its career. And with many of the major local studs also having racing interests, some very well-bred young horses make their initial appearances here.

## THE TRACK

Right-handed. Classic oval of 1902m in circumference. Home straight – 400m.

Out of the home straight a sweeping bend takes runners to the 1400m for a straight run to just past the 1000m. A sweeping bend joins the home straight.

A chute for the 1100m start gives competitors a long straight run to the home bend.

The 1700m start is from a chute which links up with the back straight.

# GOSFORD

Racecourse Road, Gosford, New South Wales, Australia. www.gosfordracing.com.au

| FEATURE RACES | | | | | | |
|---|---|---|---|---|---|---|
| Gosford Cup | L | 2100M | TURF | 3YO+ | HCP | JAN |
| Gosford Guineas | L | 1200M | TURF | 3YO | SWP | APR |
| Pacesetter Stakes | L | 1200M | TURF | 3YO+ | HCP | JUN |

**Situated 76km north of Sydney, Gosford has its origins as a convict settlement in the early 1820s. Today the rapidly growing city is the administrative capital for the Central Coast region of New South Wales.**

The area is a very popular tourist destination in the summer with its many beaches and hidden coves.

The first meeting was held on the Gosford course in 1913. The track boasts excellent facilities including a new grandstand that offers panoramic views, making it one of the most user-friendly provincial tracks in Australia.

The traditional highlight is the Gosford Cup. The Gosford Guineas is the most valuable race on the calendar.

## THE TRACK

Right-handed. Triangular course with a tight circumference of 1710m. Home straight – 250m.

Out of the home straight runners turn right at the 1600m. It is a straight run to the 1100m where the track turns sharply right onto the back of the course. It is then another straight run to the home bend at the 400m.

## FEATURE RACE

### GOSFORD CUP

Previous winners include **DENISE'S JOY (1977)**, Auckland Cup winner **FOUNTAINCOURT (1984)**, **COMRADE (1991)** won the Toorak Hcp (1991), **SPRINT BY (1995)** won the Doncaster Hcp (1996) and **IRON HORSE (1997)** won the Epsom Hcp that year.

# WYONG

Howarth Street, Wyong, New South Wales, Australia. www.wyongraceclub.com.au

| FEATURE RACES | | | | | | |
|---|---|---|---|---|---|---|
| Wyong Gold Cup | L | 2100M | TURF | 3YO+ | HCP | SEPT |
| Mona Lisa Stakes | L | 1350M | TURF | 3YO+F&M | SWP | SEPT |

**Wyong is a major northern suburb of the Central Coast region of New South Wales, 89km north-east of Sydney.**

Racing in the area can be traced back to 1875, and racing at the site of the current course began in 1912.

Wyong is a lovely course and has good facilities with the Members' Grandstand constructed in 1991.

The Wyong Gold Cup meeting is a two-day fixture held in September.

## THE TRACK

Right-handed. Circular course of 1791m in length. Home straight – 295m.

Out of the home straight, runners take a tight bend to the 1600m then it is a straight run until about the 1350m mark before a right-hand bend to the 1200m. A short run follows to the turn at the 1000m. From there runners are basically on a bend all the way to the short home straight.

Races up to 1350m start from a chute that joins the side of the course, giving a straight run of about 550m. The 1200m start is also from this chute.

The Cup starts at the top of the home straight.

# ALBURY

Fallon Street, North Albury, NSW, Australia. www.alburyracing.com.au

| FEATURE RACE | | | | |
|---|---|---|---|---|
| Albury Gold Cup | L | 2000M | TURF | 3YO+ | MAR |

**The major regional city of Albury is situated on the north side of the Murray River, which divides New South Wales and Victoria.**

Racing provides the premier social events on the calendar in Albury, in particular the two-day Albury Gold Cup meeting, scheduled annually in March.

The Albury Gold Cup was elevated to Listed grade in 2011.

Also very popular is the meeting on the first Tuesday in November, which gives the locals the opportunity to stage their own Melbourne Cup party.

## THE TRACK

Right-handed. Circular turf course of 2100m with a home straight of 400m.

Runners are on a bend for virtually the entire circuit so inside draws are favoured from all starting positions.

# WAGGA WAGGA

Cnr Travers and Moorong Streets, Wagga Wagga,
New South Wales, Australia.
www.mtcwagga.com.au

## FEATURE RACE

| Wagga Wagga Gold Cup | L | 2000M | TURF | OPEN | HCP | MAY |
|---|---|---|---|---|---|---|

Wagga Wagga is located midway between
Australia's two largest cities, Sydney
and Melbourne, on the banks of the
Murrumbidgee River. It is the largest
inland centre in New South Wales.

In 1849 the town was marked out and officially ratified as a village. The Murrumbidgee
Turf Club was promptly formed and the first
race meeting took place before year's end.

The club maintains its traditional two-day
meeting in May, culminating with the
running of the historic Wagga Gold Cup –
one of Australia's oldest horse races – on the
first Friday of the month.

The Wagga Town Plate is ungraded but
is a time-honoured sprint race, run on the
Thursday.

The carnival is the highlight on the social
calendar in the Riverina and is Wagga Wagga's
premier tourist attraction.

## THE TRACK

Right-handed. Large triangular course of
2200m in length. Home straight – 420m.

Out of the straight it is sharp right then a
straight run from the 2100m to the 1600m
before a sharp right turn and another straight
run from the 1300m until just before the
800m. A much wider bend of almost 400m
takes runners onto the home straight.

Chute starts at the 1000m and 1600m
provide only very short runs to the first turn.

The 1400m chute gives a long run of
600m before runners are on the home bend.

# EAGLE FARM

Hampden Street, Ascot, Queensland, Australia. www.brc.com.au

*I*t is unique to find two separate racetracks side by side anywhere in the world, let alone within the city limits of a major capital, but that is the case with Brisbane's Eagle Farm and Doomben racecourses.

The colony of Queensland became a free settlement in 1859 and a course was cleared and laid out at Cooper's Plains for a three-day meeting that same year. The Queensland Turf Club was formed in 1863 and constructed the course at Eagle Farm, conducting its first meeting in 1865.

Independent rival clubs, the Queensland Turf Club (Eagle Farm) and the Brisbane Turf Club (Doomben), merged to create the Brisbane Racing Club in 2009 – ending the Hatfield–McCoy relationship that had long previously endured – to present a unified force in Queensland racing.

Most of the major races in the state are run during the rich winter carnival in May and June, with many top-class raiders from the southern states adding depth and quality to the strong local contingent.

It is also common practice for trainers based in the southern states to spell horses in the warmer climate of Queensland during the winter months.

On a weekly basis, city racing in Brisbane provides some of the most competitive racing in the nation with large acceptances and capacity fields the order of the day.

Eagle Farm is the premier track in Queensland, with a number of Group 1 races staged in June, including the Stradbroke Hcp – one of Australia's premier sprint races – run on the same day as the Brisbane Cup (Group 2), which was first run in 1866 and continues to be a highlight.

## THE TRACK

Right-handed. The course is a classic oval of 2027m in circumference and a home straight of 434m.

Out of the straight, runners are on a bend until the 1400m. It is a straight run to the wide home turn at the 1000m.

The 1000m start is from a chute that allows only a 100m run to the home bend. The 1200m start is on the course proper, with a run of 200m to the turn. Inside barriers are preferable from both of these start points.

Races of 1600m begin from a chute from the back straight, giving a run of 600m to the home turn.

The Brisbane Cup start, now at the 2400m, begins at the top of the home straight.

It is generally considered a fair course with back-markers having an equal chance.

## FEATURE RACES

### STRADBROKE HANDICAP

Brisbane's premier race first run in 1890.

Dual winners include **BABEL (1895, 96)**, **GOLD TIE (1918, 19)**, **HIGHLAND (1925, 26)**, **PETROL LAGER (1934, 35)**, **LUCKY RING (1949, 50)**, **DAYBREAK LOVER (1984, 86)**, **ROUGH HABIT (1991, 92)** and **BLACK PIRANHA (2009, 10)**.

Other notables include **WIGGLE (1958)**; **WINFREUX (1965)**; **CABACHON (1968)** won the Epsom Hcp (1967) and Doomben Cup (1970); **DIVIDE AND RULE (1970)**; **RAJAH SAHIB (1971)**; **TRITON (1972)**; **IMPOSING (1979)**; **WATNEY (1981)**; **GREY RECEIVER (1982)** was a dual winner of The Galaxy (1981, 82); **ALL OUR MOB (1994)** won the Newmarket Hcp (1995), Mackinnon Stakes (1986), All Aged Stakes (1997); **CAMPAIGN KING (1988)**; **DANE RIPPER (1997)**; and **PRIVATE STEER (2003)** won the Doncaster Hcp and All Aged Stakes (2004).

### QUEENSLAND DERBY

First run in 1868, notable winners include **FLORENCE (1871)**; **LOUGH NEAGH (1931)** won the Brisbane Cup (1936) and was a three-time winner of both the Chipping Norton Stakes (1933, 36, 37) and Ranvet Stakes (1933, 36, 37); **TULLOCH (1957)**; **PERSIAN LYRIC (1960)** won the Canterbury

## FEATURE RACES

| | | | | | | |
|---|---|---|---|---|---|---|
| STRADBROKE HCP | G1 | 1400M | TURF | 3YO+ | HCP | JUN |
| QUEENSLAND DERBY | G1 | 2400M | TURF | 3YO | SW | JUN |
| QUEENSLAND OAKS | G1 | 2400M | TURF | 3YOF | SW | JUN |
| WINTER STAKES | G1 | 1400M | TURF | 4YO+F&M | SW | JUN |
| THE TJ SMITH | G1 | 1600M | TURF | 2YO | HCP | JUN |
| BRISBANE CUP | G2 | 2400M | TURF | 3YO+ | HCP | JUN |

Guineas, ATC Australian Derby (1960) and Stradbroke Hcp (1961); **ROYAL SOVEREIGN (1964)** won the ATC Australian Derby and Victoria Derby that year; **TAILS (1968)**; **DOUBLE CENTURY (1979)** won the Sydney Cup (1979); **KINGSTON TOWN (1980)**; **STRAWBERRY ROAD (1983)**; **HANDY PROVERB (1986)** won the Victoria Derby (1985); **ROUGH HABIT (1990)**; **DODGE (1998)** won the Epsom Hcp (1998); and **FREEEMASON (2000)**.

## QUEENSLAND OAKS

First run 1951, memorable winners include 1956 Melbourne Cup winner **EVENING PEAL (1955)**, **BRIGHT SHADOW (1968)** won the Tancred Stakes (1970), **ANALIE (1973)**, **DENISE'S JOY (1976)**, **SURROUND (1977)**, **NOVEMBER RAIN (1981)** won the VRC Oaks (1980) and ATC Australian Oaks (1981), **TRISCAY (1991)**, **JOIE DENISE (1995)**, **ARCTIC SCENT (1996)** won the Caulfield Cup (1996) and **ETHEREAL (2001)** took out the Caulfield–Melbourne Cup double (2001).

## THE TJ SMITH

Inaugurated in 1893 as the Claret Stakes, the race was known as the Castlemaine Stakes when upgraded to Group 1 status in 1985. The event was renamed The TJ Smith in 1999.

Since its elevation to Group 1, winners include **FLOTILLA (1987)**, who won the Australian Guineas (1988) and Chipping Norton Stakes (1989); **ZEDITAVE (1988)**; **SLIGHT CHANCE (1992)**; **MAHOGANY (1993)**; **SHOW A HEART (2000)** won the Caulfield Guineas (2000), Toorak Hcp (2001) Stradbroke Hcp (2002) and is surprisingly one of Australia's last stallions descended from the Star Kingdom line, which was for so long the country's dominant breed; and **DARCI BRAHMA (2005)**.

Darren Gauci returns to scale after winning the 2005 Stradbroke Handicap

# DOOMBEN

Hampden Street, Ascot, Queensland, Australia. www.brc.com.au

Falvelon and Damien Oliver

*T*he *Doomben racecourse is situated in the Brisbane suburb of Ascot.*

Racing was first conducted in 1933 under the auspices of the Brisbane Turf Club until the merger with the neighbouring QTC at Eagle Farm in 2009 to form the Brisbane Racing Club. The BRC now oversees and co-ordinates operations at both of Brisbane's city courses.

After the sale of the Albion Park track, major works were undertaken in 1982 to upgrade facilities.

The Queensland winter carnival in May and June is the highlight, with Doomben taking the spotlight in May.

Both Doomben and Eagle Farm are thriving training centres with trainers having the option to use either course on a daily basis. Doomben features three turf courses for training including the course proper, which is in occasional use. The larger Eagle Farm complex also has three turf tracks plus sand and dirt training tracks and a swimming pool.

## THE TRACK

Right-handed. Oval track with a circumference of 1715m. The home straight is 350m.

Out of the straight, runners are on a bend until the 1300m. It is a straight run of 400m to the turn, which takes them to the home straight.

The Doomben 10,000 start at the 1350m is from a chute from the back straight, providing a run of 450m to the home bend.

The 1600m chute joins the bend out of the home straight after only a short run of 50m.

The 2200m start for the Doomben Cup is from a chute at the top of the home straight.

Inside draws and on-pace runners are generally favoured from all starts at the course.

## FEATURE RACES

### DOOMBEN CUP

First run in 1933; **ROUGH HABIT (1991–93)** holds the record of three successive victories.

Dual winners include **EARLWOOD (1959, 60)** and **SCENIC SHOT (2009, 11)**.

Other notable winners include **BERNBOROUGH (1946), SAMSON (1962), WINFREUX (1966), BORE HEAD (1967), DIVIDE AND RULE (1970), TAILS (1971), CHEYNE WALK (1976)** won the Queensland Derby, Spring Champion Stakes, **GREY AFFAIR (1977) MARCEAU (1978)**.

**DANDY ANDY (1987)** went on to score a boil-over win in the Australian Cup (1988) defeating Vo Rogue and Bonecrusher; **DURBRIDGE (1994); DANEWIN (1995); JUGGLER (1996); MIGHT AND POWER (1998); INTERGAZE (1999); DEFIER (2004)** won the George Main Stakes, ATC Queen Elizabeth Stakes (2006) and was twice runner-up in the Cox Plate; and **METAL BENDER**

## FEATURE RACES

| DOOMBEN CUP | G1 | 2200M | TURF | 3YO+ | WFA | MAY |
|---|---|---|---|---|---|---|
| DOOMBEN 10,000 | G1 | 1350M | TURF | 3YO+ | WFA | MAY |
| BTC CUP | G1 | 1200M | TURF | 3YO+ | WFA | MAY |
| CHAMPAGNE CLASSIC | G2 | 1200M | TURF | 2YO | SW | MAY |

(2010).

### DOOMBEN 10,000

First run in 1933, it was the first sprint race in Australia to offer £10,000 in prize money.

Notable winners include **LOUGH NEAGH (1934), BERNBOROUGH (1946), AQUANITA (1961), WINFREUX (1965), BAGUETTE (1971), MAYBE MAHAL (1977), MANIKATO (1979), SOVEREIGN RED (1981), CAMPAIGN KING (1988), FLITTER (1994), TAKEOVER TARGET (2007), HOT DANISH (2010)** and **SEA SIREN (2012)**.

Dual winners include **BLACK ONYX (1969, 70)**, and **PRINCE TRIALIA (1990, 91)** and **CHIEF DE BEERS (1995, 98)** – the ultimate track specialist. He won 20 of his 51 starts – with all 20 wins at Doomben. A champion at this track where he often lumped big weights, he ran well but remarkably never won a race at any other track in his illustrious career.

**FALVELON (2001, 02)** was unbeaten in seven runs as a 2yo and went on to become a dual winner of the BTC Cup (2000, 03) and the Hong Kong Sprint (2001, 02).

**APACHE CAT (2008, 09)** was a popular horse with his unusual white markings. He won 19 races – eight at Group 1 level including the Australian Guineas (2006), Lightning Stakes, BTC Cup, TJ Smith Stakes (2008) and consecutive Australia Stakes (2008, 09), then a Group 1.

### BTC CUP

Run since 1964, the race was elevated to Group 1 in 2006. Winners since include **APACHE CAT (2008), BLACK CAVIAR (2011)** and **SEA SIREN (2012)**.

# GOLD COAST

Racecourse Drive, Surfers Paradise, Queensland, Australia. www.gctc.com.au

Ha Ha wins the Magic Millions 3YO Classic

still be pinching themselves that two of the country's heavy-hitters walked in the door with a plan to put the second-tier course on the world racing map.

The club was granted a stand-alone Saturday meeting in 2002 and runs the best of its graded races on this day in early May.

## THE TRACK

Right-handed. The track has a circumference of 1885m and a home straight of 400m.

Out of the straight, runners turn quickly to the 1700m. It is a short run to the 1500m where the track bends again until the 1350m. It is then a straight run of about 350m to the home bend. Approaching halfway around, the home bend straightens for 100m then turns again until the home straight.

The course has a number of chute starts.

Chute for the 900m races joins the home bend.

The 1100m chute gives only a short run to the first bend.

The 1250m chute is a run of 250m to the first bend.

The 1800m start is from a chute that gives a 300m run before the turn to the top of the course.

Races over 2400m begin from a chute at the top of the home straight.

While not as accentuated from the 1400m and 2400m starts, inside draws are a big advantage and on-speed runners are always preferable here from all other start positions. Back-markers often find it difficult to make ground wide on the course.

The city of the Gold Coast is located 94km south of Brisbane, but the Gold Coast area stretches for 57km of glorious coastline. With its beautiful climate, world-famous beaches, 100,000 hectares of national parks and reserves, 860km of accessible waterways and canals, golf courses and theme parks, it is the holiday venue for 10 million tourists every year.

The Gold Coast is always in holiday mode with bustling nightlife and lively restaurants and bars.

In the 1890s the cane fields at nearby Bundall were cleared and the first meeting in the area was run.

Racing at the current site began in 1946 and the Gold Coast is now a thriving racing and training centre with 700 horses in work and some very prominent names among the local training ranks.

Since 1971 racing has been conducted every Saturday, and while mostly in the restricted grades, the local trainers generally have some promising young horses coming through. All seemed to be on an even keel until the mid 1980s.

Advertising guru John Singleton and retail king Gerry Harvey are both self-made men who have amassed fortunes in business, and as long-time racing partners, became two of

Australia's most successful owner-breeders. It was their concept to stage a quality yearling sale on the Gold Coast in 1986, the Magic Millions Sale, and to put on a million-dollar race the following year exclusively for 2yos purchased at the sale, with a view to building a whole race card just for sales graduates in the ensuing years.

The idea of a major race restricted to horses bought at a specific sale was as controversial as it was innovative. It was also a highly ambitious plan, but those who questioned its viability were to doubt the business acumen and entrepreneurial nous of men renowned for it and with the resources to back it up.

The concept also relied on producing good-quality horses and inaugural Magic Millions 2yo Classic winner, **SNIPPETS (1987)**, proved to be a top-class winner of seven stakes races with Group 1 wins in the ATC Sires' Produce (1987), Oakleigh Plate, The Galaxy (1988). He became a very good sire in his own right.

The reputation of the sales was cemented and it is now a yearling sale of international significance. The multi-million-dollar race card, perfectly timed at the height of the holiday season in January, is one of the highlights on the Australian calendar.

The concept is now common all over the world and the Gold Coast Turf Club must

# Sunshine Coast

170 Pierce Avenue, Meridan Plains, Queensland.
www.sctc.com.au

| FEATURE RACES | | | | | | |
|---|---|---|---|---|---|---|
| Caloundra City Cup | L | 2400M | TURF | 3YO+ | HCP | JUN–JUL |
| Glasshouse HCP | L | 1400M | TURF | 3YO+ | HCP | JUN–JUL |
| Sunshine Coast Guineas | L | 1600M | TURF | 3YO | | JUN–JUL |
| Summer Cup | L | 1400M | TURF | 3YO+ | HCP | FEB |

The Sunshine Coast, north of Brisbane, is one of Australia's busiest tourist spots with its many famous beaches and is a rapidly growing area.

The city of Caloundra is located 90km north of Brisbane and is home to Corbould Park racecourse. Situated on the outskirts of the town, the track was opened in 1985 and is an impressive racing complex with great facilities, manicured gardens and interesting architecture. It was the first major course built outside the Brisbane metropolitan area in 50 years.

A total of $42m has been spent on the facility to date, including the installation of a synthetic Cushion track in 2008. Forty light towers were erected in 2009 to enable night meetings under lights.

The semi-tropical climate produces a high annual rainfall in the area and the establishment of the all-weather track has not only guaranteed that racing can continue unabated all year round, but has seen the Sunshine Coast Turf Club secure 70 race fixtures annually.

Racing is currently conducted every Sunday and every third Friday, catering almost exclusively for racing in the restricted grades, with the major race days scheduled separately.

Highlight day is Caloundra City Cup day held in late June or early July, with three Listed races on the card including the Cup. One of the best-attended days is the meeting on Melbourne Cup day when the course throws a Cup party of its own.

## THE TRACK

Right-handed. The track is a triangular oval in shape. The circumference of the turf track is 1967m.

The home straight is 400m.

Past the winning post it is a sweeping right-handed bend that takes runners to the 1600m. The track bends right again approaching the 1200m before a straight run to the 800m. A long sweeping bend of 400m joins the home straight.

The ground falls 6m after the turn out of the straight until just past the 1100m then rises back up by 6m from the top of the bend into the home straight to the winning post.

There are five separate chutes for race starts over 850m, 1000m, 1400m, 1600m and 1800m.

The inner Cushion Track is 1760m with a run in also of 400m.

# Ipswich

219 Brisbane Road, Bundamba, Queensland, Australia. www.ipswichturfclub.com.au

| FEATURE RACES | | | | | | |
|---|---|---|---|---|---|---|
| Ipswich Cup | L | 2150M | TURF | 3YO+ | HCP | JUN |
| Eye Liner Stakes | L | 1350M | TURF | 3YO+ | HCP | JUN |
| Gai Waterhouse Classic | L | 1350M | TURF | 3YO+F&M | HCP | JUN |

Ipswich Racecourse is located in the metropolitan suburb of Bundamba, 32km from Brisbane.

Formerly the Bundamba Racecourse, it is one of the oldest venues for racing in Queensland, with its first meeting staged in 1859. The origins of the Ipswich Turf Club date back to 1890.

Highlight fixture is Ipswich Cup Day in mid June, which features three Listed races.

## THE TRACK

Right-handed. Circular track of 1746m in circumference. Home straight – 300m.

The turn out of the home straight takes runners to the 1500m. It is then a straight run of 200m to the 1300m. From the 1300m runners are virtually on a bend all the way to the home straight.

Chute starts at the 1200m and 1350m join the course at the top of the track.

The 1666m starting chute links up with the course just after the turn out of the home straight.

The Cup start at the 2150m is from a chute at the top of the home straight.

Inside draws and on-pace are generally the recipe for success at this venue.

# Toowoomba

Hursley Road, Toowoomba, Queensland, Australia.
www.toowoombaturfclub.com

| FEATURE RACE | | | | | | |
|---|---|---|---|---|---|---|
| Weetwood HCP | L | 1200M | AWT | 3YO+ | HCP | MAR |

Situated 127km west of Brisbane, the garden city of Toowoomba is one of Australia's largest inland centres.

Racing was first staged here at Clifford Park in 1862 under the auspices of the Darling Downs Jockey Club. The Toowoomba Turf Club was formed in 1882 and staged its first meeting that year.

Toowoomba made history by running the Toowoomba Cup under lights in 1992. It was the first Australian track to run a night race, and in 1996 the course hosted Australia's first-ever night race meeting.

The turf track was replaced with an all-weather Cushion track in 2009. The combination of floodlights and the synthetic course have seen Toowoomba become the 'home of twilight racing,' with races here every Saturday night throughout the year. The track now hosts up to 60 meetings annually.

An integral part of Toowoomba's history revolves around champion Bernborough. Barred from racing on metropolitan tracks due to doubts over his true ownership, Bernborough did his early racing here at

Toowoomba where he won six races.

The ban was finally lifted when Bernborough was sold as a 6yo. He then went on a winning spree, with victory in 15 consecutive races. His racing style thrilled the public as he would drop out to the back of the field then produce an astonishing turn of foot to mow down his opposition – often carrying big weights and always against top company.

His wins in 1946 included the Chipping Norton Stakes, Ranvet Stakes, All Aged Stakes, Newmarket Hcp carrying 9st 13lb (63kg), Doomben 10,000, Doomben Cup under the steadier of 10st 10lb (68kg), Futurity Stakes and Caulfield Stakes. His record of eight consecutive wins at Group 1 level stood until 2013.

In the end his tally stood at 26 wins from 37 starts, and while Queensland has produced many of Australia's great champions none is considered greater than Bernborough. Upon retirement he was sold to legendary movie producer Louis B Mayer to stand at stud in Lexington, Kentucky, where he had reasonable success. He was one of five inaugural inductees to the Australian Hall of Fame.

## THE TRACK

Right-handed. All-weather. The course is rectangular with a circumference of 1750m. The home straight is 360m.

Out of the straight, runners are on a bend to the 1650m point and then it is a straight run until a right-hand bend at about the 1350m. It is then a straight run of 200m to the 1000m. Runners are then on a long sweeping bend until the home straight.

There are chutes from all four sides of the course, allowing starts from the 9000m, 1300m, 1600m and 2100m. The 1000m start is from a spur that joins the top of the course. Inside draws for races up to 1200m are highly advantageous.

Bernborough

# BIRDSVILLE

Remotely located almost 1600km west of Brisbane on the border of northern South Australia, the outback town of Birdsville is home to one of Australia's most celebrated race meetings.

Formerly known as Diamantina Crossing, Birdsville was an outpost centre for stock routes in the 1870s and was established as a collection point for tolls from cattlemen as they drove their herds across the state borders.

Many of Australia's early explorers travelled through here and a number of monuments acknowledge the achievements of historic figures who passed through, such as Burke and Wills, and Captain Charles Sturt.

Conducted annually on the first weekend in September, the two-day Birdsville meeting begins on the Friday and culminates with the running of the 1600m Birdsville Cup on the Saturday. The Cup was first run in 1882 as a race for stockhorses and hacks.

The Birdsville Cup meeting sees the local population of around 300 swell to 6000 for the event. The meeting importantly raises funds for the Royal Flying Doctor Service, which provides transport and assistance for

people in remote areas who require regular or emergency medical attention.

The course is situated on a claypan alongside the Birdsville sand dunes. The track is 2000m in circumference. In recent times barrier stalls have replaced the drop of a hat as the preferred starting method.

Owing to its remote location and the fact that the roads surrounding Birdsville are all unsealed, light aircraft is the popular method of transport for most of those in attendance.

In 2010 the Saturday races were cancelled due to a storm that deluged the track and closed the airport and roads. Consequently the large crowd was flooded in for almost a week with no way in or out. The party continued unfettered as fortunately beer stocks at the Birdsville Pub held out. Cigarettes were not in as plentiful supply and the last packet in the town had to be auctioned, with the winning bid lodged at $175.

Many events are held in the town to coincide with the Cup, with lots of entertainment, fashions on the field, and for those who consider themselves handy with their fists, the legendary Fred Brophy Boxing Troupe is annually in attendance.

# MORPHETTVILLE

Morphett Road, Morphettville, South Australia. www.sajc.com.au

*A*delaide is the capital city of South Australia and the fifth-largest in Australia. Racing here dates back to 1838, with the first meeting conducted on a narrow plain below West Terrace.

The Adelaide suburb of Morphettville, 10km from the city centre, is the headquarters for racing in South Australia. Racing commenced here in 1875 and the course was purchased outright by the club in 1889.

Since the closure of the South Australian Jockey Club's former base at the Victoria Park course in 2008 and then the Cheltenham Park course in 2009, it is the only metropolitan course located in Adelaide.

To cope with year-round racing, an inner track was opened in 2009, known as the Morphettville Parks circuit.

In a world first, a retractable hydraulic winning post was also installed to service both courses, so that the post can be moved between the two tracks with minimal damage to the racing surfaces.

The infield of the track features a wetlands area, which is used as a water catchment for irrigation of the course.

Adelaide Cup day in March was proclaimed a public holiday for the city in 1973. While the race was downgraded to Group 2 status in 2007, this time-honoured 3200m race with a history dating back to 1864 remains the social highlight of the Adelaide racing calendar. Racing in Adelaide rises a number of notches in April, when all of the city's Group 1 races are run.

## THE TRACK

Left-handed. The outer Morphettville track is an irregular or triangular oval shape with a circumference of 2307m and a home straight of 340m.

All of the feature races are conducted on the outer track.

Out of the straight, runners are on a bend to the 1750m. It is a straight run of over 500m before the turn to the side of the course, then a run of 400m to the home turn.

The 1200m chute provides a run of about 600m to the home turn. The chute start for the 1800m races joins the back of the course, with a run of 500m before the first bend.

2000m races begin from a spur that links up with the top of the bend out of the home straight, providing a run of only 150m until the first bend. Inside draws are a considerable advantage.

The Adelaide Cup start at the 3200m gives only a very short run to the home turn. While the distance of the race offsets the barrier draws to an extent, a low draw is still preferable.

Morphettville is considered one of Australia's fairest tracks.

The inner Morphettville Parks track has a circumference of 2100m and a run in of 305m. The tighter circuit can play more to on-pace runners.

It should be noted that there is no 1400m start on the outer track, so races listed at that distance on a Morphettville card are run on the inner Morphetville Parks track.

## FEATURE RACES

### THE GOODWOOD

The Goodwood is a top-class sprint race with an esteemed history dating back to 1881. It is considered the premier race in South Australia.

A handicap race since its inception, the conditions of the race were changed to set weights plus penalties in 2007 to maintain its status as a Group 1 race. Since then the race has been won by the great sprinters **TAKE-OVER TARGET (2009)** and **BLACK CAVIAR (2012)**.

Earlier winners include **AURIE'S STAR (1940)**; **ROYAL GEM (1946)**; **MATRICE (1956)**; and **BOMBER BILL (2003)**, who was a winner of 23 races.

Dual winners include **MOSTYN (1894, 95)** and **MUSKET BELLE (1911, 12)**.

| FEATURE RACES | | | | | | |
|---|---|---|---|---|---|---|
| THE GOODWOOD | G1 | 1200M | TURF | 3YO+ | SWP | APR |
| AUSTRALASIAN OAKS | G1 | 2000M | TURF | 3YOF | SW | APR |
| SOUTH AUSTRALIAN DERBY | G1 | 2500M | TURF | 3YO | SW | APR |
| ROBERT SANGSTER STAKES | G1 | 1200M | TURF | 3YO+F&M | WFA | APR |
| ADELAIDE CUP | G2 | 3200M | TURF | 3YO+ | HCP | MAR |

Adelaide turns out to see Black Caviar win the Robert Sangster Stakes

## AUSTRALASIAN OAKS

Notable winners include **ROSE OF KINGSTON (1982)**, who won the inaugural running; Caulfield Cup winners **IMPOSERA (1988)** and **MANNERISM (1991)**; **EPISODE (1999)**; **ZARITA (2008)** also won the SA Derby (2008).

## SOUTH AUSTRALIAN DERBY

First run in 1860 at the old Thebarton course a number of South Australian Derby winners have gone on to success in the Melbourne Cup, including **TIM WHIFFLER (1865)**, **THE ASSYRIAN (1880)**, **AURARIA (1895)**, **GATUM GATUM (1961)** and **SUBZERO (1992)**.

Other prominent winners include **LORD SETAY (1919)**, who won the Toorak Hcp (1920); **DAYANA (1972)** won the Victoria Derby, WA Derby (1972), Perth Cup (1973); **STORMY REX (1977)** won the

Victoria Derby, WA Derby and Kingston Town Stakes that year; **BREWERY BOY (1981)** won the Victoria Derby (1981) as did **REBEL RAIDER (2009)**; **COUNT CHIVAS (1995)** won the Sydney Cup (1996); and **MUMMIFY (2007)**.

## ROBERT SANGSTER STAKES

First run in 1983, the race became a Group 1 in 2005.

**ALINGHI (2005)** won the first edition at Group 1 level, and **BLACK CAVIAR (2012)** created history in this race as she extended her unbeaten streak to 20 wins to eclipse the Australasian record of 19 consecutive victories jointly held by Desert Gold and Gloaming.

# MURRAY BRIDGE

Maurice Road, Murray Bridge, South Australia, Australia. www.racingmurraybridge.com

Murray Bridge is a busy centre located 78km east of Adelaide at the crossing of the Princes Highway and the Murray River.

The river town services the surrounding agriculture and with its lovely climate is a hub for angling, houseboating and water sports of all kinds.

The Murray Bridge Racing Club was formed in 1899 and racing at the current site, just 3km from the Murray River, was first held in 1914.

The feature event is the Murray Bridge Gold Cup, run over 1600m every October.

## THE TRACK

Left-handed. Oval course with a circumference of 1850m with a run home of 400m.

Out of the straight a long sweeping bend takes runners to the 1400m. The back straight is slightly curved with another long sweeping bend at the 1050m taking runners onto the home straight.

# BALAKLAVA

Racecourse Road, Balaklava, South Australia. www.balaklavaracingclub.com.au

| FEATURE RACE | | | | | |
| --- | --- | --- | --- | --- | --- |
| Balaklava Cup | L | 1600M | TURF | 3YO+ | SEPT |

The town of Balaklava is located 92km north of Adelaide.

The course staged its first meeting in 1904 after the formation of the Balaklava Racing Club the previous year. The highlight is Balaklava Cup day in September.

## THE TRACK

Left-handed. The course is an oval-shaped turf track with a circumference of 2053m. The home straight is 453m.

# OAKBANK

Oakwood Road, Oakbank, South Australia. www.oakbankracingclub.com.au

The Adelaide Hills, 49km from Adelaide, is the spectacular setting for one of Australia's oldest and most iconic race meetings, the Oakbank Easter Racing Carnival.

This unique two-day meeting, run annually on Easter Saturday and Easter Monday since 1876, combines jumps and flat racing. With well over 100,000 people in attendance across the two days, it is officially the largest picnic race meeting in the world and the home of jumps racing in South Australia.

The tiny population of Oakbank swells exponentially, as paddocks adjacent to the course are transformed into camping grounds for the many families and groups taking up residence over the Easter holiday weekend. Family activities are scheduled throughout the weekend, and there are carnival rides on the infield of the track for the kids and the young at heart.

The highlight is the historic Great Eastern Steeple, one of Australia's richest jumps races,

2010 Great Eastern winner It's a Dud

run on the Monday in front of a crowd of 70,000. Run over a gruelling 4950m, it is the nation's most colourful and spectacular race, set against a beautiful backdrop, as competitors tackle the quirky and undulating hill course that features famous jumps, including the Fallen Log.

Other major jumps events include the Von Dousa Steeplechase and Classic Hurdle. Flat racing highlights are the Listed Oakbank Stakes over 1100m and the Onkaparinga Cup for the stayers. The meeting also stages a 3600m race – the longest race on the flat in Australia.

The course was only in operation for those two days each year in its long and esteemed history until 2009, when two extra fixtures were added – a prelude meeting to the Easter carnival in March and a Christmas meeting in late December.

## THE TRACK

Left-handed. Undulating, irregular oval-shaped course. The flat course is 1800m in length, with an extended course for the jumping events. The track rises steadily on the jumps course as runners turn out of the straight and head to the top of the track.

The home straight is approximately 360m. The home bend has a pronounced downhill run into the straight.

# ASCOT

70 Grandstand Road, Ascot, West Australia. www.perthracing.com.au

*P*erth is Australia's fourth-largest city and capital of Western Australia.

Racing was first staged in 1836 on a course laid out at Guildford, 16km from the capital, and featured a race for thoroughbred horses only.

Racing now takes place at Ascot, West Australia's principal racetrack, just east of the Perth CBD on the southern bank of the Swan River. The suburb of Ascot was named after the racecourse.

The course is affectionately known as the Grand Old Lady, having hosted its first meeting in 1848. The West Australian Turf Club, formed in 1852, now operates under the banner of Perth Racing.

Perth metropolitan racing is shared between Ascot and nearby Belmont, with racing season at Ascot between October and April. Belmont conducts all metropolitan fixtures throughout the rest of the year. All of Western Australia's Group 1 races are staged at Ascot.

The spotlight falls on racing here for the summer carnival throughout November and December with many rich races on offer, attracting some of the top horses from the eastern states.

Perth racing is very competitive and the standard in the upper grades is always high.

Evidence of that is provided during the carnival every year, as the locals are always extremely hard to beat on their home turf, often taking the lion's share of the spoils.

The warm climate and low rainfall on this part of the western seaboard almost invariably ensure firm to hard ground.

The Perth Cup, now a Group 2 over a shortened 2400m, is run annually on New Year's Day and remains the highlight fixture, alongside the Railway Stakes meeting in November.

## THE TRACK

Left-handed. The course is an irregular oval shape of 2000m in length with a run home of 300m. The track rises slightly from the 400m to the winning post.

Out of the straight a short bend takes runners to the 1800m. It is a straight run of about 300m until a bend that straightens at the 1100m. Then it is another straight run to the long home bend at the 700m.

The 1200m start is from a chute that links up with side of the course, giving a run of 500m to the home turn.

Separate chutes for the 1400m, 1500m and 1600m starts give only a short run to the first bend.

The Perth Cup start at the 2400m begins from a chute at the top of the home straight.

Back-markers can find it very difficult to come around the field, with riders generally searching for inside runs. Consequently the course can often suit on-pace runners, especially when the prevailing wind is from the east. Inside draws are preferable from most starting positions.

## FEATURE RACES

### RAILWAY STAKES

The Railway Stakes is the premier event on the calendar, and the stakes were raised to make it a million-dollar race in 2007.

First run in 1887, prominent winners include dual Perth Cup winner **WANDERING WILLIE (1890)**; **AUSTRALIAN (1901)** also won the Perth Cup (1901); **AQUANITA (1959)**; **TUDOR MAK (1966, 67)** went back to back; **LA TRICE (1968)** was a dual winner of the Winterbottom Stakes (1970, 71); **MILLEFLEURS (1972)** won the Queen of the Turf Stakes and MRC Invitation Stakes (1973); **MARJOLEO (1979)** took out The Goodwood (1980); **IKO (1987)**; 1987 Caulfield Guineas winner **MARWONG (1988)** broke the 1600m track record; and **BETTER LOOSEN UP (1989)**.

Trained in Perth by Fred Kersley, **NORTHERLY (2000)** is one of the great horses of the modern era and a winner of 19 of his 37 starts, including nine wins at Group 1. A dual winner of the Underwood Stakes (2001, 02), Australian Cup (2001, 03) and the Cox Plate (2001, 02) he also won the Caulfield Stakes (2001) and the Caulfield Cup (2002) defying all challengers for the entire length of the straight, carrying top weight. His performance to back up a week later and win a second Cox Plate left even the master trainer Bart Cummings in awe.

| FEATURE RACES | | | | | | | |
|---|---|---|---|---|---|---|---|
| RAILWAY STAKES | G1 | 1600M | TURF | 3YO+ | HCP | 1887 | NOV |
| WINTERBOTTOM STAKES | G1 | 1200M | TURF | 3YO+ | WFA | 1952 | NOV |
| KINGSTON TOWN CLASSIC | G1 | 1800M | TURF | 3YO+ | WFA | 1976 | DEC |
| PERTH CUP | G2 | 2400M | TURF | 3YO+ | HCP | 1885 | JAN |

Northerly, pictured here winning the 2002 Cox Plate

**OLD COMRADE (2001)** was a dual winner of the Kingston Town Classic (2000, 01) and defeated Northerly to win the Australian Cup in 2002, giving WA the quinella in the race; **SNIPER'S BULLET (2009)** won the Stradbroke Hcp (2007) and the Kingston Town Classic (2009); and **LUCKYGRAY (2011)**.

## KINGSTON TOWN CLASSIC

Inaugurated in 1976 the race has been run under numerous sponsor names until 2007 when the name was changed to honour the deeds of the great Kingston Town, who won this race in 1982 at his final appearance on a racetrack.

Many famous names have won the race including **STORMY REX (1977)**, **MIGHTY KINGDOM (1979)**, **SOVEREIGN RED (1980)**, 1983 Victoria Derby winner **BOUNTY HAWK (1983)**, **MILITARY PLUME (1986)** also won the Australian Guineas (1987), **VO ROGUE (1988)** and **BETTER LOOSEN UP (1989)**.

Dual winners include **FAMILY OF MAN (1976, 78)**, **SUMMER BEAU (1996, 97)**, **OLD COMRADE (2000, 01)**, **NICONERO (2006, 08)** won the Australian Cup (2009) and twice won the Futurity Stakes (2008, 09) and **PLAYING GOD (2010, 11)**.

## WINTERBOTTOM STAKES

Run since 1952, the race was elevated to Group 1 in 2011.

Notable winners include **PLACID ARK (1987)**, who went to Melbourne as a 3yo and became the first horse ever to win the autumn sprint treble of the Lightning Stakes, Oakleigh Plate and Newmarket Hcp (1987); champion sprinting mare **MISS ANDRETTI (2005)** won the Manikato Stakes (2006), Lightning Stakes, Newmarket Hcp and King's Stand Stakes (2007); **TAKEOVER TARGET (2008)**; and dual winner **ORTENSIA (2009, 11)** also won the Al Quoz Sprint and Nunthorpe Stakes (2012).

# BELMONT PARK

Victoria Park Drive Exit, Belmont, West Australia.
www.perthracing.com.au

Miss Andretti, pictured winning the 2007 Kings Stand Stakes

## FEATURE RACES

| ROMA CUP | G3 | 1200M | TURF | 2YO+ | WFA | MAY |
|---|---|---|---|---|---|---|
| BELMONT SPRINT | G3 | 1400M | TURF | 3YO+ | HCP | JUN |
| HYPERION STAKES | G3 | 1600M | TURF | 3YO+ | WFA | JUN |
| STRICKLANU STAKES | G3 | 2000M | TURF | 3YO+ | WFA | JUL |

The West Australian Turf Club also operates racing at the second of Perth's city courses in the inner suburb of Belmont, east of the Perth CBD.

Belmont Park stages all metropolitan racing during winter and into spring, with racing season from April to October.

While the weather outside may be cool, facilities at Belmont are enclosed and the river backdrop provides a lovely setting. Excellent drainage allows racing to continue unabated throughout the season.

While the major races are held at Ascot, this is not to suggest that the top Perth horses all sit it out for half of the year. Belmont stages plenty of open-class racing with more than a dozen Group and Listed events over the six months.

## THE TRACK

Left-handed. The course is an oval shape with a circumference of 1699m and a home straight of 333m.

Out of the straight, runners are on a bend to the 1300m. It is a straight run of 400m along the back of the course to the home turn.

The 1000m start is from a chute that gives only a short run before joining the home turn. The 2800m start is also located in this chute, 100m further back.

The 1600m races begin from a spur that jumps virtually onto the turn out of the home straight, so runners are on a bend for the first 300m of the race.

The 2400m races begin from a chute at the top of the home straight.

Low draws and, in particular, on-pace runners are always well suited.

# BUNBURY

Corner Blair Street and Brittain Road, Bunbury, West Australia. www.bunburyturfclub.com.au

## FEATURE RACES

| Bunbury Cup | L | 2200M | TURF | 3YO+ | HCP | MAR |
|---|---|---|---|---|---|---|
| Bunbury Patrons Plate | L | 1400M | TURF | 3YO | HCP | MAR |
| Bunbury Stakes | L | 1400M | TURF | 3YO+ | HCP | MAR |

The port city of Bunbury is located near the mouth of the Collie River, 175km south of Perth. It is West Australia's third–most populated city, exceeded only by Perth and Mandurah.

Racing in Bunbury occurs between November and April. The club conducts around 20 meetings and the main races are run in February and March. The course has excellent amenities for the public.

The highlight Bunbury Cup meeting is in mid March and its honour roll includes **ROGAN JOSH (1998)**, who was transferred to the Bart Cummings stable for his successful tilt at the Melbourne Cup (1999); and Australian Cup (1995) winner **STARSTRUCK (1994)**.

While racing is only conducted during a five-month period, Bunbury has multiple turf and sand training tracks to provide a year-round facility for the more than 60 trainers based on the track.

## THE TRACK

Left-handed. The course is circular with a circumference of 1796m. Home straight – 348m.

Leaving the home straight, runners are on a circular course that turns virtually all the way back to the home straight.

Chute starts from the 1200m, 1400m and 1675m all provide only short runs to the circle.

On-pace runners and inside draws are preferable here.

# KALGOORLIE

Meldrum Avenue, Kalgoorlie, Western Australia, Australia. www.kbrc.com.au

## FEATURE RACES

| Kalgoorlie Gold Cup | L | 2300M | TURF | 3YO+ | HCP | SEPT |
|---|---|---|---|---|---|---|
| Boulder Cup | L | 1760M | TURF | 3YO+ | HCP | SEPT |
| Hannan's HCP | L | 1400M | TURF | 3YO+ | HCP | SEPT |

The town of Kalgoorlie, about 600km east of Perth, was established following the discovery of gold in the area in 1893. With its reserves of gold and particularly nickel, it remains a major mining centre.

The first race meeting was staged here in 1896. Racing in the area was conducted on a number of tracks, some quite makeshift.

The courses at Kalgoorlie, Coolgardie and Boulder emerged as the main venues with all conducting meetings at their respective tracks. A circuit known as The Round was established to share the meetings among the courses and give each equal benefit of the best weather and conditions.

World War I brought about the closure of the Coolgardie track and the Boulder course was commandeered by the army to be used as a training base during World War II. Consequently the Boulder Racing Club held its meetings at the Kalgoorlie course and a merger of the two clubs was convened in 1953 to form the Kalgoorlie–Boulder Racing Club.

The Coolgardie Racing Club still holds two race days per year on the Kalgoorlie track.

Kalgoorlie's two-day meeting in September is still known as The Round and provides very good quality racing with three Listed events, including the Kalgoorlie Cup and Boulder Cup. The feature sprint is the Hannan's Handicap, named after Paddy Hannan, who was among the trio of men who first found gold in the region.

## THE TRACK

Left-handed. The course is square with a circumference of 1934m. Home straight – 320m.

Leaving the run home it is a straight run from the 1700m until the bend at the 1300m. Another bend is encountered at the 800m to the side of the track. It is a short run from the 600m to the very shallow bend into the home straight.

Inside draws tend to be advantaged from most start positions.

The 1400m start is from a chute that joins the back of the course, providing a straight run of 600m to the first bend.

The Boulder Cup start at the 1760m is from a chute that links up with the turn out of the straight.

The 2300m start is from a chute at the top of the home straight.

# PINJARRA

Racecourse Road, Pinjarra, West Australia.
www.pinjarrapark.com.au

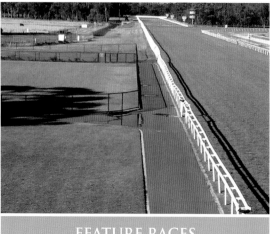

| FEATURE RACES | | | | | | |
|---|---|---|---|---|---|---|
| Pinjarra Cup | L | 2300M | TURF | 3YO+ | HCP | MAR–APR |
| Pinjarra Stakes | L | 1300M | TURF | 3YO+ | HCP | MAR |

Pinjarra is situated 86km south of Perth. The expansive lawns and shady trees of the course provide an idyllic and relaxed rural setting for racing against the spectacular backdrop of the Darling Range Escarpment.

Pinjarra Park is the most picturesque course in Western Australia and its proactive marketing department organise many theme days and live music events to complement their race meetings.

Major works on the track were completed in 2008 with the turns widened and re-cambered, and improvements made to the irrigation and drainage systems.

Feature race days are in autumn.

## THE TRACK

Left-handed. Oval-shaped track with a circumference of 1837m and a run in of 336m.

Out of the straight a sweeping bend takes runners to just before the 1300m. It is a straight run to about the 900m, where another sweeping bend leads to the home straight.

Races from 1400m to 1800m start on a chute from the back straight providing long runs to the first bend.

1000m races are held on the straight course, which runs slightly uphill. The Pinjarra Cup start at the 2300m is also located on the straight course.

It is considered quite a fair racetrack.

# NORTHAM

175 Yilgarn Avenue, Northam, West Australia.
www.northamraceclub.com

| FEATURE RACES | | | | | |
|---|---|---|---|---|---|
| Northam Sprint | L | 1100M | TURF | 3YO+ | APR |
| Northam Cup | L | 1600M | TURF | 3YO+ | OCT |

Northam is situated 97km north-east of Perth in the heart of the Avon Valley.

The racecourse is located by the Mortlock River to the east of the town, with racing conducted most Thursdays from late April until early November.

## THE TRACK

Left-handed. Oval turf track with a circumference of 2017m. Home straight – 425m.

# HOBART

Goodwood Road, Glenorchy, Tasmania, Australia.
www.tasracingclub.com.au

| FEATURE RACES | | | | | | |
|---|---|---|---|---|---|---|
| HOBART CUP | G3 | 2200M | TURF | 3YO+ | HCP | FEB |
| BOW MISTRESS TROPHY | G3 | 1200M | TURF | 3YO+F&M | SW | FEB |
| Tasmanian Derby | L | 2200M | TURF | 3YO | SW | FEB |
| Strutt Stakes | L | 2100M | TURF | 3YOF | SW | FEB |
| Thomas Lyons Stakes | L | 1400M | TURF | 3YO+ | WFA | FEB |
| Elwick Stakes | L | 1100M | TURF | 2YO | SW | FEB |
| Hobart Guineas | L | 2100M | TURF | 3YO | SW | JAN |

Hobart is the capital of the island state of Tasmania, directly south of the Australian mainland's south-east coast. Located in the foothills of Mount Wellington on the estuary of the Derwent River, the beautiful city was originally settled as a penal colony in 1803.

Having obtained the lease, the Tasmanian Racing Club held its first meeting on the course in 1874 and the venue quickly enjoyed great popularity, which encouraged the TRC to buy the course outright.

In recent times racing in Tasmania has progressed significantly with the establishment of a summer racing carnival that now offers big prize money over January and February at both of Tasmania's main venues, Hobart and

Launceston. Many good-quality entrants from the mainland complement the best of the local horses to provide competitive racing in this picturesque environment.

The Hobart Cup is a race with a long history, having first been run in 1876. Melbourne cup winners **THE ASSYRIAN (1883)** and **PIPING LANE (1972)** have taken out the race.

**BRALLOS** won back-to-back Hobart and Launceston Cups in 1976 and 1977.

Also referred to as the Elwick Racecourse; a $20m redevelopment of the facility in 2004 included an upgrade to the heritage-listed grandstand, a new bookmakers' enclosure and the installation of harness racing and greyhound tracks on the infield.

## THE TRACK

Left-handed. Egg-shaped oval track with a circumference of 1990m. Home straight – 350m.

Leaving the home straight a long, wide bend of approximately 800m swings all of the way to the 1100m. It is a straight run to the home turn approaching the 600m.

The 1200m start is from a chute that joins the back straight, giving a long run to the home bend.

Separate chutes for the 1400m and 1600m starting positions provide only a short run to the first turn.

The 2400m start is from a chute at the top of the home straight.

# LAUNCESTON

Jellicoe Road, Mowbray, Tasmania, Australia.
www.tasmanianturfclub.com

| FEATURE RACES | | | | | | |
|---|---|---|---|---|---|---|
| LAUNCESTON CUP | G3 | 2400M | TURF | 3YO+ | HCP | FEB |
| Tasmanian Guineas | L | 1600M | TURF | 3YO | SW | JAN |
| Gold Sovereign Stakes | L | 1200M | TURF | 2YO | SW | FEB |
| Tasmanian Oaks | L | 2100M | TURF | 3YOF | SW | FEB |
| Mowbray Stakes | L | 1600M | TURF | 3YO+ | WFA | FEB |
| Vamos Stakes | L | 1400M | TURF | 3YO+F&M | SW | FEB |
| Premium Stakes | L | 1200M | TURF | 3YO+ | WFA | JAN–FEB |
| Newmarket HCP | L | 1200M | TURF | 3YO+ | HCP | NOV |

Launceston is the second–most populated city in Tasmania, and is situated in the Tamar Valley of northern Tasmania, 45km south of Bass Strait and 163km north of the state's capital, Hobart.

Launceston is renowned for its great surrounding beauty with many heritage sites and the unspoilt environs of its wilderness areas and national parks making it an increasingly popular destination for tourists.

Formerly known as Mowbray racecourse, the track is only 3km from the heart of Launceston.

The Tasmanian summer racing carnival gets into full swing in January and February with many good prize-money races on the schedule and more than $3 million in stakes up for grabs.

The rich Launceston Cup in February is the highlight.

## THE TRACK

Left-handed. The track is an irregular rectangle in shape. It is 1830m in length with a run home of only 230m.

Out of the straight a wide bend takes runners to the 1500m for a straight run until just past the 1200m. It is a run of about 200m to the bend at the top of the course,

which straightens again around the 700m point for the run to the home turn.

Chutes for the 1600m and 2600m starts both provide a run of about 400m before the first bend.

The 1200m races start from a chute at the top of the course giving a run of 200m before turning.

Gate speed and a low draw are advantageous.

# AUSTRALIA
## AUSTRALIAN CAPITAL TERRITORY

# CANBERRA

Randwick Road, Lyneham, ACT, Australia .
www.thoroughbredpark.com.au

| FEATURE RACES | | | | | | |
|---|---|---|---|---|---|---|
| Black Opal Stakes | L | 1200M | TURF | 3YO | SWP | MAR |
| Canberra Cup | L | 2000M | TURF | 3YO+ | HCP | MAR |
| Canberra Guineas | L | 1400M | TURF | 3YO | SW | MAR |
| National Sprint | L | 1400M | TURF | 3YO+ | HCP | MAR |

After the federation of Australia in 1901, its two largest cities and fierce rivals Melbourne and Sydney both lay claim to being Australia's capital city. It was decided that the Australian capital and federal seat of power should be independent of both, and the site of Canberra – 280km south-west of Sydney and 660km north-east of Melbourne – was agreed upon as a compromise location, with the new capital city to be designed from scratch.

Thoroughbred Park is the venue for racing in the Australian Capital Territory. Located in the heart of Canberra, the track has been redeveloped in recent years to improve the course proper with wider bends and new irrigation and drainage systems installed. Major works have been carried out on the grandstand, now an excellent facility, and an inner synthetic Acton track has been added.

Canberra Cup Day in March is the highlight meeting, with Canberra's feature races all run on the day.

## THE TRACK

Right-handed. Oval-shaped track of 1815m in length. Home straight – 400m.

Out of the straight, runners are on a bend until the 1400m. It is a straight run to the 1000m then a long, wide bend takes runners to the home straight.

Separate chute starts for the 1000m and 1200m starts only provide a short run to the first bend.

The chute for the 1600m start gives runners a 600m straight run to the home turn.

The remodelling of the track has made it a fairer course, although outside draws can still sometimes be difficult, especially from the sprint starts.

The all-weather Acton track is 1620m in length. Home straight – 380m.

## FEATURE RACES

### BLACK OPAL STAKES

The Black Opal Stakes is Canberra's top 2yo race with notable winners including **BLAZING SADDLES (1977)**, who won the Blue Diamond Stakes; as did **PAINT (1996)**; **CLAN O'SULLIVAN (1992)** was the first locally trained horse to win; **ST COVET (1994)** won the ATC Sires' Produce Stakes and Caulfield Guineas (1994); and **CATBIRD (1999)** won the Golden Slipper.

### CANBERRA CUP

Prominent winners of the Canberra Cup include **FOXSEAL (1984)**, who won the Brisbane Cup (1985); **NICHOLAS JOHN (1982)** won the Metropolitan Hcp (1982); champion **SUPER IMPOSE (1992)**; **IRON HORSE (1998)** won the Epsom Hcp (1997); and **BLUTIGEROO (2008)** who won the Tancred Stakes (2007).

# FANNIE BAY

Dick Ward Drive, Fannie Bay, Northern Territory, Australia. www.darwinturfclub.org.au

### FEATURE RACES

| Darwin Cup | 2000M | AWT | OPEN | HCP | AUG |
|---|---|---|---|---|---|
| Palmerston Sprint | 1200M | AWT | OPEN | HCP | AUG |

Official racing in the blistering heat of the Northern Territory began in Darwin in 1955 with the establishment of the Darwin Turf Club. The Darwin Cup was first run the following year.

While the course at Fannie Bay does not host Group or Listed racing, the Darwin Cup is a celebrated race with excellent prize money and crowds of over 20,000 in attendance annually.

The Darwin Cup Carnival currently comprises eight days of racing held over five weeks, culminating with the Cup, held on the first Monday in August.

Punters from all over Australia make the pilgrimage to the Northern Territory's biggest party. With Darwin's soaring temperatures and humidity, hydration is the key and the majority of patrons are ready and willing to take up the challenge.

Many activities are organised to keep the influx of tourists amused and the annual Darwin Cup Ball is the city's premier social event.

## THE TRACK

Left-handed. The course is an irregular oval shape and has a circumference of 1725m. Home straight – 375m.

Officially an all-weather track, the surface is actually a mixture of sand and sump oil.

With the tight nature of the track and horses (and riders) back in the field sometimes resenting the kickback, on pace is generally the place to be.

# ELLERSLIE

80 Ascot Avenue, Remuera, New Zealand. www.ellerslie.co.nz

*N*ew Zealand has long established itself as one of the world's great racing and breeding centres, having produced many champion horses who have gone on to success, not only here and in Australia but also around the world. The same can be said of its highly respected horsemen and women who have constantly matched it with the world's best.

The city of Auckland in the North Island of New Zealand is the largest city in the country and home to its premier racing venue, Ellerslie. Racing has been conducted in this beautiful setting since 1942, and became an annual fixture in 1949.

There are currently seven races staged at the elite level. The main events are all run during the summer and autumn, including the New Zealand Derby and the historic Auckland Cup, which was first run in 1874 and is considered the premier staying contest in New Zealand.

Ellerslie also stages the two major jumps events in New Zealand – the Great Northern Steeplechase and the Great Northern Hurdles. The Great Northern Steeplechase is run over the gruelling distance of 6400m, which makes it the longest race in Australasia. The eastern side of the steeplechase course features a very testing run up Ellerslie Hill, which competitors must climb three times during the Great Northern. There are 25 fences to negotiate.

## THE TRACK

Right-handed. Egg-shaped oval with a circumference of 1845. Home straight of 380m.

Out of the straight a right-hand bend takes runners to the 1500m. It is a run of 400m to the sweeping 700m home bend.

The 1600m start is from a chute that joins the back straight giving a 500m run to the bend.

The 2400m races begin from a chute at the top of the home straight.

The 1200m start on the course proper gives only a short run of 100m to the home bend.

## FEATURE RACES

### AUCKLAND CUP

**ARIEL (1876, 78, 79)** and **NELSON (1885–87)** both scored hat-tricks.

Dual winners include **BLUE JACKET (1899, 1900)**, **ALL RED (1908, 09)**, **CUDDLE (1935, 36)**, **CHEVAL DE VOLEE (1938, 39)**, **IL TEMPO (1969, 70)** and **PRIZE LADY (2006, 07)**.

Other notables include **BEAU VITE (1940)**, who was a dual Cox Plate winner (1940, 41); **KINDERGARTEN (1942)** won the New Zealand Derby, Wellington Cup (1941) and twice won the Easter Hcp (1941, 42); **YEMAN (1958)** also won the Cox Plate (1958); **APOLLO ELEVEN (1973)** won the Tancred Stakes, Sydney Cup, ATC Queen Elizabeth Stakes (1973) and was a dual winner of the Chipping Norton Stakes (1973, 75).

**BLUE DENIM (1980)** was second in the Melbourne Cup (1980) and won the Tancred Stakes, ATC Queen Elizabeth Stakes (1981); **CASTLETOWN (1992)** won the New Zealand Derby, (1989), Caulfield Stakes (1992) and three Wellington Cups (1991, 92, 94); **MILTAK (1994)** won the New Zealand Oaks (1993), Tancred Stakes (1994); and **JEZABEEL (1998)** won the Melbourne Cup that year.

### NEW ZEALAND DERBY

The race was combined with the Great Northern Derby in 1973.

Winners since include **FURY'S ORDER (1973)**, who won the Cox Plate (1975); **BALMERINO (1975)** won 22 of 46 starts including the New Zealand 2000 Guineas (1975), Ranvet Stakes, Brisbane Cup (1976), New Zealand Stakes, Ormond Memorial (1977) and ran second to Alleged in the Arc.

**BONECRUSHER (1985)** won 18 of 44 including the ATC Australian Derby, Caulfield Stakes, Tancred Stakes, Underwood Stakes, Cox Plate (1986), Australian Cup

| FEATURE RACES | | | | | | | |
|---|---|---|---|---|---|---|---|
| ZABEEL CLASSIC | G1 | 2000M | TURF | OPEN | WFA | 1985 | DEC |
| RAILWAY STAKES | G1 | 1200M | TURF | 3YO+ | SWP | 1890 | JAN |
| NEW ZEALAND DERBY | G1 | 2400M | TURF | 3YO | SW | 1860 | MAR |
| AUCKLAND CUP | G1 | 3200M | TURF | 3YO+ | HCP | 1874 | MAR |
| ELLERSLIE SIRES' PRODUCE | G1 | 1200M | TURF | 2YO | SW | 1964 | MAR |
| NEW ZEALAND STAKES | G1 | 2000M | TURF | 3YO+ | WFA | 1975 | MAR |
| EASTER HANDICAP | G1 | 1600M | TURF | 3YO+ | HCP | 1874 | APR |

(1997) and twice won the New Zealand Stakes (1986, 88).

**SURFERS PARADISE (1990)** won the New Zealand 2000 Guineas (1990), Rosehill Guineas, New Zealand Stakes, Cox Plate (1991); **THE PHANTOM CHANCE (1992)** also won the Cox Plate (1993); **XCELLENT (2004)** won the Mudgway Stakes, Ormond Memorial, New Zealand Stakes (2005); **JIMMY CHOUX (2011)** won the New Zealand 2000 Guineas (2010), Rosehill Guineas, Horlicks Plate and Ormond Memorial (2011).

## NEW ZEALAND STAKES

Inaugurated in 1975, dual winners include **McGINTY (1983, 84)**, who also won the Canterbury Guineas, Caulfield Stakes, Thorndon Mile (1983), Ranvet Stakes (1984); **BONECRUSHER (1986, 88)**; and **SOLVIT (1993, 94)**.

Other notables include **BALMERINO (1977)**; **LA MER (1979)**; **TIDAL LIGHT (1987)** also won the New Zealand Derby (1986), Canterbury Guineas (1987); **RIVERINA CHARM (1990)** won the MRC Thousand Guineas (1988), Rosehill Guineas, Canterbury Guineas (1989); **SURFERS PARADISE (1991)**; **TALL POPPY (2001)**; **XCELLENT (2005)**; **SIR SLICK (2008)**; and **OCEAN PARK (2013)**.

## RAILWAY STAKES

**MR TIZ (1989–91)** won three in succession; and dual winners include **HUNTING CRY (1929, 30), GAY**

**BLONDE (1934, 36)**, **BRONWEN (1939, 40)**, **RIZZIO (1948, 49)** and **YAHABEEBE (1957, 58)**.

Other prominent winners include **LOYALTY (1893)**; **RENOWN (1900)**; **BLUE BLOOD (1974)**; **SHIFNAL CHIEF (1975)**; **TUDOR LIGHT (1977)**; **ARBRE CHENE (1980)**; and **GOLD HOPE (1981)**, who also won the Doncaster Hcp and All Aged Stakes (1982).

## EASTER HANDICAP

**SLEEPY FOX (1944–47)** won it four times in succession; and dual winners include **YATAPA (1879, 80)**; **IMPULSE (1889, 91)**; **REX (1898, 99)**; **REREMOANA (1925, 26)**; **KINDERGARTEN (1941, 42)**; **WAIPARI (1960, 61)**; and **VEYRON (2011, 12)**.

Other notables include superior weight carrier **ADVANCE (1900)**, **ABORIGINE (1909)**, **HUNTING CRY (1931)**, **KIWI CAN (1975)**, **TUDOR LIGHT (1976)**, **GREY WAY (1977)** and **SHIVAREE (1981)**.

## ZABEEL CLASSIC

ZABEEL had 19 starts for 7 wins with a Group 1 victory in the 1990 Australian Guineas. His impact off the track was remarkable as a sire of more than 100 stakes winners including Melbourne Cup victors Efficient and Jezabeel, Caulfield Cup winners Sky Heights and Railings, Cox Plate winners Octagonal and Savabeel, and Might And Power, who won all three of those

races. Zabeel also sired Hong Kong star Vengeance Of Rain.

Dual winners of the race include Japan Cup winner **HORLICKS (1988, 90)** and **STAR DANCER (1995, 96)**.

Other notables include **WAVERLEY STAR (1986)**; **GIOVANA (2002)**; **LASHED (2004)**; **SHEZ SINSATIONAL (2011)** also won the WAIRC International Stakes, Ormond Memorial, Auckland Cup (2012); and **VEYRON (2012)**.

## ELLERSLIE SIRES' PRODUCE STAKES

Established in 1964, the race is currently run as the Ford Diamond Stakes. Notable winners include **RAJAH SAHIB (1968)**, who won the Caulfield Guineas, Cox Plate (1968), Stradbroke Hcp, Doncaster Hcp (1971); **DARYL'S JOY (1969)**; **LONGFELLA (1972)** won the Rosehill Guineas, Manawatu Sires' Produce (1972), CF Orr Stakes (1973); **VICE REGAL (1976)**; **VITE CHEVAL (1983)** won the Doncaster Hcp, Manikato Stakes (1984), MRC Futurity Stakes, All Aged Stakes (1985); **SPYGLASS (1987)** won the Auckland Cup (1989); **BALLROOM BABE (1995)**; and **MAROOFITY (2003)**.

# TRENTHAM

10 Racecourse Road, Trentham, Upper Hutt, New Zealand. www.trentham.co.nz

## FEATURE RACES

| | | | | | | | |
|---|---|---|---|---|---|---|---|
| NZ OAKS | G1 | 2400M | TURF | 3YOF | SW | 1969 | MAR |
| TELEGRAPH HCP | G1 | 1200M | TURF | 3YO+ | HCP | 1891 | MAR |
| CAPTAIN COOK STAKES | G1 | 1600M | TURF | 3YO+ | WFA | 1973 | DEC |
| THORNDON MILE | G1 | 1600M | TURF | 3YO+ | HCP | 1932 | JAN |
| WELLINGTON GUINEAS | G2 | 1500M | TURF | 3YO+ | SW | 1940 | OCT |
| WELLLINGTON CUP | G2 | 2400M | TURF | 3YO+ | HCP | 1874 | OCT |
| WAKEFIELD CHALLENGE STAKES | G2 | 1200M | TURF | 2YO | SW | 1962 | JAN |

_L_ocated on the south-west tip of the North Island, Wellington is the capital city of New Zealand. The first official meeting in the area dates back to 1840, and the Wellington Jockey Club was formed a year later on the anniversary of the inaugural fixture. Racing is now conducted under the auspices of the Wellington Racing Club.

Many venues were used for racing in and around Wellington until 1906 when the course was permanently established at the current site at Trentham, just 38km from Wellington International Airport.

Trentham is host to some of New Zealand's great races including the Wellington Cup meeting in January, which is the most popular annual fixture with the Thorndon Mile also on the card. The New Zealand Oaks is also run at the course.

New Zealand-bred Phar Lap was based here briefly en route to the USA in 1931, and large crowds flocked to the course every day in the early hours to catch a glimpse of the legendary horse on the training track as he prepared for his overseas assault.

## THE TRACK

Left-handed. The track is a slightly irregular oval shape with a circumference of just under 2000m. The home straight is 450m.

Out of the straight runners are on a bend to the 1600m. It is then a straight run to the home bend at the 1000m. A spur joins the home straight, which provides the starts for races up to 1200m.

## FEATURE RACES

### NEW ZEALAND OAKS

First won by **MAYO GOLD (1969)**, other prominent winners include **LA MER (1977)**, **TANG (1979)**, **MILTAK (1993)**, **SNAP (1994)**, **TYCOON LIL (1998)** and **PRINCESS COUP (2007)**.

### CAPTAIN COOK STAKES

One of New Zealand's premier races and has been won by many great horses including **GLENGOWAN (1973)** and **MICKEY'S TOWN (1991)**.

**ROUGH HABIT (1992)** was a winner of 29 races, including eleven Group 1s. His victories included the Queensland Derby (1990), ATC Queen Elizabeth Stakes (1992), Caulfield Stakes (1994), two Stradbroke Hcps (1991, 92) and three Doomben Cups (1991–93); **TIT FOR TAAT (2002)** won the New Zealand 2000 Guineas, Levin Classic (2000), Waikato Sprint, Telegraph Hcp (2003).

**MUFHASA (2011)** won the Waikato Sprint (2009), Otaki-Maori (2010), Toorak Hcp, Futurity Stakes, Challenge Stakes (2011), Windsor Park Plate (2012) and is a dual winner of the Telegraph Hcp (2009, 11).

### THORNDON MILE

Notable winners include **MCGINTY (1983)**, who won the Canterbury Guineas, Caulfield Stakes (1983), Ranvet Stakes (1984) and two New Zealand Stakes (1983, 84); **TALL POPPY (2001)**; **GIOVANA (2002)**; **MAROOFITY (2005)**; **SIR SLICK (2009)**; and dual winner **HAUGHTY WINNER (1938, 40)**.

# RICCARTON PARK

165 Racecourse Road, Sockburn, New Zealand. www.riccartonpark.co.nz

Katie Lee

*H*istoric Riccarton Park is located just west of the Christchurch CBD and has been in operation since 1855. Modern amenities complement the typically beautiful New Zealand setting, which offers spectacular views over the Canterbury Plains towards the Southern Alps.

Canterbury Racing is one of the most respected racing organisations in New Zealand and makes its base here at Riccarton. Riccarton Park is also one of the major training facilities on the South Island.

New Zealand Cup Week in November is one of the country's premier race meetings with not only the running of the Cup, but also two of New Zealand's top races for 3yos – the 1000 Guineas and the 2000 Guineas.

The Riccarton Racecourse Hotel is not only a great venue to refresh but also a place of unusual interest. It is said to be haunted by the ghost of its former publican, Donald Fraser, who was murdered there in 1933.

## THE TRACK

Left-handed. The course is a slightly irregular oval shape of approximately 2400m in length. Home straight of 450m.

Out of the home straight, runners are on a bend until just past the 1800m. It is a straight run of 150m before the track doglegs left giving a straight run of 400m to the wide home bend at the 1100m. Out of the home bend at the 600m point, the track straightens for 150m before a slight dogleg into the home straight proper.

Sprint races of up to 1200m start from an angled chute that joins the bottom of the home bend. It is a straight run of 500m from the 1200m start.

The New Zealand Cup start at the 3200m also begins from this chute, giving a run of about 100m before the bend.

## FEATURE RACES

### NEW ZEALAND 2000 GUINEAS

Held at Riccarton Park since 1973 when won by **FURY'S ORDER (1973)**, who also took out the New Zealand Derby (1973) and Cox Plate (1975).

Other notables include **BALMERINO (1975)**; **VICE REGAL (1976)**; **UNCLE REMUS (1977)**; **LITTLE BROWN JUG (1979)**; **SURFERS PARADISE (1990)**; **VEANDERCROSS (1991)**; **HERO (1996)**; **TIT FOR TAAT (2000)**; **KING'S CHAPEL (2003)** won the Telegraph Hcp, Otaki-Maori (2004); **DARCI BRAHMA (2005)** won the QTC TJ Smith Classic (2005), Otaki-Maori (2006), Telegraph Hcp, Waikato Sprint (2007); and **JIMMY CHOUX (2010)**.

### NEW ZEALAND 1000 GUINEAS

Also run at Riccarton since 1973, prominent winners include **OUR FLIGHT (1982)**, who also won the New Zealand Derby and Levin Classic that year; **CANTERBURY BELLE (1984)** took out the Stradbroke Hcp (1985); **SNAP (1993)**; **TYCOON LIL (1997)**; **SEACHANGE (2005)**; **DAFFODIL (2008)**; and **KATIE LEE (2009)** brought up the 1000 Guineas–2000 Guineas double.

# HASTINGS

300 Prospect Road, Hastings, Hawke's Bay, New Zealand. www.hawkesbayracing.co.nz

●Starcraft

*The city of Hastings lies 20km inland from the port city of Napier on the east coast of the North Island. Operated by the Hawke's Bay Racing Club, the course at Hastings has a proud history with racing conducted in this lovely park location since 1866.*

The standard here is excellent with three Group 1 races currently staged during the very popular spring carnival throughout September and October. The track becomes the social hub of the area during this time and the locals attend in force with many availing themselves of the marquees that line the home straight.

The Ormond Spring Classic – formerly known as the Kelt Capital – is regarded as one of the premier weight-for-age contests in New Zealand. While prize money levels for the race have not been sustained in recent years, it is still a race known for its quality.

Other calendar highlights include the New Year's Day fixture, which is pitched toward families and always attracts strong numbers, as well as Cup day in April.

Hawke's Bay is one of the premier wine regions in New Zealand with many a famous drop produced locally.

## THE TRACK

Left-handed. The course is a rectangular oval of 1600m in circumference. Home straight of 375m.

Out of the straight, runners are on a bend until the 1100m mark, then it is a run of 400m to the home bend.

The bends into and out of the run home straighten for 100m at the mid point.

The 1200m start is from a chute that joins the back straight.

The 1400m chute provides only a very short run before linking up with the turn out of the straight, and a 2000m chute is located at the top of the home straight.

## FEATURE RACES

### KIT ORMOND MEMORIAL SPRING CLASSIC

Registered as the Ormond Memorial Stakes, the race was sponsored up until recently and known as the Kelt Capital Stakes.

Established in 1920 the race was run until 1930 and then revived in 1955. It has been won by many of New Zealand's great names.

**GAME (1969–71)** won the race three times, as did **PICAROON (1960, 61, 63)**.

Dual winners include all-time great **GLOAMING (1922, 25)**, who had 67 starts for 57 wins and nine seconds. He won 19 consecutive races and was successful in the New Zealand Derby, New Zealand 2000 Guineas (1918), ATC Australian Derby (1919) and Mackinnon Stakes (1924).

Other dual winners include **DUTY FREE (1973, 76)**; **LA MER (1978, 79)**; **COMMISSIONAIRE (1983, 84)**; **MR LOMONDY (1986, 89)**; and **PRINCESS COUP (2007, 08)**.

Champion **REDCRAZE (1955)** was a winner of 32 races including the Turnbull Stakes (1955), Metropolitan Hcp, Caulfield Stakes, Caulfield Cup (1956), Ranvet Stakes, Cox Plate (1957); **SYNTAX (1956)** won 19 of 34 starts including the New Zealand 2000 Guineas (1955), New Zealand Derby (1956), Memsie Stakes, Turnbull Stakes Underwood Stakes (1957); **BALMERINO (1977)**; **CASTLETOWN (1991)**; **VEANDERCROSS (1992)**; **CALM HARBOUR (1993)**; **SOLVIT (1994)**; **XCELLENT (2005)**; and **JIMMY CHOUX (2011)**.

### HORLICKS PLATE

Champion mare Horlicks was a six-time winner at Group 1 level and in 1989 became the first and

currently only New Zealand horse to win the Japan Cup.

Formerly run as the Stoney Bridge Stakes, the race is currently known as the Windsor Park Plate.

Dual winners include **HELLO DOLLY (2001, 02)** and **SEACHANGE (2006, 07)**.

Notable winners include **GREY WAY (1976)**, who won 51 races from 164 starts including the Easter Hcp, Thorndon Mile (1977); **VICE REGAL (1979)** won the New Zealand 2000 Guineas, Diamond Stakes (1976), JJ Liston Stakes (1977), Manikato Stakes (1978), Ormond Memorial (1979); **STARCRAFT (2004)**; **PRINCESS COUP (2008)**; **DAFFODIL (2009)**; **JIMMY CHOUX (2011)**; and **MUFHASA (2012)**.

### HAWKE'S BAY CHALLENGE STAKES

First run in 1991, the race was known until recently as the Mudgway Stakes.

**SEACHANGE (2006, 07)** won it twice.

Other notables include **ROUGH HABIT (1991)**; **SURFERS PARADISE (1992)**; **CALM HARBOUR (1993)**; **SNAP (1994)** won the New Zealand 1000 Guineas, Manawatu Sires' Produce, (1993), New Zealand Oaks (1994), Waikato Sprint (1995); **VIALLI (1996)**.

Outstanding mare **SUNLINE (2002)** is one of New Zealand's greatest ever. Winner of 32 of 48 career starts, including 13 victories at the elite level. She won the Flight Stakes (1988), Manikato Stakes, Hong Kong Mile (2000) and was dual winner of the Doncaster Hcp (1999, 2002), Cox Plate (1999, 2000), Coolmore Classic (2000, 02), All Aged Stakes (2000, 02) and the Waikato Sprint (2001, 02).

She was four times New Zealand Horse of the Year (1999–2002) and thee times Australian Horse of the Year (2000–02). Sunline was undefeated in 10 starts in New Zealand.

**STARCRAFT (2004)**; **XCELLENT (2005)**; **MUFHASA (2011)**; and **OCEAN PARK (2012)** also won the Underwood Stakes, Caulfield Stakes, Cox Plate (2012) and New Zealand Stakes (2013).

# TE RAPA

Te Rapa Road, Hamilton, New Zealand. www.teraparacing.co.nz

Sunline holds off Fairy King Prawn in the Hong Kong Mile

Other notable winners include **COPPER BELT (1978)**; **MARCH LEGEND (1979)**; **POETIC PRINCE (1989)** won the Cox Plate (1988), ATC Queen Elizabeth Stakes, Tancred Stakes (1989); **MR TIZ (1991)** was three-time winner of the Railway Stakes (1989–91), dual winner of the Telegraph Hcp (1989, 90) and won The Galaxy (1991); **VEANDERCROSS (1993)**; **SNAP (1995)**; **ALLEGRO (1996)**; **TIT FOR TAAT (2003)**; **DARCI BRAHMA (2007)**; and **SEACHANGE (2008)**.

## INTERNATIONAL STAKES

**COMMISSIONAIRE (1983–85)** posted a hat-trick of wins.

Other notable winners include **SAILING HOME (1972)**, ridden to victory by Lester Piggott; **BATTLE HEIGHTS (1974)**; **OOPIK (1976)** won the Sydney Cup (1976).

**LA MER (1978)** won 24 of her 43 career starts including the Manawatu Sires' Produce (1976), New Zealand Oaks (1977), Ormond Memorial Stakes twice (1978, 79) and the New Zealand Stakes (1979); **SHIVAREE (1979)** won the Tancred Stakes, ATC Queen Elizabeth Stakes (1979), Easter Hcp (1981); **BONECRUSHER (1986)**; **THE PHANTOM CHANCE (1993)** won the New Zealand Derby (1992), Cox Plate (1993); **THE PHANTOM (1994)** won the Underwood Stakes (1990), Mackinnon Stakes (1993); **SIR SLICK (2007)**; **SHEZ SINSATIONAL (2012)**; and **SANGSTER (2013)** won the Victoria Derby (2011) and Auckland Cup (2013).

Te Rapa lies to the north-west of Hamilton on the North Island of New Zealand.

It is one of New Zealand's more prominent venues with racing mostly conducted by the Waikato Racing Club, which stages the major races.

The Cambridge Jockey Club races here three times a year and the Taumaranui Club also stage their annual meeting at the course in July.

Highlight fixture is International Day in September, which features both of the Group 1 races run at the course plus the Sir Tristram Fillies Classic (Group 2).

Te Rapa is also one of the main jumps venues in the country with the premier jumps days held in May and National Jumps Day scheduled for the end of September, which is the culmination of the New Zealand jumping season.

A recent innovation is the Cheltenham Dream Series for jumpers. It is a points-based competition for jumps horses that takes in a number of races across the nation. Up for grabs is the opportunity of assisted passage and entry to feature races at the Cheltenham Gold Cup festival in the UK.

Waikato Cup day remains one of the most popular with the locals.

## THE TRACK

Left-handed. Classic oval of 1788m in length. Home straight – 425m.

The 1600m start is from a chute that joins the back straight.

A chute from the top of the home straight provides the starting point for the 2400m races.

## FEATURE RACES

### WAIKATO SPRINT

Inaugurated in 1974, dual winners include **COURIER BAY (1987, 88)**, **SUNLINE (2001, 02)**, **SEDECREM (2004, 05)** and **MUFHASA (2009, 11)**.

# OTAKI

Te Roto Road, Otaki, New Zealand. www.otakimaoriracing.co.nz

Kings Chapel

## FEATURE RACES

| OTAKI-MAORI WFA STAKES | G1 | 1600M | TURF | 3YO+ | FEB |
|---|---|---|---|---|---|
| LEVIN TURF CLASSIC | G1 | 1600M | TURF | 3YO | NOV–DEC |

## FEATURE RACES

### OTAKI-MAORI WFA STAKES

Dual winners include **POETIC PRINCE (1988, 89)** and **JAVELIN (1992, 93)**.

The race has also been won by **WESTMINSTER (1990)**, who won the Cantala Stakes (1988), Manikato Stakes (1989); **ROUGH HABIT (1991)**; **ALLEGRO (1995)**; **HERO (1999)**; **KING'S CHAPEL (2004)**; **DARCI BRAHMA (2006)**; **SIR SLICK (2007)**; and **MUFHASA (2010)**.

### LEVIN TURF CLASSIC

Notable winners include **OUR FLIGHT (1982)**; **BURLETTA (1983)**; **BONECRUSHER (1985)**; **VEANDERCROSS (1991)**; **O'REILLY (1996)**; **TIT FOR TAAT (2000)**; **RUSSIAN PEARL (2003)** won the Hong Kong Stewards Cup (2006); and **WAHID (2005)** won the New Zealand Derby (2006).

*T*he town of Otaki is located in the central lower North Island, 70km north of Wellington in the Kapiti Coast region.

The Otaki-Maori Racing Club conducts its meetings here and is the only remaining indigenous racing club in New Zealand, having been in existence since 1886. The club held its first official meeting the following year, although racing in the area can be traced back to the 1840s.

In these times the European population in the area was very sparse and the crowds and competitors were almost exclusively of Maori origin.

Throughout its history Otaki has been a very well-patronised course with the facilities often struggling to accommodate the large crowds.

Significant improvements were made to public amenities during the 1970s and a new grandstand completed in 1990.

The Levin Racing Club also stages its meetings at Otaki and both clubs stage a Group 1 event annually.

## THE TRACK

Left-handed. Pear-shaped oval of approximately 1600m. Home straight – 350m.

Out of the straight, runners are on a bend until the 1200m. Straight run of almost 400m to the home bend.

Chute start from the 1400m joins the back straight giving a run of nearly 600m to the home turn.

The 1600m chute only provides only a short run before linking up with the bend out of the home straight.

# AWAPUNI

Awapuni Racecourse Road, Awapuni, New Zealand.
www.awapuniracing.co.nz

## FEATURE RACES

| | | | | | |
|---|---|---|---|---|---|
| MANAWATU SIRES' PRODUCE STAKES | G1 | 1400M | TURF | 2YO | MAR–APR |
| AWAPUNI GOLD CUP | G2 | 2000M | TURF | 3YO+ | MAR–APR |
| MANAWATU CLASSIC | G3 | 2000M | TURF | 3YO | MAR–APR |
| MARTON METRIC MILE | G3 | 1600M | TURF | 3YO+ | SEPT |
| EULOGY STAKES | G3 | 1600M | TURF | 3YOF | DEC |
| MANAWATU CUP | G3 | 2300M | TURF | 3YO+ | DEC |
| MANAWATU CHALLENGE STAKES | G3 | 1400M | TURF | 3YO+ | DEC |

**Awapuni is a rural township in Palmerston North's central region, on the North Island.**

The course is situated to the west of the town and this beautiful park location is the venue for many local racing clubs including the Marton Jockey Club, Rangitikei Racing Club, Fielding Jockey Club and most prominently, the Manawatu Racing Club, which stages the premier meeting on the Awapuni calendar and has a history dating back to 1880.

The Manawatu Sires' Produce Stakes in late March or early April is New Zealand's richest Group 1 race for 2yos.

The course has undergone major redevelopments in recent times and remains very popular with large crowds in attendance for the feature days, in particular the Sires' Produce fixture and the festive December meeting staged just days before Christmas.

## THE TRACK

Left-handed. Oval-shaped track of 1800m in circumference. Home straight – 400m.

Out of the straight, runners are on a bend until the 1300m, then it is a straight run of 500m to the home bend.

The 1600m start is from a chute joining the back straight allowing a run of 800m before the turn.

A chute for the 2600m starting position gives only a very short run before linking up with the home bend.

## FEATURE RACE

Established in 1908, notable winners include **DESERT GOLD (1915)**, who won 36 of 59 starts and famously set an Australasian record of 19 consecutive wins, equalled shortly after by Gloaming but unsurpassed until 2012 by Black Caviar. Desert Gold also won the New Zealand Derby, New Zealand 1000 Guineas, New Zealand 2000 Guineas (1915), All Aged Stakes (1918) and the Awapuni Gold Cup three times in succession (1916–18).

**EASTLAND (1917)** won the New Zealand 2000 Guineas (1917), New Zealand Derby (1918); **LIMERICK (1926)** was a winner of more than 20 stakes races including the Chipping Norton Stakes, All Aged Stakes (1928), and was dual winner of the Ranvet Stakes (1927, 28) and ATC Queen Elizabeth Stakes (1927, 28); **GAY BALLERINA (1930)** won the ATC Australian Oaks (1930); **GOLDEN HAIR (1933)** won the VRC Oaks (1933); **DEFAULTER (1938)** won the New Zealand 2000 Guineas (1938), ATC Queen Elizabeth Stakes, Chipping Norton Stakes, Wellington Cup, New Zealand Derby (1939); **PASSIVE (1956)** won the New Zealand 1000 Guineas, New Zealand 2000 Guineas (1956), New Zealand Derby (1957); **MAYO GOLD (1968)** won the New Zealand Oaks (1969) Railway Stakes (1970); **DARYL'S JOY (1969)**; **LA MER (1976)**; **SNAP (1993)**; **BALLROOM BABE (1995)**; **HAPPYANUNOIT (1998)**; **MAROOFITY (2003)**; and **KEENINSKY (2004)**.

# TE AROHA

Racecourse Road, Te Aroha, New Zealand.
http://racingtearoha.trac.co.nz

## FEATURE RACE

| | | | | |
|---|---|---|---|---|
| NZ THOROUGHBRED BREEDERS' STAKES | G1 | 1600M | TURF | 3YO+F&M | APR |

**The rural town of Te Aroha is situated in the Waikato region, 53km north-east of Hamilton on the North Island.**

The Te Aroha course is noted for its picturesque outlook, which takes in towering palm trees and the stunning backdrop of Mount Te Aroha. The locals pride themselves on providing great racing with good old-fashioned country hospitality.

The racing surface at Te Aroha is one of the best in the land and the track itself is considered a very fair test with the home straight one of the longest in New Zealand.

The New Zealand Thoroughbred Breeders' Stakes in April is one of the richest races for fillies and mares in the nation and undoubtedly the highlight on the calendar here.

In 1999 the Te Aroha Jockey Club voted to join the TRAC group, which oversees the running of a number of courses in the region. The Te Aroha Jockey Club now conducts its meetings under the banner of Racing Te Aroha.

## THE TRACK

Right-handed. Oval track with a circumference of approximately 1900m. Home straight of 500m.

Out of the straight, runners are on a bend to the 1400m. It is then a straight run of 450m to the home turn.

The 1600m start is from a back straight chute providing a run of 600m until the home bend.

The 1200m chute gives a run of 300m to the turn.

## FEATURE RACE

One of the premier weight-for-age contests in New Zealand for fillies and mares.

Multiple winners include three-time winner **ORCHIDRA (1978, 79, 81)** and dual winners **TUDOR LIGHT (1976, 77)**, **WAIKIKI (1990, 91)**, **AIMEE JAY (1998, 99)** and **SAINT CECILE (2001, 02)**.

Tall Poppy

Other notables include **SWELL TIME (1973)**, who won the Caulfield Cup (1973); **GOLD HOPE (1981)** won the Railway Stakes (1981), Doncaster Hcp, All Aged Stakes (1982); **TALL POPPY (1999)** won the Waikato Sprint (2000), Thorndon Mile and New Zealand Stakes (2001).

# AVONDALE

90 Ash Street, Avondale, New Zealand.
www.ajc.co.nz

## FEATURE RACES

| AVONDALE CUP | G2 | 2400M | TURF | 3YO+ | FEB |
|---|---|---|---|---|---|
| AVONDALE GUINEAS | G2 | 2100M | TURF | 3YO | FEB |

Avondale is a suburb of Auckland and racing in the area can be traced back to 1864.

The Avondale Jockey Club was formed in 1889, with the first meeting staged the next year. At this time Avondale was a rural area on the outskirts of Auckland and the establishment of the racecourse instigated the development of the town, with many businesses opening in and around the track to cater for the expected influx of visitors.

The feature Avondale Cup was inaugurated the same year as the opening of the track in 1890 and has been won by many good horses. Most famous of those is Even Stevens, who won the race in 1961 before going on to claim the Caulfield Cup–Melbourne Cup double the following year.

The Avondale Guineas is a 3yo race of good quality with many well-performing horses proceeding towards the New Zealand Derby.

Extensive works to resurface the track and install improved drainage systems have been undertaken in recent times. Racing resumed in 2012 after a three-year closure, which allowed the new racing surface to consolidate.

Entry to the course on race days is free of charge.

## THE TRACK

Right-handed. Oval-shaped course with a circumference of 1800m. Home straight – 400m.

Out of the straight, runners are on a bend until just past the 1400m. It is a straight run of 400m to the home bend.

The chute start at the 1600m allows a straight run of 650m to the home bend.

# PUKEKOHE PARK

242-250 Manukau Road, Pukekohe, New Zealand.
www.countiesracing.co.nz

## FEATURE RACES

| AUCKLAND THOROUGHBRED | G2 | 1400M | TURF | 3YO+F&M | NOV |
|---|---|---|---|---|---|
| COUNTIES CUP | G2 | 2100M | TURF | 3YO+ | NOV |

Pukekohe is located on the southern outskirts of Auckland between Manukau Harbour and the Waikato River.

Constructed on 39ha of pastoral land, the course staged the first meeting in New Zealand with an operational tote in 1924.

Initially established by the Franklin Racing Club, the course is currently run under the auspices of the Counties Racing Club.

In 1962, the track joined forces with the New Zealand International Grand Prix Organisation to also stage motor racing events.

Pukekohe is also a major training venue and home base of the jockey school for apprentice riders.

## THE TRACK

Right-handed. Classic oval of 1800m in circumference. Home straight – 475m.

A 1600m chute joins the back straight.

# MATAMATA

7555 State Highway 27, RD3, Matamata, New Zealand. www.matamataracingclub.co.nz

## FEATURE RACE

| MATAMATA BREEDERS' STAKES | G2 | 1200M | 2YOF | 1970 | FEB |
|---|---|---|---|---|---|

The eastern Waikato township of Matamata is one of New Zealand's major training and breeding centres.

Set against the stunning rural backdrop of the Kaimai Ranges, Matamata is home to many of New Zealand's top trainers. The course contains ten separate training tracks to accommodate the 700 horses that are based there.

The area has also become a popular tourist attraction as one of the main filming locations for Peter Jackson's *Lord of the Rings*.

The course is located only 2km south of the town. The main races are staged in February, including the Matamata Breeders' Stakes, which is currently one of the richest races for 2yo fillies in New Zealand.

The Matamata Cup is held annually in October.

## THE TRACK

Left-handed. Classic oval with a circumference of about 1700m. Home straight – 350m.

The turn out of the home straight takes runners to the 1400m. It is a run of 500m to the home bend.

Back straight chute for the 1600m start.

The 2030m start is from a chute at the top of the home straight.

# TAURANGA

1381 Cameron Road, Greerton, New Zealand.
racingtauranga.trac.co.nz

## FEATURE RACES

| JAPAN–NEW ZEALAND INTERNATIONAL TROPHY | G2 | 1600M | TURF | 3YO+ | MAR |
|---|---|---|---|---|---|
| THAMES VALLEY STAKES | G3 | 1600M | TURF | 3YO+ | NOV |

The port city of Tauranga on the North Island is the largest in the Bay of Plenty region and one of the fastest growing in New Zealand.

The racecourse is located on the southern outskirts of Tauranga.

The prime fixture on the calendar here is in March and features the Japan–New Zealand International Trophy run at Group 2 level.

The course is operated in partnership with TRAC Incorporated, which provides assistance to a number of clubs with business and sponsorship management and planning and marketing of race days.

## THE TRACK

Right-handed. The track has a circumference of approximately 1800m. Home straight – 350m.

Out of the straight, runners are on a bend until the 1400m before a run of 425m to the home bend.

Chute start for the 1600m gives a run of more than 600m to the home turn.

## PUKEKURA RACEWAY

Roagan Street, New Plymouth, New Zealand.
www.taranakiracing.co.nz

| FEATURE RACES | | | | | |
|---|---|---|---|---|---|
| TARANAKI CUP | G3 | 1800M | TURF | 3YO+ | FEB |
| TARANAKI 2YO CLASSIC | G3 | 1200M | TURF | 2YO | FEB |

New Plymouth on the west coast of the North Island is the main city in the Taranaki region.

The Pukekura course is located in the heart of the CBD and features stunning views, with both ocean and mountain aspects.

Taranaki Thoroughbred Racing Incorporated conducts its meetings here and the premier day is in mid February, with the two major races staged at this fixture.

## THE TRACK

Left-handed. A 1600m oval-shaped course. Home straight – 375m.

Out of the straight, runners are on a bend to the 1200m. It is then a straight run of 350m to the wide home bend.

The 1400m races start from a chute that joins the back straight.

The 1600m start is from a spur that links up with the top of the bend out of the home straight.

The 2000m races start from a chute at the top of the home straight.

## ARAWA PARK

Fenton Street, Rotorua, New Zealand.
www.progroupracing.com.au/new-zealand-race courses/arawa-park-racecourse

| FEATURE RACE | | | | | |
|---|---|---|---|---|---|
| ROTORUA CUP | G3 | 2200M | TURF | 3YO+ | MAY |

The city of Rotorua is situated in the Bay of Plenty area of the North Island of New Zealand, on the southern shores of Lake Rotorua.

This stunning location is the home of Arawa Park racecourse.

The main race days are the very popular Summer Festival fixture, held annually on 27 December, and Rotorua Cup day in early May.

Arawa Park is a good all-year track as it tends to dry quickly due to the thermal volcanic soil on which the course was constructed.

## THE TRACK

Left-handed. The course is an irregular oval with a circumference of 1582m. Home straight – 280m.

Out of the home straight, runners are on a bend until just after the 1300m. It is then a straight run until approaching the 800m onto the long sweeping bend into the home straight.

The 1400m chute joins the back straight providing a run of nearly 600m to the home bend.

Chute at the 1500m joins the turn out of the home straight.

The 1900m start is from a chute that links up with the home straight.

The start at the 2200m is from a chute that gives only a short straight run before joining the home bend just before the turn.

## HAWERA

Waihi Road, Hawera, New Zealnd.
www.progroupracing.com.au/new-zealand-race courses/hawera-racecourse

| FEATURE RACE | | | | | |
|---|---|---|---|---|---|
| EVERGREEN STAKES | G3 | 1400M | TURF | 3YO+F&M | OCT |

Hawera is situated 75km south of New Plymouth in the Taranaki region on the west coast of the North Island.

The area is best known for its famous landmark, the volcanic Mount Egmont, and the adjacent Egmont National Park.

The Egmont Racing Club was established in 1882 and stages its meeting here at the Hawera racecourse, which is located only a short distance from the centre of town.

Admission to all race meetings at Hawera is free of charge.

## THE TRACK

Left-handed. Oval course of 1800m in length. Home straight – 425m.

Out of the home straight, runners are on a bend until the 1200m. It is then a straight run of 400m to the home turn.

The 1400m start is from a chute that joins the back straight.

A spur for races over 1600m gives a run of 400m before bending left at the 1200m point.

Races over 2400m begin from a chute at the top of the home straight.

# WANGANUI

19 Purnell Street, Wanganui, New Zealand.
www.wjc.co.nz

## FEATURE RACES

| | | | | | |
|---|---|---|---|---|---|
| Wanganui Cup | L | 2040M | TURF | 3YO+ | DEC |
| Wanganui Guineas | L | 1340M | TURF | 3YO | SEPT |

**Wanganui is situated on the west coast of New Zealand's North Island.**

The course is only minutes from the centre of Wanganui and has been in operation since 1848, making it the oldest course in New Zealand still racing on its original site.

The sand-based soil provides excellent drainage and Wanganui is known as a course that races very well during the winter.

## THE TRACK

Left-handed. Oval-shaped track with a circumference of 1700m. Home straight – 350m.

Chute start from the 1350m joins the back straight.

The 1600m chute joins the bend out of the home straight.

A chute that joins the top of the home bend provides the release point for races over 800m and 2400m.

# RUAKAKA

Peter Snell Road, Ruakaka, New Zealand. www.
ruakakaracing.co.nz

## FEATURE RACES

| | | | | | |
|---|---|---|---|---|---|
| WESTBURY STUD CHALLENGE STAKES | L | 1200M | TURF | 3YO | SEPT |

The town of Ruakaka is situated 30km south of Whangarei on the coast of Bream Bay.

The Whangarei Racing Club conducts its meetings at the seaside location of the Ruakaka course. The grandstands provide sweeping views of the coastline and beyond.

The sand-based soil ensures that Ruakaka is an excellent wet-weather course.

It is also a popular training centre with trainers able to avail themselves of the beach as well as the course facilities.

Feature days are Whangarei Cup day in July and the Fashion Fiesta meeting in September.

## THE TRACK

Right-handed. Classic oval of just over 1800m. Home straight – 500m.

The 1600m start is from a chute that joins the back straight.

A chute for the 1000m start links up with the home bend.

# FOXTON

37 State Highway 1, Foxton, New Zealand.
www.progroupracing.com.au/new-zealand-race
courses/foxton-racecourse

## FEATURE RACE

| | | | | |
|---|---|---|---|---|
| Castletown Stakes | 1200M | TURF | 2YO | JUN |

**The rural town of Foxton is on the lower west coast of the North Island, near the Manawatu River.**

Racing in this picturesque and relaxed setting takes place three times a year in June and August, with the feature meeting held on the Queen's Birthday holiday in June.

The Foxton course is situated north of the township between Levin and Palmerston North.

## THE TRACK

Left-handed. Classic oval of approximately 1800m in circumference. Home straight – 350m.

The 1400m races begin from a chute from the back straight.

# GORE

132 Gore Mataura Highway, Charlton, New Zealand.
www.gallopsouth.co.nz

## FEATURE RACE

| | | | | |
|---|---|---|---|---|
| Gore Guineas | L | 1335M | TURF | 3YO | JAN |

**Gore is located 64km north-east of Invercargill in the southern region of New Zealand's South Island.**

While the town of Gore is better known as a venue for trout fishing and the home of country music in New Zealand, the Gore Racing Club currently stages three meetings annually at the course, located just south of the township.

Two meetings are held in January and one in May.

The 53ha site is also used as a training facility.

## THE TRACK

Left-handed. The course has a circumference of just over 1600m. Home straight – 300m.

Gloaming

# MEYDAN

Meydan City, Dubai. www.dubairacingclub.com

*N*ot many countries would decide that a better racing facility is required than the one at Nad Al Sheba, but in Dubai nothing stands still.

Completed in 2010, the Meydan racecourse was built to be the focal point of the still developing Meydan City and every year the skyline has visibly moved towards the course.

Meydan is the most amazing and adventurous racing project ever undertaken in its sheer size and grandeur. With its futuristic, space-age features it is vast, extravagant and ahead of its time.

The new grandstand is nearly a mile long and the seven-star Meydan Hotel is situated on the course itself, just past the winning post. If they wish, guests can take in the all of the excitement without leaving their suites, as all rooms provide an unimpeded view of the track.

Racing season is from November until March, with the Dubai World Cup as its finale. It is the richest race in the world and is staged on the world's richest race night.

World Cup Night generates tremendous atmosphere and excitement. For any trainer or rider from around the globe who wants to make a name for themselves, this is the place they have to be.

With the eyes of the racing world watching and the enormous prize money on offer, all parties are there to play for keeps. Riders need to be on their game as they fight for positions, which once established are not willingly surrendered.

Betting is against the law in Dubai but such is the magnitude of the racing and the spectacle that the lack of wagering in no way detracts from the night.

The welcome ceremony is always a highlight, with its laser and light shows and stunning fireworks display. Sheik Mohammed is committed to ensuring that each year's extravaganza surpasses the previous.

Not many would have the idea to assemble the cream of the world's thoroughbreds in the one place and set off fireworks around them, but as everything in Dubai, it works brilliantly.

Meydan is a wonder in our time and an absolute must see. In a word: wow!

## THE TRACK

Left-handed. The turf course is 2400m in circumference. The home straight is 450m.

Out of the straight, runners are on a bend until the 1700m. It is a straight run of more than 700m to the home bend.

Races from 1800m to 2000m begin from a chute that links up with the top of the back straight.

Straight sprint course of 1200m joins the home straight. The release point for races over 3200m is also located on this chute.

The inner Tapeta all-weather track is 1750m in length. Home straight – 400m.

Chute start for races over 1500m joins the back straight.

The 1600m chute is a diagonal spur that doglegs onto the top of the back straight.

## FEATURE RACES

### DUBAI WORLD CUP

Notable winners include **CIGAR (1996)**, who confirmed his superstar status; **SINGSPIEL (1997)**; **SILVER CHARM (1998)** after wins in the Kentucky Derby and Preakness (1997).

**DUBAI MILLENNIUM (2000)** won the Queen

| FEATURE RACES | | | | | |
|---|---|---|---|---|---|
| DUBAI WORLD CUP | G1 | 2000M | AWT | NH4YO+&SH3YO+ | MAR |
| AL QUOZ SPRINT | | 1200M | TURF | 3YO+ | MAR |
| DUBAI DUTY FREE | G1 | 1800M | TURF | NH4YO+&SH3YO+ | MAR |
| DUBAI SHEEMA CLASSIC | G1 | 2400M | TURF | 3YO+ | MAR |
| DUBAI GOLDEN SHAHEEN | G1 | 1200M | AWT | 3YO+ | MAR |
| AL MAKTOUM CHALLENGE – ROUND 3 | G1 | 2000M | AWT | 3YO+ | MAR |
| JEBEL HATTA STAKES | G1 | 1800M | TURF | NH4YO+&SH3YO+ | MAR |
| GODOLPHIN MILE | G2 | 1600M | AWT | NH4YO &SH3YO+ | MAR |
| UAE DERBY | G2 | 1800M | AWT | 3YO | MAR |

Elizabeth II Stakes, Prix Jacques Le Marois (1999), Prince of Wales's Stakes (2000);

**CAPTAIN STEVE (2001)**; **STREET CRY (2002)**; **PLEASANTLY PERFECT (2004)** followed up his win in the Breeders' Cup Classic (2003); **ELECTROCUTIONIST (2006)**; **INVASOR (2007)**; **CURLIN (2008)**; **WELL ARMED (2009)** won the final running at Nad Al Sheba by a stunning 14 lengths; **VICTOIRE PISA (2011)**; and **ANIMAL KINGDOM (2013)**.

## DUBAI SHEEMA CLASSIC

Notable winners include **FANTASTIC LIGHT (2000)**; **STAY GOLD (2001)** won the Hong Kong Vase (2001); **NAYEF (2002)**; **SULAMANI (2003)**; **PHOENIX REACH (2005)**; **HEART'S CRY (2006)**; **VENGEANCE OF RAIN (2007)**; **SUN CLASSIQUE (2008)**; **DAR RE MI (2010)**; **REWILDING (2011)**; **CIRRUS DES AIGLES (2012)**; and **ST NICHOLAS ABBEY (2013)**.

## DUBAI DUTY FREE

Notable winners include **JIM AND TONIC (2001)**; South African mare **IPI TOMBE (2003)**; **PAOLINI (2004)**; **ELVSTROEM (2005)**; **DAVID JUNIOR (2006)**; **ADMIRE MOON (2007)**; **JAY PEG (2008)**; **GLADIATORUS (2009)**; and **PRESVIS (2011)**.

## AL QUOZ SPRINT

**JJ THE JET PLANE (2009, 11)** won the race twice; **JOY AND FUN (2010)** won for Hong Kong; and **ORTENSIA (2012)** stormed home from last to claim the prize.

## DUBAI GOLDEN SHAHEEN

Notables include dual winner **CALLER ONE (2001, 02)**; **PROUD TOWER TOO (2006)** won the Malibu Stakes (2005); and **ROCKET MAN (2006)** launched Singapore onto the world racing map.

The Jabel Hatta Stakes and the Al Maktoum Challenge (Round 3) are new additions to the Group 1 ranks.

Monterosso wins the 2012 Dubai World Cup

# ABU DHABI

Abu Dhabi, United Arab Emirates.
www.emiratesracing.com

Sheikh Zayed bin Sultan al-Nahayan

## FEATURE RACES

| ABU DHABI CHAMPIONSHIP | G2 | 2200M | TURF | 3YO+ | | MAR |
|---|---|---|---|---|---|---|
| National Day Cup | L | 1600m | TURF | NH3YO+&SH4YO+ | | Dec |
| His Highness The President Cup | L | 1400m | TURF | NH4YO+&SH3YO+ | | Dec |

The Abu Dhabi Equestrian Club was formed by the President, His Highness Sheik Zayed bin Sultan al-Nahyan in 1976, originally as a riding club.

The turf course was laid for racing in 1980 and was used for private meetings scheduled for state occasions, with events exclusively for the purebred Arabian horses.

The course began to stage open meetings in 1991 and was completely refurbished three years later with the installation of a fibreturf track to replace the grass, as well as lighting to enable night racing.

## THE TRACK

Right-handed. Classic oval fibreturf course with a circumference of 2000m. The home straight is 400m.

Chute start for races over 1600m joins the back straight.

The 1000m chute links up with the top of the home bend.

# JEBEL ALI

Al Barisha, Dubai, United Arab Emirates. www.emiratesracing.com

## FEATURE RACES

| Jebel Ali Stakes | L | 1950m | AWT | 3YO+ | | Jan |
|---|---|---|---|---|---|---|
| Jebel Ali Mile | L | 1600m | AWT | SH3YO+&NH4YO+ | | Jan |
| Jebel Ali Sprint | L | 1000m | AWT | 3YO+ | | Mar |

The Jebel Ali course is located 15 minutes from the city of Dubai.

Opened in 1990 the course has magnificent facilities and prides itself on a more relaxed atmosphere, akin to a garden party. The dress code here is smart casual. An extra level was added to the grandstand in 1995.

Racing is conducted from November until March with meetings scheduled every second Friday during the season. There are generally six races on the program.

## THE TRACK

Right-handed. Horseshoe-shaped all-weather track with a circumference of 2200m. The home straight is 900m with an uphill run to the winning post.

Straight course caters for races up to 1400m.

Races from 1600m to 1950m begin from a chute that joins the back straight.

# QATAR

Al Furousiya Street, Al Rayyan, Doha, Qatar.
www.qrec.gov.qa

Qatar is an emerging and upwardly mobile country in the Middle East.

As the latest member of the oil set it has a lot of new money and racing is beginning to gather momentum.

The Qatar Racing and Equestrian Club formed in 1975 and the Al Rayyan racecourse has been built and re-built a number of times in the short period of its existence.

Despite a limited horse population the quality of racing is good and well patronised. Horses are being imported and bred locally in growing numbers and the training facility is state of the art.

The course features a turf track and an inner sand track, which is being used more frequently as race dates and extra fixtures are added every year.

The season is conducted from May to October, with racing every Thursday throughout plus a Wednesday meeting once a month. Race cards are generally split between the thoroughbreds and Arabians.

The highlight is the Qatar International Equine Festival, which has been staged since 2000 with excellent prize money.

Feature races for the thoroughbreds are the Qatar Derby, HH The Emir's Trophy and the HH The Heir Apparent Trophy.

## THE TRACK

Right-handed. Main turf course has a circumference of 1800m. Home straight – 400m.

# CHURCHILL DOWNS

700 Central Avenue, Louisville, Kentucky, USA. www.churchilldowns.com

*L*ocated on the Falls of the Ohio River, near the border of Kentucky and Indiana, Louisville is Kentucky's largest city. The Churchill Downs racecourse is the home of America's most famous race, the Kentucky Derby.

Colonel Meriwether L Clark travelled to England where he attended many race meetings, including The Derby meeting at Epsom, and held talks with officials such as the legendary Admiral Rous. Upon his return he leased 80 acres of land from his uncles, John and Henry Churchill, to lay out a racecourse.

The inaugural fixture was held in 1875, with a race card constructed around three feature races – the Kentucky Derby, Kentucky Oaks and the Clark Handicap.

A garland of roses was presented to the first Derby victor, Aristides, and since then the Run for the Roses has established itself as the premier race on the US calendar. Every winner of the Kentucky Derby is a story to be inscribed into racing folklore.

A record crowd of 163,628 was on hand to witness the 100th running of the race in 1974, won by Cannonade.

Racing season at Churchill Downs comprises a spring meeting from April to July, which includes the two-week Kentucky Derby Festival in May, and the fall meeting during October and November.

Hundreds of millions of dollars have been spent upgrading and expanding facilities in the past decade to provide world-class amenities for the public.

The Kentucky Derby Museum opened to the public in 1985 and since then has received more than 4 million visitors. The course was granted National Historic Landmark status the following year. A famous feature of the course is the twin-spire grandstand, which was commissioned in 1895.

## THE TRACK

Left-handed. One-mile dirt oval. Home straight – 412yds.

A 1-mile chute joins the back straight.

Long runs to the first turn from all starts except the $1\frac{1}{16}$ or $5\frac{1}{2}$ furlong start, which has a short run of 162yds to the first turn.

The Matt Win Turf Course is a 7-furlong inner turf track with a home straight of 407yds.

## FEATURE RACES

### KENTUCKY DERBY

America's greatest race and first leg of the US 3yo Triple Crown – the pinnacle of US racing – which also comprises the Preakness Stakes at Pimlico, and the Belmont Stakes.

Winners of the Triple Crown include **SIR BARTON (1919)**, **GALLANT FOX (1930)**, **OMAHA (1935)**, **WAR ADMIRAL (1937)**, **WHIRLAWAY (1941)**, **COUNT FLEET (1943)**, **ASSAULT (1946)**, **CITATION (1948)**, **SECRETARIAT (1973)**, **SEATTLE SLEW (1977)** and **AFFIRMED (1978)**.

Those to have won the Kentucky Derby–Preakness Stakes double include **BURGOO KING (1932)**, **BOLD VENTURE (1936)**, **PENSIVE (1944)**, **TIM TAM (1958)**, **CARRY BACK (1961)**, **NORTHERN DANCER (1964)**, **KAUAI KING (1966)**, **FORWARD PASS (1968)**, **MAJESTIC DANCE (1969)**, **CANONERO (1971)**, **SPECTACULAR BID (1979)**, **PLEASANT COLONY (1981)**, **SUNDAY SILENCE (1989)**, **SILVER CHARM (1997)**, **REAL QUIET (1998)**, **CHARISMATIC (1999)**, **WAR EMBLEM (2002)**, **FUNNYCIDE (2003)**, **SMARTY JONES (2004)**, **BIG BROWN (2008)** and **I'LL HAVE ANOTHER (2012)**.

Winners of the Kentucky Derby–Belmont Stakes double include **JOHNSTOWN (1939)**, **SHUT OUT (1942)**, **MIDDLEGROUND (1950)**, **NEEDLES (1956)**, **CHATEAUGAY (1963)**, **RIVA RIDGE (1972)**, **BOLD FORBES (1976)**, **SWALE (1984)**, **ALYSHEBA (1987)** and **THUNDER GULCH (1995)**.

Other notable winners include **HINDOO (1881)**, who won 30 of 35 starts; **APOLLO (1882)** won

| FEATURE RACES | | | | | | | |
|---|---|---|---|---|---|---|---|
| KENTUCKY DERBY | G1 | 9F | DIRT | 3YO | SW | 1875 | MAY |
| KENTUCKY OAKS | G1 | 9F | DIRT | 3YOF | SW | 1875 | MAY |
| HUMANA DISTAFF | G1 | 7F | DIRT | 4YO+F&M | ASS | 1987 | MAY |
| WOODFORD RESERVE TURF CLASSIC | G1 | 9F | TURF | 4YO+ | WFA | 1987 | MAY |
| STEPHEN FOSTER HCP | G1 | 9F | DIRT | 3YO+ | HCP | 1982 | JUN |
| CLARK HCP | G1 | 9F | DIRT | 3YO+ | HCP | 1875 | NOV |

24 of 54 and remains the only horse ever to win the Kentucky Derby not having raced as a 2yo; **BEN BRUSH (1896)** would become one of the most influential sires in US history; **OLD ROSEBUD (1914)** had 80 starts for 40 wins including the Carter Hcp and Clark Hcp (1917); **REGRET (1915)** was the first of only three fillies ever to win.

**EXTERMINATOR (1918)** won 50 of 99 starts including the Saratoga Cup four times; **ZEV (1923)** also won the Belmont Stakes, and defeated English Derby winner Papyrus in a famous match race in 1923; **BLACK GOLD (1924)** is buried in the infield at New Orleans Fair Grounds; **REIGH COUNT (1926)** sired Triple Crown winner **COUNT FLEET (1943)** and won the Coronation Cup (1929); **TWENTY GRAND (1931)** won the Belmont Stakes, ran second in the Preakness Stakes, and also won the Wood Memorial Stakes, Travers Stakes and Jockey Club Gold Cup that year.

**BROKER'S TIP (1933)** is the only horse to have recorded the Kentucky Derby as its only win.

**SWAPS (1955)** had 25 starts for 19 wins including the Santa Anita Derby, Hollywood Derby (1955) and Hollywood Gold Cup (1956). He ran world-record times on five occasions at distances ranging from a mile to 13 furlongs, including 1:33:2 for the mile in winning the Argonaut Hcp (1956).

The extraordinary **NORTHERN DANCER (1964)** won 14 of 18 starts including the Flamingo Stakes, Blue Grass Stakes, Florida Derby, Preakness Stakes and ran third in the Belmont Stakes. He became the world's most successful and influential sire of the 20th century.

**LUCKY DEBONAIR (1965)** won the Santa Anita Derby, Blue Grass Stakes (1965), Santa Anita Hcp (1966); and **FOOLISH PLEASURE (1975)** won the Champagne Stakes (1974), Wood Memorial (1975), Donn Hcp, Suburban Hcp (1976).

**GENUINE RISK (1980)** was only the second filly ever to win. She ran second in the Preakness and Belmont to be the only filly ever to be placed in all three legs of the Triple Crown.

**SUNNY'S HALO (1983)** won that year's Arkansas Derby and Super Derby; **FERDINAND (1986)** won the Breeders' Cup Classic, Hollywood Gold Cup (1987); **ALYSHEBA (1987)** won nine races at Group 1 level including the Preakness (1987) and the Breeders' Cup Classic (1988), and holds the track record for 10 furlongs at both Belmont and Meadowlands; **WINNING COLORS (1988)** was the third of the three fillies to win.

**SUNDAY SILENCE (1989)** won the Santa Anita Derby, Super Derby, Preakness Stakes and ran second in the Belmont (1989). Also won the Breeders' Cup Classic (1989) California Stakes (1990), and is one of the greatest sires in Japanese history, winning the sire's title every year from 1995 to 2007. His progeny include Dance In The Dark (sire of Delta Blues), Deep Impact, Zenno Rob Roy, Hat Trick and Stay Gold – sire of Japanese Triple Crown winner Orfevre.

**UNBRIDLED (1990)** won the Breeders' Cup Classic (1990); **THUNDER GULCH (1995)** won the Swaps Stakes, Florida Derby, Belmont Stakes, Travers Stakes and ran third in the Preakness. He was leading sire in North America in 2001. **STREET SENSE (2007)** won the Breeders' Cup Juvenile (2006).

## KENTUCKY OAKS

**PRINCESS DOREEN (1924)** won 34 races during her career and was the champion filly then mare in the USA from 1924 to 1926. She retired as leading female money-winner in history.

**BLACK MARIA (1926)** was also champion filly/mare on three occasions; **WISTFUL (1949)**; **REAL DELIGHT (1952)** is a Hall of Famer who won eight consecutive stakes races in 1952; **LALUN (1955)** dam of Never Bend and Bold Reason; **CICADA (1962)** won 18 stakes races including the Spinaway Stakes, Frizette Stakes (1961) Mother Goose Stakes, Beldame Stakes, Acorn Stakes (1962). She is the only filly ever to be named champion as a 2, 3 and 4yo.

**DARK MIRAGE (1968)** was the first winner of the Fillies' Triple Crown; three-time champion filly or mare **SUSAN'S GIRL (1972)** won 29 races – 24 in stakes company – including the Acorn Stakes, Santa Anita Oaks, Gazelle Stakes (1972), Santa Margarita Invitational Stakes (1973), Apple Blossom Hcp, Gamely Stakes (1975) and was dual winner of the Beldame Stakes (1972, 75) and Spinster Stakes (1973, 75).

**DAVONA DALE (1979)** was the first filly ever to win both the National and New York Triple Tiaras.

**BOLD 'N' DETERMINED (1980)** had 20 starts

for 16 wins, with six at Grade 1 level including the Chandelier Stakes (1979), Spinster Stakes, Coaching Club American Oaks, Santa Anita Oaks, Acorn Stakes (1980), Apple Blossom Hcp (1981); **PRINCESS ROONEY (1983)**; **OPEN MIND (1989)** won eight Grade 1 races including the Fillies' Triple Crown (1989) and the Breeders' Cup Juvenile Fillies (1998); **LITE LIGHT (1991)** won the Chandelier Stakes (1990), Las Virgenes Stakes, Santa Anita Oaks and Coaching Club American Oaks (1991).

**SILVERBULLETDAY (1999)** was champion filly as both a 2yo and 3yo, and winner of the Breeders' Cup Juvenile Fillies, Alcibiades Stakes, Ashland Stakes (1998), Gazelle Stakes, Alabama Stakes (1999).

**ASHADO (2004)** won the Spinaway Stakes (2003), Breeders' Cup Ladies' Classic, Coaching Club American Oaks (2004), Ogden Phipps Hcp, Beldame Stakes (2005).

**RAGS TO RICHES (2007)** was World Champion Filly in 2007 after becoming only the third filly in history to win the Belmont Stakes.

Star **RACHEL ALEXANDRA (2009)** won the race by a record margin of 20¼ lengths. She was the first filly ever to win the Woodward Stakes (2009), the second filly in history to win the Preakness Stakes (2009) and the second filly to win the Haskell invitational (2009) when successful by 6 lengths.

**BLIND LUCK (2010)** won the Chandelier Stakes, Hollywood Starlet Stakes (2009), Las Virgenes Stakes, Alabama Stakes (2010) and Vanity Invitational Hcp (2011).

## TURF CLASSIC STAKES

First run in 1987, the race was elevated to Grade 1 status in 1998.

Since then prominent winners include **BEAT HOLLOW (2002)**, who won the Grand Prix de Paris (2000), Manhattan Hcp, Arlington Million (2002); **ENGLISH CHANNEL (2006)** won 13 of 22 starts including the Breeders' Cup Turf (2007) and twice won both the United Nations Stakes (2006, 07) and the Joe Hirsch Invitational (2006, 07); **SKY CONQUEROR (2007)** was a dual winner of the Northern Dancer Stakes (2006, 07); **EINSTEIN (2008, 09)** went back to back, was also a dual winner of the Gulfstream Park Turf Hcp (2006, 08) and won the Santa Anita Hcp (2009).

## CLARK HANDICAP

Named after Colonel M Lewis Clark, founder of the Louisville Jockey Club, which constructed the course at Churchill Downs.

In the early days of the race there was a close link with the Kentucky Derby as the race was restricted to 3yos until 1901 and run at the same track over a slightly shorter distance.

Horses to also win the Kentucky Derby include

Triple Crown winner Seattle Slew

**HINDOO (1881)**, **BUCHANAN (1884)**, **SPOKANE (1889)**, **RILEY (1890)**, **AZRA (1892)**, **CHANT (1894)**, **HALMA (1895)**, **PLAUDIT (1898)**, **LIEUT. GIBSON (1900)**, **HIS EMINENCE (1901)**, **OLD ROSEBUD (1914)**, **EXTERMINATOR (1918)**, **WHIRLAWAY (1942)** and **SILVER CHARM (1998)**.

Dual winners include **HODGE (1915, 16)**, **BOLD FAVORITE (1968, 69)** and **BOB'S DUSTY (1977, 78)**.

Other notables include **FALSETTO (1879)**, sire of three Kentucky Derby winners; **KING'S DAUGHTER (1910)** won the Kentucky Oaks (1906) as did **WISTFUL (1951)**; **SWOON'S SON (1956)** was a winner of 30 of 51 starts.

Former Chilean Horse of the Year **LIDO PALACE (2002)** won the Whitney Hcp (2002) and twice won the Woodward Stakes (2001, 02); **SAINT LIAM (2004)** won the Breeders' Cup Classic (2005), as did **BLAME (2009)**; **EINSTEIN (2008)**; **WISE DAN (2011)** won the Woodbine Mile, Shadwell Turf Mile, Breeders' Cup Mile (2012); and **SHACKLEFORD (2012)** won the Preakness (2011) and Metropolitan Hcp (2012).

## STEPHEN FOSTER HANDICAP

Named after composer Stephen Foster who penned the tune 'My Old Kentucky Home', which is played as competitors parade onto the track for the Kentucky

Derby. Among his many popular and enduring songs, Foster also wrote 'Oh Susanna', 'Camptown Races' and 'Jeanie with the Light Brown Hair'.

First run in 1982, the race was elevated to Grade 1 status in 2002. Since then prominent winners include Dubai World Cup winner **STREET CRY (2002)**; **SAINT LIAM (2005)**; **BLAME (2010)**; and **CURLIN (2008)** won the Arkansas Derby, Preakness, Breeders' Cup Classic (2007), Woodward Stakes, Dubai World Cup (2008) and was a dual winner of the Jockey Club Gold Cup (2007, 08).

## HUMANA DISTAFF

First run in 1987 the race was upgraded to Grade 1 level in 2002.

Notables since include **SIGHTSEEK (2003)**, dual winner of the Beldame Stakes (2003, 04) and Ogden Phipps Hcp (2003, 04) and winner of the Ruffian Hcp (2004); and **INFORMED DECISION (2009)**, who won the Breeders' Cup Filly & Mare Turf Sprint the same year.

# PIMLICO

5201 Park Heights Avenue, Baltimore, Maryland, USA. www.pimlico.com

*Pimlico in Baltimore, Maryland, was originally founded by settlers from inner London who named the town after their old local pub.*

In 1868, a dinner party of racing enthusiasts was held, including Maryland Governor Oden Bowie. A number of the guests owned yearlings and they agreed over the course of the evening that the party would reconvene two years hence to stage a race for their horses, with a rich prize for the winner.

Governor Bowie vowed to build an outstanding facility for the race and became instrumental in the decision to construct a course in Baltimore.

Situated west of Jones Falls, on 70 acres of land purchased by the Maryland Jockey Club, Pimlico staged its first race in 1870 and is only pre-dated by Saratoga as the oldest course in the USA.

The Dinner Party Stakes was held at the inaugural meeting, won by a horse called Preakness.

A small rise in the infield was a popular position to view the races and the track was commonly known as Old Hilltop. The infield quickly became a lively setting and a fashionable rendezvous point for the social set, who would gather for champagne lunches on race days. With the advent of film cameras, the hill was removed in 1938 to provide a clear view of the back of the course, but the Old Hilltop nickname still remains.

Pimlico was one of the few courses that survived the anti-gambling lobby of 1910, when racing was banned in all states across the US, except Kentucky and Maryland.

Racing at Pimlico comes alive in May for the running of the legendary Preakness Stakes, the second leg of the US Triple Crown for 3yos. Most of the major events at the course are run over two days in mid May, which culminates with the Preakness.

From the opening of the course, the ornate and elegant Old Clubhouse was the place to be on Preakness day, with patrons attired in the height of fashion as they enjoyed the sumptuous menu and silver service. Tragedy occurred in 1966 when the building was destroyed by fire, along with virtually all of the course's records and prized memorabilia. A replica of the Old Clubhouse was built on the infield.

The tradition of painting the colours of the Preakness winner onto the weather vane began in 1909 and continues with the weather vane now situated atop the replica Clubhouse.

While the Preakness Stakes is the only Grade 1 race conducted at the course, Pimlico has been the site of many legendary races. In 1877 the US House of Representatives adjourned for the only time in its history to watch a horse race – The Great Race at Pimlico – between Parole, Ten Broeck and Tom Ochiltree, won by Parole.

On 1 November 1938 the American match race of the century was staged between Triple Crown winner War Admiral and Seabiscuit in the Pimlico Special, with Seabiscuit producing a famous upset victory. The race was the subject of the 2003 movie *Seabiscuit*, one of the great motion pictures about horseracing.

In 2007, a record crowd of over 121,000 people was in attendance on Preakness Day to witness the win of Curlin.

## THE TRACK

Left-handed. One-mile dirt oval with a run in of 384yds.

Seven-furlong inner turf track.

## FEATURE RACES

| PREAKNESS STAKES | G1 | 9½F | DIRT | 3YO | MAY |
|---|---|---|---|---|---|
| BLACK-EYED SUSAN STAKES | G2 | 9F | DIRT | 3YOF | MAY |
| DIXIE STAKES | G2 | 9F | TURF | 3YO+ | MAY |
| PIMLICO SPECIAL | G3 | 9½F | DIRT | 3YO | MAY |
| PIMLICO DISTAFF STAKES | G3 | 8½F | DIRT | 3YO+F&M | MAY |
| MARYLAND SPRINT HCP | G3 | 6F | DIRT | 3YO+ | MAY |
| GALLORETTE HCP | G3 | 8½F | TURF | 3YO+F&M | MAY |

Seabiscuit defeats War Admiral

## FEATURE RACE

### PREAKNESS STAKES

Notable winners who have forged their reputation outside of the Triple Crown races include **TOM OCHILTREE (1875)**, who won 21 of 33 starts; **THE BARD (1886)** won 27 of 47; **EFFENDI (1909)** was the first to have its racing colours painted on to the weather vane; **DISPLAY (1926); VICTORIAN (1928); MATE (1931)**; and **HEAD PLAY (1933)**.

**CHALLEDON (1939)** won 20 of 44 including the Hollywood Gold Cup, Whitney Hcp (1940); **ALSAB (1942); POLYNESIAN (1945)** had 58 starts for 27 wins; **HILL PRINCE (1950)** won 17 of 30 including the Wood Memorial Stakes, Jockey Club Gold Cup (1950); **BOLD RULER (1957); BALLY ACHE (1960); TOM ROLFE (1965); MASTER DERBY (1975)** won 16 of 33 career starts; **ELOCUTIONIST (1976); CODEX (1980)**.

**DEPUTED TESTIMONY (1983)** won the Haskell Invitational (1983); **SNOW CHIEF (1986)** won the FrontRunner Stakes, Hollywood Futurity (1985), Florida Derby and Santa Anita Derby (1986); **SUNDAY SILENCE (1989); SUMMER SQUALL (1990); TIMBER COUNTRY (1995); SILVER CHARM (1997); BERNADINI (2006); CURLIN (2007)**; and **LOOKIN' AT LUCKY (2010)** won the Del Mar Futurity, FrontRunner Stakes, Hollywood Futurity (2009) and Haskell Invitational (2010).

# BELMONT PARK

2150 Hempstead Turnpike, Elmont, New York, USA. www.nyra.com/belmont

*E*lmont in Nassau County on Long Island, New York is the location of Belmont Park – one of the elite racetracks of the USA.

Nearly all of America's great champions have competed on the course, which hosts some of the most legendary races in the country including the third leg of the US Triple Crown for 3yos, the Belmont Stakes, which is held in June.

Situated on 430 acres, the course was built by a group of investors including August Belmont Jnr and William C Whitney. Their vision was to build a grand course in the style of the great English tracks. The course opened in 1905, and racing was initially conducted in the clockwise direction.

Since 1955, New York's three major tracks at Belmont, Saratoga and Aqueduct have been under the control of the not-for-profit New York Racing Association.

The old grandstand was considered unsafe, so was demolished and completely rebuilt in 1963 to comfortably accommodate crowds in excess of 100,000. More than 120,000 were on hand in 2004 to witness the unsuccessful attempt by Smarty Jones to claim the elusive Triple Crown.

Two meetings are conducted annually at Belmont Park. The first meeting is held from April to July and the second over September and October.

The course features a display dedicated to Woody Stephens, who trained five consecutive winners of the Belmont Stakes from 1982 to 1986.

Visitors can also book in for Breakfast at Belmont, which allows race fans to enjoy breakfast while watching the horses go through their paces on the training track. The package also includes a ride through the stable area by tram, a paddock show and a starting gate demonstration.

Famously, over 150,000 people attended the track in 1910 to witness an aerial show featuring the legendary aviation pioneers, the Wright Brothers.

Belmont is the largest course in the USA.

## THE TRACK

Left-handed. One-and-a-half-mile dirt oval. Home straight – 366yds.

The Belmont Stakes start at the mile and a half begins from a chute that joins the back straight. The inner turf track is 11 furlongs.

## FEATURE RACES

| | | | | | | |
|---|---|---|---|---|---|---|
| ACORN STAKES | G1 | 8F | DIRT | 3YOF | SW | 1931 MAY |
| METROPOLITAN HCP | G1 | 8F | DIRT | 3YO+ | HCP | 1891 MAY |
| MOTHER GOOSE STAKES | G1 | 8½F | DIRT | 3YOF | SW | 1957 JUN |
| BELMONT STAKES | G1 | 12F | DIRT | 3YO | SW | 1867 JUN |
| MANHATTAN HCP | G1 | 10F | TURF | 3YO+ | HCP | 1887 JUN |
| JUST A GAME STAKES | G1 | 8F | TURF | 3YO+F&M | ASS | 1992 JUN |
| MAN O' WAR STAKES | G1 | 11F | TURF | 3YO+ | WFA | 1959 JUL |
| JOE HIRSCH TURF CLASSIC INVITATIONAL | G1 | 12F | TURF | 3YO+ | WFA | 1977 SEPT |
| GARDEN CITY STAKES | G1 | 9F | TURF | 3YOF | SWP | 1978 SEPT |
| JOCKEY CLUB GOLD CUP | G1 | 2M | DIRT | 3YO+ | WFA | 1919 SEPT |
| VOSBURGH STAKES | G1 | 6F | DIRT | 3YO+ | ASS | 1940 SEPT–OCT |
| JAMAICA HCP | G1 | 9F | TURF | 3YO | HCP | 1929 OCT |
| BELDAME STAKES | G1 | 9F | DIRT | 3YO+F&M | WFA | 1939 OCT |
| FRIZETTE STAKES | G1 | 8F | DIRT | 2YOF | WFA | 1945 OCT |
| CHAMPAGNE STAKES | G1 | 8F | DIRT | 2YO | ASS | 1867 OCT |
| FLOWER BOWL INVITATIONAL STAKES | G1 | 10F | TURF | 3YO+F&M | ASS | 1978 OCT |

# FEATURE RACES

## BELMONT STAKES

The third and longest leg of the US 3yo Triple Crown, it was first run in 1867 at the Jerome Park racecourse in The Bronx, which had been built by stock-market speculator Leonard Jerome, with the financial backing of August Belmont Snr.

The race was conducted at Morris Hill racecourse from 1891 until the opening of Belmont Park in 1905.

The inaugural running was taken out by **RUTHLESS (1867)**, one of only three fillies ever to win, alongside **TANYA (1905)** and **RAGS TO RICHES (2007)**.

Winners of the Preakness Stakes–Belmont Stakes double include **DUKE OF MAGENTA (1878)**, **BELMAR (1895)**, **MAN O' WAR (1920)** won this race by 20 lengths, **PILLORY (1922)**, **BIMELECH (1939)**, **NATIVE DANCER (1953)**, **NASHUA (1955)**, **DAMASCUS (1957)**, **LITTLE CURRENT (1974)**, **RISEN STAR (1988)**, **HANSEL (1991)**,

**TABASCO CAT (1994)**, **POINT GIVEN (2001)** and **AFLEET ALEX (2005)**.

Other notables include **FENIAN (1869)**, owned by August Belmont Snr. His son August Belmont Jnr would win it four times with **HASTINGS (1896)**, grandsire of Man O' War; **MASTERMAN (1902)**; **FRIAR ROCK (1916)**; and **HOURLESS (1917)**.

**HARRY BASSETT (1871)** won 22 of 36 starts; **SPENDTHRIFT (1879)**; **HANOVER (1887)** had 50 starts for a record of 32–14–2 and retired as leading US money winner; **HENRY OF NAVARRE (1894)** won 29 of 42 runs;

**COMMANDO (1901)**; **PETER PAN (1907)**; **COLIN (1908)** was undefeated in a 15-start career; influential sire **SWEEP (1910)**; **PRINCE EUGENE (1913)** made it a record eight wins for trainer James G Rowe Sr; **GREY LAG (1921)**; **CRUSADER (1926)** won the Jockey Club Gold Cup (1926) and twice won the Suburban Hcp (1926, 27); **BLUE LARKSPUR (1929)**; **GRANVILLE (1936)**; **GALLANT MAN (1957)**; **SWORD DANCER (1959)**; **JAIPUR (1962)**; **ARTS AND LETTERS (1969)**.

**SECRETARIAT (1973)** set a world record time (2:24:00) and winning margin of 31 lengths, both of which still stand; **TEMPERENCE HILL (1980)**; **CONQUISTADOR CIELO (1982)** was the first of trainer Woody Stephens's five in a row; **CREME FRAICHE (1985)**; Canadian **VICTORY GALLOP (1998)**; **EASY GOER (1989)** won 14 of 20 starts; **GO AND GO (1990)** for Dermot Weld; **AP INDY (1992)** won the Breeders' Cup Classic (1992); **LEMON DROP KID (1999)**; and **DROSSELMEYER (2010)** also won the Breeders' Cup Classic (2011).

## JOCKEY CLUB GOLD CUP

First run in 1919; the inaugural running was won by **PURCHASE (1919)**.

Legendary champion **KELSO (1960–64)** is the greatest horse in the history of the race with five consecutive victories. A winner of 39 of 63 starts including three-time winner of both the Woodward Stakes (1961–63) and the Whitney Hcp (1961, 63, 65)

At it again: Affirmed defeats Alydar

Man O' War

Goodbye

and a dual winner of the Suburban Hcp (1961, 63). Kelso still holds the world-record time for 2 miles on dirt, set during his fifth victory in the Jockey Club Gold Cup of 1964. Five-time US Horse of the Year (1960–64).

Dual winners include **MAD HATTER (1921, 22)**; **FIRETHORN (1935, 37)** brought up the first of ten wins in the race for Eddie Arcaro; **DARK SECRET (1933, 34)**; **NASHUA (1955, 56)**, whose second win made it a record seven victories for trainer Jim Fitzsimmons; **SHUVEE (1970, 71)** won the Triple Tiara and is the only filly to win; **SLEW O' GOLD (1983, 84)**; **CREME FRAICHE (1986, 87)** also won the Belmont Stakes; **SKIP AWAY (1996, 97)**; **CURLIN (2007, 08)** and **FLAT OUT (2011, 12)**.

Triple Crown winners successful in the race include **GALLANT FOX (1930)**, **WAR ADMIRAL (1938)**, **WHIRLAWAY (1942)**, **CITATION (1948)** and **AFFIRMED (1979)**.

Kentucky Derby winners include **REIGH COUNT (1928)**, **TWENTY GRAND (1931)**, **PONDER (1949)**, and **FUNNYCIDE (2004)**, who also won the Preakness (2004).

Belmont Stakes winners include **MAN O' WAR (1920)**, **CRUSADER (1926)**, **PAVOT (1946)**, **PHALANX (1947)**, **COUNTERPOINT (1951)**, **ONE COUNT (1952)**, **HIGH GUN (1954)**, **GALLANT MAN (1957)**, **SWORD DANCER (1959)**, **ARTS AND LETTERS (1969)**, **TEMPERENCE HILL (1980)**, **EASY GOER (1989)**, **COLONIAL AFFAIR (1994)** and **SUMMER BIRD (2009)**.

Other notables include **CHANCE PLAY (1927)**; influential **PRINCEQUILLO (1943)**; **HILL PRINCE (1950)** won the Preakness (1950); **BUCKPASSER (1966)** was a winner of 25 of 31 races, including 15 wins on end before being beaten at his only run on turf; **DAMASCUS (1967)** won the

Belmont, Preakness, Wood Memorial Stakes, Woodward Stakes and the Travers Stakes by 22 lengths (1967); **FOREGO (1974)**.

**EXCELLER (1978)** won Grand Prix de Paris (1976) and Coronation Cup (1977), and defeated Seattle Slew and Affirmed in this race to be the only horse ever to beat two Triple Crown champions in the one race; **JOHN HENRY (1981)**; **VANLANDINGHAM (1985)** won the Stephen Foster Hcp, Suburban Hcp and Washington DC International (1985); **CIGAR (1995)**; and **BERNADINI (2006)** also won Preakness (2006).

## CHAMPAGNE STAKES

A 2yo race that has long unearthed potential champions. The race has been run over a number of distances in its 150-year history, and is currently staged over a mile.

Triple Crown winners **COUNT FLEET (1942)** and **SEATTLE SLEW (1976)** both took it out.

Those who went on to claim the Kentucky Derby include **AZRA (1891)**, **BEN BRUSH (1895)**, **PLAUDIT (1897)**, **BUBBLING OVER (1925)**, **FOOLISH PLEASURE (1974)** and **SEA HERO (1992)**.

Horses to also win the Belmont Stakes include **COLIN (1907)**, **GREY LAG (1920)**, **EASY GOER (1988)**, **BIRDSTONE (2003)** and **UNION RAGS (2011)**.

Winners of the Preakness include **MATE (1930)**, **ALSAB (1941)** and **TIMBER COUNTRY (1994)**, who also won the Breeders' Cup Juvenile.

**CAPOT (1948)** won the Preakness and Belmont; **RIVA RIDGE (1971)** and **SPECTACULAR BID (1978)** won the Kentucky Derby and Preakness; **POT O' LUCK (1944)**, **ROMAN BROTHER (1963)** and **BUCKPASSER (1965)** all won the Jockey Club Gold Cup; **FLY SO FREE (1990)**, **WAR PASS (2007)**,

**UNCLE MO (2010)** and **SHANGHAI BOBBY (2012)** all won the Breeders' Cup Juvenile.

Other prominent winners include **ENDURANCE BY RIGHT (1901)**, who won 16 of 18; **CLEOPATRA (1919)** won the Alabama Stakes, Coaching Club American Oaks (1920); **SARAZEN (1923)** won 27 of 55 starts including the Carter Hcp, Manhattan Hcp (1924), Metropolitan Hcp (1926); **DONOR (1946)**; **NEVER BEND (1962)**; **BOLD LAD (1964)**; **ALYDAR (1977)**; **DEVIL'S BAG (1983)**; **FORTY NINER (1987)** won the Haskell Invitational and Cigar Mile (1988); **DEHERE (1993)**; and **MARIA'S MON (1995)** sire of Kentucky Derby winners Monarchos (2001) and Super Saver (2010).

## ACORN STAKES

The Acorn Stakes is the first leg of the US Triple Tiara for fillies. Up until 2009 the series also comprised the Mother Goose Stakes and the Coaching Club American Oaks. From 2010 the Alabama Stakes became the third leg with the deletion of the Mother Goose from the series.

More changes are currently being mooted to dispense with history and make the New York–based series a more national competition.

Winners of the Triple Tiara include **DARK MIRAGE (1968)**, **SHUVEE (1969)**, **CHRIS EVERT (1974)**, **RUFFIAN (1975)**, **DAVONA DALE (1979)**, **MOM'S COMMAND (1985)**, **OPEN MIND (1989)** and **SKY BEAUTY (1993)**.

Other notables include **TOP FLIGHT (1932)** who had 16 starts for 12 wins. Undefeated from 7 starts at two, she won the Spinaway Stakes (1931), Coaching Club American Oaks and Alabama Stakes (1932); **TWILIGHT TEAR (1944)** won 18 of 24; great mare **GALLORETTE (1945)** won 21 races including the Metropolitan Hcp, Beldame Stakes (1946), Carter Hcp and Whitney Hcp (1948). **BOWL OF FLOWERS (1961)** won the Frizette Stakes (1960), Spinster Stakes and Coaching Club American Oaks (1961).

**CICADA (1962)** won 23 of 42 including the Spinaway Stakes, Frizette Stakes (1961), Kentucky Oaks and Mother Goose Stakes (1962);

**SUSAN'S GIRL (1972); BOLD N DETERMINED (1980); MEADOW STAR (1991)** won the Breeders' Cup Juvenile Fillies (1990); **INSIDE INFORMATION (1994)** won the Breeders' Cup Ladies' Classic (1995), as did **ROUND POND (2005)**.

**SHARP CAT (1997)** won the Del Mar Debutante Stakes, Hollywood Starlet Stakes (1996), Zenyatta Stakes, Las Virgenes Stakes, Santa Anita Oaks (1997), Beldame Stakes, Clement L Hirsch Stakes and Ruffian Hcp (1998).

## MOTHER GOOSE STAKES

First run in 1957; Mother Goose was a winner of the Belmont Futurity in 1924.

Prominent winners include **IDUN (1958); BERLO (1960)** won the Beldame Stakes, Coaching Club American Oaks, Gazelle Stakes (1960); **CICADA (1962); OFFICE QUEEN (1970); LIFE'S MAGIC (1984)** won the Chandelier Stakes (1983), Beldame Stakes, Alabama Stakes (1984), Breeders' Cup Ladies' Classic (1985); **GO FOR WAND (1990)** won the Breeders' Cup Juvenile Fillies (1989), Ashland Stakes, Alabama Stakes, Beldame Stakes, Test Stakes (1990); **MEADOW STAR (1991)**.

**SERENA'S SONG (1995)** won 11 Grade 1 races including the Chandelier Stakes, Hollywood Starlet Stakes (1994), Las Virgenes Stakes, Gazelle Stakes, Santa Anita Oaks, Haskell Invitational, Beldame Stakes (1995), Ogden Phipps Hcp, Santa Maria Hcp and Santa Monica Stakes (1996); **AJINA (1997)** won the Breeders' Cup Ladies' Classic (1997); **MUSIC NOTE (2008)**; and **RACHEL ALEXANDRA (2009)** won by a record 19¼ lengths.

## MAN O' WAR STAKES

In any discussion regarding the greatest horses in the history of the USA, the name Man O'War is always most prominent.

As a 2yo he was a winner of 9 of 10 starts and desperately unlucky when second in the other, followed by an unbeaten 11-start campaign as a 3yo. The Triple Crown was not recognised as such at the time, and Man O'War bypassed the Kentucky Derby, but was seemingly invincible with easy wins in the Preakness, Belmont Stakes (by 20 lengths) and Jockey Club Gold Cup of 1920.

By the end of his 3yo campaign, Man O'War had run out of willing opponents, with only one rival prepared to line up in both of his final two starts. He travelled to Canada for his swansong – a match with 1919 Triple Crown champion Sir Barton, whom he defeated by 7 lengths, being eased down.

His final record stood at 20 wins from 21 career starts. At stud he was highly influential and became leading sire. Despite producing only 379 named foals over 22 seasons, he sired 64 stakes winners.

Run since 1959, its dual winners include **MAJESTY'S PRINCE (1983, 84), SOLAR SPLENDOR (1991, 92), WITH ANTICPATION (2001, 02)** and **GIO PONTI (2009, 10)**.

Other notables include champion South African horse **HAWAII (1969)**, who had 28 starts for 21 wins and sired 1980 Epsom Derby winner Henbit; **RUN THE GAUNTLET (1971)** sire of 39 stakes winners including Ascot Gold Cup winner Ardross; **SECRETARIAT (1973)**; dual UK Horse of the Year **DAHLIA (1974); SNOW KNIGHT (1975)** won The Epsom Derby (1974); **THEATRICAL (1987)** won the Breeders' Cup Turf (1987) and sire of 18 G1 winners including 2002 Melbourne Cup winner Media Puzzle; **YANKEE AFFAIR (1989); DAYLAMI (1998); FANTASTIC LIGHT (2000); BETTER TALK NOW (2005)** won the Breeders' Cup Turf (2004); and **DOCTOR DINO (2007)** was a dual winner of the Hong Kong Vase (2007, 08).

## JOE HIRSCH TURF CLASSIC INVITATIONAL STAKES

A mile-and-a-half turf race named after racing journalist and founding president of the National Turf Writers Association, Joe Hirsch.

Dual winners include top French filly **APRIL RUN (1981, 82); VAL'S PRINCE (1997, 99)**; and Breeders' Cup Turf (2007) winner **ENGLISH CHANNEL (2006, 07)**.

**WAYA (1978)** won the Prix de l'Opera (1977), Flower Bowl Invitational, Diana Stakes, Man O'War Stakes (1978), Beldame Stakes (1979).

**ALL ALONG (1983)** won the Arc de Triomphe, Prix Vermeille (1982), Canadian International, Washington DC International (1983).

**JOHN HENRY (1984)** won 39 races and was four-times US Champion Turf horse (1980, 81, 83, 84), Three-time winner of the Charles Whittingham Memorial (1980, 81, 84), dual winner of the Santa Anita Hcp (1981, 82) and Arlington Million (1981, 84), winner of the Jockey Club Gold Cup (1981), and also won the Oak Tree Turf Championship three times in succession (1980–82).

**MANILA (1986), THEATRICAL (1987), TIKKANEN (1994)** and **BUCK'S BOY (1998)** were all winners of the Breeders' Cup Turf; **SULAMANI (2003); KITTEN'S JOY (2004); CAPE BLANCO (2011)** won the Irish Derby, Irish Champion Stakes (2010), Man O'War Stakes and Arlington Million (2011).

## VOSBURGH STAKES

An open sprint race named after Walter S Vosburgh, turf historian and former Jockey Club handicapper.

**JOE SCHENCK (1940, 41)** won the first two editions; other dual winners are **DR FAGER (1967, 68)** and **SEWICKLEY (1989, 90)**.

Other notable winners include **BOLD RULER (1957)**, who won the Preakness, Wood Memorial Stakes (1957), Carter Hcp, Suburban Hcp (1958); **AFFECTIONATELY (1964)** had 52 starts for 28 wins; **TA WEE (1969)** won 15 of 21 including the Prioress Stakes and Test Stakes (1969); **FOREGO (1974); MY JULIET (1976)** won 24 of 36 starts; **KING'S SWAN (1986); HOUSEBUSTER (1991); LANGFUHR (1996); ARTAX (1999)** won the Breeders' Cup Sprint (1999); **LEFT BANK (2001)** won the Cigar Mile (2001), Whitney Hcp (2002); **GHOSTZAPPER (2003)** also won the Woodward Stakes, Metropolitan Hcp and Breeders' Cup Classic to be highest ranked horse in the world in 2004; and **HENNY HUGHES (2006)**.

## FRIZETTE STAKES

Frizette was a stakes winner and important foundation mare from the early 20th century.

Prominent winners include **IDUN (1957)** who won 17 of 30 starts including the Mother Goose Stakes, Gazelle Stakes; **BOWL OF FLOWERS (1960); CICADA (1961); TOSMAH (1963); SHUVEE (1968); FORWARD GAL (1970);** and **NUMBERED ACCOUNT (1971)**.

**LA PREVOYANTE (1972)** is in the Canadian Hall of Fame as a winner of 25 out of 39 career starts and was undefeated in 12 starts as a 2yo; **LAKEVILLE MISS (1977); HEAVENLY CAUSE (1980)** won the Kentucky Oaks (1981); **PRINCESS ROONEY (1982); MISS OCEANA (1983); PERSONAL ENSIGN (1986); MEADOW STAR (1990); HEAVENLY PRIZE (1993); STORM FLAG FLYING (2002); INDIAN BLESSING (2007);** and **DEVIL MAY CARE (2009)**.

## BELDAME STAKES

Beldame was a great filly from the turn of the 20th century who won 12 of 14 starts as a 3yo. The Beldame Stakes is one of the great races for fillies and mares in the USA. Established in 1939, it is run over 9 furlongs.

There have been several dual winners including **FAIRY CHANT (1940, 41), NEXT MOVE (1950, 52), GAMELY (1968, 69), SUSAN'S GIRL (1972, 75), DESERT VIXEN (1973, 74), LOVE SIGN (1980, 81), LADY'S SECRET (1985, 86), PERSONAL ENSIGN (1987, 88)** and **SIGHT SEEK (2003, 04)**.

Other notable winners include **GALLORETTE**

(1946); **BUT WHY NOT (1948)** won the Alabama Stakes, Acorn Stakes (1947), Personal Ensign Stakes (1949); **REAL DELIGHT (1952)** won the Kentucky Oaks and Coaching Club American Oaks (1952).

LALUN (1955) won the Kentucky Oaks, dam of Bold Reason and Never Bend – sire of Mill Reef; **LEVEE (1956)**, dam of **SHUVEE (1970)**; **TEMPTED (1959)** won the Alabama Stakes (1958) and twice won the Diana Stakes (1959, 60).

BERLO (1960) won the Gazelle Stakes, Mother Goose Stakes, Coaching Club American Oaks (1960); **CICADA (1962)**; **TOSMAH (1964)**; **WHAT A TREAT (1965)**, dam of Be My Guest who would become one of the foundation sires responsible for transforming Ireland's Coolmore Stud into one of the world's largest breeding operations; **WAYA (1979)**; **DANCE NUMBER (1983)**, dam of Rhythm; **LIFE'S MAGIC (1984)** won the Chandelier Stakes (1983), Mother Goose Stakes, Alabama Stakes (1984), Breeders' Cup Ladies' Classic (1985); **GO FOR WAND (1990)**; **SERENA'S SONG (1995)**; **SHARP CAT (1998)**; **BEAUTIFUL PLEASURE (1999)** won the Breeders' Cup Ladies' Classic (1999) and twice won the Personal Ensign Stakes (1999, 2000).

ASHADO (2005) won the Kentucky Oaks, Coaching Club American Oaks, Breeders' Cup Ladies' Classic (2004) and Ogden Phipps Hcp (2005); **FLEET INDIAN (2006)** won 13 of 17; **COCOA BEACH (2008)** won the UAE Oaks, UAE 1000 Guineas and Matriarch Stakes (2008); **MUSIC NOTE (2009)** won the Gazelle Stakes, Mother Goose Stakes, Coaching Club American Oaks (2008), Ballerina Stakes (2009); **HAVRE DE GRACE (2011)**; and **ROYAL DELTA (2012)** is a dual winner of the Breeders' Cup Ladies' Classic (2011, 12).

## NEW YORK HANDICAP TRIPLE

The New York Handicap Triple consists of the Metropolitan Handicap (8f), Grade 2 Brooklyn Handicap (12f) and Grade 2 Suburban Hcp (10f).

Four horses have won the Triple: **WHISK BROOM (1913)**, **TOM FOOL (1953)**, **KELSO (1961)** and **FIT TO FIGHT (1984)**.

## METROPOLITAN HANDICAP

The Met Mile was first run in 1891.

DEVIL DIVER (1943–45) made it a hat-trick.

Dual winners include **MAD HATTER (1921, 22)**, **EQUIPOISE (1932, 33)**, **STYMIE (1947, 48)**, **FOREGO (1976, 77)** and **GULCH (1987, 88)**.

Those to also win the Belmont Stakes include **BOWLING BROOK (1898)**, **THE FINN (1916)**, **NATIVE DANCER (1954)**, **HIGH GUN (1955)**, **GALLANT MAN (1958)**, **SWORD DANCER (1959)**, **ARTS AND LETTERS (1969)** and **CONQUISTADOR CIELO (1982)**.

Other notables include **KING JAMES (1909)**, who

won 24 of 57 starts; **GREY LAG (1923)**; **SARAZEN (1926)**; **BLACK MARIA (1927)**; **QUESTIONNAIRE (1931)**; **EIGHT THIRTY (1941)** won 16 of 27 including the Travers Stakes, Whitney Hcp (1939); **GALLORETTE (1946)**.

BALD EAGLE (1960) was a dual winner of the Washington DC International (1959, 60); **CARRY BACK (1962)** won the Kentucky Derby and Preakness (1961); **GUN BOW (1965)** won the Whitney Hcp, Woodward Stakes (1964), Donn Hcp (1965); **BOLD LAD (1966)**; **BUCKPASSER (1967)**; **IN REALITY (1968)** won 14 of 27; **NODOUBLE (1970)**; **COX'S RIDGE (1978)**; **FAPPIANO (1981)**; **CRIMINAL TYPE (1990)** won the Hollywood Gold Cup (1990); **IN EXCESS (1991)**.

HOLY BULL (1994) also won the Florida Derby, Blue Grass Stakes, Haskell Invitational, Travers Stakes and Woodward Stakes that year; **LANGFUHR (1997)**; **GHOSTZAPPER (2005)**; **SILVER TRAIN (2006)** won the Breeders' Cup Sprint (2005); **CORINTHIAN (2007)** won the Breeders' Cup Dirt Mile (2007); **QUALITY ROAD (2010)** won the Florida Derby (2009), Donn Hcp, Woodward Stakes (2010); and **SHACKLEFORD (2012)** won the Preakness (2011).

## MANHATTAN HANDICAP

Inaugurated in 1887, **BOLINGBROKE (1940, 42, 43)** holds the mark with three wins in the race.

Dual winners include **FIREARM (1899, 1900)**, **ROSEBEN (1905, 06)**, **THE FINN (1915, 16)**, **NATURALIST (1918, 20)**, **LITTLE CHIEF (1922, 23)**, **DARK SECRET (1933, 34)** and **MILESIUS (1988, 89)**.

Other notables include legendary mare **FIRENZE (1888)**, who had 82 starts for 47–21–9; incredible **RACELAND (1890)** had 70 wins from 130 starts; **HENRY OF NAVARRE (1895)**; **BELMAR (1896)**; **SARAZEN (1924)**; **VICTORIAN (1928)** won the Preakness (1928), Agua Caliente (1930); **DEVIL DIVER (1944)**; **STYMIE (1946)**; **DONOR (1949)**; **HIGH GUN (1954)**; **ROUND TABLE (1959)** had 66 starts for 43 wins including the Dixiana Breeders' Futurity (1956), Blue Grass Stakes, Hollywood Gold Cup (1957), Santa Anita Hcp, Agua Caliente (1958), twice won the United Nations Stakes (1957, 59) and an influential stallion; **ROMAN BROTHER (1965)**; **QUICKEN TREE (1968)** won the Jockey Club Gold Cup that year.

SNOW KNIGHT (1975) won the Epsom Derby (1974), Man O'War Stakes, Canadian International (1975); **SKY CLASSIC (1992)**; **STAR OF COZZENE (1993)** won the Arlington Million, Man O'War Stakes, United Nations Stakes (1993); **PARADISE CREEK (1994)** won the Hollywood Derby (2002), Washington DC International, Arlington Million, Turf Classic Stakes (1994); **CHIEF BEARHEART (1998)** won the Canadian International, Breeders' Cup Turf (1997); **BEAT HOLLOW (2002)**

won the Grand Prix de Paris (2000), Turf Classic Stakes, Arlington Million (2002); **BETTER TALK NOW (2007)**; and **GIO PONTI (2009)**.

## FLOWER BOWL INVITATIONAL STAKES

Flower Bowl was a handy mare from the 1950s and influential dam of Bowl Of Flowers.

The inaugural winner was **WAYA (1978)**, and subsequent winners include **PEARL NECKLACE (1979)**, who won the Gazelle Stakes (1977), Ogden Phipps Hcp, Diana Stakes (1979); **RIVER MEMORIES (1989)** won the Canadian International (1987); **SOARING SOFTLY (1999)** took out the Breeders' Cup Filly & Mare Turf (1999); German-bred **KAZZIA (2002)** won the 1000 Guineas, The Oaks (2002); **STACELITA (2011)** won the Prix Saint-Alary, Prix de Diane, Prix Vermeille (2009), Prix Jean Romanet (2010), Beverly D Stakes (2011); and **RISKAVERSE (2004, 05)** won the race twice.

## JAMAICA HANDICAP

Established in 1929, the race was upgraded to Grade 1 level in 2009.

## GARDEN CITY STAKES

Upgraded to Grade 1 status in 1999, it has since been won by **PERFECT STING (1999)**, winner of the Breeders' Cup Filly & Mare Turf (2000); and **SAMITAR (2012)**, who won the Irish 1000 Guineas (2012).

## JUST A GAME STAKES

Just A Game was Champion Female Horse in the USA in 1980.

Established in 1994, the race became a Grade 1 in 2008.

Winners since include **VENTURA (2008)**, who won the Breeders' Cup Filly & Mare Sprint, Madison Stakes (2008), Santa Monica Stakes, Woodbine Mile, Matriarch Stakes (2009); and **TAPITSFLY (2012)** won the Breeders' Cup Juvenile Fillies' Turf (2009).

# SANTA ANITA PARK

285 W Huntington Drive, Arcadia, California, USA. www.santaanita.com

*A*rcadia, in Los Angeles County, is just 13 miles from downtown Los Angeles. It is the location of one of the world's greatest and most famous racetracks – Santa Anita Park.

Racing in the area dates back to the days of the Spanish Dons, who raced their horses on the site.

EJ 'Lucky' Baldwin amassed enormous wealth having fortuitously received shares in a mining company, in lieu of a debt, just before the major discovery of gold in Nevada in 1849. He purchased the Santa Anita Ranch in 1875 and conducted his own races there for many years before building an official racecourse in 1907 on his private land.

Baldwin died two years later and the track lay dormant until 1933 when pari-mutuel betting was legalised and a syndicate headed by local dentist Charles H Strub and movie mogul Hal Roach formed the Los Angeles Turf Club and constructed the current course on the site.

Roach – producer of the films of Harold Lloyd, Laurel and Hardy, Abbott and Costello, as well as movies including *Of Mice and Men* – was of the belief that big stake money was the key to attracting the best horses. His strategy was an immediate success. The Santa Anita Handicap would become the first race in the USA to be staged for a purse of $100,000 and, along with the Santa Anita Derby, Santa Anita Oaks and Santa Margarita Stakes, was run on the first day of the inaugural fall meeting in 1935.

Seabiscuit was trained on the course and 78,000 turned out for his emotion-charged final race here, but the record attendance was in 1985 when more than 85,000 people saw Lord At War propel Bill Shoemaker past an unprecedented $100m in stakes as a rider.

Due to California's favourable weather, plenty of racing is conducted at the track with the season from October until April.

## FEATURE RACES

| | | | | | | | |
|---|---|---|---|---|---|---|---|
| LAS VIRGENES STAKES | G1 | 8F | DIRT | 3YOF | SW | 1981 | MAR |
| FRANK E KILROE MILE | G1 | 8F | TURF | 4YO+ | HCP | 1960 | MAR |
| SANTA MAGARITA INVITATIONAL | G1 | 9F | DIRT | 4YO+F&M | ASS | 1935 | MAR |
| SANTA ANITA HCP | G1 | 10F | DIRT | 4YO+ | HCP | 1935 | MAR |
| SANTA ANITA DERBY | G1 | 9F | DIRT | 3YO | SW | 1935 | APR |
| SANTA ANITA OAKS | G1 | 8½F | DIRT | 3YOF | SW | 1935 | APR |
| ZENYATTA STAKES | G1 | 8½F | DIRT | 3YO+F&M | ASS | 1993 | OCT |
| RODEO DRIVE STAKES | G1 | 10F | TURF | 3YO+F&M | SW | 1977 | OCT |
| FRONTRUNNER STAKES | G1 | 8½F | DIRT | 2YO | ASS | 1970 | OCT |
| CHANDELIER STAKES | G1 | 8½F | DIRT | 2YOF | ASS | 1969 | OCT |
| AWESOME AGAIN STAKES | G1 | 9F | DIRT | 3YO+ | SW | 1981 | OCT |
| SANTA ANITA SPRINT CHAMPIONSHIP | G1 | 6F | DIRT | 3YO+ | ASS | 1985 | OCT |
| MALIBU STAKES | G1 | 7F | DIRT | 3YO | ASS | 1952 | DEC |
| LA BREA STAKES | G1 | 7F | DIRT | 3YOF | ASS | 1974 | DEC |

## BREEDERS' CUP RACES

| | | | | |
|---|---|---|---|---|
| BREEDERS' CUP CLASSIC | G1 | 10F | DIRT | 3YO+ |
| BREEDERS' CUP DIRT MILE | G1 | 8F | DIRT | 3YO+ |
| BREEDERS' CUP FILLY & MARE SPRINT | G1 | 7F | DIRT | 3YO+F&M |
| BREEDERS' CUP JUVENILE | G1 | 8½F | DIRT | 2YOC&G |
| BREEDERS' CUP JUVENILE TURF | G1 | 8F | TURF | 2YOC&G |
| BREEDERS' CUP MILE | G1 | 8F | TURF | 3YO+ |
| BREEDERS' CUP SPRINT | G1 | 6F | DIRT | 3YO+ |
| BREEDFRS' CUP TURF | G1 | 12F | TURF | 3YO+ |
| BREEDERS' CUP FILLY & MARE TURF | G1 | 10F | TURF | 3YO+F&M |
| BREEDERS' CUP JUVENILE FILLIES | G1 | 8½F | DIRT | 2YOF |
| BREEDERS' CUP JUVENILE FILLIES TURF | G1 | 8F | TURF | 2YOF |

While the March meeting remains the annual highlight, Santa Anita is the regular host of the two-day Breeders' Cup meeting held in November. Inaugurated in 1984, the Breeders' Cup program was designed as the showcase meeting on the US calendar and is the undisputed championship of American racing.

Set against the majestic San Gabriel mountains, Santa Anita is also one of the most beautiful locations for a racecourse anywhere in the world. A memorable spectacle is an early morning visit to the track, where visitors can see champion horses working on the course at dawn as the California sun rises over the mountains. Highly recommended.

While Los Angeles is known for its glitz and glamour, the Santa Anita course is wonderfully traditional and positively reeks of history.

## THE TRACK

Left-handed. One-mile dirt oval. Home straight – 330yds.

Inner turf course of ⁹⁄₁₀ of a mile.

The Hillside Turf Course is a downhill 6½ furlong course.

## FEATURE RACES

### SANTA ANITA HANDICAP

The Santa Anita Handicap was inaugurated in 1935 and is considered the premier older age contest in California and one of the most important races in the USA.

In scenes rarely witnessed on a racecourse **SEABIS-CUIT (1940)**, with Red Pollard aboard, capped a remarkable return to the racetrack with his swansong in this race. Both were mobbed on return to the enclosure by the 78,000 adoring fans in attendance. His 33 career victories enabled him to retire as all-time leading money winner.

Dual winners of the race include **JOHN HENRY (1981, 82)**, **MILWAUKEE BREW (2002, 03)** and **LAVA MAN (2006, 07)**.

Other notables include **ROUND TABLE (1958)**; **HILL RISE (1965)**; Kentucky Derby winner **LUCKY DEBONAIR (1966)**; **NODOUBLE (1969)**; **QUICKEN TREE (1970)**; Chilean stars **COUGAR (1973)** and **MALEK (1998)**; Triple Crown hero **AFFIRMED (1979)**; **SPECTACULAR BID (1980)**; **BROAD BRUSH (1987)**; **ALYSHEBA (1988)**; Champion Argentine miler **LORD AT WAR (1985)**.

**BEST PAL (1992)** won six Grade 1 races including the Hollywood Gold Cup. Other winners to also take out the Hollywood Gold Cup include **KAYAK (1939)**; **NOOR (1950)**; **REJECTED (1954)**; **PROVE IT (1961)**; **ACK ACK (1971)**; **GREINTON (1986)** and **GAME ON DUDE (2011)**, who was also a dual winner of the Awesome Again Stakes (2011, 12).

**FREE HOUSE (1999)** won the FrontRunner Stakes, Santa Anita Derby (1997), Pacific Classic Stakes (1998); **TIZNOW (2001)** was a dual winner of the Breeders' Cup Classic (2000, 01); and **EINSTEIN (2009)** won the Clark Hcp (2008) and twice won the

Turf Classic Stakes, Gulfstream Park Turf Classic Stakes and the Woodford Reserve Turf Classic (2008, 09).

## SANTA ANITA DERBY

Considered the most important lead-up race to the Kentucky Derby on the West Coast.

Winners to go on to Derby success include **HILL GAIL (1952)**, **DETERMINE (1954)**, **SWAPS (1955)**, **LUCKY DEBONAIR (1965)**, **MAJESTIC PRINCE (1969)**, **AFFIRMED (1978)**, **SUNDAY SILENCE (1989)** and **I'LL HAVE ANOTHER (2012)**.

Preakness winners include **CANDY SPOTS (1963)**; **CODEX (1980)**; **SNOW CHIEF (1986)**; **POINT GIVEN (2001)** also won the Belmont, as did **AVATAR (1975)**; **AP INDY (1992)** won the Belmont Stakes, Breeders' Cup Classic (1992); **STAGEHAND (1938)** narrowly defeated Seabiscuit in the Santa Anita Hcp that year; **YOUR HOST (1950)** sired Kelso; **SILKY SULLIVAN (1958)** came from 28 lengths behind.

**SILVER SPOON (1959)** became the first of only two fillies ever to win the Santa Anita Derby and the Santa Anita Oaks – the second being **WINNING COLORS (1988)**, who also won the Kentucky Derby.

**TOMPION (1960)**; **HILL RISE (1964)**; **BOLD-NESIAN (1966)**, grandsire of Seattle Slew; **SHAM (1973)**; **SKYWALKER (1985)** won the Breeders' Cup Classic (1986); Puerto Rican hero **MISTER FRISKY (1990)**; **BROCCO (1994)** won the Breeders' Cup Juvenile (1993); **FREE HOUSE (1997)**; and **CASTLEDALE (2004)** was a Grade 1 winner on dirt and turf.

## SANTA ANITA OAKS

Formerly known as the Santa Susana Stakes.

Winners who also took out the Kentucky Oaks include **BLUE NORTHER (1964)**; **BOLD 'N DETERMINED (1980)**; **LITE LIGHT (1991)**; and Belmont Stakes winner **RAGS TO RICHES (2007)**, who was rated World Champion Filly that year.

Other notable winners include Louis B Mayer's three-time champion filly **BUSHER (1942)**, **SILVER SPOON (1959)**, **LAMB CHOP (1963)**, **TURKISH TROUSERS (1971)**, **SUSAN'S GIRL (1972)**, **WINNING COLORS (1988)**, **SERENA'S SONG (1995)** and **SHARP CAT (1997)**;

Breeders' Cup Juvenile Fillies winners include **ELIZA (1993)** and **STARDOM BOUND (2009)**.

## SANTA MARGARITA INVITATIONAL STAKES

Fillies and mares race established in 1935. Originally a handicap, the race became an invitational event in 1968.

Dual winners include **OUR BETTERS (1956,**

57); **CURIOUS CLOVER (1964, 65)**; **BAYAKOA (1989, 90)** and **PASEANA (1992, 94)**.

Other prominent winners include **FAIRY CHANT (1940)**; **BUSHER (1945)**; **TWO LEA (1950)** and **PRINCESSNESIAN (1969)** both won the Hollywood Gold Cup; **BED O' ROSES (1952)**; **SILVER SPOON (1960)**; **GAMELY (1968)**; **GALLANT BLOOM (1970)** won 16 of 22 starts with 12 wins in succession; **TURKISH TROUSERS (1972)**; **SUSAN'S GIRL (1973)**; star Canadian mare **GLORIOUS SONG (1980)**; **LADY'S SECRET (1986)**; **NORTH SIDER (1987)**.

**JEWEL PRINCESS (1997)** and **LIFE IS SWEET (2009)** both won the Breeders' Cup Ladies' Classic, **MANISTIQUE (1999)**, **AZERI (2002)**, **NASHOBA'S KEY (2008)** and **ZENYATTA (2010)**.

## SANTA MONICA STAKES

Dual winners include **CHOP HOUSE (1964, 65)**, **PAST FORGETTING (1982, 83)** and **PINE TREE LANE (1987, 88)**.

Other notables include **SILVER SPOON (1960)**; **GAMELY (1969)**; **TYPECAST (1972)** won 21 races including the Gamely Stakes, Charles Whittingham Memorial, Man O' War Stakes (1972); **SERENA'S SONG (1996)**; four-time Grade 1 winner **AFFLUENT (2003)**; and **VENTURA (2009)** won the Just A Game Stakes, Madison Stakes (2008), Woodbine Mile, Matriarch Stakes, Breeders' Cup Filly & Mare Sprint (2009).

## LAS VIRGENES STAKES

Notable winners include **ALTHEA (1984)**, who won the Hollywood Starlet Stakes (1983), Santa Anita Oaks, Arkansas Derby (1984); **FRAN'S VALENTINE (1985)** won the Santa Anita Oaks and Kentucky Oaks; **LITE LIGHT (1994)**; **SERENA'S SONG (1995)**; **SHARP CAT (1997)**; **RAGS TO RICHES (2007)**; **STARDOM BOUND (2009)**; and **BLIND LUCK (2010)**.

## FRANK E KILROE MILE

Mile race on the turf, inaugurated in 1960 as the Arcadia Handicap.

Notable winners include top Australian **DARYL'S JOY (1971)**, who won the Manawatu Sires' Produce, Ellerslie Diamond Stakes, Cox Plate, Victoria Derby and defeated Vain in the Moonee Valley Stakes (1969); **THE AXE (1973)** won the Canadian International and Man O' War Stakes that year; **GA HAI (1975, 76)** is the only dual winner to date; **CAUCASUS (1977)** won the Irish St Leger (1975), Manhattan Hcp (1976); **PERRAULT (1982)** was a multiple stakes winner in France and also won the Arlington Million and

Goldikova

Hollywood Gold Cup (1982); **EXCELLER (1978)**; **STRAWBERRY ROAD (1986)**; **PRIZED (1990)** won the Breeders' Cup Turf (1989).

**FLY TILL DAWN (1992)** won four Grade 1 races including the Washington DC International (1990); Brazilian champ **REDATTORE (2003)**; **SWEET RETURN (2005)** won the Hollywood Derby (2003), Charles Whittingham Memorial, Eddie Read Stakes (2005); **MILK IT MICK (2006)** won the Dewhurst Stakes (2003); **KIP DEVILLE (2007)** won the Maker's Mark Mile (2007, 08) twice and the Breeders' Cup Mile (2007); **GIO PONTI (2009)**; and **PROVISO (2010)** became the first filly to win.

## MALIBU STAKES

Established in 1952, it is a 7-furlong race for 3yos that has been a springboard for many top young horses.

Winners include filly **A GLEAM (1953)**; Kentucky Derby winner **DETERMINE (1955)**; **ROUND TABLE (1957)**; **HILLSDALE (1958)**; **TOMPION (1960)**; **NATIVE DIVER (1962)**; **BUCKPASSER (1966)**; **DAMASCUS (1968)**; **ANCIENT TITLE (1974)** won 25 of 57 starts with five Grade 1 wins; **J.O. TOBIN (1978)**; **SPECTACULAR BID (1980)**.

**PRECISIONIST (1984)** won six times at Grade 1 level including the Breeders' Cup Sprint (1995); ill-fated **FERDINAND (1986)** won the Kentucky Derby (1986), Hollywood Gold Cup, Breeders' Cup Classic (1987); **PLEASANT TAP (1990)** won the Jockey Club Gold Cup (1992); **DIXIE UNION (2000)** won the Haskell Invitational (2000); **SOUTHERN IMAGE (2003)**; and **BOB BLACK JACK (2008)** holds the track records at Santa Anita for both 6 and 7 furlongs.

## CHANDELIER STAKES

First run in 1969 as the Oak Leaf Stakes, the name was changed in 2012. The race for 2yo fillies is an automatic qualifier for the Breeders' Cup Juvenile Fillies.

Notable winners include **IN THE AIR (1978)**, who won the Ruffian Hcp, Alabama Stakes (1979) and twice won the Vanity Invitational (1979, 80); **BOLD 'N DETERMINED (1979)**; **LIFE'S MAGIC (1983)**; **SACAHUISTA (1986)** also won the Breeders' Cup Ladies' Classic (1987); **LITE LIGHT (1990)**;

PHONE CHATTER (1993) won the Breeders' Cup Juvenile Fillies (1993); SERENA'S SONG (1994); CHILUKKI (1999); and COMPOSURE (2002) won the Santa Anita Oaks and Las Virgenes Stakes (2003).

## LA BREA STAKES

Seven-furlong race for 3yo fillies, first run in 1974.

Prominent winners include five-time Grade 1 winner FAMILY STYLE (1987); VERY SUBTLE (1988) won the Breeders' Cup Sprint (1987); SPAIN (2000) won the Breeders' Cup Ladies' Classic that year; AFFLUENT (2001); GOT KOKO (2002); and INDIAN BLESSING (2008) won the Breeders' Cup Juvenile Fillies (2007).

## ZENYATTA STAKES

Established in 1993 as the Lady's Secret Stakes, it was up graded to Grade 1 status in 2007.

ZENYATTA (2008–10) won three in a row during her sensational record-equalling streak of 19 consecutive victories – 13 of those at Grade 1 level. She was also a three-time winner of the Clement L Hirsch Stakes (2008–10) and the Vanity Invitational (2008–10), dual winner of the Apple Blossom (2008, 10) and victorious in the Breeders' Cup Ladies' Classic (2008) and Breeders' Cup Classic (2009).

It is history now that she was narrowly defied in her bid for 20 consecutive wins by Blame in the Breeders' Cup Classic of 2010, but her second-place money saw her retire as leading money-winner of all time, and she is regarded as one of the greatest horses in the history of US racing.

Among her many honours, Zenyatta was named by *Sports Illustrated* as top female horse in history and she was twice runner-up in the Female Athlete of the Year category, as voted by the Associated Press.

Zenyatta

# SARATOGA

267 Union Avenue, Saratoga Springs, New York, USA. www.nyra.com/saratoga

*Opened in 1863, only a month after the Battle of Gettysburg, Saratoga racecourse is one of the USA's most famous venues for racing.*

The historic city is famous for its architecture and mineral baths and is the site of over a thousand buildings that are listed on the National Register of Historic Places.

The first meeting was instigated by former boxing champion, John 'Old Smoke' Morrissey, who was also a fierce gambler, raconteur and future congressman. It was staged on the old Oklahoma track, which had previously been used for trots racing.

After the success of the inaugural meeting, Morrissey enlisted friends including William Travers to form the Saratoga Association, which purchased the land directly across Union Avenue and constructed the current course and a permanent grandstand on the 350-acre site. The Oklahoma track was converted into a training facility.

Saratoga is now the oldest course in continual operation in the USA with many of its traditional grandstands and clubhouses still intact.

Each summer the population of Saratoga triples and the course stages its meeting from July to September. Consequently race-goers can experience the historic charm of the track in a relaxed atmosphere while viewing absolutely top-class racing.

Many of America's time-honoured Grade 1 races are conducted here including the Travers Stakes, Alabama Stakes, Whitney Handicap, Test Stakes and the Coaching Club American Oaks. The Woodward Stakes is one of the country's premier open events.

The infield features a gazebo and a lake, and every year the colours of the Travers Stakes winner are painted onto a canoe stationed on the lake.

Spectators are afforded a close-up look at runners as they make their way from the paddock to the track along a path through the picnic grounds. The many provided picnic tables are always in strong demand and are generally available on a first-come, first-served basis. Also available is the opportunity to partake in the natural waters from an active mineral spring.

Saratoga was famously the scene of Man O' War's only defeat on a racetrack, by the aptly named Upset in the 1919 Sanford Memorial Stakes. Gallant Fox and Secretariat also had their colours lowered here.

The course features three tracks – the main

| FEATURE RACES | | | | | | | |
|---|---|---|---|---|---|---|---|
| COACHING CLUB AMERICAN OAKS | G1 | 9F | DIRT | 3YOF | SW | 1917 | JUL |
| DIANA STAKES | G1 | 9F | TURF | 3YO+F&M | HCP | 1939 | JUL |
| WHITNEY HCP | G1 | 9F | DIRT | 3YO+ | HCP | 1928 | AUG |
| PRIORESS STAKES | G1 | 6F | DIRT | 3YOF | ASS | 1948 | AUG |
| ALFRED G VANDERBILT HCP | G1 | 6F | DIRT | 3YO+ | HCP | 1985 | AUG |
| SWORD DANCER INVITATIONAL HCP | G1 | 12F | TURF | 3YO+ | ASS | 1975 | AUG |
| ALABAMA STAKES | G1 | 10F | DIRT | 3YOF | SW | 1872 | AUG |
| BALLERINA STAKES | G1 | 7F | DIRT | 3YO+F&M | ASS | 1979 | AUG |
| TRAVERS STAKES | G1 | 10F | DIRT | 3YO | SW | 1864 | AUG |
| TEST STAKES | G1 | 7F | DIRT | 3YOF | ASS | 1922 | AUG |
| KING'S BISHOP STAKES | G1 | 7F | DIRT | 3YO | ASS | 1984 | AUG |
| PERSONAL ENSIGN STAKES | G1 | 10F | DIRT | 3YO+F&M | SWP | 1948 | AUG |
| RUFFIAN HCP | G1 | 8½F | DIRT | 3YO+F&M | WFA | 1976 | SEPT |
| WOODWARD STAKES | G1 | 9F | DIRT | 3YO+ | WFA | 1954 | SEPT |
| FOREGO HCP | G1 | 7F | DIRT | 3YO+ | HCP | 1980 | SEPT |
| SPINAWAY STAKES | G1 | 7F | DIRT | 3YOF | ASS | 1881 | SEPT |

dirt oval and two turf tracks. Steeplechase races are conducted on the inner turf course every Thursday during the season, with the feature the G1 New York Turf Writer's Cup. Twilight fixtures are a fairly recent addition, having been scheduled since 2006.

## THE TRACK

Left-handed. Main Track – 9-furlong dirt oval. The Mellon Turf Track is a one-mile turf oval. The inner turf track is approximately 7½ furlongs.

## FEATURE RACES

### TRAVERS STAKES

First run in 1864, it is a historic race with the winning owner awarded the Man O'War trophy and their colours painted on the famous canoe. Man O'War won the 1920 edition of the race. The race is the richest run at Saratoga with a purse of $1 million and has been won by many of the greats of US racing.

**KENTUCKY (1864)** won the inaugural running and 21 of 23 career starts.

The race has been won by many Classic winners including Triple Crown champion **WHIRLAWAY (1941)**, dual Classic winners include **DUKE OF MAGENTA (1878)**, **MAN O'WAR (1920)**, **TWENTY GRAND (1931)**, **SHUT OUT (1942)**, **NATIVE DANCER (1953)**, **THUNDER GULCH (1995)** and **POINT GIVEN (2001)**.

**BADEN-BADEN (1877)**, **HINDOO (1881)**, **AZRA (1892)**, **OMAR KHAYYAM (1917)**, **SEA HERO (1993)** and **STREET SENSE (2007)** were Kentucky Derby winners. **BERNADINI (2006)** won the Preakness.

**RUTHLESS (1867)**, **KINGFISHER (1870)**, **HARRY BASSETT (1871)**, **JOE DANIELS (1872)**, **HENRY OF NAVARRE (1894)**, **GRANVILLE (1936)**, **ONE COUNT (1952)**, **GALLANT MAN (1957)**, **SWORD DANCER (1959)**, **QUADRANGLE (1964)** sire of Susan's Girl; **HAIL TO ALL (1965)**, **DAMASCUS (1967)**, **ARTS AND LETTERS (1969)**, **TEMPERENCE HILL (1980)**, **EASY GOER (1989)**, **LEMON DROP KID (1999)**, **BIRDSTONE (2004)** and **SUMMER BIRD (2009)** all won the Belmont Stakes.

Other notable winners include **FALSETTO (1879)**, sire of three Kentucky Derby winners; **HERMIS (1902)** had 55 starts for 28 wins; **BROOMSTICK (1904)** influential sire of Regret – the first filly to win the Kentucky Derby – and the legendary Tippity Witchet, who had a phenomenal 266 starts for 78 wins, 52 seconds and 42 thirds. Tippity Witchet was

an iron horse who was one of the top juveniles of his year winning 14 of 20 starts and was still winning at the age of 14. He won on 27 different tracks in the USA, Canada, Mexico and Cuba over distances ranging from 6 furlongs to a mile and a half.

**ROAMER (1914)** had 39 career wins; **SPUR (1916)**; **SUN BRIAR (1918)**, influential sire of Sun Beau and Pompey; **LITTLE CHIEF (1922)** was a dual winner of the Manhattan Hcp (1922, 23); **EIGHT THIRTY (1939)** won 16 of 27; **ARISE (1949)**; **BATTLEFIELD (1951)**; **FISHERMAN (1954)**; **TOMPION (1960)**; **JAIPUR (1962)** ran a track record to narrowly defeat Ridan in a classic down-the-stretch battle; **BUCKPASSER (1966)**; **BOLD REASON (1971)**; **WAJIMA (1975)**; **HONEST PLEASURE (1976)**; **ALYDAR (1978)**; **RUNAWAY GROOM (1982)** became the only horse ever to defeat all three winners of the that year's Triple Crown in the one race.

Four-time Grade 1 winner **PLAY FELLOW (1983)**; **CHIEF'S CROWN (1985)** won the Breeders' Cup Juvenile (1984); **JAVA GOLD (1987)**; **FORTY NINER (1988)**; **RHYTHM (1990)** won the Breeders' Cup Juvenile (1989); **HOLY BULL (1994)**; **CORONADO'S QUEST (1998)**; **MEDAGLIA D'ORO (2002)**; and **FLOWER ALLEY (2005)**, sire of I'll Have Another.

### WHITNEY HANDICAP

The Whitney family has been synonymous with thoroughbred racing in the USA for more than a century. Many members of this prominent family have long been involved in racing administration and have owned multiple winners of all of the American Classics. William C Whitney also owned 1901 Epsom Derby winner Volodyovsky.

HP Whitney won this race with **WHICHONE (1930)** and CV Whitney won it on four occasions with **EQUIPOISE (1932)**, **COUNTERPOINT (1952)**, **STATE DINNER (1980)** and **SILVER BUCK (1982)**.

**DISCOVERY (1934–36)** recorded a hat-trick, as did **KELSO (1961, 63, 65)**. **COMMENTATOR (2005, 08)** is a dual winner.

Other notables include inaugural winner **BLACK MARIA (1928)**; **BATEAU (1929)** won the Gazelle Stakes, Coaching Club American Oaks (1928); **WAR ADMIRAL (1938)**; **EIGHT THIRTY (1939)**; **CHALLEDON (1940)**; **FENELON (1941)** won the Jockey Club Gold Cup (1940); **DEVIL DIVER (1944)** won 22 of 47 including the Dixiana Breeders' Futurity (1941), Carter Hcp, Manhattan Hcp (1943) and three successive Metropolitan Hcps (1943–45); **STYMIE (1946)**; **GALLORETTE (1948)**; **PIET (1950)** scored three consecutive wins in the Jamaica Hcp (1949–51).

**TOM FOOL (1953)** won 21 of 30 career races including the NY Handicap Triple Crown that year;

**CARRY BACK (1962)**; **DR FAGER (1968)**; **KEY TO THE MINT (1972)**; **ONION (1973)** defeated Secretariat; **ANCIENT TITLE (1975)**; **ALYDAR (1978)**; **FIO RITO (1981)** won 28 of 50 starts; **ISLAND WHIRL (1983)** won the Malibu Stakes, Woodward Stakes (1982), Hollywood Gold Cup (1983); **SLEW O' GOLD (1984)**; **TRACK BARRON (1985)** won four races at Grade 1; **LADY'S SECRET (1986)**; **JAVA GOLD (1987)**; **PERSONAL ENSIGN (1988)**; **EASY GOER (1989)**; **CRIMINAL TYPE (1990)**.

**IN EXCESS (1991)** was the first horse since Kelso to sweep the Metropolitan Hcp, Suburban Hcp, Whitney Hcp and Woodward Stakes in the same year; **SULTRY SONG (1992)** won the Woodward Stakes, Hollywood Gold Cup (1992); **COLONIAL AFFAIR (1994)** won the Belmont Stakes and Jockey Club Gold Cup (1983).

**AWESOME AGAIN (1998)**; **VICTORY GALLOP (1999)**; **LEMON DROP KID (2000)**; Chilean Triple Crown winner **LIDO PALACE (2001)**; **LEFT BANK (2002)** won the Cigar Mile, Vosburgh Stakes (2001); **MEDAGLIA D'ORO (2003)**; **ROSES IN MAY (2004)** won the Dubai World Cup (2005), as did **INVASOR (2006)**; **LAWYER RON (2007)** won the Arkansas Derby (2006), Woodward Stakes (2007); **BLAME (2010)** won the Clark Hcp (2009), Stephen Foster Hcp and denied Zenyatta in the Breeders' Cup Classic (2010); and **FORT LARNED (2012)** also won the Breeders' Cup Classic (2012).

### WOODWARD STAKES

Named after prominent owner William Woodward Sr, long-time chairman of the United States Jockey Club. The race has been run at all three NYRA tracks at Aqueduct, Belmont and moved to Saratoga in 2006. It is one of the premier weight-for-age contests in the US.

Great names to have won include **FOREGO (1974–77)**, who won the race four years in succession; **KELSO (1961–63)** won it three times; and dual winners include **SWORD DANCER (1959, 60)**, **SLEW O' GOLD (1993, 94)**, **CIGAR (1995, 96)** and **LIDO PALACE (2001, 02)**.

Other notable winners include **PET BULLY (1954)**, **CLEM (1958)**, **GUN BOW (1964)**, **ROMAN BROTHER (1965)**, **BUCKPASSER (1966)**, **DAMASCUS (1967)**, **ARTS AND LETTERS (1969)**, **PERSONALITY (1970)**, **WEST COAST SCOUT (1971)**, **KEY TO THE MINT (1972)**, **SEATTLE SLEW (1978)**, **AFFIRMED (1979)**, **SPECTACULAR BID (1980)**, **PLEASANT COLONY (1981)**, **PRECISIONIST (1986)**, **ALYSHEBA (1988)**, **EASY GOER (1989)**, **BERTRANDO (1993)**, **HOLY BULL (1994)**, **SKIP AWAY (1998)**, **LEMON DROP KID (2000)**, **MINESHAFT (2003)**, **GHOSTZAPPER (2004)**, **SAINT LIAM (2005)**, **CURLIN (2008)**, **QUALITY ROAD (2011)**, **RACHEL ALEXANDRA (2009)** and **HAVRE DE GRACE (2011)** are the only fillies to have won.

## ALABAMA STAKES

Established in 1872, the race is currently a leg of the Triple Tiara.

Winners of this race who have taken out the Triple Tiara include **SHUVEE (1969)**; **MOM'S COMMAND (1985)**; **OPEN MIND (1989)**, who also won the Breeders' Cup Juvenile Fillies (1988) and Kentucky Oaks (1989); and **SKY BEAUTY (1993)**.

Other notable winners include **MISS WOODFORD (1883)** who won 37 of 48; **BELDAME (1904)**; **MASKETTE (1909)**; **SUNBONNET (1919)** won the Kentucky Oaks (1919); **CLEOPATRA (1920)**; **TOP FLIGHT (1932)**; **BARN SWALLOW (1933)** won the Kentucky Oaks; **VAGRANCY (1942)**; **BUT WHY NOT (1947)**; **BUSANDA (1950)**, dam of Buckpasser; **PARLO (1954)** won the Beldame Stakes, Personal Ensign Stakes (1954) and Delaware Hcp (1955); **TEMPTED (1958)** was a dual winner of the Diana Stakes (1959, 60); **PRIMONETTA (1961)** won 17 of 25 starts; **WHAT A TREAT (1965)**; **GAMELY (1967)**.

Canadian Hall of Famers **FANFRELUCHE (1970)** and **LAURIES DANCER (1971)**; **SUMMER GUEST (1972)**; **DESERT VIXEN (1973)**; **WHITE STAR LINE (1978)** won the Kentucky Oaks; **IT'S IN THE AIR (1979)**; **LOVE SIGN (1980)**; **LIFE'S MAGIC (1984)**; **GO FOR WAND (1990)**.

**VERSAILLES TREATY (1991)** won the Gazelle Stakes, Test Stakes, Ruffian Hcp (1991); **BANSHEE BREEZE (1998)**; **SILVERBULLETDAY (1999)**; **BLIND LUCK (2010)**; and dual Breeders' Cup Ladies' Classic winner **ROYAL DELTA (2011)**.

## SPINAWAY STAKES

Historic contest for 2yo fillies, first run in 1881.

Notable winners include **MISS WOODFORD (1882)**; **LOS ANGELES (1887)** had 110 starts for 48 wins; **TANYA (1904)** was the second filly ever to win the Belmont Stakes (1905); **MASKETTE (1908)**; **GOOSE EGG (1929)**, dam of Kentucky Derby winner Shut Out; **TOP FLIGHT (1931)**; **MAR-KELL (1941)**; influential broodmare **ALANESIAN (1956)**.

**CICADA (1961)**; **AFFECTIONATELY (1962)** won 28 of 52 starts; **FORWARD GAL (1970)**; **NUMBERED ACCOUNT (1971)** won 14 of 22 including the Frizette Stakes, (1971), Spinster Stakes, Test Stakes, Prioress Stakes (1972); **LA PREVOYANTE (1972)**; **RUFFIAN (1974)**.

**DEARLY PRECIOUS (1975)** won 12 of 16 starts; **FAMILY STYLE (1985)**; **MEADOW STAR (1990)**; **COUNTESS DIANA (1997)** won the Breeders' Cup Juvenile Fillies (1997); **ASHADO (2003)** won the Kentucky Oaks, Breeders' Cup Ladies'

Classic, Coaching Club American Oaks (2004), Ogden Phipps Hcp and Beldame Stakes (2005).

## TEST STAKES

Three-year-old fillies race, first run in 1922. Notables include **SUNTICA (1932)**, who won the Kentucky Oaks (1932); **VAGRANCY (1942)**; **CANADIANA (1953)** won 20 races; **MOCASSIN (1966)**; **GAMELY (1967)**; **TA WEE (1969)**; **NUMBERED ACCOUNT (1972)**; **DESERT VIXEN (1973)**; **MY JULIET (1975)**; **WHITE STAR LINE (1978)**; **LOVE SIGN (1980)**; **LADY'S SECRET (1985)**; **VERY SUBTLE (1987)**.

**SAFELY KEPT (1989)** won 24 of 31 starts including the Breeders' Cup Sprint; **GO FOR WAND (1990)**; **VERSAILLES TREATY (1991)**; **JERSEY GIRL (1998)** won 9 of 11 including the Mother Goose Stakes, Acorn Stakes; **INDIAN BLESSING (2008)**; and **TURBULENT DESCENT (2011)**.

## DIANA STAKES

Inaugurated in 1939. Fillies and mares event conducted on the turf.

It has had several dual winners including **MISS GRILLO (1946, 47)**, **SEARCHING (1956, 58)**, **TEMPTED (1959, 60)**, **SHUVEE (1970, 71)**, **HUSH DEAR (1982, 83)**, **GLOWING HONOR (1988, 89)** and **FOREVER TOGETHER (2008, 09)**.

Other notables include **BUSANDA (1952)**; **MISTY MORN (1955)**, dam of Bold Lad; **OPEN FIRE (1966)**; **GAMELY (1969)**; **WAYA (1978)**; **PEARL NECKLACE (1979)**; **JUST A GAME (1980)**; **STARINE (2001)**; and **MY TYPHOON (2007)**.

## COACHING CLUB AMERICAN OAKS

Second leg of the Triple Tiara, the race has been won by many of the top fillies. While the Triple Tiara races have been subject to change, the Coaching Club American Oaks has been a constant in the series.

Triple Tiara winners include **DARK MIRAGE (1968)**, **SHUVEE (1969)**, **CHRIS EVERT (1974)**, **RUFFIAN (1975)**, **DAVONA DALE (1979)**, **MOM'S COMMAND (1985)**, **OPEN MIND (1989)** and **SKY BEAUTY (1993)**.

Other prominent winners include **CLEOPATRA (1920)**; **PRINCESS DOREEN (1924)** won 34 races including the Kentucky Oaks; **BATEAU (1928)**; **TOP FLIGHT (1932)**; **BLACK HELEN (1935)** won 15 of 22 races; **VAGRANCY (1942)**; **TWILIGHT TEAR (1944)**; **WISTFUL (1949)**; **NEXT MOVE (1950)**; **REAL DELIGHT (1952)**; **BERLO (1960)**; **BOWL OF FLOWERS (1961)**; **LAMB CHOP**

**(1963)**; **SUMMER GUEST (1972)**; **LAKEVILLE MISS (1978)** won four races at Grade 1; **BOLD 'N DETERMINED (1980)**; **LITE LIGHT (1991)**; **MY FLAG (1996)** won the Breeders' Cup Juvenile Fillies (1995); **AJINA (1997)** won the Breeders' Cup Ladies' Classic (1997); **BANSHEE BREEZE (1998)**; **ASHADO (2004)**; **MUSIC NOTE (2008)**; **DEVIL MAY CARE (2010)**; and **IT'S TRICKY (2011)**.

## PRIORESS STAKES

Named after Prioress, recorded as the first American thoroughbred to win in England when she took out the Cesarewitch in 1857.

Won by **NEXT MOVE (1950)**; **GRECIAN QUEEN (1953)**; **PRIMONETTA (1961)**; **WHAT A TREAT (1965)**; **DARK MIRAGE (1968)**; **TA WEE (1969)**; **NUMBERED ACCOUNT (1972)**; **WINDY'S DAUGHTER (1973)** won the Acorn Stakes, Mother Goose Stakes (1973); **DEARLY PRECIOUS (1976)**; **TEMPEST QUEEN (1978)** won the Mother Goose Stakes, Spinster Stakes and Gazelle Stakes that year; top broodmare **FALL ASPEN (1979)**; **SAFELY KEPT (1989)**; **CLASSY MIRAGE (1993)** won 13 of 25 starts; **XTRA HEAT (2001)**; and **INDIAN BLESSING (2008)**.

## ALFRED G VANDERBILT HANDICAP

Alfred G Vanderbilt was a prominent owner, breeder and administrator. He was chairman of the board of the NYRA and owned many champions including Discovery, Next Move, Bed O' Roses and the great Native Dancer. As owner of Pimlico he organised the famous match between Seabiscuit and War Admiral.

The race is an open sprint handicap over 6 furlongs. It was upgraded to Group 1 status in 2010.

## SWORD DANCER INVITATIONAL HANDICAP

Sword Dancer is in the US Hall of Fame. He won 15 races including the Belmont Stakes, Jockey Club Gold Cup, Metropolitan Hcp, Travers Stakes and was a dual winner of the Woodward Stakes (1959, 60).

Inaugurated in 1975, the race has been run as an invitational since 1994. Since then winners include **AWAD (1997)**, **HONOR GLIDE (1999)** and **BETTER TALK NOW (2004)**.

**WITH ANTICIPATION (2001, 02)**, **GRAND COUTURIER (2007, 08)** and **TELLING (2009, 10)** all won it twice.

## BALLERINA STAKES

Ballerina won the inaugural Maskette Stakes in 1954.

Notable winners include **DAVONA DALE (1980)**;

LOVE SIGN (1981); LADY'S SECRET (1985); CLASSY MIRAGE (1995); MARYFIELD (2007) won the Breeders' Cup Filly & Mare Sprint (2007); MUSIC NOTE (2009); TURBULENT DESCENT (2012); and SHINE AGAIN (2001, 02) made it successive victories.

## FOREGO STAKES

Forego is one of the all-time champions. Three-time US Horse of the Year from 1974 to 1976, he won 34 races from 57 starts including 24 stakes races, 14 of those at Group 1 level including four successive Woodward Stakes (1974–77), three wins in the Brooklyn Hcp (1974–76) when it was a Group 1, Jockey Club Gold Cup (1974), and dual winner of the Carter Hcp (1974, 75), Metropolitan Hcp (1976, 77) and the former Widener Hcp (G1) at Hialeah (1974, 75).

Dual winners include **GROOVY (1986, 87)** and **QUICK CALL (1988, 89)**.

Other prominent winners include **FAPPIANO (1981)**; **HOUSEBUSTER (1991)**; **RUBIANO (1992)** and **AFFIRMED SUCCESS (1998)** both won the Vosburgh Stakes, Carter Hcp and Cigar Mile; **NOT SURPRISING (1995)**; **LANGFUHR (1996)**; **ORIENTATE (2002)** won the Breeders' Cup Sprint (2002); and **MIDNIGHT LUTE (2007)** is a dual winner of the Breeders' Cup Sprint (2007, 08).

## KING'S BISHOP STAKES

King's Bishop won 11 of 28 career starts including the Carter Hcp.

Winners include **HOUSEBUSTER (1990)**, **HONOR AND GLORY (1996)**, **TALE OF THE CAT (1997)**, **FORESTRY (1999)**, **MORE THAN READY (2000)**, **SQUIRTLE SQUIRT (2001)** won the Breeders' Cup Sprint that year, **LOST IN THE FOG (2005)** won his first ten career starts, **HENNY HUGHES (2007)** and **HARD SPUN (2008)**.

## PERSONAL ENSIGN STAKES

Inaugurated as the Firenze Handicap at the Jamaica racecourse in 1948, the race became the Personal Ensign Stakes in 1997.

Personal Ensign was an eight-time Grade 1 winner in her undefeated 13-start career, which produced wins in this race in 1986, Whitney Hcp, Ogden Phipps Hcp, Breeders' Cup Ladies Classic (1988) as well as two Beldame Stakes (1987, 88). She produced G1 winners Miner's Mark, Traditionally, My Flag and G1-placed Our Emblem – sire of War Emblem.

Dual winners include **POLITELY (1967, 68)**, **LIE LOW (1974, 75)** and **BEAUTIFUL PLEASURE (1999, 2000)**.

Other notable winners include **BUT WHY NOT (1949)**; **NEXT MOVE (1952)**; **PARLO (1954)**;

**LAMB CHOP (1963)**; **OBEAH (1970)** twice won the Delaware Hcp (1969, 70); **RELAXING (1980)**, dam of Easy Goer; **COLONIAL WATERS (1989)** brought up a record eight wins in the race for Angel Cordero Jr; **HEAVENLY PRIZE (1995)** won eight times at Grade 1 including the Gazelle Stakes, Beldame Stakes, Alabama Stakes (1994), Apple Blossom, Ogden Phipps Hcp (1995); **STORM FLAG FLYING (2004)** won the Breeders' Cup Juvenile Fillies (2002); and **GINGER PUNCH (2008)** won the Breeders' Cup Ladies Classic (2007).

## RUFFIAN HANDICAP

Ruffian was a champion filly who captured the imagination of the American public as she went undefeated through her first 10 starts in 1974 and 1975, setting many speed records and claiming the US Filly Triple Crown. She led in all of her races and had never been passed, showing an enormous will to win.

In one of the great tragedies of US racing she fatally broke down in front of an adoring crowd of 50,000 who had turned out at Belmont to witness the match race against that year's Kentucky Derby winner, Foolish Pleasure. While again in the lead, Ruffian snapped her right foreleg but refused to stop running, sparking almost unrivalled scenes of grief on a US racetrack.

She is buried in the Belmont Park infield with her nose pointing to the winning post. Considered by many as the top US female racehorse of the 20th century, she was the subject of the 2007 ABC telemovie *Ruffian*, starring Sam Shepard as Ruffian's trainer Frank Whitely.

The race was transferred to Saratoga in 2010.

Dual winner **LADY'S SECRET (1985, 86)** was US Horse of the Year in 1986 after winning a record eight Grade 1 races in one season. She was also a dual winner of the Beldame Stakes (1985, 86) and winner of the Whitney Hcp, Santa Margarita Invitational and Breeders' Cup Ladies' Classic (1986).

Other notables include inaugural winner **REVIDERE (1976)**, who won the Gazelle Stakes and Coaching Club American Oaks that year; **IT'S IN THE AIR (1979)**; **GENUINE RISK (1980)**; **RELAXING (1981)**; **BAYAKOA (1989)**; **VERSAILLES TREATY (1992)**; **SKY BEAUTY (1994)**; **INSIDE INFORMATION (1995)**; **YANKS MUSIC (1996)**; **SHARP CAT (1998)**; **SIGHTSEEK (2004)**; and **GINGER PUNCH (2007)**.

# KEENELAND

4201 Versailles Road, Lexington, Kentucky, USA. www.keeneland.com

*The renowned Keeneland racecourse is one of the world's greatest racetracks. Located off Highway 60 in the renowned bluegrass country of Lexington, the horse capital of the world.*

Jack Keene was an eminent horseman from a well-heeled Lexington family, who spent time overseas as a trainer in Russia and Japan. On returning to the US in 1916 Keene laid out a course on his property for use as a private training track.

After many years of fluctuating fortunes and the closure of the old Lexington track in 1933, Keene agreed to sell the 147-acre property to the newly established Keeneland Association for less than market value plus some stock options so that a new track could be built. It was a gesture that was largely responsible for the revival of racing in the USA at that time.

The Association converted Keene's historic mansion into a clubhouse and set about building a functional course and stands, which enabled it to open to the public in 1936.

The privately owned Keeneland Association was unique in that it was formed as a not-for-profit organisation for the benefit of horsemen, which re-invests its money into increased purses, new facilities and infrastructure. It also makes charitable donations to the community. This corporate structure has seen prize money constantly on the increase and capital improvements undertaken on an ongoing basis right throughout its history. Directors of the Association serve in an honorary capacity.

Since its inception, Keeneland has also been a major venue for horse sales, with the September yearling sales long considered the premier thoroughbred sale in the world. Crowned heads and racing royalty from around the globe are always in attendance.

The course was officially listed as a National Historic Landmark in 1996 and prides itself as a rural setting with cosmopolitan clientele, and it is indeed a beautiful setting for the world-class competition that it provides.

Racing at Keeneland is conducted in April and October. Meetings are generally scheduled from Wednesday to Sunday every week during the season. The highlight of the spring is the Blue Grass Stakes, while the fall feature is the Spinster Stakes.

In recent years the course has seen the upgrading of a number of races to Grade 1 status including the Shadwell Turf Mile, Jenny Wiley Stakes, Madison Stakes, Alcibiades Stakes, Maker's Mark Mile, Dixiana Breeders' Futurity and First Lady Stakes.

The course is open all year round and the public is always welcome to visit the historic grounds during the off-season.

## THE TRACK

Left-handed. Main Track is an 8½ furlong Polytrack oval with a home stretch of 412yds.

A 4½ furlong chute is known as the Headley Course, while the 7-furlong chute is

| FEATURE RACES | | | | | | | |
|---|---|---|---|---|---|---|---|
| ASHLAND STAKES | G1 | 8½F | AWT | 3YOF | SW | 1936 | APR |
| MADISON STAKES | G1 | 7F | AWT | 4YOF&M | ASS | 2002 | APR |
| MAKER'S MARK MILE | G1 | 8F | TURF | 4YO+ | ASS | 1989 | APR |
| JENNY WILEY STAKES | G1 | 8½F | TURF | 4YO+F&M | ASS | 1989 | APR |
| BLUE GRASS STAKES | G1 | 9F | AWT | 3YO | SW | 1911 | APR |
| ALCIBIADES STAKES | G1 | 8½F | AWT | 2YOF | SW | 1952 | OCT |
| SHADWELL TURF MILE | G1 | 8F | TURF | 3YO+ | ASS | 1986 | OCT |
| FIRST LADY STAKES | G1 | 8F | TURF | 3YO+F&M | ASS | 1998 | OCT |
| DIXIANA BREEDERS' FUTURITY | G1 | 8½F | AWT | 2YO | SW | 1910 | OCT |
| SPINSTER STAKES | G1 | 9F | AWT | 3YO+F&M | WFA | 1956 | OCT |
| QUEEN ELIZABETH II CHALLENGE CUP STAKES | G1 | 9F | TURF | 3YOF | ASS | 1984 | OCT |

referred to as the Beard Course.

The Turf Track is 7½ furlongs in circumference with a run in of 396yds.

# FEATURE RACES

## BLUE GRASS STAKES

Originally run at the Kentucky Association course at Lexington from 1911 to 1926, the event was revived by Keeneland in 1937. The race for 3yo is one of the main precursors to the Kentucky Derby and a genuine Grade 1 in its own right.

Winners to go on and claim the Run for the Roses include **BUBBLING OVER (1926)**, **SHUT OUT (1942)**, **TOMMY LEE (1959)**, **LUCKY DEBONAIR (1965)**, **DUST COMMANDER (1970)** and **STRIKE THE GOLD (1991)**.

**BRONZEWING (1911)** won the Kentucky Oaks. **CHATEAUGAY (1963)** and **RIVA RIDGE (1972)** won the Kentucky Derby and Belmont; **NORTHERN DANCER (1964)**, **FORWARD PASS (1968)** and **SPECTACULAR BID (1979)** won the Kentucky Derby and Preakness; **BIMELECH (1940)** won the Preakness and Belmont; **SHERLUCK (1961)** and **ARTS AND LETTERS (1969)** won the Belmont; **FAULTLESS (1947)**, **MASTER DERBY (1975)**, **SUMMER SQUALL (1990)** and **PRAIRIE BAYOU (1993)** all won the Preakness.

Other notables include the remarkable **BULL LEA (1938)**, sire of seven US Hall of Fame horses – Armed, Twilight Tear, Citation, Coaltown, Bewitch, Two Lea and Real Delight. Also sire of Canadian Hall of Famer Bull Page, who was in turn sire of Flaming Page – dam of Nijinsky. Bull Lea was also sire of Kentucky Derby winners Hill Gail and Iron Leige.

**COALTOWN (1948)** won 23 of 39 career starts; **ROUND TABLE (1957)**, **TOMPION (1960)**, **RIDAN (1962)**, **HONEST PLEASURE (1976)**, **ALYDAR (1978)**, **CHIEF'S CROWN (1985)**, **HOLY BULL (1994)**, **SKIP AWAY (1996)**, **PULPIT (1997)**, **MANIFEE (1999)** and **PEACE RULES (2003)** both won the Haskell Invitational, and **DULLAHAN (2012)** won the Dixiana Breeders' Futurity (2011) and Pacific Classic Stakes (2012).

## SPINSTER STAKES

Run annually in October, the Spinster Stakes has long been one of the premier contests for fillies and mares in the USA and a launching pad towards the Breeders' Cup.

Many of America's top females have won the race. Dual winners include **BORNASTAR (1957, 58)**, **SUSAN'S GIRL (1973, 75)**, **BAYAKOA (1989, 90)** and **TAKE CHARGE LADY (2002, 03)**.

Other notables include **BOWL OF FLOWERS (1961)**, **PRIMONETTA (1962)**, mighty **LAMB CHOP (1963)**, **OLD HAT (1964)** won 35 races; **OPEN FIRE (1966)**, **GALLANT BLOOM (1969)**, **NUMBERED ACCOUNT (1972)**, **SUMMER GUEST (1974)**, **BOLD 'N DETERMINED (1980)**, **GLORIOUS SONG (1981)**, **TRACK ROBBERY (1982)**, **PRINCESS ROONEY (1984)**, **SACAHUISTA (1987)**, **PASEANA (1993)**, **INSIDE INFORMATION (1995)**, **BANSHEE BREEZE (1998)** and **AZERI (2004)**.

## ASHLAND STAKES

Ashland was the name of the property of politician Henry Clay, who represented Kentucky in both the Senate and House of Representatives, where he served as Speaker. He was Secretary of State from 1825 to 1829 and three times ran for president.

The race was part of the inaugural fixture at Keeneland in 1936 won by **MYRTLEWOOD (1936)**.

Other prominent winners include **BEWITCH (1948)**, **REAL DELIGHT (1952)**, **BLUE NORTHER (1964)**, **DOUBLE DELTA (1969)**, **OPTIMISTC GAL (1976)** won seven races at G1, **CANDY ECLAIR (1979)** won 15 of 23; **PRINCESS ROONEY (1983)**, **GO FOR WAND (1990)**, **INSIDE INFORMATION (1994)**, **MY FLAG (1996)**, **SILVERBULLETDAY (1999)**, **TAKE CHARGE LADY (2002)** and **EVENING JEWEL (2010)**.

## QUEEN ELIZABETH II CHALLENGE CUP STAKES

Turf race inaugurated in 1984 to commemorate Queen Elizabeth II's visit to Keeneland. The race was awarded Grade 1 status in 1990.

Winners since include **RYAFAN (1997)**, **PERFECT STING (1999)** won 14 of 21 starts including the Breeders' Cup Filly & Mare Turf (2000) and **AFFLUENT (2001)**.

# HOLLYWOOD PARK

1050 South Prairie Avenue, Inglewood, California . www.betfairhollywoodpark.com

*T*he inner Los Angeles suburb of Inglewood is the location of the Hollywood Park racecourse, which held its first meeting in 1938.

The Hollywood Turf Club was formed with Warner Brothers mogul, Jack L Warner, as its chairman.

Among its initial shareholders were some of the biggest names in Hollywood including Walt Disney, Bing Crosby, Samuel Goldwyn, Darryl Zannuck and Ralph Bellamy. Al Jolson was on the original board of directors, and Mervin Le Roy was a director at Hollywood Park from 1941 until his passing in 1987.

Not surprisingly, in1941, the course was the first to introduce film patrol footage to be viewed by stewards.

The turf course was opened in 1969 and the track was quick to take advantage of a change in legislation four years later to allow race meetings to be conducted on Sundays.

Legendary horse Citation became the first to pass $2 million in prize money when successful in the Hollywood Gold Cup of 1974. Only nine years later John Henry became the first to surpass $4 million with victory in the Hollywood Turf Cup.

In 1984 Hollywood Park hosted the inaugural Breeders' Cup meeting, with 64,625 people on hand to witness the spectacle.

Refurbishments in 1991 included the construction of a European-style garden paddock and the addition of an infield lake. The six-race Turf Festival was staged for the first time that year.

To comply with Californian law, the course was the first in the state to replace the traditional dirt surface with a synthetic Cushion Track in 2007.

Racing at Hollywood Park is scheduled from April to July and then November and December.

## THE TRACK

Left-handed. Main Track is an oval all-weather Cushion Track of 9 furlongs. The run in is 330yds.

The Turf track is a one-mile oval, also with a home straight of 330yds.

## FEATURE RACES

### HOLLYWOOD GOLD CUP

The Hollywood Gold Cup was established in the track's inaugural year and its honour roll is brimming with champions.

**SEABISCUIT (1938)** won the first edition. He was the first of many horses who would win the race on their way to claiming the title of Horse of the Year. Others include **CHALLEDON (1940)**, **CITATION (1951)**, **SWAPS (1956)**, **ROUND TABLE (1957)**, **ACK ACK (1971)**, **AFFIRMED (1979)**, **FERDINAND (1987)**, **CRIMINAL TYPE (1990)**, **CIGAR (1995)** and **SKIP AWAY (1998)**.

Multiple winners include **NATIVE DIVER (1966–68)** and **LAVA MAN (2005–07)**, who both registered a hat-trick.

Other notables include **KAYAK (1939)**, **HAPPY ISSUE (1944)** was the first female to win, and **TWO LEA (1952)** and **PRINCESSNESIAN (1968)** are the only other females to have won.

**TRIPLICATE (1946)**, owned by Fred Astaire; top Australian **SHANNON (1948)**; **NOOR (1950)**; **ROYAL SERENADE (1953)** was a dual winner of the Nunthorpe Stakes (1951, 52) and won the Diamond Jubilee Stakes (1952); **REJECTED (1955)**; **GALLANT MAN (1958)**; **HILLSDALE (1959)**; **PROVE IT (1962)**.

## FEATURE RACES

| CHARLES WHITTINGHAM MEMORIAL HCP | G1 | 10F | TURF | 3YO+ | ASS | 1969 | JUN |
|---|---|---|---|---|---|---|---|
| VANITY HCP | G1 | 9F | AWT | 3YO+F&M | ASS | 1940 | JUN |
| TRIPLE BEND INVITATIONAL HCP | G1 | 7F | AWT | 3YO+ | HCP | 1952 | JUN |
| SHOEMAKER MILE STAKES | G1 | 8F | TURF | 3YO+ | ASS | 1938 | JUN |
| HOLLYWOOD GOLD CUP | G1 | 10F | AWT | 3YO+ | HCP | 1938 | JUN |
| AMERICAN OAKS | G1 | 10F | TURF | 3YOF | SW | 2002 | JUN |
| MATRIARCH STAKES | G1 | 8F | TURF | 3YO+F&M | ASS | 1981 | NOV |
| HOLLYWOOD DERBY | G1 | 10F | TURF | 3YO | SW | 1938 | NOV |
| HOLLYWOOD STARLET STAKES | G1 | 8½F | AWT | 2YOF | ASS | 1974 | DEC |
| HOLLYWOOD FUTURITY | G1 | 8½F | AWT | 2YO | SW | 1981 | DEC |
| HOLLYWOOD TURF CUP STAKES | G1 | 12F | TURF | 3YO+ | ASS | 1981 | DEC |

FOUR-AND-TWENTY (1961); BOLD REASON (1971); CRYSTAL WATER (1976); FLYING PASTER (1979); CODEX (1980).

ROYAL HEROINE (1983) won the Prix de l'Opera (1983), Breeders' Cup Mile (1984); PARADISE CREEK (1992) won the Washington DC International, Arlington Million, Manhattan Hcp, Turf Classic Stakes (1994); MARLIN (1996) won the Secretariat Stakes, Arlington Million (1997); SUBORDINATION (1997); JOHAR (2002) won the Breeders' Cup Turf (2003); SWEET RETURN (2003), SHOWING UP (2006) won the Secretariat Stakes and Jamaica Hcp (2006).

## CHARLES WHITTINGHAM MEMORIAL HANDICAP

Established in 1969 as the Hollywood Invitational Turf Handicap and renamed in 1999 to honour Hall of Fame trainer Charles Whittingham, who prepared the winner of this race on seven occasions.

JOHN HENRY (1980, 81, 84) and ACCLAMATION (2010–12) have both won the race three times.

Other notables include FORT MARCY (1969); COUGAR (1971); TYPECAST (1972); Champion mare DAHLIA (1976); EXCELLER (1978); ERINS ISLE (1983) won the Curragh Tattersalls Gold Cup (1981); RIVLIA (1987) was a three-time Grade 1 winner; GREAT COMMUNICATOR (1988) won the Breeders' Cup Turf that year; STEINLEN (1989) won the Arlington Million, Breeders' Cup Mile (1989); 1990 Epsom Derby winner QUEST FOR FAME (1992); BIEN BIEN (1993) won four Grade 1 races; SANDPIT (1996); STORMING HOME (2003) won the Champion Stakes at Ascot (2002), John Henry Turf Championship (2003); and SWEET RETURN (2005).

Californian-bred LAVA MAN (2006) was a three-time winner of the Hollywood Gold Cup (2005–07), dual winner of the Santa Anita Hcp (2006, 07) and won the Pacific Classic Stakes and Awesome Again Stakes (2006).

## HOLLYWOOD FUTURITY

First run in 1981, the race became the first to ever offer a $1 million purse for 2yos in 1983.

Notable winners include ROVING BOY (1982), who won the FrontRunner Stakes, Del Mar Futurity (1982); SNOW CHIEF (1985); TEJANO (1987) became the first 2yo in the USA to post $1 million in stakes earnings; KING GLORIOUS (1988) won 8 of 9 starts including the Haskell Invitational (1989); BEST PAL (1990); AP INDY (1991); REAL QUIET (1997); CAPTAIN STEVE (1999); POINT GIVEN (2000); LOOKIN' AT LUCKY (2009).

Santa Anita Derby winners include TEMPERATE SIL (1986), BROTHER DEREK (2005) and PIONEEROF THE NILE (2008).

COLORADO KING (1964) won the Durban July (1963); Canadian Hall of Fame horse KENNEDY ROAD (1973); ANCIENT TITLE (1975); CRYSTAL WATER (1977); EXCELLER (1978); PERRAULT (1982); BLUSHING JOHN (1989) won the Poule d'Essai des Poulains (1988); BEST PAL (1993); GENTLEMAN (1997) won three G1 races in Argentina including the Gran Premio Nacional (1995) and three G1 races in the USA; REAL QUIET (1999); CONGAREE (2003); and GAME ON DUDE (2012).

## HOLLYWOOD DERBY

Also inaugurated in 1938, it is one of the premier 3yo contests in the USA.

Kentucky Derby winners successful in the race include SWAPS (1955), RIVA RIDGE (1972) and AFFIRMED (1978).

Other notables include fillies BUSHER (1945); HONEYMOON (1946) took out the Hollywood Derby–Oaks double; and A GLEAM (1952); REJECTED (1953); ROUND TABLE (1957);

Sunday Silence

Cup Turf (1992); **CHAMPS ELYSEES (2008)** won the Northern Dancer Turf Stakes (2008) and Canadian International (2009).

First run in 1981; **FLAWLESSLY (1991–93)** posted a hat-trick.

Other notables include **KILIJARO (1981)**; **ROYAL HEROINE (1984)**; **RYAFAN (1997)** won the Prix Marcel Boussac (1996), Falmouth Stakes, Nassau Stakes, Rodeo Drive Stakes, Queen Elizabeth II Challenge Cup (1997); **HAPPYANUNOIT (1999)**; **STARINE (2001)** won the Breeders' Cup Filly & Mare Turf (2002), as did **INTERCONTINENTAL (2004)**; **COCOA BEACH (2008)**; and **VENTURA (2009)**.

## SHOEMAKER MILE STAKES

Inaugurated in 1938 as the Premiere Handicap, the race was renamed in 1990 after Hall of Fame jockey Bill Shoemaker. It was upgraded to Grade 1 level in 2000.

Notable winners include **SILIC (1999, 2000)**, who went back to back; **REDATTORE (2003)**; **CASTLEDALE (2005)**; and **THE TIN MAN (2007)** was a dual winner of the John Henry Turf Championship (2002, 06) and won the Arlington Million (2006).

## AMERICAN OAKS

Inaugurated in 2002, the race became a Grade 1 in 2004.

**PANTY RAID (2007)** was a Grade 1 winner on turf and dirt.

## TRIPLE BEND INVITATIONAL HANDICAP

Inaugurated in 1952 as the Lakes and Flowers Handicap. Triple Bend ran a world-record time for 7 furlongs on the dirt in winning the Santa Anita Handicap in 1972. The race was upgraded to Grade 1 status in 2005.

**PORTERHOUSE (1955, 56)** won the race twice.

## VANITY INVITATIONAL HANDICAP

**ZENYATTA (2008–10)** holds the benchmark with three consecutive wins.

Dual winners include **ANNIE-LU-SAN (1957, 58)**, **CONVENIENCE (1972, 73)**, **IT'S IN THE AIR (1979, 80)** and **AZERI (2002, 03)**.

Horses to also win the Breeders' Cup Ladies' Classic include Azeri; **PRINCESS ROONEY (1984)**; **BAYAKOA (1989)**, who won the Ladies' Classic twice; **PASEANA (1992)**; **JEWEL PRINCESS (1996)**; **ESCANA (1998)**; and **ZENYATTA**.

Other prominent winners include **HAPPY ISSUE (1944)**, **BUSHER (1945)**, **HONEYMOON (1947)**, **NEXT MOVE (1950)**, **BEWITCH (1951)**, **TWO LEA (1952)**, **SILVER SPOON (1960)**, **LINITA (1962)**, **GAMELY (1968)**, **TRACK ROBBERY (1981)**, **HOLLYWOOD STORY (2006)**, **NASHOBA'S KEY (2007)** and **BLIND LUCK (2011)**.

## GAMELY STAKES

Established in 1939 as the Long Beach Handicap, the name was changed in 1976 to honour Hall of Fame filly Gamely, who won 16 races including the Alabama Stakes, Test Stakes (1967) Vanity Invitational, Santa Margarita Invitational (1968), Diana Stakes (1969) and twice won the Beldame Stakes (1968, 69).

Dual winners include **TIPPING TIME (1970, 72)** and **ASTRA (2000, 02)**.

Other notables include **TYPECAST (1972)**; **SUSAN'S GIRL (1975)**; **WISHING WELL (1980)**, dam of Sunday Silence; **KILIJARO (1981)** won the Phoenix Stakes (1978), Prix du Moulin de Longchamp, Rodeo Drive Stakes (1980), Matriarch Stakes (1981); **ESTRAPADE (1985)** won the Rodeo Drive Stakes

(1985), Arlington Million, John Henry Turf Championship (1986).

**TOUSSAUD (1993)** influential dam of Chester House and Empire Maker; **HOLLYWOOD WILDCAT (1994)** won the Del Mar Oaks, Breeders' Cup Ladies' Classic (1993) and was dual winner of the Zenyatta Stakes (1993, 94); **HAPPYANUNOIT (2001)** won the Manawatu Sires' Produce (1998), First Lady Stakes, Matriarch Stakes (1999); and **NOCHES DE ROSA (2004)** won the Chilean Oaks (2001).

## HOLLYWOOD STARLET STAKES

Notable winners include **ALTHEA (1983)**; **OUTSTANDINGLY (1984)** won the Breeders' Cup Juvenile Fillies (1984); **VERY SUBTLE (1986)** won the Breeders' Cup Sprint (1987); **SERENA'S SONG (1994)**; **CARA RAFAELA (1995)**, dam of Bernadini; **SHARP CAT (1997)**; **BIENAMADO (2000)** gave Chris McCarron his eighth win in the race; **HOLLYWOOD STORY (2003)** is the only maiden to win; **BLIND LUCK (2009)**; and **TURBULENT DESCENT (2010)** won the Test Stakes, Santa Anita Oaks and Ballerina Stakes (2011).

## HOLLYWOOD TURF CUP STAKES

Dual winners include **ALPHABATIM (1984, 86)**, who won the Racing Post Trophy at Doncaster (1983); and Argentinean **LAZY LODE (1998, 99)**.

Other notable winners include **PROVIDENTIAL (1981)**, who won the Criterium de Saint-Cloud (1979), Washington DC International (1981); **JOHN HENRY (1983)**; **GREAT COMMUNICATOR (1988)**; **ITSALLGREEKTOME (1990)** won the Hollywood Derby (1990); filly **MISS ALLEGED (1991)** won the Breeders' Cup Turf (1991); **BIEN BIEN (1992)**; **FRAISE (1993)** won the Breeders'

# DEL MAR

2260 Jimmy Durante Boulevard, Del Mar, California, USA . www.dmtc.com

*The beautiful coastal city of Del Mar is located 20 miles north of San Diego and is one of California's most popular resort areas.*

Bing Crosby enlisted a group of friends including actors Pat O'Brien, Jimmy Durante, Oliver Hardy and Seabiscuit's owner Charles S Howard to fund the construction of a racecourse at Del Mar, which opened in 1937.

Crosby was in attendance to personally greet race-goers at the gate for its inaugural meeting, which featured a match race between Seabiscuit and colt Ligaroti, who won the inaugural Inglewood Handicap at Hollywood Park. In an enthralling encounter, Seabiscuit prevailed by a nose. It was the first-ever thoroughbred race to be broadcast nationally, by NBC radio.

The course quickly established itself as playground for the stars with Hollywood glitterati regularly in attendance, including legendary figures WC Fields, Dorothy Lamour, Don Ameche and Ava Gardner. Lucille Ball and Desi Arnez also owned and raced horses here.

In 1953 Del Mar staged its richest meeting to that date with ten stakes races worth $130,000 each. Hall of Fame jockey Bill Shoemaker won five of them. Three years later at this course, John Longden posted winner number 4871 to surpass the riding record of Sir Gordon Richards. Longden was again on hand at Del Mar in 1970 to congratulate Shoemaker when he booted home winner 6033 to in turn break Longden's all-time record.

In 1993 a modern grandstand was constructed with the new facility still maintaining the old Spanish charm of the course.

Racing season 'where the turf meets the surf' and 'no one is in a hurry but the horses' takes place over seven weeks from mid July until early September with many Grade 1 races conducted.

There are currently five races included in the Breeders' Cup series, with automatic entry for winners of the Pacific Classic, Clement L Hirsch Handicap, Del Mar Futurity as well as Grade 2 races the Del Mar Handicap and San Diego Handicap.

The $1 million Pacific Classic Stakes in August is the most valuable race on the calendar.

While the lustre of Hollywood may have dimmed in recent decades, this perhaps only demonstrates that they don't make Hollywood stars like they used to, and Del Mar remains one of premier racetracks in the USA.

## THE TRACK

Left-handed. Main Track is a one-mile Polytrack oval. Home straight – 330yds.

The Jimmy Durante Turf Course – 7 furlong turf track.

## FEATURE RACES

| PACIFIC CLASSIC STAKES | | | | | | |
|---|---|---|---|---|---|---|

Dual winners include **TINNER'S WAY (1994, 95)** and **SKIMMING (2000, 01)**, both prepared by Robert J Frankel, and **RICHARD'S KID (2009, 10)**.

Other notables include **BEST PAL (1991)**; **BERTRANDO (1993)**; **DARE AND GO (1996)** produced a stunning upset to defy Cigar a 17th consecutive victory; **GENTLEMAN (1997)**; **FREE HOUSE (1998)** won the FrontRunner Stakes (1996), Santa Anita Derby (1997), Santa Anita Hcp (1999).

Sidney and Jenny Craig's **CANDY RIDE (2003)** began his undefeated 6 start career in Argentina where he had two G1 victories. He won this race ridden by Hall of Fame jockey Julie Krone. She was the first female rider to win a Classic race when she won the Belmont in 1993, and ten years later became the first to win a Breeders' Cup race.

## FEATURE RACES

| | | | | | | | |
|---|---|---|---|---|---|---|---|
| EDDIE READ STAKES | G1 | 9F | TURF | 3YO+ | ASS | 1974 | JUL |
| BING CROSBY HCP | G1 | 6F | AWT | 3YO+ | HCP | 1946 | JUL |
| CLEMENT L HIRSCH HCP | G1 | 8½F | AWT | 3YO+F&M | ASS | 1937 | AUG |
| DEL MAR OAKS | G1 | 9F | TURF | 3YOF | ASS | 1957 | AUG |
| PACIFIC CLASSIC STAKES | G1 | 10F | AWT | 3YO+ | SW | 1991 | AUG |
| DEL MAR DEBUTANTE STAKES | G1 | 7F | AWT | 2YOF | SW | 1951 | SEPT |
| DEL MAR FUTURITY | G1 | 7F | AWT | 2YO | SW | 1948 | SEPT |

Bing Crosby greets a surprised first customer

PLEASANTLY PERFECT (2004) was dual winner of the Awesome Again Stakes (2002, 03) and winner of the Breeders' Cup Classic (2003), Santa Anita Hcp, Dubai World Cup (2004); BORREGO (2006); LAVA MAN (2007); ACCLAMATION (2011) was a three-time winner of the Charles Whittingham Memorial (2010–12) and dual winner of the Eddie Read Hcp (2011, 12).

## EDDIE READ STAKES

Established in 1974, the race achieved Grade 1 status in 1988.

Winners since include dual victors FASTNESS (1995, 96), SPECIAL RING (2003, 04) and ACCLAMATION (2011, 12).

Other notables include FLY TILL DAWN (1990), TIGHT SPOT (1991) won the Arlington Million (1991), MARQUETRY (1992) won the Hollywood Gold Cup (1991), KOTASHAAN (1993) won the Breeders' Cup Turf (1993), Brazilian JOE WHO (1999), REDATTORE (2001) and SWEET RETURN (2005).

## DEL MAR OAKS

First run in 1957, it was upgraded to Grade 1 in 1994.

Winners since include five-time Grade 1 winner TWICE THE VICE (1994), who also took out the Apple Blossom, Santa Margarita Invitational (1996), Vanity Invitational (1997); ANTESPEND (1996) won the Las Virgenes Stakes, Santa Anita Oaks (1996); GOLDEN APPLES (2001) won the Beverly D Stakes, Rodeo Drive Stakes (2002); and MAGICAL FANTASY (2008) won four races at Grade 1.

## BING CROSBY HANDICAP

Inaugurated in 1946, the race was upgraded to Grade 1 level in 2005.

## CLEMENT L HIRSCH STAKES

Clement L Hirsch initiated the establishment of New York's Oak Tree Racing Association. Inaugurated in 1937 as the Chula Vista Handicap, the race has been a permanent fixture on the calendar since 1973 and became a Grade 1 in 2009. Notable winners include ZENYATTA (2008–10), who made it a hat-trick, and two-time champion AZERI (2002, 03).

## DEL MAR DEBUTANTE STAKES

First run in 1951, the 2yo fillies' race was upgraded to a Grade 1 in 1999.

Winners since include CHILUKKI (1999) and Breeders' Cup Juvenile Fillies winners HALFBRIDLED (2003) and STARDOM BOUND (2008).

TERLINGUA (1978) is the dam of Storm Cat.

## DEL MAR FUTURITY

Established in 1948 and upgraded to Grade 1 in 2007, it has been won since by 2008 Breeders' Cup Juvenile winner MIDSHIPMAN (2008) and LOOKIN' AT LUCKY (2009).

# AQUEDUCT

110-00 Rockaway Blvd, Jamaica, New York, USA. www.nyra.com/aqueduct

*Opened in September 1894, Aqueduct is the only track located within the city limits of New York.*

The course was constructed by the Queens County Jockey Club on land leased near the former site of the conduit that carried water from Long Island to Ridgewood Reservoir.

The course gained prominence under the presidency of Phillip Dwyer who acquired adjacent land, completely rebuilt the grandstands and extended the track during his reign between 1905 and 1917.

In 1956 the course was completely torn down for major renovations at a cost of $33 million – an enormous sum by the standards of the day – and re-opened in September 1959.

An inner dirt track was added in 1975 to cater for winter racing.

Aqueduct was to be shut down in 2007 but a rally from the local community and the sale of adjacent real estate in 2009 prevented the closure.

Memorably, Secretariat paraded here for the public for the very last time before his retirement in 1973. Cigar began his 16-race winning streak when switched to the dirt for the first time with two wins here. They are just two of the many great champions to grace the Aqueduct track.

The course also played host to the Breeders' Cup in 1985.

Now under the auspices of the New York Racing Association, The Big A, as it is affectionately known, remains one of the premier tracks in the USA with top-class racing right throughout the season, held from October to April.

## THE TRACK

Left-handed the complex consists of three tracks.

The Main Track is a dirt course with a circumference of 9 furlongs. Home straight of 384yds.

A chute on the back straight allows mile races to be run with only one turn.

The inner Dirt Track is exactly 1 mile long. Unusually, due to the configuration of the turns, the straight on the inner track is slightly longer at 391yds.

The Turf Track is the innermost course with a circumference of just over 7 furlongs.

## FEATURE RACES

| FEATURE RACES | | | | | | | |
|---|---|---|---|---|---|---|---|
| WOOD MEMORIAL STAKES | G1 | 9F | DIRT | 3YO | SW | 1925 | APR |
| CARTER HANDICAP | G1 | 7F | DIRT | 3YO+ | HCP | 1895 | APR |
| CIGAR MILE HANDICAP | G1 | 8F | DIRT | 3YO+ | HCP | 1988 | NOV |
| GAZELLE STAKES | G1 | 9F | DIRT | 3YOF | ASS | 1887 | NOV |
| TOP FLIGHT HCP | G2 | 8½F | DIRT | 3YO+F&M | ASS | 1940 | MAR |
| JEROME STAKES | G2 | 8F | DIRT | 3YO | ASS | 1866 | APR |
| DISTAFF HCP | G2 | 6F | DIRT | 3YO+F&M | ASS | 1954 | APR |
| DEMOISELLE STAKES | G2 | 8F | DIRT | 2YOF | ASS | 1908 | NOV |
| RED SMITH HCP | G2 | 11F | TURF | 3YO+ | ASS | 1960 | NOV |
| REMSEN STAKES | G2 | 9F | DIRT | 2YO | HCP | 1904 | NOV |
| GO FOR WAND HCP | G2 | 8F | DIRT | 3YO+F&M | ASS | 1954 | NOV |
| NASHUA STAKES | G2 | 8F | DIRT | 2YO | ASS | 1975 | NOV |

## FEATURE RACES

### WOOD MEMORIAL STAKES

This $1 million, 9-furlong race for 3yos is one of the five major precursors to the Kentucky Derby. Many winners of the race have gone on to glory in the Derby with four of those capturing the Triple Crown: **GALLANT FOX (1930)**, **COUNT FLEET (1943)**, **ASSAULT (1946)** and **SEATTLE SLEW (1977)**.

**TWENTY GRAND (1931)**, **HIGH QUEST (1934)**, **JOHNSTOWN (1939)**, **HOOP JR (1945)**, **PHALANX (1947)**, **HILL PRINCE (1950)**, **NATIVE DANCER (1953)**, **NASHUA (1955)**, **BOLD RULER (1957)**, **QUADRANGLE (1964)**, **AMBEROID (1966)**, **DAMASCUS (1967)**, **PERSONALITY (1970)**, **FOOLISH PLEASURE**

Cigar wins the Dubai World Cup

LAMB CHOP (1963) was a winner of the Coaching Club American Oaks, Spinster Stakes, Personal Ensign Stakes, Santa Anita Derby (1963); **WHAT A TREAT (1965)** won the Beldame Stakes, Alabama Stakes and Prioress Stakes (1965).

**GALLANT BLOOM (1969)** won 16 of 22 including the Spinster Stakes (1969), Santa Margarita Invitational and Santa Maria Hcp (1970); **FORWARD GAL (1971)** won the Frizette Stakes and Spinaway Stakes (1970); **REVIDERE (1976)** won the Coaching Club American Oaks, Ruffian Hcp (1976); **PEARL NECKLACE (1977)**.

**MISS OCEANA (1984)** was a six-time winner at Grade 1 level; **SERENA'S SONG (1995)**; **MY FLAG (1996)** won the Breeders' Cup Juvenile Fillies (1995), Ashland Stakes, Coaching Club American Oaks (1996); **SILVERBULLETDAY (1999)**; **MUSIC NOTE (2008)** won the Mother Goose Stakes, Coaching Club American Oaks (2008), Ballerina Stakes, Beldame Stakes (2009); **AWESOME FEATHER (2011)** won the Breeders' Cup Juvenile Fillies (2010).

Great fillies **FAIRY CHANT (1940)**, **NEXT MOVE (1950)**, **SUSAN'S GIRL (1972)**, **DESERT VIXEN (1973)** and **LOVE SIGN (1980)** are all dual winners of the Beldame Stakes.

(1975), **BOLD FORBES (1976)**, **PLEASANT COLONY (1981)**, **EASY GOER (1989)**, **FUSA-ICHI PEGASUS (2000)** and **EMPIRE MAKER (2003)** all were winners of Triple Crown races.

Other notables include influential **POMPEY (1926)**, **FIGHTING FOX (1938)** won the Jamaica Hcp and Carter Hcp (1939), **MARKET WISE (1941)** won 19 career races including the Jockey Club Gold Cup (1941), **OLYMPIA (1949)** was a champion broodmare sire, **JEWEL'S REWARD (1958)** gave Eddie Arcaro a record nine wins in the race, **ANGLE LIGHT (1973)** defeated Sham and Secretariat.

**PLUGGED NICKLE (1980)** won the Florida Derby and Vosburgh Stakes (1980); **SLEW O' GOLD (1983)**; **BROAD BRUSH (1986)**; **GULCH (1987)** won the Breeders' Cup Sprint (1988); **UNBRI-DLED'S SONG (1996)** won the Breeders' Cup Juvenile (1995); **CORONADO'S QUEST (1998)** won the Travers Stakes, Haskell Invitational (1998); and **CONGAREE (2001)**.

Sunny Jim Fitzsimmons holds the training honours with seven wins.

## CARTER HANDICAP

Historic open handicap over 7 furlongs dating back to 1895 when the stake was put up by Brooklyn contractor and tugboat captain William Carter.

The Carter Handicap of 1944 earned a unique place in US racing history when **BOSSUET**, **BROWNIE** and **WAIT A BIT** hit the line locked together to record the nation's only triple dead heat in a stakes race.

The inaugural winner was **CHARADE (1895)**,

who won 30 races including the Test Stakes (1891) and Metropolitan Hcp (1893).

Dual winners include **AUDACIOUS (1920, 21)**, **OSMAND (1928, 29)**, **FLYING HEELS (1930, 31)**, **FOREGO (1974, 75)** and **LITE THE FUSE (1995, 96)**.

Other notable winners include **BELDAME (1904)**; **ROSEBEN (1906)** won 52 of 111 starts including two Metropolitan Hcps (1905–06); the legendary **ROAMER (1914)** won 39 races and broke many track records; **OLD ROSEBUD (1917)** won 40 of 80 starts including the Kentucky Derby (1914); **SARAZEN (1924)**; **KING SAXON (1935)** was a winner of 28 races; **FIGHTING FOX (1939)**; **DEVIL DIVER (1943)**; **GALLORETTE (1948)**.

**ARISE (1951)** won the Canadian International and Travers Stakes (1949), **TOM FOOL (1953)**, **BOLD RULER (1958)**, **GULCH (1988)**, **HOUSEBUSTER (1991)**, **LANGFUHR (1997)**, **ARTAX (1999)** won the Breeders' Cup Sprint that year, **CONGAREE (2003)** and **KODIAK KOWBOY (2009)**.

## GAZELLE STAKES

Established in 1887 at the Gravesend Racecourse, this historic contest for 3yo fillies was transferred to Aqueduct in 1917 and most editions were run here until 1968, when it was transferred to Belmont Park. The race returned to Aqueduct in 2009.

Legendary winners include **FIRENZE (1887)**; **BELDAME (1904)**; **MASKETTE (1909)**; **VAGRANCY (1942)**; **GRECIAN QUEEN (1953)** won the Coaching Club American Oaks, Delaware Hcp and Prioress Stakes that year; **IDUN (1958)**;

## CIGAR MILE HANDICAP

Originally known as the NYRA Stakes, the name was changed in 1997 to honour the deeds of champion dirt horse Cigar, whose two victories at Aqueduct in 1994 kicked off his streak of 16 consecutive successes. Cigar's 7-length win in the NYRA Stakes here that year was his first at Grade 1 level.

Cigar also won the Hollywood Gold Cup, Jockey Club Gold Cup, Breeders' Cup Classic (1995), Dubai World Cup (1996); was a dual winner of the Donn Hcp (1995, 96) and Woodward Stakes (1995, 96); and was a two-time Horse of the Year (1995, 96).

Fittingly Cigar's regular partner, Jerry Bailey, maintains the benchmark in this race, having ridden the winner on five occasions over a ten-year period.

Notable winners include inaugural victor **FORTY NINER (1988)**, **CIGAR (1994)**, **LEFT BANK (2001)**, **CONGAREE (2002, 03)** went back to back, **DISCREET CAT (2006)** and **KODIAK KOWBOY (2009)**.

# ARLINGTON PARK

2200 Euclid Avenue, Arlington Heights, Illinois, USA. www.arlingtonpark.com

*A*rlington Heights is located in Cook County, Illinois, 25 miles west of downtown Chicago.

Founded in 1927 by Harry D 'Curly' Brown, picturesque Arlington Park is one of the premier tracks in the USA with a history of staying ahead of the curve in racecourse innovation.

In that regard its impressive list of credits includes becoming the first track to install a public address system. In 1933 the first all-electric totalisator was installed here, in 1934 it was the first track in Illinois to run turf races, in 1936 one of the world's first photo finish cameras was installed and in 1981 it hosted the world's first million-dollar race, the Arlington Million.

During the 1980s the club successfully adopted an aggressive marketing campaign to promote the course as a family entertainment venue.

It has also taken a leading role internationally by exchanging races with leading tracks in England and Japan and participating in global racing conferences to further international racing with a view to establishing a worldwide racing series.

Pat Day set the course alight in 1989 when he rode eight winners on the nine-race card.

Arlington Park merged with Churchill Downs Inc in 2000.

Racing season is from May to September, with the feature events conducted in August All three Grade 1 races are staged on the turf.

Arlington is also a major training base with stabling for over 2000 horses.

## THE TRACK

Left-handed. Nine-furlong Polytrack oval. Home straight – 342yds.

Inner turf oval of 1 mile, also with a straight of 342yds.

## FEATURE RACES

### ARLINGTON MILLION

The Arlington Million was the first race in the world to offer a purse of $1 million. The inaugural edition in 1981 was taken out by **JOHN HENRY (1981, 84)**, the only multiple winner of the race.

Other notables include French raiders **PERRAULT (1982)**, who won the Hollywood Gold Cup (1982); and **ESTRAPADE (1986)**, who won the Gamely Stakes (1985), Clement L Hirsch Turf Championship (1986); **MANILA (1987)**; **GOLDEN PHEASANT (1990)** won the Japan Cup (1991); **STAR OF COZZENE (1993)**; **PARADISE CREEK (1994)**; **AWAD (1995)** won the Secretariat Stakes (1993), Manhattan Hcp (1995), Sword Dancer Invitational (1997); **SILVANO (2001)** won the QE II Cup in Hong Kong (2001); **BEAT HOLLOW (2002)**; **SULAMANI (2003)**; **POWERSCOURT (2005)** won the Tattersalls Gold Cup at The Curragh (2004); **THE TIN MAN (2006)** was a dual winner of the Clement L Hirsch Turf Championship (2002, 06) and won the Shoemaker Mile (2007); **GIO PONTI (2009)**; and **CAPE BLANCO (2011)**.

### BEVERLY D STAKES

First run in 1987, notable winners include nine-time Grade 1 winning **FLAWLESSLY (1993)** and twice champion French filly **HATOOF (1994)**.

### SECRETARIAT STAKES

Secretariat is the only genuine rival to Man O' War as the USA's greatest horse of all time. The Triple Crown winner broke race records in winning the Kentucky Derby and the Preakness, then set a world record of 2:24:00 for a mile and a half on dirt in winning the Belmont Stakes by a record 31 lengths. To date, no other horse has ever broken 2:25:00 on dirt.

He won 16 of 21 career starts, was the subject of a movie, a postage stamp, and was voted by ESPN as the 35th greatest athlete of the 20th century. Man O' War (84th) and Citation (97th) are the only other horses nominated. Secretariat is the only non-human admitted to the Kentucky Athletic Hall of Fame.

Run since 1974, notable winners include **MAC DIARMIDA (1978)**, who won the Canadian International, Washington DC International (1978); **HAWKSTER (1989)** won the FrontRunner Stakes (1988), Del Mar Derby, Clement L Hirsch Turf Championship (1989) and would later set a world record 2:22:8 for a mile and a half on turf; **AWAD (1993)**; **MARLIN (1996)** won the Hollywood Derby (1996), Arlington Million (1997);

| FEATURE RACES | | | | | | | |
|---|---|---|---|---|---|---|---|
| ARLINGTON MILLION | G1 | 10F | TURF | 3YO+ | WFA | 1974 | AUG |
| BEVERLY D STAKES | G1 | 9½F | TURF | 3YO+F&M | SW | 1967 | AUG |
| SECRETARIAT STAKES | G1 | 10F | TURF | 3YO | HCP | 1974 | AUG |
| AMERICAN DERBY | G2 | 9½F | TURF | 3YO | HCP | 1884 | JUL |

**KICKEN KRIS (2003)** won the Arlington Million (2004); **KITTEN'S JOY (2004)** set a track record; **SHOWING UP (2006)** won the Hollywood Derby and Jamaica Hcp that year; and **TREASURE BEACH (2011)** won the Irish Derby.

## AMERICAN DERBY (G2)

Dating back to 1884, the American Derby has a history of attracting some of the biggest names of the US turf. The honor roll includes **CAVALCADE (1934)**, **CITATION (1948)**, **NATIVE DANCER (1953)**, **ROUND TABLE (1957)**, **BUCKPASSER (1966)**, **DAMASCUS (1967)** and **BOLD REASON (1971)**.

# GULFSTREAM PARK

901 S Federal Highway, Hallandale Beach, Florida, USA. www.gulfstreampark.com

*The beautiful town of Hallandale Beach in Broward County on the south-east coast of Florida is the location of one of America's most important racetracks, Gulfstream Park.*

The course staged one race meeting in 1939 but lay idle until taken over by James Donn Sr in 1944. Under his guidance major construction works were undertaken, and the Florida Derby and Donn Handicap established. Three generations of the Donn family would control the track for 30 years and were responsible for engineering and maintaining the track's rise to prominence.

Gulfstream Park hosts all of the races in the Sunshine Millions series. Inaugurated in 2003, the series is restricted to horses bred in Florida and California. With the strength of the local breeding industries in both states the races provide top competition and more than a measure of interstate rivalry.

The course has also hosted the Breeders' Cup meeting on a number of occasions and is remembered as the track where Bill Shoemaker rode the last winner of his illustrious career in 1990.

While the course has undergone many ownership changes in recent times, Gulfstream Park remains one of the premier tracks in the USA.

Racing season is December through April with the feature Grade races in February and the Florida Derby held in early March.

## THE TRACK

Left-handed. The track underwent a major reconstruction in 2004 to lengthen the layout and now consists of a 9-furlong dirt oval and a 1-mile inner turf track.

The back straight has a chute that accommodates mile races on the dirt.

## FEATURE RACES

| FEATURE RACES | | | | | | | |
|---|---|---|---|---|---|---|---|
| GULFSTREAM PARK TURF HCP | G1 | 9F | TURF | 4YO+ | HCP | 1986 | FEB |
| DONN HCP | G1 | 9F | DIRT | 4YO+ | HCP | 1959 | FEB |
| FLORIDA DERBY | G1 | 9F | DIRT | 3YO+ | SW | 1952 | MAR |
| FORWARD GAL STAKES | G2 | 7F | DIRT | 3YOF | ASS | 1981 | JAN |
| HUTCHESON STAKES | G2 | 7F | DIRT | 3YO | ASS | 1954 | FEB |
| GULFSTREAM PARK SPRINT | G2 | 7F | DIRT | 4YO+ | ASS | 1972 | FEB |
| DAVONA DALE STAKES | G2 | 9F | DIRT | 3YOF | ASS | 1981 | FEB |
| MAC DIARMIDA HCP | G2 | 11F | TURF | 4YO+ | ASS | 1995 | FEB |
| FOUNTAIN OF YOUTH STAKES | G2 | 9F | DIRT | 3YO | ASS | 1988 | MAR |
| GULFSTREAM PARK HCP | G2 | 8F | DIRT | 4YO+ | ASS | 1946 | MAR |
| SWALE STAKES | G2 | 7F | DIRT | 3YO | ASS | 1985 | MAR |
| INSIDE INFORMATION HCP | G2 | 7F | DIRT | 4YO+F&M | ASS | 1976 | MAR |
| HONEY FOX HCP | G2 | 8F | TURF | 3YO+F&M | HCP | 1985 | MAR |
| PAN AMERICAN HCP | G2 | 12F | TURF | 4YO+ | HCP | 1962 | MAR |
| GULFSTREAM OAKS | G2 | 9F | DIRT | 3YOF | ASS | 1971 | MAR |

## FEATURE RACES

### FLORIDA DERBY

The Florida Derby currently offers a $1 million purse and winners of this race generally go on to compete in the Kentucky Derby, so it has an impressive history dating back to 1952.

Derby Day is also the main social event on the calendar in South Florida.

Winners who have gone on to win the Kentucky Derby include **NEEDLES (1956)**, **TIM TAM (1958)**, **CARRY BACK (1961)**, **NORTHERN DANCER (1964)**, **FORWARD PASS (1968)**, **SPECTACULAR BID (1979)**, **SWALE (1984)**, **UNBRIDLED (1990)**, **THUNDER GULCH (1995)**, **MONARCHOS (2001)**, **BARBARO (2006)** and **BIG BROWN (2008)**.

Other winners that have claimed Triple Crown races include **NASHUA (1955)**, **BALLY ACHE (1960)**,

CANDY SPOTS (1963), SNOW CHIEF (1986) and **EMPIRE MAKER (2003)**.

Other notables include **RIDAN (1962)**, **IN REALITY (1967)**, **HONEST PLEASURE (1976)**, **ALYDAR (1978)**, **PLUGGED NICKLE (1980)**, **TIMELY WRITER (1982)**, **PROUD TRUTH (1985)** won the Breeders' Cup Classic (1985), **CRYP-TOCLEARANCE (1987)** also won the Donn Hcp (1989), **FLY SO FREE (1991)** won the Breeders' Cup Juvenile (1990).

**HOLY BULL (1994)** won 13 of 16. His 3yo campaign also included wins in the Blue Grass Stakes, Metropolitan Hcp, Haskell Invitational, Travers Stakes and Woodward Stakes (1994); **UNBRIDLED'S SONG (1996)** won the Breeders' Cup Juvenile (1995); and **QUALITY ROAD (2009)**.

## DONN HANDICAP

Established in 1959, the race is named in honour of the Donn family.

It is a 9-furlong race on the dirt with a list of winners that includes dual victors

**ONE-EYED-KING (1959, 60)**, **PISTOLS AND ROSES (1993, 94)** and **CIGAR (1995, 96)**.

Other notable winners include **FOREGO (1974)**; **FOOLISH PLEASURE (1976)**; **DEPUTY MINISTER (1983)**; **CREME FRAICHE (1986)**; **LITTLE BOLD JOHN (1987)** won 38 of 105 career starts; **JADE HUNTER (1988)**; **SKIP AWAY (1998)** won the Blue Grass Stakes, Woodbine Million, Haskell Invitational (1996), Breeders' Cup Classic (1997), two Jockey Club Gold Cups (1996, 97) defeating Cigar in the first of those victories, Woodward Stakes, Hollywood Gold Cup, Gulfstream Park Hcp (1998) and was three times a champion horse.

**CAPTAIN STEVE (2001)** won the Dubai World Cup (2001); **MEDAGLIA D'ORO (2004)**; **SAINT LIAM (2005)** won the Breeders' Cup Classic (2005); Uruguayan national hero **INVASOR (2007)**; and **QUALITY ROAD (2010)** won the Florida Derby (2009), Metropolitan Hcp and Woodward Stakes (2010).

Jerry Bailey piloted the winner six times between 1988 and 2004.

## GULFSTREAM PARK TURF HCP

Gulfstream Park's premier turf race, first run in 1986.

**EINSTIEN (2006, 08)** is a dual winner of the race.

Other notable winners include **CELTIC ARMS (1996)**, who won the Prix du Jockey Club (1994); **YAGLI (1999)**; **ROYAL ANTHEM (2000)** won the Canadian International (1998) International Stakes at York (1999); **JAMBALAYA (2007)** won the Arlington Million (2007); and **KIP DEVILLE (2009)**.

# OAKLAWN PARK

Central Ave, Hot Springs, Arkansas. www.oaklawn.com

Azeri wins the Breeders' Cup Ladies' Classic

## FEATURE RACES

| APPLE BLOSSOM HCP | G1 | 8½F | DIRT | F&M | HCP | 1958 | APR |
|---|---|---|---|---|---|---|---|
| ARKANSAS DERBY | G1 | 9F | DIRT | 3YO | SW | 1936 | APR |
| REBEL STAKES | G2 | 8½F | DIRT | 3YO | SW | 1961 | MAR |
| FANTASY STAKES | G2 | 8½F | DIRT | 3YOF | SW | 1973 | APR |
| OAKLAWN HCP | G2 | 9F | DIRT | OPEN | HCP | 1946 | APR |

*The popular spa town of Hot Springs is located in Garland County, Arkansas. Hot Springs National Park is the USA's oldest federal park reserve.*

Opened in 1905, Oaklawn Park is the premier course in Arkansas and has played host to many of the great champions. The track has gone from strength to strength throughout its proud history and is now considered one of the top ten racetracks in the USA.

The Arkansas Racing Commission was formed in 1935 to manage the course after legislation was changed to allow the resumption of racing in the state.

Oaklawn is now home to the Racing Festival of the South. Instituted in 1974, a stakes race is run every day over the final seven programs, with the climax the Arkansas Derby.

The course also houses a state-of-the-art training facility and in 2008 underwent a $3 million addition to transform it into the largest gaming facility in Arkansas.

Racing season is from January through April, with the main races run towards the back of the season.

## THE TRACK

Left-handed. One-mile dirt oval. Home straight – 385yds.

## FEATURE RACES

### ARKANSAS DERBY

First run in 1936, the Arkansas Derby has of recent times elevated in prestige to become one of the major lead-up races to the 3yo Triple Crown. A bonus of $5 million was added in 2004 for any horse who could win the Rebel Stakes (Grade 2), the Arkansas Derby and the Kentucky Derby. This incentive has created greater participation by top-class 3yos and has seen the race upgraded to a Grade 1 event in 2010.

**SUNNY'S HALO (1983)** was the first winner of the race to go on to take the Kentucky Derby.

Since the institution of the bonus, winners have included **SMARTY JONES (2004)**, who went on to collect the bonus; **AFLEET ALEX (2005)** won the Belmont Stakes and the Preakness Stakes; **CURLIN (2007)** won the Preakness, Breeders' Cup Classic (2007) and the Dubai World Cup (2008).

Third place-getter in 2009, Summer Bird subsequently took the Belmont Stakes.

Earlier notables include **ELOCUTIONIST (1976)**, who was the first winner of the race to also take out a Triple Crown race by winning the Preakness; **NODOUBLE (1968)**; **TEMPERENCE HILL (1980)**; **TANK'S PROSPECT (1985)**; and **VICTORY GALLOP (1998)**.

## APPLE BLOSSOM HANDICAP

The Apple Blossom Handicap is an 8½ furlong race for fillies and mares dating back to 1958.

The record for wins is held by **AZERI (2002–04)** with three consecutive victories. Azeri's brilliant 2002 victory catapulted her to the top of the American ratings, confirming the status of the race.

**PASEANA (1992, 93)** and **ZENYATTA (2008, 10)** have both won it twice.

Other prominent winners include **SUSAN'S GIRL (1975)**; **NORTHERNETTE (1978)**; **BOLD 'N DETERMINED (1981)**; **TRACK ROBBERY (1982)** won 22 of 59 career starts; **BAYAKOA (1989)**; **NINE KEYS (1994)** was the first of six winners in the race for jockey Mike Smith; **ESCENA (1998)** won the Breeders' Cup Ladies' Classic that year; **BANSHEE BREEZE (1999)** won the Alabama Stakes, Coaching Club American Oaks, Spinster Stakes (1998); and **HAVRE DE GRACE (2011)**.

# MONMOUTH PARK

175 Oceanport Avenue, Oceanport, New Jersey, USA.
www.monmouthpark.com

Curlin

## FEATURE RACES

| | | | | | | |
|---|---|---|---|---|---|---|
| HASKELL INVITATIONAL HCP | G1 | 9F | DIRT | 3YO | SWP | 1968 AUG |
| UNITED NATIONS STAKES | G1 | 11F | TURF | 3YO+ | HCP | 1953 JUL |
| MOLLY PITCHER STAKES | G2 | 8½F | DIRT | 3YO+F&M | ASS | 1946 JUL |
| MONMOUTH STAKES | G2 | 9F | TURF | 3YO+ | ASS | 2008 JUN |
| MONMOUTH CUP | G2 | 8F | DIRT | 3YO+ | ASS | 1977 JUL |

Oceanport in Monmouth County is the venue for racing in New Jersey.

Monmouth Park originally opened in 1870 but ran into financial trouble after only three years, forcing it to shut down. Races resumed in 1882 but the track was once again closed in 1894 after pari-mutuel betting was outlawed in New Jersey. The track re-opened in 1946 after new legislation provided for regulation of horse racing.

Following the purchase of the Monmouth Park Jockey Club by the New Jersey Sports and Exposition Authority in 1986, many of the course's historic races were reinstated, including the Monmouth Cup. Dating back to 1884, the race was renamed the Phillip H Iselin Handicap after the man who, along with Amory Haskell, led the rebirth and resurgence of racing in New Jersey.

In 1951 the Molly Pitcher Handicap at

Monmouth Park was the first race ever to be televised live in colour.

Monmouth Park is a grand old seaside course renowned for its old-style New Jersey elegance and manicured gardens. Racing season is from May to September and meetings here have a relaxed holiday atmosphere.

The top class Haskell Invitational Stakes, run in August, is always the most popular race day on the schedule.

## THE TRACK

Left-handed. The Main Track is a 1-mile dirt oval with two chutes that provide the starting positions for races over 6 furlongs and 10 furlongs.

The inner Turf Track has a circumference of 7 furlongs, with a hedge acting as the inside rail when the movable rail is not employed.

A diagonal inner chute accommodates the starts for races between 1 and 1¼ mile.

A separate chute provides for 5½ furlong races on the turf course.

## FEATURE RACES

### HASKELL INVITATIONAL STAKES

The Haskell Invitational Stakes is an invitation-only dirt race over 9 furlongs for 3yos and is one of the top races on the US racing calendar. It was named in honour of Armory Haskell who campaigned heavily in the 1940s for the legislative changes that led to the resumption of horseracing in New Jersey.

The scheduling of the race between the Triple Crown races and the Breeders' Cup meeting, plus its million-dollar purse and bonuses for Grade 1 winners just for lining up at the start, provides owners with plenty of incentive to run. Inaugurated in 1968, the race became an invitation-only event in 1981.

Kentucky Derby winners to have won it include **WAR EMBLEM (2002)** and **BIG BROWN (2008)**. **COASTAL (1979)**, **BET TWICE (1987)** and **TOUCH GOLD (1997)** all won the Belmont; **DEPUTED TESTIMONY (1983)**, **RACHEL ALEXANDRA (2009)** and **LOOKIN' AT LUCKY (2010)** won the Preakness; and **POINT GIVEN (2001)** won both.

Other notables include **WAJIMA (1975)**, **FORTY NINER (1988)**, **HOLY BULL (1994)**, **SERENA'S SONG (1995)** was a winner of 11 Grade 1 races and was the first filly to win, **SKIP AWAY (1996)**, **CORONADO'S QUEST (1998)**, **DIXIE UNION (2000)** and **PEACE RULES (2003)**.

## UNITED NATIONS STAKES

The United Nations Stakes is Monmouth's biggest turf race with a rich history.

Several horse have won the race twice including **ROUND TABLE (1957, 59)**, **MONGO (1962, 63)**, **MANILA (1986, 87)**, Brazilian champ **SANDPIT (1995, 96)**, **ENGLISH CHANNEL (2006, 07)** and **PRESIOUS PASSION (2008, 09)**.

Other notables include **CLEM (1958)**, who defeated Round Table; **TV LARK (1960)** won the Washington DC International (1961); **ASSAGAI (1966)**; **DR FAGER (1968)**; South African star **HAWAII (1969)** won 21 of 28 starts and sired 1980 Epsom Derby winner Henbit; and **FORT MARCY (1970)** finally won after three consecutive placings in the race, and also won the Charles Whittingham Memorial (1969), Man O' War Stakes (1970) and twice won the Washington DC International (1967, 70).

**RUN THE GAUNTLET (1971)**; **HALO (1974)**, influential sire of Sunday Silence; **ROYAL GLINT (1975)**; **YANKEE AFFAIR (1989)**; **SKY CLASSIC (1992)**; **STAR OF COZZENE (1993)**; **LURE (1994)** twice won the Breeders' Cup Mile (1992, 93); **YAGLI (1999)** and **BETTER TALK NOW (2005)**.

# DELAWARE PARK

777 Delaware Park Boulevard, Wilmington, Delaware, USA. www.delawarepark.com

## FEATURE RACES

| | | | | | | |
|---|---|---|---|---|---|---|
| DELAWARE HCP | G1 | 10F | DIRT | 3YO+F&M | HCP | JUL |
| DELAWARE OAKS | G2 | 8½F | DIRT | 3YOF | | JUL |
| OBEAH HCP | G3 | 9F | DIRT | 3YO+F&M | | JUN |
| ROBERT G DICK MEMORIAL HCP | G3 | 11F | TURF | 3YO+F&M | HCP | JUL |
| KENT STAKES | G3 | 9F | TURF | 3YO | | SEPT |

Situated at the confluence of the Christina River and Brandywine Creek, the city of Wilmington is the largest in the state of Delaware.

The Delaware Park course, expertly designed by William DuPont Jr, was constructed in 1937 and originally featured two steeplechase courses and quickly became known for its saddling and picnic grove areas as well as its architecture.

After initial success, the course began to flounder during the 1980s and was closed down in 1982. It re-opened in 1984 and a decade later the course mounted a campaign to increase the number of tracks receiving the live broadcast of Delaware Park races, which saw betting turnover increase significantly.

Changes in legislation to allow it to conduct football betting and gaming also helped revive the fortunes of the track and prize money received a major boost.

The rise back to prominence was completed when the track regained its Grade 1 status in 2013, with the upgrading of the Delaware Handicap to the elite level.

Racing season is scheduled from April to October, with the Del 'Cap run in mid to late July.

The complex also features an 18-hole championship golf course.

## THE TRACK

Left-handed. One-mile dirt oval. Home straight – 332yds.

Inner turf track of 7 furlongs.

## FEATURE RACE

### DELAWARE HANDICAP

A major race for the fillies and mares, it was first run in 1937 as the New Castle Handicap. The race name was amended in 1955.

Dual winners include **ENDINE (1958, 59)**, **OBEAH (1969, 70)**, **BLESSING ANGELICA (1971, 72)**, **SUSAN'S GIRL (1973, 75)** and **NASTIQUE (1988, 89)**.

Other notables include **MISS GRILLO (1948)**, **BUSANDA (1951)**, **GRECIAN QUEEN (1953)**, **PARLO (1955)**, **FLOWER BOWL (1956)**, **PRINCESS TURIA (1957)** won the Kentucky Oaks, **QUILL (1960)**, **AIRMANS GUIDE (1961)**, **OLD HAT (1964)**, **OPEN FIRE (1966)**, **POLITELY (1968)**, **OPTIMISTIC GAL (1976)**, **LATE BLOOMER (1978)**, **RELAXING (1981)**, **JAMEELA (1982)** won 27 of 58, **COUP DE FUSIL (1987)**, **FLEET INDIAN (2006)**, **HYSTERICA-LADY (2008)**, **BLIND LUCK (2011)** and **ROYAL DELTA (2012)**.

# PARX

3001 Street Road, Bensalem, Pennsylvania, USA.
www.parxracing.com

Smarty Jones

### FEATURE RACES

| | | | | | | |
|---|---|---|---|---|---|---|
| COTILLION HCP | G1 | 8½F | DIRT | 3YOF | ASS | 1969 SEPT |
| PENNSYLVANIA DERBY | G2 | 9F | DIRT | 3YO | SW | 1977 SEPT |
| DR JAMES PENNY MEMORIAL HCP | G3 | 8½F | TURF | 3YO+F&M | HCP | 2000 JUL |
| SMARTY JONES CLASSIC | G3 | 8½F | DIRT | 3YOC | ASS | 2008 SEPT |
| TURF MONSTER HCP | G3 | 5F | TURF | 3YO+ | HCP | 2002 SEPT |

The township of Binsalem is located in Bucks County in southern Pennsylvania.

Situated on 417 acres, the racecourse opened in 1974 and was originally known as Keystone Racetrack before it was renamed Philadelphia Park in 1984.

Since 2009 it has operated under the moniker of Parx Casino and Racing, which may not overly enthuse fans of the English language, but punters are well catered for as it is the largest gaming complex in Pennsylvania.

Racing here is conducted right throughout the year, with highlights the Grade 1 Cotillion Handicap and the Pennsylvania Derby (Grade 2), which currently boasts prize money of $1 million.

During the warmer months the Picnic Grove provides a great atmosphere for an outing to the track.

Smarty Jones is the pride of the locally trained brigade, and the global attention that he attracted to Binsalem during his Triple Crown

attempt of 2004 is regarded as crucial to the passing of the Bill – in July of that year – that allowed casino gambling in the state of Pennsylvania and guaranteed the survival of the track.

## THE TRACK

Left-handed. One-mile dirt oval with 7-furlong and 10-furlong chutes.

The 7-furlong turf inner track has a 9-furlong chute.

## FEATURE RACE

### COTILLION HANDICAP

Only recently upgraded to Grade 1 level, top fillies to have won include inaugural winner **SHUVEE (1969)**, **OFFICE QUEEN (1970)** won 16 races, **SUSAN'S GIRL (1975)**, **MY JULIET (1975)**, **JOSTLE (2000)**, **ASHADO (2004)** and **HAVRE DE GRACE (2010)**.

# CALDER

21001 NW 27th Avenue, Miami Gardens, Florida, USA. www.calderracecourse.com

### FEATURE RACES

| | | | | | |
|---|---|---|---|---|---|
| PRINCESS ROONEY HCP | G1 | 6F | DIRT | 3YO+F&M | ASS 1985 |
| CARRY BACK STAKES | G2 | 6F | DIRT | 3YO | ASS 1975 |
| LA PREVOYANTE HCP | G2 | 12F | TURF | 3YO+ | HCP 1976 |
| SMILE SPRINT HCP | G2 | 6F | DIRT | 3YO+ | ASS 1984 |
| WL MCKNIGHT HCP | G2 | 12F | TURF | 3YO+ | HCP 1973 |

Calder racecourse is located at Miami Gardens and named after real estate developer Stephen A Calder, who founded the track in 1971. The course is home to Miami's Festival of the Sun.

The racing calendar runs from April until January and provides plenty of top-class racing with the highlight the Grade 1 Princess Rooney Stakes, run in July.

Since 1982 Calder has also run the Florida Stallion Stakes series, which is open to eligible Florida-bred 2yos, with three races each over increasing distances for the colts and also the fillies.

In June 2005 top Panamanian rider Eddie Castro set a North American record here when he booted home nine winners on a ten-race program.

## THE TRACK

Left-handed. One-mile dirt oval.
Seven-furlong inner turf track.

## FEATURE RACES

### PRINCESS ROONEY STAKES

Princess Rooney won 17 of 21 starts including the Frizette Stakes (1982), Ashland Stakes (1983), Vanity Invitational Hcp, Spinster Stakes, Clement L Hirsch Hcp and Breeders' Cup Distaff (1984). She was the first winner of a Breeders' Cup race to be admitted to the Hall of Fame.

Inaugurated in 1987, the event was upgraded to Grade 1 status in 2006. The race winner receives automatic entry into the Breeders' Cup Filly & Mare.

### SMILE SPRINT HANDICAP

A notable sprint race on the dirt track, with winners **ORIENTATE (2002)** and **BIG DRAMA (2010)** going on to win the Breeder's Sprint Cup.

### WL McKNIGHT HCP

While the accent at Calder is on speed, the premier staying races are the La Prevoyante Handicap and the WL McKnight Handicap, both Grade 2 races over a mile and a half on the turf.

Probably the most notable winner of the McKnight is dual Ascot Gold Cup victor **DRUM TAPS (1990)**.

Noted front-running stayer **PRESIOUS PASSION (2007, 08)** is the only multiple winner. Presious Passion was denied the hat-trick in 2009, running second to former Canadian International Stakes hero, **CLOUDY'S NIGHT (2009)**.

# FAIR GROUNDS

1751 Gentilly Boulevard, New Orleans, Louisiana, USA. www.fairgroundsracecourse.com

## FEATURE RACES

| | | | | | |
|---|---|---|---|---|---|
| RISEN STAR STAKES | G2 | 8½F | DIRT | 2YO | FEB |
| FAIR GROUNDS OAKS | G2 | 8½F | DIRT | 3YOF | MAR |
| NEW ORLEANS HCP | G2 | 8½F | DIRT | 4YO+ | MAR |
| MERVYN H MUNTZ MEMORIAL HCP | G2 | 9F | TURF | 4YO+ | MAR |
| LOUISIANA DERBY | G2 | 9F | DIRT | 3YO | MAR |
| RACHEL ALEXANDRA STAKES | G3 | 8½F | DIRT | 3YOF | FEB |
| MINESHAFT HCP | G3 | 8½F | DIRT | 4YO+ | FEB |
| FAIR GROUNDS HCP | G3 | 9F | TURF | 4YO+ | FEB |

Historic Fair Grounds racecourse is situated off the Interstate 610, in the mid-city area of New Orleans, only a short distance from the CBD and the French Quarter.

Fair Grounds is located on the site of the original Union Racecourse – one of the oldest in the USA, having been laid out in 1852.

The first thoroughbred meeting was staged the following year, though racing has hardly been continuous on the site. Fair Grounds has a history like no other. The course has suffered many closures. Fire, flood, the Civil War, the Spanish–American War, the Great Depression, World War II, internal bickering, local rivalries and government legislation have all threatened the course during its long history. Like many American courses, it has also narrowly avoided the threat of property developers.

Many colourful characters have frequented the track, including riverboat gamblers, champion prize fighters and Pat Garrett – the man who shot Billy the Kid – raced a stable here. President Ulysses S Grant attended in 1880 and Frank James, brother of Jesse, was a commission agent for one of the major local stables around the turn of the 20th century.

Many great champions have raced here.

Fabled harness horse, Flora Temple, the 'bob-tailed nag' depicted in Stephen Foster's song, 'Camptown Races' started here in 1859. Legendary mare Pan Zareta, who won 76 races from 151 starts, passed away in her stall at Fair Grounds in 1918, and is buried in the infield here. Tippity Witchet won many races here.

In the modern era the track has undergone major capital works with a $27 million grandstand opened in 1997 and purchase of the course by Churchill Downs Inc in 2004.

Racing season is from November to March, and the course stages many Graded and Listed races with very good prize money on offer throughout. The signature race is the Louisiana Derby, which has a history dating back to 1898 and a current purse of $1 million.

During January the course hosts a very popular mixed meeting. In addition to the regular thoroughbred card, race-goers are treated to the spectacle of zebra races and ostrich races, although none of those is currently rated at Graded or Listed level.

## THE TRACK

Left-handed. One-mile dirt oval.
Inner turf track of 7 furlongs.

## FEATURE RACE

### LOUISIANA DERBY

Notable winners include Kentucky Derby winners **BLACK GOLD (1924)** and **GRINDSTONE (1996)**,

**MASTER DERBY (1975)** won the Preakness, **GOLDEN ACT (1979)** won the Canadian International (1979), **RISEN STAR (1988)** won the Preakness and Belmont, **DISPERSAL (1989)** and **PEACE RULES (2003)**.

# HAWTHORNE

3501 S Laramie Avenue, Cicero, Illinois, USA.
www.hawthorneracecourse.com

| FEATURE RACES | | | | | | | |
|---|---|---|---|---|---|---|---|
| HAWTHORNE GOLD CUP | G2 | 10F | DIRT | 3YO+ | HCP | 1928 | OCT |
| ILLINOIS DERBY | G3 | 9F | DIRT | 3YO | SW | 1923 | APR |
| SIXTY SAILS HCP | G3 | 9F | DIRT | 3YO+F&M | ASS | 1976 | APR |
| HAWTHORNE DERBY | G3 | 9F | TURF | 3YO | ASS | 1965 | OCT |

Cicero is located in Cook County, Illinois. The Hawthorne racecourse was built by Chicago businessman and thoroughbred owner Edward Corrigan, and began operations in 1891.

While the track enjoyed popularity in its early days progress was halted by a fire in 1902, which completely destroyed the grandstand, and then by government legislation that forced the closure of the track in 1905.

Despite a number of attempts, racing did not permanently return to the venue until 1922.

Racing season runs from February to April and October to December. During September the course stages the Illinois Festival of Racing, with events for locally bred horses.

The traditional highlight is the valuable Hawthorne Gold Cup, run in October, with a solid gold cup traditionally awarded to the winner.

## THE TRACK

Left-handed. One-mile dirt oval with a long home straight of 440yds.

Inner turf course of 7 furlongs.

## FEATURE RACE

### HAWTHORNE GOLD CUP

First run in 1928, it is a top race that has been won by some great horses. **SUN BEAU (1929–31)** made it a hat-trick, and dual winners include **ROUND TABLE (1957, 58)**, **NODOUBLE (1968, 69)** and **CRYPTO-CLEARANCE (1988, 89)**.

Other notables include inaugural winner **DISPLAY (1928)**, who won the Preakness (1926) and Jockey Club Gold Cup (1927); **EQUIPOISE (1933)**; **DISCOVERY (1935)**; **CHALLEDON (1939)**; **REJECTED (1954)**; **DEDICATE (1956)**; **KELSO (1960)**; **TV LARK (1961)**; **DR FAGER (1967)**; **DROLL ROLE (1972)** won the Canadian International, Washington DC International (1972); **ROYAL GLINT (1975)**; **BLACK TIE AFFAIR (1990)**; **BUCK'S BOY (1997)** won the Breeders' Cup Turf (1998); **AWESOME AGAIN (1998)**; and **AWESOME GEM (2009)** won the Hollywood Gold Cup (2010).

# TAMPA BAY DOWNS

11225 Race Track Road, Tampa, Florida, USA.
www.tampabaydowns.com

| FEATURE RACES | | | | | | | |
|---|---|---|---|---|---|---|---|
| TAMPA BAY DERBY | G2 | 8½F | DIRT | 3YO | ASS | 1981 | MAR |
| SAM F DAVIS STAKES | G3 | 8½F | DIRT | 3YO | ASS | 1981 | FEB |
| ENDEAVOUR STAKES | G3 | 8½F | TURF | 4YO+F&M | ASS | 2000 | FEB |
| TAMPA BAY STAKES | G3 | 8½F | TURF | 4YO+ | ASS | 1987 | FEB |
| HILLSBOROUGH STAKES | G3 | 9F | TURF | 3YO+F&M | ASS | 1999 | MAR |

Tampa Bay is a natural harbour on the west-central coast of Florida and home to Tampa Bay Downs racetrack, which opened in 1926. It is the only track on the west coast of Florida.

After being commandeered by the US Army as a training base during World War II, the course was left in a state of disrepair and badly in need of maintenance and redevelopment before racing could resume.

The track re-opened in 1946 following the installation of electric starting stalls, photo finish equipment and an electronic tote board.

Racing season on the Oldsmar Oval is from December until May, and it is a popular venue with the climate typically conducive. The highlight fixture is Festival Day in March, featuring the Tampa Bay Derby.

In recent times betting turnover has risen due to an increase in turf races now being scheduled here.

The course also features a museum-quality exhibition devoted to Seabiscuit in the Legends Bar.

## THE TRACK

Left-handed. One-mile dirt oval.

Seven-furlong inner turf track, which has a quarter-mile inner chute.

### TAMPA BAY DERBY

First run in 1981, the race was upgraded to a Grade 2 event in 2011.

**STREET SENSE (2007)** and **SUPER SAVER (2010)** both won en route to victory in the Kentucky Derby.

# GOLDEN GATE FIELDS

11 Eastshore Highway, Albany, California, USA.
www.goldengatefields.com

| FEATURE RACES | | | | | | | |
|---|---|---|---|---|---|---|---|
| SAN FRANCISCO MILE STAKES | G2 | 8F | TURF | 4YO+ | SW | 1948 | APR |
| EL CAMINO DERBY | G3 | 9F | AWT | 3YO | ASS | 1980 | FEB |
| BERKELEY HCP | G3 | 8½F | AWT | 3YO+ | ASS | 1948 | JUN |
| ALL AMERICAN STAKES | G3 | 9F | AWT | 3YO+ | ASS | 1968 | NOV |

Albany in California is just a short distance from Oakland, San Francisco, and the famous Napa Valley wine country.

Opened in 1941, the elegant Golden Gate Fields racecourse is situated on the eastern shoreline of the San Francisco Bay, which provides a spectacular setting for very good quality racing.

It is the only major racetrack in northern California since the closure of Bay Meadows in 2008.

Racing takes place from May to June and October to January.

## THE TRACK

Left-handed. The Main Track is a one-mile oval Tapeta track. Home straight – 333yds.

Lakeside Turf Course of 9⁄10 of a mile.

# FEATURE RACES

## SAN FRANCISCO MILE STAKES

First run in 1948, the race has been won by many top horses, none better than **CITATION (1950)**.

Other prominent winners include **DETER-MINE (1955)**, who won the Kentucky Derby (1954); **VIKING SPIRIT (1965)**; **FIGONERO (1971)** won the Gran Premio San Isidro (1968) and Hollywood Gold Cup (1969); **TIGHT SPOT (1992)** won the Arlington Million (1991); **REDATTORE (2001)**; **SUANCES (2002)** was a winner of the Prix Jean Prat (2000); **SINGLETARY (2004)** won the Breeders' Cup Mile (2004); and **BATTLE DANCE (1957, 58)** and **NATIVE DIVER (1963, 67)** both won it twice.

## SILKY SULLIVAN HANDICAP

Silky Sullivan's name entered the American vernacular through his deeds as a fast-finishing back-marker in the 1950s. Legendary for giving away enormous starts in his races, he could not keep up early, often coming from 30 lengths behind the bunch to win. Silky won 12 out of his 27 starts including the Santa Anita Derby (Grade 1) and the Golden Gate Futurity, and was a folk hero to the American public.

His name became a byword. To 'do a Silky' entered the vernacular as a description for any situation that required making a run from a seemingly impossible position. He became the first horse ever buried in the infield at Golden Gate Fields.

Silky Sullivan

# COLONIAL DOWNS

10515 Colonial Downs Parkway, New Kent, Virginia, USA. www.colonialdowns.com

## FEATURE RACES

| | | | | | | |
|---|---|---|---|---|---|---|
| VIRGINIA DERBY | G2 | 10F | TURF | 3YO | ASS | 1998 JUL |
| VIRGINIA OAKS | G3 | 9F | TURF | 3YOF | ASS | 2004 JUL |
| ALL ALONG STAKES | G3 | 9F | TURF | 3YO+F&M | ASS | 1985 JUL |

Located in New Kent, Virginia, and surrounded by beautiful countryside, Colonial Downs is a spectacular setting for racing.

Established in 1997, the course is a multi-purpose venue that caters for thoroughbreds, harness racing and steeplechase racing.

Unique Colonial Downs is one of the larger tracks in the USA, with most of its racing conducted on the 9-furlong turf course. The turf layout is the widest turf course in the country at 60yds across and can accommodate larger than usual fields for a US track.

The 10-furlong dirt track is the country's second largest behind Belmont but is used mainly for harness racing.

Racing takes place each week from Wednesday to Sunday over June and July, with the premier event the Virginia Derby in July.

## THE TRACK

Left-handed. The dirt track is a 10-furlong oval. The Secretariat Turf Course is 9 furlongs in circumference. Home straight of 430yds.

There is also an inner turf course of 7 furlongs.

## FEATURE RACE

### VIRGINIA DERBY

The Virginia Derby is the richest and most important race on the Virginia racing calendar and is gathering in status. A Grade 2 event on turf, it is a leg of the Grand Slam of Grass, which currently offers a $2 million bonus for any 3yo who can sweep four races: the Colonial Turf Cup and Virginia Deby at Colonial Downs, the Secretariat Stakes at Arlington and the Breeders' Cup Turf.

Run since 1998, notable winners of the race include **KITTEN'S JOY (2004)**, who won the Secretariat Stakes and the Joe Hirsch Invitational (2004); **ENGLISH CHANNEL (2005)**; **RED GIANT (2007)** ran a world record for 10 furlongs on the turf in the Clement L Hirsch Turf Championship (2008); and **GIO PONTI (2008)**, winner of the Manhattan Hcp, Frank E Kilroe Mile, Arlington Million (2009) and dual winner of both the Man O'War Stakes (2009, 10) and the Shadwell Turf Mile (2010, 11).

# LAUREL PARK

Route 198 and Racetrack Road, Laurel, Maryland, USA. www.laurelpark.com

## FEATURE RACES

| | | | | | | |
|---|---|---|---|---|---|---|
| BARBARA FRITCHIE HCP | G2 | 7F | DIRT | 3YO+F&M | ASS | 1952 FEB |
| GENERAL GEORGE HCP | G3 | 7F | DIRT | 3YO+ | ASS | 1973 FEB |

The city of Laurel is located midway between Washington DC and Baltimore in Prince George's County, Maryland.

Laurel Park races were originally founded as part of the Laurel Four County Fair in 1911. The course was purchased three years later by James Butler, who installed Colonel Matt Wynn as general manager. Wynn had successfully established the Kentucky Derby as the nation's premier race and would engineer a rise to prominence for the Laurel course.

The track rose in prestige once again under the auspices of John Schapiro, who broke new ground in 1952 when he instigated the first race ever designed to attract international participants – the Washington DC International Stakes on the turf. The race put the track on the world racing map and succeeded in its aim with visiting runners winning 21 of the 43 editions before the demise of the race in 1995.

The course is currently a regular host of one of the state's biggest racing attractions. Maryland Millions Day in October is one of the most well-attended race days at the track with a great festival atmosphere and an 11-race card for horses by stallions who stand in Maryland.

Inaugurated in 1986 and the brainchild of sports journalist Jim McKay, the highlight of these races is the Maryland Million Classic, run over 9 furlongs on the dirt track.

While state-bred showcase days are now commonplace, the Maryland Millions was the first of its kind in the USA and is a model that has been successfully imitated across the USA and in other parts of the world. While the restricted nature of these races generally prevents them from any sort of Graded or Listed status, there is no doubting their popularity and positive effect on local breeding industries.

In recent times the track has fought a battle to survive financial stresses, which has seen the downgrading of its only Grade 1 race, but has continued to outlay significant sums for regular renovations and upgrades to its course and facilities.

Racing season is from September until March, with the annual feature races run in February.

## THE TRACK

Left-handed. Nine-furlong oval that has two winning-post positions.

The first finish line gives a straight run from the home turn of 363yds, while the second finish position provides a run in of 473yds.

The inner turf track has a circumference of 7f 84yds with a 363yd straight.

In 2005 the dirt track was completely refurbished and the turf track widened from 75ft to 142ft.

## FEATURE RACE
### BARBARA FRITCHIE HANDICAP

The story goes that Barbara Fritchie was 95 years old when she risked her life with an open gesture of defiance toward the Confederate Army as they marched through Maryland en route to the Battle of Gettysburg. Whether the story is legend or myth is a matter of conjecture, but the tale of her defiant waving of the Union flag became a symbol of the American Civil War

Established in 1952, dual winners of the race include **TOO BALD (1968, 69)**, **SKIPAT (1979, 81)**, **TWIXT (1973, 74)** and **XTRA HEAT (2002, 03)**. Other notables include top fillies **TOSMAH (1966)**, **PROCESS SHOT (1970)** and **TAPPIANO (1989)**.

# HOOSIER PARK

4500 Dan Patch Circle, Anderson, Indiana, USA. www.hoosierpark.com

| FEATURE RACES | | | | | | | |
|---|---|---|---|---|---|---|---|
| INDIANA DERBY | G2 | 8½F | DIRT | 3YO | ASS | 1995 | OCT |
| INDIANA OAKS | G2 | 8½F | DIRT | 3YOF | ASS | 1995 | OCT |

Hoosier Park racecourse is located in the Madison County city of Anderson in the central region of Indiana.

Local businessman and long-time Anderson resident Virgil Cook donated 110 acres of land to the city so that a racecourse could be built. Churchill Downs took up the licence and the track staged its inaugural meeting in 1994, with a harness-racing fixture.

The Indiana Derby and Indiana Oaks were established the following year and remain the signature races at the course, both run in October.

Churchill Downs sold its interests in 2007 and Hoosier Park was converted into a combined racetrack and casino shortly after.

The thoroughbred racing season is conducted season from August to October.

## THE TRACK

Left-handed. Seven-furlong dirt oval. Home straight – 418yds.

## FEATURE RACE
### INDIANA DERBY

The Indiana Derby is the richest race on the calendar. Established in 1995, it has been won by **ORIENTATE (2001)**, **PERFECT DRIFT (2002)** and **LOOKIN' AT LUCKY (2010)**.

# MOUNTAINEER PARK

Mountaineer Cir, New Cumberland, West Virginia, USA. www.mtrracetrack.com

| FEATURE RACE | | | | | | | |
|---|---|---|---|---|---|---|---|
| WEST VIRGINIA DERBY | G2 | 9F | DIRT | 3YO | SWP | 1981 | AUG |

New Cumberland in Hancock County is situated on the north shore of the Ohio River in West Virginia.

The course at Mountaineer Park is conveniently located between Pittsburg and Cleveland.

Charles Town president Al Boyle instigated the construction of the track, which began operating in 1951 as Waterford Park racecourse. Following its sale in 1992, the track was renamed Mountaineer Park.

Two years later, after a change in legislation, the Mountaineer course was transformed into a resort and casino. The resulting increase in revenue flows has driven substantial and much-needed improvements to the track and also increased prize money to allow it to successfully compete with the neighbouring courses.

The signature race is the highly valuable Grade 2 West Virginia Derby held in August, with around a dozen Listed races also staged during the March to December racing season.

## THE TRACK

Left-handed. Main Course is a one-mile, oval-shaped track.

The Turf Track is a 7-furlong inner course.

## FEATURE RACE
### WEST VIRGINIA DERBY

Notable winners include **MIRACLE HILL (1967)**, winner of 24 races, and **ARCHITECT (1979)**, who won 13 of 24 career starts.

# LOUISIANA DOWNS

8000 East Texas Avenue, Bossier City, Louisiana, USA. www.harrahslouisianadowns.com

| FEATURE RACE | | | | | | | |
|---|---|---|---|---|---|---|---|
| SUPER DERBY | G2 | 9F | DIRT | 3YO | SW | 1980 | SEPT |

Bossier City is located in the Ark-La-Tex region of north-western Louisiana and is the home of Louisiana Downs racecourse.

Instigated and constructed by developer Edward DeBartolo Sr, the track staged its first meeting in 1974.

Racing season is conducted from May to September, with the highlight the Super Derby in September.

The course also hosts quarter-horse racing from January to March.

## THE TRACK

Left-handed. One-mile dirt oval. Home straight – 337yds.

Inner turf track of 7f 17yds.

## FEATURE RACE
### SUPER DERBY

First run in 1980, the race was run as a Grade 1 until 2002. A number of winners have been successful in the 3yo Classic races including Kentucky Derby winners **SUNNY'S HALO (1983)**, **ALYSHEBA (1987)** and **SUNDAY SILENCE (1989)**.

**TEMPERENCE HILL (1980)**, **CREME FRAICHE (1985)** and **EDITOR'S NOTE (1996)** won the Belmont, and **GATE DANCER (1984)** took out the Preakness.

Other notables include **ISLAND WHIRL (1981)**, **SEEKING THE GOLD (1988)**, **ARCH (1998)** and **TIZNOW (2000)**.

# PRESQUE ISLE DOWNS

8199 Perry Highway, Erie, Pennsylvania, USA. www.presqueisledowns.com

| FEATURE RACES | | | | | |
|---|---|---|---|---|---|
| PRESQUE ISLE DOWNS MASTERS STAKES | G2 | 6½F | AWT | 3YO+F&M | SEPT |
| Inaugural Stakes | L | 6F | AWT | 3YOF | MAY |
| Tom Ridge Stakes | L | 6F | AWT | 3YO | MAY |
| Satin And Lace Stakes | L | 5½F | AWT | 3YO+F&M | JUN |
| Windward Stakes | L | 8F | AWT | 3YO+F&M | JUL |
| Presque Isle Mile Stakes | L | 8F | AWT | 3YO+ | SEPT |
| Presque Isle Debutante Stakes | L | 6F | AWT | 2YOF | SEPT |
| HBPA Stakes | L | 8F | AWT | 3YO+F&M | SEPT |
| Fitz Dixon Jr Memorial Juvenile Stakes | L | 6½F | AWT | 2YO | SEPT |

Erie, on the south-central shores of Lake Erie in the state's north-west, is the fourth-largest city in Pennsylvania.

The newly opened Presque Isle Downs is the venue for racing with the season conducted from May until September. It was the first course in the USA to install a synthetic Tapeta surface track.

The main race is the Presque Isle Downs Masters Stakes, run in May since the inaugural 2007 meeting.

## THE TRACK

Left-handed. One-mile oval. Tapeta surface. Home straight – 354yds.

## FEATURE RACE
### PRESQUE ISLE DOWNS MASTERS STAKES

A Grade 2 race for fillies and mares, it has been won twice by **INFORMED DECISION (2009, 10)**. She also won the Madison Stakes, Humana Distaff and Breeders' Cup Filly & Mare Sprint (2009). **GROUPIE DOLL (2012)** likewise won the Madison Stakes, Humana Distaff and Breeders' Cup Filly & Mare Sprint (2012).

# CHARLES TOWN

750 Hollywood Drive, Charles Town, West Virginia, USA. www.hollywoodcasinocharlestown.com

| FEATURE RACES | | | | | |
|---|---|---|---|---|---|
| CHARLES TOWN CLASSIC STAKES | G2 | 9F | DIRT | 4YO+ | APR |
| Sugar Maple Stakes | L | 7F | DIRT | 4YO+F&M | APR |
| Robert R Hilton Memorial Stakes | L | 7F | DIRT | 3YO+ | APR |
| Red Legend Stakes | L | 7F | DIRT | 3YO | JUN–JUL |
| Charles Town Oaks | L | 7F | DIRT | 3YOF | SEPT |

Charles Town racecourse is situated in Jefferson County, West Virginia.

Albert and Joseph Boyle spent the princely sum of $160,000 to construct a racetrack in 1933, convinced that people would attend the only northern track open for racing during the winter months.

Charles Town quickly enjoyed enormous popularity with large crowds in attendance, boosted by the train service from nearby Baltimore, and racing flourished right throughout World War II.

Presidential candidate John F Kennedy staged one of his major rallies here in 1960.

The course has raced year round since 1972 and is one of the busiest in the country with meetings generally staged five days a week.

Since its purchase in 1997, the facility has had $175 million invested to transform it into a massive gaming and hotel complex.

The highlight is the Charles Town Classic Stakes, run in April. A 9-furlong race established in 2009, prize money for the race was increased to $1.5 million in 2013 to make it the richest race in the USA, aside from the Kentucky Derby and Breeders' Cup Championships. With the lift in purse, it appears destined to become one of America's top races. Research won the first two editions.

The course stages good-quality racing with more than a dozen Listed races, and a series of short course events dubbed the Sprint Festival. Virginia Breeders' Classic Day is also a highlight.

## THE TRACK

Left-handed. The main track is a 6-furlong dirt oval. Run in of 220yds.

# TURFWAY PARK

7500 Turfway Road, Florence, Kentucky, USA.
www.turfway.com

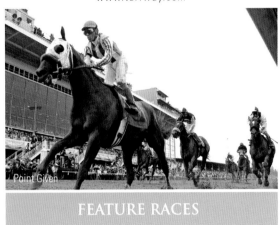

Point Given

### FEATURE RACES

| SPIRAL STAKES | G3 | 9F | AWT | 3YOC&G | ASS | 1972 MAR |
|---|---|---|---|---|---|---|
| BOURBONETTE OAKS | G3 | 8F | AWT | 3YOF | ASS | 1983 MAR |

Florence in Boone County, near the Ohio River, is the venue for racing in Northern Kentucky.

Racing in the area dates back to 1833, with the opening of the Latonia Racecourse, just 10 miles from the present site. Latonia had a proud history and the Latonia Derby long held a position as one of the country's premier 3yo events, but the track was forced to close in 1939.

Latonia re-opened its doors at the new location in Florence in 1959. When Jerry Carroll purchased the course in 1986 it underwent a major facelift and the name was changed to Turfway Park.

In 2005, Turfway was the first course in the USA to install an all-weather Polytrack, which enables racing throughout the season which is conducted from December to March.

The course is also the setting for the 2005 comedy film *Racing Stripes*.

The Spiral Stakes is far and away the most valuable race on the calendar, with a current purse of $500,000.

## THE TRACK

Left-handed. One-mile Polytrack oval. Home straight – 323yds.

## FEATURE RACE

### SPIRAL STAKES

Notable winners include **BROAD BRUSH (1986)**, **SUMMER SQUALL (1990)**, **HANSEL (1991)** won the Preakness and the Belmont, **LIL E TEE (1992)** won the Kentucky Derby, **PRAIRIE BAYOU (1993)** took out the Preakness, **SERENA'S SONG (1995)** is the only mare to win, **HARD SPUN (2007)** and **ANIMAL KINGDOM (2011)** won the Kentucky Derby (2011) and Dubai World Cup (2013).

# PRAIRIE MEADOWS

1 Prairie Meadows Drive, Altoona, Iowa, USA.
www.prairiemeadows.com

### FEATURE RACES

| IOWA DERBY | | G3 | 8½F | DIRT | 3YO | JUN |
|---|---|---|---|---|---|---|
| IOWA OAKS | | G3 | 8½F | DIRT | 3YOF | JUN |
| PRAIRIE MEADOWS CORNHUSKER HCP | | G3 | 9F | DIRT | 3YO+ | JUN |

Polk County, in the heart of Iowa, is the location of the Prairie Meadows racecourse.

The track was constructed on 157 acres of pastoral land adjacent to the Adventureland Amusement Park following the legalisation of pari-mutuel betting in Iowa in 1983. The inaugural meeting was staged in 1989.

In 1995 Prairie Meadows became the country's first combined racetrack and slot machine casino, by then under the control of Polk County, which operates the course as a not-for-profit organisation to benefit the local community in the Des-Moines area.

Since then the track has contributed over $1 billion in grants, donations to charitable institutions and taxes to local government. Revenues raised also funded the construction of the Iowa Events Center, as well as being re-invested into construction of new facilities for the Prairie Meadows course.

Racing is staged from April to August, with

the major races run in June. There are many Listed events and races for locally bred horses conducted right throughout the season.

The course also hosts quarter-horse racing.

## THE TRACK

Left-handed. One-mile dirt oval. Home straight – 330yds.

## FEATURE RACES

### PRAIRIE MEADOWS CORNHUSKER HANDICAP

Originally established in 1966 at the Ak-Sar-Ben course, which closed in 1995, notable winners of the race include **GATE DANCER (1985)**, who won the Preakness (1984); **DISPERSAL (1990)**, winner of the Cigar Mile (1989), Woodward Stakes (1990); Breeders' Cup Classic winner **BLACK TIE AFFAIR (1991)**; **SIR BEAR (2000)** won 19 races including the Cigar Mile (1998), Metropolitan Hcp (1999) and Gulfstream Park Hcp (2001); and **ROSES IN MAY (2004)** won the Dubai World Cup (2005).

### IOWA DERBY

First run in 1989, it has been won by **CAPTAIN STEVE (2000)**, who won the Dubai World Cup (2001) and **HANSEN (2012)**, who won the Breeders' Cup Juvenile the previous year.

# LONE STAR

1000 Lone Star Parkway, Grand Prairie, Texas, USA.
www.lonestarpark.com

Ouija Board

### FEATURE RACES

| TEXAS MILE STAKES | G3 | 8F | DIRT | 3YO+ | ASS | 1997 APR |
|---|---|---|---|---|---|---|
| LONE STAR PARK HCP | G3 | 8½F | DIRT | 3YO+ | ASS | 1997 MAY |
| OUIJA BOARD HCP | G3 | 8F | TURF | 3YO+F&M | ASS | 1997 MAY |

Ghostzapper

Opened in 1997 in front of a crowd of more than 21,000 people, Lone Star Park is the premier venue for racing in Texas.

Located in Grand Prairie, midway between Dallas and Fort Worth, the setting combined with the Spanish baroque architecture gives the course a highly distinctive atmosphere.

A major upgrade of the barns and stabling complex took place in 2002, and the course received the ultimate accolade of being selected to host the Breeders' Cup Championships in 2004.

Racing season occurs between April and July. The Texas Mile Stakes was elevated to Grade 3 level in 1999 to become the first Graded stakes race ever run in Texas.

## THE TRACK

Left-handed. One-mile dirt oval. Home straight – 310yds.

Seven-furlong turf inner track. Home straight – 300yds.

## FEATURE RACES

### TEXAS MILE STAKES

**LITTLEBITLIVELY (1998, 99)** won it twice, but apart from that it has proved a hard race to win with some defeats more notable than victories. The 1998 Kentucky Derby and Preakness Stakes winner Real Quiet ran second in 1999 and Skip Away – US Horse of the Year (1998) and Champion 3yo Colt (1996) – was beaten into third place in 1997.

### LONE STAR PARK HANDICAP

**CONGAREE (2002)** went on to win the Cigar Mile twice (2002, 03) and the Hollywood Gold Cup (2003), and **BOB AND JOHN (2007)** also won the Wood Memorial Stakes (2006).

### OUIJA BOARD HANDICAP

Originally run in 1997 as the Fort Worth Handicap, the race has undergone a number of name changes in its short history and was renamed again in 2007 to honour the deeds of champion mare Ouija Board. Ouija Board was a winner of seven G1 races including the Epsom Oaks, Breeders Cup Filly & Mare Turf and the Hong Kong Vase, and she was twice named European Horse of the Year (2004, 06).

**WASTED TEARS (2009–11)** has made the race her own with three consecutive victories.

## DELTA DOWNS

2717 Highway 3063, Vinton, Louisiana, USA.
www.deltadowns.com

### FEATURE RACES

| DELTA JACKPOT STAKES | G3 | 8½F | DIRT | 2YO | NOV |
|---|---|---|---|---|---|
| DELTA PRINCESS STAKES | G3 | 8F | DIRT | 2YOF | NOV |
| Jean Lafitte Stakes | L | 8F | DIRT | 2YO | OCT |
| My Trusty Cat Stakes | L | 7F | DIRT | 2YOF | OCT |
| Delta Mile Stakes | L | 8F | DIRT | 3YO+ | NOV |
| Treasure Chest Stakes | L | 8F | DIRT | 3YO+F&M | NOV |

The town of Vinton in the Calcasieu Parish of Louisiana is home to the Delta Downs racecourse.

Situated on a 220-acre countryside site, the tight 6-furlong course was opened in 1973, primarily as a track for quarter-horse races, which are still conducted.

Racing season at Delta Downs is from October until April, with most of its feature races in mid November, including the $1 million Delta Jackpot – a Grade 3 race for 2yos. The race was won by Big Drama in 2008, who went on to take out the Breeders' Cup Sprint in 2010.

In the 1990s, when changes to the laws allowed, the track was purchased and redeveloped into a casino and gaming facility.

The devastation of Hurricane Katrina in 2005 forced the closure of the track for six months while extensive repairs were carried out.

## THE TRACK

Left-handed. Six-furlong dirt oval. Home straight – 220yds.

There are separate start chutes for races over 5 furlongs and 9 furlongs.

## KENTUCKY DOWNS

5629 Nashville Road, Franklin, Kentucky, USA.
www.kentuckydowns.com

### FEATURE RACES

| KENTUCKY CUP TURF STAKES | G3 | 12F | TURF | 3YO+ | SEPT |
|---|---|---|---|---|---|
| Kentucky Cup Turf Dash Hcp | L | 6F | TURF | 3YO+ | SEPT |
| Kentucky Cup Ladies' Turf Stakes | L | 8F | TURF | 3YO+F&M | SEPT |
| Franklin-Simpson Stakes | L | 8F | TURF | 3YO+ | SEPT |
| Kentucky Downs Ladies' Marathon Stakes | L | 10½F | TURF | 3YO+F&M | SEPT |

The city of Franklin is located in the very south of Kentucky on the border of Tennessee, 40 miles north of Nashville. It is an area with a colourful history.

During the 19th century the practice of duelling to settle disputes was still legal in Kentucky but not in Tennessee, and the border town of Franklin became host to an area known as the Dueling Grounds.

When the practice was outlawed the land reverted to more useful agricultural purposes. In the 1980s a group of investors purchased the 260-acre property to build a European style racetrack for steeplechase racing.

This unique course opened in 1990 and was a complete departure from the usual dirt ovals across the country, with a turf layout based on that of Doncaster.

In 1992 the course was altered to also

host flat racing. All black type racing here is conducted on the flat.

Originally established as the Dueling Grounds racecourse, the name was changed to Kentucky Downs in 1997 after management of the track was taken over by Turfway Park.

Kentucky Downs annually stages only a handful of meetings in September, with the highlight the Grade 3 Kentucky Cup Turf Handicap over a mile and a half.

## THE TRACK

Left-handed. A slightly undulating turf course in the shape of an ice-cream cone. Circumference of 10½ furlongs. The home straight is approximately a quarter of a mile.

Out of the straight a sharp left-handed turn takes runners to the mile pole. It is then a run of almost 2 furlongs to a sweeping bend that joins the home stretch.

The mile-and-a-half start is located at the top of the home straight.

# SAM HOUSTON PARK

7575 North Sam Houston Parkway, West Houston, Texas, USA. www.shrp.com

| FEATURE RACE | | | | | | |
|---|---|---|---|---|---|---|
| JOHN B CONNALLY TURF HCP | G3 | 9F | TURF | 4YO+ | HCP | JAN |

Sam Houston was the first and third president of the independent republic of Texas in the mid 19th century. He was one of the key figures who paved the way for the inclusion of Texas into the United States.

Sam Houston Park staged its inaugural meeting in 1994 and now races from January to March.

The highlight race to this point in time has been the Grade 3 John B Connally Turf Cup Stakes, which is a 9-furlong race for 4yos and up and is currently the only Grade stakes run.

It seems likely that this will not be the case for long with the establishment of the

Houston Ladies' Classic in 2013. The inaugural running offered a purse of $400,000 – currently double that of the John B Connally – suggesting that the new race for fillies and mares (4yo+) may soon assume the mantle of feature race at the course.

Sam Houston Park is also building up its schedule of races for the locally bred horses and appears to be climbing the ranks of racecourses in the US.

The track also conducts quarter-horse racing and the season directly follows the thoroughbred meet.

## THE TRACK

Left-handed. One-mile dirt oval. Home straight – 318yds.

Inner turf track of 7 furlongs.

# ELLIS PARK

3300 US 41, Henderson, Kentucky, USA. www.ellisparkracing.com

| FEATURE RACE | | | | | |
|---|---|---|---|---|---|
| GARDENIA STAKES | G3 | 8F | DIRT | 3YO+F&M | AUG |

Ellis Park is located by the twin bridges on the Indiana side of the Ohio River, although it is officially in Kentucky. While the Ohio River forms the border between Kentucky and Indiana, the state border is based on the course of the river as it existed at the time Kentucky became a state in 1792. An earthquake in 1812 altered the course of the Ohio, leaving the land that would accommodate Ellis Park separated from the remainder of Kentucky.

Opened in 1922 the track was originally named Dade Park after AB 'Barrett' Dade, who was a director of the Green River Jockey Club, which had purchased the land and established the track.

Plagued by financial woes in its early years, the Green River Jockey Club went broke and in 1925 the track was bought at a Kentucky county

bankruptcy auction for $35,000 by James A Ellis. The track was renamed in his honour in 1954, shortly before his passing in 1956.

The course has proved resilient, having survived the flooding of the Ohio River in 1937. Much of the track and its facilities were severely damaged by a major tornado in 2005.

Despite reconstruction Ellis Park still proudly exudes its old-world charm.

In 2006 the track was bought by local Kentucky businessman Ron Geary, who reinstated the 4 July opening date but has struggled in recent times with dwindling prize money and acceptors. This has seen a scaling back of race dates with the season now limited to July and August.

## THE TRACK

Left-handed. Nine-furlong dirt track with a home straight of 392yds.

Chutes for the 7-furlong and one-mile starts.

One-mile turf inner track.

# EMERALD DOWNS

2300 Emerald Downs Drive, Auburn, Washington. www.emeralddowns.com

| FEATURE RACES | | | | | |
|---|---|---|---|---|---|
| LONGACRES MILE HCP | G3 | 8F | DIRT | 3YO+ | AUG |
| Washington Oaks | L | 9F | DIRT | 3YOF | AUG |
| Emerald Downs Derby | L | 9F | DIRT | 3YO | AUG |

Auburn is a suburb of the metropolitan area of Seattle in King's County, Washington.

Emerald Downs is a modern facility opened in 1996 to replace the Longacres course, which had been in operation for about 60 years until its closure in 1992.

The initial racing surface was deemed to be substandard, so a $1 million upgrade was undertaken in 1997.

Situated between Seattle and Tacoma in the Auburn Valley and with the majestic Mount

Rainier as a backdrop, Emerald Downs is the major track in the Pacific North-east.

Racing season is from April to September, with a score of Listed races conducted over the duration, and the highlight Grade 3 Longacres Mile in August.

Worthy of mention is West Seattle Boy, who won 21 races at the course.

## THE TRACK

Left-handed. One-mile dirt oval. Home straight – 330yds.

## FEATURE RACE

### LONGACRES MILE

First run in 1935 at the former Longacres course, the race is a Grade 3 and currently an automatic qualifying race for the Breeders' Cup Dirt Mile.

Dual winners include **AMBLE IN (1946, 48)**, **TROOPER SEVEN (1980, 81)** and **SIMPLY MAJESTIC (1988, 89)**.

Other notables include **VIKING SPIRIT (1964)**, who won the Carter Hcp, Bing Crosby Stakes and Shoemaker Mile (1965).

**CHINOOK PASS (1982)** was a winner of 16 of 25 starts including the Bing Crosby Stakes. He set a US record time of 55:2:00 for 5 furlongs at Longacres in 1982 and was voted Washington State Horse of the Century.

**SKYWALKER (1986)** won the Santa Anita Derby and Breeders' Cup Classic (1986); **SKY JACK (2003)** – out of a Skywalker mare – won the Hollywood Gold Cup (2003), as did **AWESOME GEM (2011)**, who followed up his Hollywood Gold Cup win from the previous year.

# REMINGTON PARK

1 Remington Place, Oklahoma City, Oklahoma, USA.
www.remingtonpark.com

## FEATURE RACES

| | | | | | |
|---|---|---|---|---|---|
| Oklahoma Derby | L | 9F | DIRT | 3YO | SEPT–OCT |
| Governor's Cup | L | 9F | DIRT | 3YO+ | AUG |
| Remington Park Sprint Championship Hcp | L | 8F | DIRT | 2YO | SEPT–OCT |
| Remington Park Oaks | L | 8½F | TURF | 3YOF | SEPT–OCT |
| Remington Green Stakes | L | 8½F | TURF | 3YO+ | SEPT–OCT |
| Clever Trevor Stakes | L | 6F | DIRT | 2YO | NOV |
| Remington MEC Mile Stakes | L | 8F | DIRT | 2YO | DEC |

Constructed by Edward J DeBartolo Sr, Remington Park is situated in the north-east side of Oklahoma City. The first meeting was conducted in 1988.

Upon its opening, Remington Park was the first American track to experiment with the installation of a synthetic track but considered the surface sub-par before reverting to a more traditional dirt track.

Racing season is from August until December with the highlight races the valuable Oklahoma Derby and the richest race in Oklahoma, the Heritage Place Futurity, worth $1 million.

## THE TRACK

Left-handed. One-mile dirt oval. Home straight – 342yds.

Seven-furlong turf inner track.

# SUNLAND PARK

1200 Futurity Drive, Sunland Park, New Mexico.
www.sunland-park.com

## FEATURE RACES

| | | | | | |
|---|---|---|---|---|---|
| SUNLAND PARK YULETIDE DERBY | G3 | 9F | DIRT | 3YO | MAR |
| Borderland Derby | L | 8½F | DIRT | 3YO | FEB |
| Sunland Park Oaks | L | 8½F | DIRT | 3YOF | MAR |
| Harry W Henson Hcp | L | 8F | DIRT | 3YO+F&M | MAR |
| Bill Thomas Memorial Hcp | L | 6½F | DIRT | 3YO+ | MAR |
| Sunland Park Hcp | L | 9F | DIRT | 3YO+ | APR |
| Riley Allison Futurity | L | 8F | DIRT | 2YO | SEPT |

Sunland Park conducted its inaugural meeting in 1959, with the track immediately popular as the region's only legalised form of betting.

The general downturn in racing during the 1990s saw a casino added to the course in 1999 under agreement with Native American casinos. The deal ensured that the gaming facility would operate under strict laws and with restricted opening hours.

The season is from December to April with racing staged a minimum four days a week during the meeting.

The feature event on the calendar is the Sunland Park Yuletide Derby, run in March, which has recently been elevated to Grade 3 level. The race was won in 2005 by Thor's Echo, who went on to win the Breeders' Cup Sprint the following season.

## THE TRACK

Left-handed. One-mile dirt oval. Home straight – 330yds.

# MEADOWLANDS

50 State Route 120, East Rutherford, New Jersey,
USA. www.thebigm.com

## FEATURE RACES

| | | | | | |
|---|---|---|---|---|---|
| CLIFF HANGER STAKES | G3 | 8½F | TURF | 3YO+ | SEPT |
| Dan Horn Stakes | L | 5F | TURF | 3YO+ | MAY |
| Who Did It And Run | L | 5F | TURF | 3YO+F&M | MAY |

East Rutherford is an inner-ring suburb of New York City in the Bergen County borough of New Jersey.

Meadowlands racetrack is world-renowned as the USA's home of harness racing and one of the world's foremost tracks in the sport. It is the venue for the famous Hambletonian Stakes for 3yo trotters.

Opened in 1976, the mile dirt track at The Big M also accommodates thoroughbred racing, which commenced the following year.

Once host to the Grade 1 Meadowlands Cup, which saw horses the calibre of Spectacular Bid and Alysheba take home the prize, the focus on the standardbreds saw racing shut down completely for a time and the Cup race moved to Monmouth Park where it is now run under the name of the new host venue.

After a three-year hiatus, thoroughbred racing was again scheduled at the Meadowlands with an experimental two-day meeting in May 2012 to coincide with the Kentucky Derby and Oaks fixtures. The track staged a mixed card of thoroughbred races, which were run in the afternoon on the turf course, followed by a full harness fixture in the evening.

It remains doubtful whether the planned thoroughbred dates will be maintained in the long term.

Chris Antly set a riding record in 1987 when he rode four winners at Aqueduct in the afternoon then followed up with five wins on the evening Meadowlands card to complete nine wins on the day.

## THE TRACK

Left-handed. One-mile dirt oval. Home stretch of exactly 300yds.

Inner turf track of 7 furlongs.

# INDIANA DOWNS

4200 N Michigan Road, Shelbyville, Indiana, USA.
www.indianadowns.com

## FEATURE RACES

| | | | | | |
|---|---|---|---|---|---|
| Oliver Stakes | L | 8F | TURF | 3YO | JUN |
| Kenneth Self Boys and Girls Club Stakes | L | 8F | TURF | 3YO+ | JUN |
| Shelby County Stakes | L | 8F | DIRT | 3YO+F&M | JUN |
| Golden Bear Stakes | L | 8½F | DIRT | 3YO+ | JUL |
| Indiana First Lady Stakes | L | 8½F | TURF | 3YOF | JUL |

The city of Shelbyville is located in the Addison Township of Shelby County, Indiana.

After several unsuccessful attempts by developer Paul Estridge Snr, permission was granted in 2001 by the Indiana Horse Racing Commission for a second race-track in Indiana.

The state-of-the-art Indiana Downs race-course opened in Shelbyville the following year.

Situated 15 miles to the south of downtown Indianapolis, Indiana Downs is a venue for thoroughbred, harness and quarter-horse racing.

The season is from April to July, with the highlight meeting in mid July featuring the Listed First Lady Stakes and the restricted Governor's Cup. The most valuable race on the calendar is the Oliver Stakes for 3yos in June.

## THE TRACK

Left-handed. One-mile dirt oval.
Seven-furlong turf inner track.

# PLEASANTON

4501 Pleasanton Avenue, Pleasanton, California,
USA. www.alamedacountyfair.com

## FEATURE RACES

| | | | | | |
|---|---|---|---|---|---|
| California Wine Stakes | L | 6F | DIRT | 3YO | JUN |
| Alameda County Fillies and Mares Hcp | L | 8½F | DIRT | 3YO+F&M | JUN–JUL |
| Alameda Hcp | L | 8½F | DIRT | 3YO+ | JUN–JUL |
| Juan Gonzales Memorial Stakes | L | 5½F | DIRT | 2YOF | JUL |
| Everett Nevin Alameda County Futurity | L | 5½F | DIRT | 2YO | JUL |

Pleasanton, in Alameda County, California is located in the San Francisco Bay area 25 miles east of downtown Oakland.

Constructed by the sons of Spaniard Don Augustin Bernal, racing at the current course at Pleasanton commenced in 1859, and it is the oldest 1-mile racetrack in the USA.

In its early history the area was known as a refuge for thieves and desperados, particularly during the Gold Rush when returning prospectors passing through were often relieved of their booty by gun-wielding bandits.

Before the transportation of horses became commonplace, Pleasanton was a popular venue for wealthy owners from the east coast to send their horses for training during the winter months to take advantage of the warmer climate.

Alameda County purchased the track in 1940. The venue hosts races for thoroughbreds, Arabians and quarter horses.

Racing is conducted annually over the three-week Alameda County Fair during June and July.

## THE TRACK

Left-handed. One-mile dirt oval.

# RUIDOSO DOWNS

461 US Highway 70, Ruidoso Downs, New Mexico.
www.raceruidoso.com

## FEATURE RACES

| First Lady Hcp | L | 6F | DIRT | 3YO+F&M | MAY |
| Free Spirit Hcp | L | 6F | DIRT | 3YO+ | JUN |
| Aspen Cup | L | 6F | DIRT | 3YOF | AUG |
| Ruidoso Derby Stakes | L | 8½F | DIRT | 3YO | SEPT |
| Ruidoso Thoroughbred Championship Hcp | L | 8½F | DIRT | 3YO+ | SEPT |

Ruidoso is located in Lincoln County, New Mexico, beside the Lincoln National Forest.

Racing at Ruidoso Downs dates back to the 1930s when regular match races were staged on a strip of land on Mr Miller's corn field. The field is the site of the current course, which officially commenced operations in 1947. Initially the course was known as Hollywood Park but when the track was acquired by Gene Hensley in 1953 the name was sensibly changed to reflect its geography.

Originally a 5-furlong oval, the track was enlarged in 1986.

While the course stages a number of Listed events for thoroughbreds, it is best known as a Grade 1 quarter-horse venue with separate straights for thoroughbred racing and quarter-horse racing. Ruidoso Downs is the home of the All American Futurity – America's richest quarter-horse race.

Racing for the thoroughbreds is conducted from May to August.

## THE TRACK

Left-handed. Seven-furlong dirt oval. Home straight – 220yds.

# EVANGELINE DOWNS

2235 Creswell Lane Extension, Opelousas, Louisiana, USA. www.evangelinedowns.com

## FEATURE RACES

| Louisiana Showcase Classic Stakes | L | 8½F | DIRT | 3YO+ | JUN–JUL |
| Louisiana Showcase Distaff | L | 8½F | DIRT | 3YO+F&M | JUN–JUL |
| DS 'Shine' Young Memorial Futurity | L | 5F | DIRT | 2YO | JUL–AUG |
| Evangeline Downs Mile Hcp | L | 8F | DIRT | 3YO+ | AUG |

Evangeline Downs racecourse opened in 1966 at Carencro but moved to its present site at Opelousas in the St Landry Parish of Louisiana in 2005.

With its modern facilities, it is a very user-friendly course for race-goers.

John Henry scored his first stakes win at the track and Hallowed Dream established a then record for a filly with her 14th consecutive victory registered in the Listed Tellike Stakes, run here at Evangeline Downs.

Racing season is from April until September with meetings conducted from Wednesday to Saturday every week.

## THE TRACK

Left-handed. One-mile dirt oval.
Seven-furlong turf inner track. The turf track has a chute for the 9-furlong start.

# TURF PARADISE

1501 W Bell Road, Phoenix, Arizona, USA. www.turfparadise.com

## FEATURE RACES

| Cotton Fitzsimmons Mile Handicap | L | 8F | TURF | 4YO+ | JAN |
| Turf Paradise Derby | L | 8½F | DIRT | 3YO | FEB |
| Phoenix Gold Cup | L | 6F | DIRT | 4YO+ | FEB |

Local businessman Walter Cluer purchased 1400 acres of barren desert on the outskirts of Phoenix in 1954 with the intention to construct a premier racing facility. Two years later his vision was complete and the first meeting was staged at the Turf Paradise racecourse.

Situated 14 miles north-west of downtown Phoenix, the track has undergone many improvements in the past decade and the landscaped grounds and mountain setting make an idyllic location.

With the weather in Arizona always fine, Turf Paradise races right through October till May. The feature Turf Paradise Derby and Phoenix Gold Cup are both run in February.

## THE TRACK

Left-handed. One-mile dirt oval. Home straight – 330yds.

Inner turf course of 7 furlongs with a chute for races over 9 furlongs.

# RETAMA PARK

1 Retalma Parkway, Selma, Texas, USA.
www.retamapark.com

## FEATURE RACES

| La Senorita Stakes | L | 8F | TURF | 2YOF | NOV |
| El Joven Stakes | L | 8F | DIRT | 2YO | NOV |
| Mistletoe Stakes | L | 8F | DIRT | 2YOF | DEC |

The city of Selma in Texas is located 18 miles north-east of San Antonio.

Opened in 1995, Retama Park hosts meetings on Fridays and Saturdays from October through December.

The course also stages quarter-horse racing.

## THE TRACK

Left-handed. One-mile dirt oval. Home straight – 330yds.

Seven-furlong turf inner track.

# FINGER LAKES

5857 State Route 96, Farmington, New York, USA.
www.fingerlakesracetrack.com

| FEATURE RACES | | | | | |
|---|---|---|---|---|---|
| Rachel Alexandra Stakes | L | 6F | DIRT | 2YOF | SEPT |
| Curlin Stakes | L | 6F | DIRT | 2YO | SEPT |

The beautiful Finger Lakes region in upstate New York is a haven for recreational activities, water sports and wineries and provides a spectacular location for racing.

Situated 25 miles south-east of Rochester and set on 450 acres the Finger Lakes thoroughbred facility staged its first meeting in 1962.

Course highlights include the appearance of legendary jockey Steve Cauthen to ride in September 1978, which drew a crowd of 11,000 and produced a record on-track wagering hold.

The record attendance was in 2007 when 2003 Kentucky Derby–Preakness winner Funnycide trounced his rivals in the Wadsworth Memorial Handicap in what would be his final racetrack appearance, witnessed by more than 12,000 people.

Racing season is from April to November and the highlight fixture is the restricted New York Derby in July. The race is currently the second leg of the Big Apple Triple for locally bred 3yos. The richest race on the calendar is the New York Breeders' Futurity.

Locally trained hero Fio Rito is buried in the infield. He won 28 of 50 starts, with 19 wins from 27 starts here at his home track. He proved himself a Grade 1 horse when he took out the Whitney Hcp in 1981.

## THE TRACK

Left-handed. One-mile dirt oval. Home straight – 320yds.
Chute starts for races at 6 furlongs and 10 furlongs.

# FRESNO

South Chance Avenue, Fresno, California, USA. www.fresnofair.com

| FEATURE RACES | | | | | |
|---|---|---|---|---|---|
| Charlie Palmer Futurity | L | 8F | DIRT | 2YO | OCT |
| Bulldog Stakes | L | 9F | DIRT | 3YO+ | OCT |

The city of Fresno is the fifth largest in California, situated 170 miles south of the state capital, Sacramento.

First held in 1884, the Big Fresno Fair is one of the biggest and longest running events in the Central Valley, with well in excess of half-a-million visitors annually.

Races are staged for thoroughbreds, quarter horses, Arabians, appaloosas and mules on a one-mile course over the two weeks of the fair.

The thoroughbred fixture contains two Listed races.

1962 Kentucky Derby winner Decidedly was trained at the Big Fresno Fair course.

## THE TRACK

Left-handed. One-mile dirt oval. Home straight – 320yds.

# FAIRPLEX PARK

Fairplex Drive, Pomona, California, USA.
www.fairplex.com/fp/horseracing

| FEATURE RACES | | | | | |
|---|---|---|---|---|---|
| Ralph M Hinds Hcp | L | 9F | DIRT | 3YO+ | SEPT |
| Pomona Derby | L | 8½F | DIRT | 3YO | SEPT |

The city of Pomona, is located 27 miles east of Los Angeles.

Racing has been staged as part of the Los Angeles County Fair since 1922. In 1933 the course was the first in Southern California to allow on-track pari-mutuel betting on live races.

The course was extended to the current 5-furlong track in 1985, providing an intimate and family-friendly setting. No binoculars are required here.

Renovations to the grandstand and clubhouse were completed the following year, when the Pomona course was officially renamed Fairplex Park.

With admission to the course included in the price of entry to the County Fair, attended by more than 1.5 million people each year, there are always plenty on hand to cheer on the competitors.

Despite the tight nature of the course, Fairplex Park hosts up to a dozen Listed races over 19 days. The most valuable of those is the Ralph M Hinds Handicap.

## THE TRACK

Left-handed. Five-furlong dirt oval. Home straight – 220 yds.

# SANTA ROSA

1350 Bennett Valley Road, San Rosa, California, USA.
www.santarosapark.com

| FEATURE RACES | | | | | |
|---|---|---|---|---|---|
| Cavonnier Juvenile Stakes | L | 6F | DIRT | 2YO | AUG |
| Wine Country Debutante Stakes | L | 6F | DIRT | 2YOF | AUG |

The beautiful city of Santa Rosa on California's north coast is the gateway to the Sonoma and Napa Valleys – California's legendary wine country.

A 90-acre section of the Sonoma County Fair Grounds was set aside in 1897 for the construction of a 1-mile oval racetrack.

Santa Rosa Park hosts a 15-day meeting during the Sonoma County Fair in July and August, which sees a number of Listed races conducted.

## THE TRACK

Left-handed. One-mile dirt oval. Home straight – 382yds.

Chute starts for races over 6 furlongs and over a mile and a quarter.

Inner turf track of 7 furlongs.

# CANTERBURY PARK

1100 Canterbury Road, Shakopee, Minnesota, USA.
www.canterburypark.com

### FEATURE RACES

| Mystic Lake Derby | L | 8F | TURF | 3YO | | | JUL |
|---|---|---|---|---|---|---|---|
| Lady Canterbury Stakes | L | 8F | TURF | 3YO+F&M | | | AUG |

The city of Shakopee in Minnesota is situated in the south-west corner of the Twin Cities metropolitan area.

Canterbury Park is the venue for racing and the course has endured a turbulent history in the short time since its opening in 1985, with numerous changes of name, ownership, and closures at various times due to financial difficulties and legislative issues.

Canterbury Park was back racing again in 2012 following an unsuccessful court challenge and another period of shut down.

Racing season is from May until September. Feature races here are run on the turf, including the Mystic Lake Derby, run in July.

### THE TRACK

Left-handed. One-mile dirt oval.

Chute starts for 6½-furlong and 10-furlong races.

Seven-furlong inner turf course.

# SUNRAY PARK

30 Road 5565, Farmington, New Mexico, USA.
www.sunraygaming.com

### FEATURE RACES

| Russell and Helen Foutz Distaff Hcp | L | 6½F | DIRT | 3YO+F&M | | | APR |
|---|---|---|---|---|---|---|---|
| San Juan County Commissioner's Hcp | L | 9F | DIRT | 3YO+ | | | JUL |

Farmington in New Mexico is situated in San Juan County, at the junction of the San Juan, Animas and La Plata rivers.

Sunray Park is the venue for horseracing with the season from April through until June.

### THE TRACK

Left-handed. Six-furlong dirt oval. Home straight – 330yds.

# THISTLEDOWN

21501 Emery Road, North Randall, Ohio, USA. www.caesars.com/thistledown

### FEATURE RACE

| OHIO DERBY | G3 | 8½F | DIRT | 3YO | SWA | 1876 | JUL |
|---|---|---|---|---|---|---|---|

Thistledown racecourse is located in North Randall, 10 miles east of Cleveland.

Racing season is from April to December, and the highlight is the Ohio Derby in July.

The track also hosts many events for locally bred horses.

### THE TRACK

Left-handed. One-mile dirt oval. Home straight – 326yds.

# ALBUQUERQUE

201 California Street Northeast Albuquerque, New Mexico, USA. www.abqdowns.com

### FEATURE RACES

| Don Juan de Onate Stakes | L | 6F | DIRT | 3YO | | | AUG |
|---|---|---|---|---|---|---|---|
| University of New Mexico Hcp | L | 8F | DIRT | 3YO+ | | | Oct |

Settled in 1706 as a Spanish colonial outpost, Albuquerque is the largest city in New Mexico and one of the highest altitude cities in the USA.

Racing occurs during the spring at The Downs in Albuquerque.

There is also a 17-day meeting during the State Fair in September.

### THE TRACK

Left-handed. One-mile dirt oval. Home straight – 372yds.

# WOODBINE

555 Rexdale Boulevard, Toronto, Ontario, Canada. www.woodbineentertainment.com

*Woodbine racecourse in Toronto is the premier racing venue in Canada.*

The original Woodbine course opened in 1874 and was in operation until 1963. Racing on the current site began in 1956 and the course became known as New Woodbine until the closure of the former track.

Woodbine is home to Canada's most valuable race, the Canadian International Stakes, as well as two legs of the Triple Crown in the Queen's Plate – the country's most historic race – and the Breeders' Stakes.

Extensive works were completed in 1993, which also added a harness-racing track.

Woodbine had the honour of hosting the Breeders' Cup meeting in 1996. It is the only course outside the USA to do so.

Racing in Canada is experiencing an extremely difficult period and is definitely at the crossroads with falling revenues and attendances the reality. Nearly all courses in the nation are currently either facing closure or fighting for their survival.

## THE TRACK

Left-handed. EP Taylor Turf Course is 12 furlongs in circumference. Home straight – 480yds.

Races over 9 furlongs start from a chute joining the back straight.

Inner Polytrack oval of 1 mile. Home straight – 325yds.

## FEATURE RACES

### CANADIAN INTERNATIONAL STAKES

Inaugurated in 1938 at the former Long Branch racecourse, the race moved to Woodbine in 1956 and became a turf race two years later.

Since then dual winners include **GEORGE ROYAL (1965, 66)**, **MAJESTY'S PRINCE (1982, 84)** and **JOSHUA TREE (2010, 12)**.

Other notable winners include **SECRETARIAT (1973)**; **DAHLIA (1974)**; Epsom Derby winner **SNOW KNIGHT (1975)**; **YOUTH (1976)** won the Prix du Jockey Club (1976), Washington

DC International (1976); **EXCELLER (1977)**; **MAC DIARMIDA (1978)**; Arc winner **ALL ALONG (1983)**; top local **SKY CLASSIC (1991)**; **SNURGE (1992)** won the St Leger (1990), Gran Premio di Milano (1991); **SINGSPIEL (1996)**; **CHIEF BEARHEART (1997)**; **ROYAL ANTHEM (1998)**; **MUTAFAWEQ (2000)** won the St Leger (1999), Grosser Preis von Berlin (2000), Coronation Cup (2001); **PHOENIX REACH (2003)** won the Hong Kong Vase (2004), Dubai Sheema Classic (2005); **SULAMANI (2004)**; **COLLIER HILL (2006)**; and **CHAMPS ELYSEES (2009)**.

### QUEEN'S PLATE

First run in 1860, it is the oldest race in Canada. It is the first leg of the Canadian Triple Crown, run over 10 furlongs on the all-weather course. The race is for Canadian-bred 3yos.

Triple Crown winners in Canada include **NEW PROVIDENCE (1959)**, **CANEBORA (1963)**, **WITH APPROVAL (1989)**, **IZVESTIA (1990)**, filly **DANCE SMARTLY (1991)** won the Breeders' Cup Ladies' Classic (1991), **PETESKI (1993)** and **WANDO (2003)**.

Other notable winners include **NETTIE (1868)**, **NORTHERN DANCER (1964)**, **KENNEDY ROAD (1971)** won the Hollywood Gold Cup (1973), **SOUND REASON (1977)**, **ALYDEED (1992)**, **AWESOME AGAIN (1997)** and **DANCETHRUTHEDAWN (2001)**.

### EP TAYLOR STAKES

First run in 1956 as the Nettie Handicap, the race for fillies and mares is now named after the former president of the Ontario Jockey Club, who was also one of the founders of the Canadian Jockey Club.

As well as being the prime mover behind the emergence of Canadian racing onto the world stage, EP Taylor is renowned internationally as the man who bred and raced Northern Dancer, and for his famous stud, Windfields Farm.

## FEATURE RACES

| | | | | | |
|---|---|---|---|---|---|
| WOODBINE MILE STAKES | G1 | 8F | TURF | 3YO+ | SEPT |
| NORTHERN DANCER BREEDERS' CUP TURF STAKES | G1 | 12F | TURF | 3YO+ | SEPT |
| NEARCTIC HCP | G1 | 6F | TURF | 3YO+ | OCT |
| EP TAYLOR STAKES | G1 | 10F | TURF | 3YO+F&M | OCT |
| CANADIAN INTERNATIONAL STAKES | G1 | 12F | TURF | 3YO+ | OCT |

Northern Dancer with Bill Shoemaker up

Runners head to the post for the centenary Queen's Plate

**KITTY'S GIRL (1957, 58)** is the only dual winner to date.

Other prominent winners include **DE LA ROSE (1981)**, who won the Hollywood Derby (1981); **L'AT-TRAYANTE (1983)** won the Irish 1000 Guineas, Poule d'Essai des Pouliches (1983); **RUBY TIGER (1990)**; **HATOOF (1992)**; **TIMARIDA (1995)** won the Prix de l'Opera (1995), Irish Champion Stakes, Beverly D Stakes (1996); **HONEY RYDER (2005)**; **ARRAVALE (2006)** won the Del Mar Oaks (2006); and **MRS LINDSAY (2007)** won the Prix Vermeille (2007).

## WOODBINE MILE

Notable winners include **PRIZED (1989)**; **IZVESTIA (1990)**; **DANCE SMARTLY (1991)**; **PETESKI (1993)**; **SKIP AWAY (1996)**; **LABEEB (1998)** won the Hollywood Derby (1995), Shoemaker Mile (1998); **VENTURA (2009)**; **COURT VISION (2010)** won the Jamaica Hcp, Hollywood Derby (2008), Shadwell Turf Mile (2009), Gulfstream Park Turf Hcp (2010), Breeders' Cup Mile (2011); and **WISE DAN (2012)**.

# HASTINGS PARK

188 North Renfrew Street, Vancouver, British Columbia, Canada. www.hastingspark.com

### FEATURE RACES

| BRITISH COLUMBIA DERBY | G3 | 9F | DIRT | 3YO | SEPT |
|---|---|---|---|---|---|
| BALLERINA STAKES | G3 | 9F | DIRT | 3YO+F&M | OCT |

Hastings Park is located four miles from the centre of Vancouver.

The course conducted its inaugural meeting in 1896. It was then known as East Park, and is the oldest track in Canada in continuous use.

The track has a splendid outlook with views of the North Shore Mountains and Burrard Inlet.

Racing takes place from April to October with the highlight events staged toward the end of the season.

## THE TRACK

Left-handed. The track is a 5½ furlong dirt oval. Home straight – 171yds.

# NORTHLANDS PARK

Wayne Gretzky Drive, Edmonton, Alberta, Canada. www.northlandspark.ca

### FEATURE RACE

| Speed To Spare Stakes | L | 11F | DIRT | 3YO+ | SEPT |
|---|---|---|---|---|---|

Situated on the North Saskatchewan River, Edmonton is the capital of the Alberta province in Canada.

Northlands Park racecourse staged its inaugural meeting in 1900.

Renovations to upgrade facilities were completed in 2005 to make it a very user-friendly course.

Racing season in Edmonton is from May to October.

## THE TRACK

Left-handed. Classic dirt oval of 5 furlongs. Home straight – 208yds.

# SAN ISIDRO

504 San Isidro Marquez Avenue, Buenos Aires Province, Argentina. www.hipodromosanisidro.com

*The historic city of San Isidro is situated in the metropolitan area of Buenos Aires. Located 22km north of the city centre, the Hipodromo San Isidro was established in 1935 under the control of the Argentina Jockey Club.*

## FEATURE RACES

| | | | | | |
|---|---|---|---|---|---|
| GP MIGUEL ALFREDO MARTINEZ DE HOZ | G1 | 2000M | TURF | 3YO+ | FEB |
| GP PAUL Y PAUL CHEVALIER | G1 | 1400M | TURF | 2YOC | APR |
| GP ELISIO RAMIREZ | G1 | 1400M | TURF | 2YOF | APR |
| GP GRAN CRITERIUM | G1 | 1600M | TURF | 2YO | MAY |
| GP DE POTRANCAS | G1 | 1600M | TURF | 2YOF | MAY |
| GP 25 DE MAYO | G1 | 2400M | TURF | 3YO+ | MAY |
| GP ESTRELLAS SPRINT | G1 | 1000M | TURF | 3YO+ | MAY |
| GP ESTRELLAS MILE | G1 | 1600M | TURF | 3YO+ | JUN |
| GP ESTRELLAS JUVENILE FILLIES | G1 | 1600M | TURF | 2YOF | JUN |
| GP ESTRELLAS JUVENILE | G1 | 1600M | TURF | 2YOC | JUN |
| GP MIL GUINEAS CONSAGRACION DE POTRANCAS | G1 | 1600M | TURF | 3YOF | AUG |
| GP DOS MIL GUINEAS CONSAGRACION DE POTRILLOS | G1 | 1600M | TURF | 3YOC | AUG |
| GP SUIPACHA | G1 | 1000M | TURF | 3YO+ | OCT |
| GP SAN ISIDRO | G1 | 1600M | TURF | 3YO+ | OCT |
| BP JOCKEY CLUB | G1 | 2000M | TURF | 3YO | OCT |
| GP COPA DE ORO | G1 | 2400M | TURF | 4YO+ | NOV |
| GP ENRIQUE ACEBAL | G1 | 2000M | TURF | 3YOF | NOV |
| GP INTERNACIONAL JOAQUIN S DE ANCHORENA | G1 | 1600M | TURF | 3YO+ | DEC |
| GP FELIX DE ALZAGA UNZUE | G1 | 1000M | TURF | 3YO+ | DEC |
| GP COPA DE PLATA ROBERTO VASQUEZ MANSILLA INTERNACIONAL | G1 | 2000M | TURF | 3YO+F&M | DEC |
| GP INTERNACIONAL CARLOS PELLEGRINI | G1 | 2400M | TURF | 3YO+ | DEC |

Argentina has a fine reputation as a horseracing and breeding nation and the course at San Isidro is a great galloping track with large expanses that provides a fair contest for horse and rider. The 148-hectare site has five training tracks and accommodation for 1800 horses in the lush surrounds.

San Isidro is host to Argentina's most important race – the Gran Premio Internacional Carlos Pellegrini – an open event over the 2400m, staged in December. The Carlos Pellegrini attracts crowds in large numbers with the record mark in excess of 102,000 people.

The course underwent a major renovation in 1979 with works to the grandstands and public facilities and the installation of a lighting system for night racing.

Around 120 meetings are held annually with fixtures scheduled on Wednesdays and weekends.

## THE TRACK

Left-handed. Main turf course has a circumference of 2783m. Home straight – 800m. Straight sprint course for 1000m races.

A diagonal chute for races over 1200m and 1400m joins the top of the home straight.

The release point for races over 2200m and 2400m is from a chute that joins the top of the back straight.

Inner sand track has two home bends. The long course is 2590m in length. When the first bend is in use, the circumference is 2200m.

Horse pool at San Isidro

## FEATURE RACE

Named after a former president of Argentina, the race has been run since 1887. Dual winners include **ATHOS (1890, 92)**, **PILLITO (1897, 99)**, **MOUCHETTE (1911, 12)** is the only mare to win twice, **MACON (1925, 26)**, **ROMANTICO (1938, 39)**, **FILON (1944, 45)**, **ACADEMICO (1946, 48)**, and **STORM MAYOR (2005, 06)**.

Argentinian Triple Crown winners to also take out this race include **PIPPERMINT (1902)**, **OLD MAN (1904, 05)** won it twice, **BOTAFOGO (1917)**, **MINERAL (1931)**, filly **LA MISSION (1940)**, **YATASTO (1951)**, **TATAN (1956)**, **MANANTIAL (1958)** and **TELESCOPINO (1978)**.

**FORLI (1966)** is one of Argentina's all-time greats. Undefeated Triple Crown winner in Argentina and highly influential sire of three-time US Horse of the Year Forego; Thatch; and dam sire of Nureyev, Swale and Precisionist.

Other notables include **PELAYO (1906)**, **SIBILA (1910)**, **MOLOCH (1921)**, **RICO (1922)**, **CONGREVE (1928)**, **COCLES (1930)**, **PAYASO (1932)**, **COTE D'OR (1933)**, **CUTE EYES (1934)**, **CAMERINO (1936)**, **TONICO (1942)**, **BANDERIN (1943)**, **DOUBTLESS (1947)** won the Saratoga Cup (1949), **MANGANGA (1955)**, **ESCORIAL (1959)**, **ARTURO A (1961)**, **CHAR-OLAIS (1964)**, **INDIAN CHIEF (1968)**, **PRAC-TICANTE (1969)** was a dual stakes winner in the USA, **SANTORIN (1973)**, **IMMENSITY (1983)** won the Brazilian Derby and Oaks, **MONTUBIO (1988)** was a Grade 1 winner in the USA, **ALGENIB (1990)**, **MUCH BETTER (1994)**, **CHULLO (1997)**, **ASIDERO (1999)**, **LATENCY (2007)** won nine Grade 1 races and **INTERACTION (2009)**.

# PALERMO

Avenue del Libertador, Buenos Aries, Argentina.
www.palermo.com.ar

## FEATURE RACES

| | | | | | |
|---|---|---|---|---|---|
| GRAN PREMIO SATURNINO J UNZUE | G1 | 1200M | DIRT | 2YOF | MAR |
| GRAN PREMIO SANTIAGO LURO | G1 | 1200M | DIRT | 2YOC | MAR |
| GRAN PREMIO ASOCIACION LATINO AMERICANA DE JOCKEY CLUBES | G1 | 2000M | DIRT | 3YO+ | MAR |
| GRAN PREMIO GILBERTO LERENA | G1 | 2000M | DIRT | 3YO+F&M | APR |
| GRAN PREMIO REPUBLICA ARGENTINA | G1 | 2000M | DIRT | 3YO+ | MAY |
| GRAN PREMIO LAS AMERICAS | G1 | 1600M | DIRT | 3YO+ | MAY |
| GRAN PREMIO CRIADORES | G1 | 2000M | DIRT | 3YO+F&M | MAY |
| GRAN PREMIO CIUDAD DE BUENOS AIRES | G1 | 1000M | DIRT | 3YO+ | MAY |
| GRAN PREMIO ESTRELLAS DISTAFF | G1 | 2000M | DIRT | 3YO+F&M | JUN |
| GRAN PREMIO ESTRELLAS CLASSIC | G1 | 2000M | DIRT | 3YO+ | JUN |
| GRAN PREMIO GENERAL SAN MARTIN | G1 | 1800M | DIRT | 4YO+ | AUG |
| GRAN PREMIO POLLA DE POTRANCAS | G1 | 1600M | DIRT | 3YOF | SEPT |
| GRAN PREMIO POLLA DE POTRILLOS | G1 | 1600M | DIRT | 3YOC | SEPT |
| GRAN PREMIO SELECCION | G1 | 2000M | DIRT | 3YOF | OCT |
| GRAN PREMIO PALERMO | G1 | 1600M | DIRT | 3YO+ | NOV |
| GRAN PREMIO MAIPU | G1 | 1000M | DIRT | 3YO+ | NOV |
| GRAN PREMIO NACIONAL | G1 | 2500M | DIRT | 3YO | NOV |

Palermo is situated to the north-east of the Buenos Aries CBD. The elegant Hipodromo Argentino de Palermo staged its first race meeting in 1876 and is the original venue for racing in Argentina.

Classic French architecture is a feature of the course, which is the home to one of the country's most historic and prestigious classics, the Gran Premio Nacional, otherwise known as the Argentina Derby. The Nacional is staged in mid November and has been run at Palermo since its inception in 1884.

The course underwent restorations after it became privately owned in 1992. There is a shopping area, French restaurants and a casino on the site.

Racing occurs right throughout the year, with meetings twice a week on Mondays and weekends. The course is equipped for night racing.

## THE TRACK

Left-handed. The main track is an oval sand course that has a circumference of 2400m. The home straight is 600m.

Straight sprint course for races up to 1100m.

# LA PLATA

Avenue 44 and 115 La Plata, Buenos Aires, Argentina.
www.hipodromolaplata.gba.gov.ar

## FEATURE RACES

| | | | | | |
|---|---|---|---|---|---|
| CLASICO SELECCION DE POTRANCAS | G1 | 2000M | DIRT | 3YOF | SEPT |
| GRAN PREMIO PROVINCIA DE BUENOS AIRES | G1 | 2200M | DIRT | 3YO | OCT |
| GRANDE PREMIO JOAQUIN V GONZALEZ | G1 | 1600M | DIRT | 3YO+ | NOV |
| GRAN PREMIO DARDO ROCHA | G1 | 2400M | DIRT | 3YO+ | NOV |

La Plata is the capital of the Province of Buenos Aries. The Hipodromo La Plata held its first meeting in 1884. The track has the distinction of being the first in Argentina to host night racing in 1964.

The highlight of the calendar is the Gran Premio Dardo Rocha, held in November. Dr Rocha was the founder of the city and instrumental in passing the ordinance that would allow the course to be constructed.

Meetings are scheduled weekly on Tuesday and Thursday and on alternate Sundays.

## THE TRACK

Left-handed. Oval sand course of 2000m in circumference. Home straight – 400m. Races over 1700m begin from a chute that joins the top of the back straight.

# BRAZIL

# CIDADE JARDIM

Linnaeus Avenue de Paula Machado, Sao Paolo, Brazil
. www.jockeysp.com.br

## FEATURE RACES

| | | | | | |
|---|---|---|---|---|---|
| GRANDE PREMIO SAO PAOLO | G1 | 2400M | TURF | 3YO+ | MAY |
| GRANDE PREMIO PRESIDENTE DA REPUBLICA | G1 | 1600M | TURF | 3YO+ | MAY |
| GRANDE PREMIO IMMENSITY | G1 | 1600M | TURF | 3YO+F&M | JUN |
| CLASICO FARWELL | G1 | 1600M | TURF | 3YO | JUN |
| GRANDE PREMIO MARGARIDA POLAK LARA | G1 | 1600M | TURF | 2YOF | JUN |
| GRANDE PREMIO COPA ABCPCC MATIAS MACHLINE | G1 | 2000M | TURF | 3YO+ | JUN |
| GRANDE PREMIO IPIRANGA | G1 | 1600M | TURF | 3YOC&F | SEPT |
| GRANDE PREMIO BARAO DE PIRACICABA | G1 | 1600M | TURF | 3YOF | SEPT |
| GRANDE PREMIO HENRIQUE DE TOLEDO LARA | G1 | 1800M | TURF | 3YOF | OCT |
| GRANDE PREMIO JOCKEY CLUB DE SAO PAOLO | G1 | 2000M | TURF | 3YOC&F | OCT |
| GRAN PREMIO DIANA | G1 | 2000M | TURF | 3YOF | NOV |
| GRANDE PREMIO DERBY PAOLISTA | G1 | 2400M | TURF | 3YOC&F | NOV |

Sao Paolo in the south-east of Brazil is the largest city in the country and one of the ten most populous in the world.

The Sao Paolo Jockey Club was founded in 1875 and began operations the following year with its first meeting at the Mooca racecourse. Sao Paolo's premier race, the Grande Premio Sao Paolo, was first run at that track in 1923. The Hipodromo Cidade Jardim or Garden City Racecourse was completed in 1941 and has been the main venue for racing in Sao Paolo ever since.

The course sees plenty of action as the season is all-year round, with racing five days a week from Thursday to Monday as well as the occasional Tuesday fixture.

The art nouveau–styled restaurant provides the best view of the races – and of the Sao Paolo city skyline.

Cicade Jardim has training facilities that accommodate 1400 horses.

## THE TRACK

Left-handed. The main turf course is 2119m in circumference. Inner sand track has a circumference of 1993m.

# GAVEA

Praca Santos Dumont, Rio de Janeiro. Brazil.
www.jcb.com.br

### FEATURE RACES

| | | | | |
|---|---|---|---|---|
| GRANDE PREMIO HENRIQUE POSSOLO | G1 | 1600M | TURF 3YOF | FEB |
| GRAND PREMO ESTADO DO RIO DE JANEIRO | G1 | 1600M | TURF 3YOC | FEB |
| GRANDE PREMIO FRANCISCO EDUARDO DE PAULA MACHADO | G1 | 2000M | TURF 3YOC&G | MAR |
| GRANDE PREMIO DIANA | G1 | 2000M | TURF 3YOF | MAR |
| GRANDE PREMIO ZELIA GONZAGA PEIXOTO DE CASTRO | G1 | 2400M | TURF 3YOF | APR |
| GANDE PREMIO CRUZEIRO DO G1 SUL-DERBY CARIOCA | G1 | 2400M | TURF 3YO | APR |
| GRANDE PREMIO JOCKEY CLUB BRASILEIRU | G1 | 1600M | TURF 2YO | JUN |
| GRANDE PREMIO JOJA ADHEMAR DEL ALMEIDA PRADO | G1 | 1600M | TURF 2YOC | JUN |
| GRANDE PREMIO ROBERTO E NELSON GRIMALDI SEABRA | G1 | 2000M | TURF 4YO+F&M | AUG |

| | | | | |
|---|---|---|---|---|
| GRANDE PREMIO MAJOR SUCKOW | G1 | 1000M | TURF 3YO+ | AUG |
| GRANDE PREMIO PRESIDENTE DA REPUBLICA | G1 | 1600M | TURF 3YO+ | AUG |
| GRANDE PREMIO BRASIL | G1 | 2400M | TURF 4YO+ | AUG |
| GRANDE PREMIO LINNEO DE PAULA MACHADO | G1 | 2000M | TURF 3YO | OCT |

Adjacent to the Rodrigo de Freitas Lagoon on the south side of Ipanema Bay, Gavea racecourse is an absolutely stunning location in the shadow of Sugarloaf Mountain and the famed statue of the Christo Redentor.

The gardens and classical architecture add an elegant ambience to the Hipodromo de Gavea, which was established in 1868.

The course is one of the main training bases in Brazil with 1500 horses stabled and trained on the track and it is home to the academy for apprentice riders.

For those wishing to visit this beautiful course, there is racing here four times a week, all year round.

## THE TRACK

Left-handed. Main turf course is a spacious, pear-shaped oval with a circumference of 2200m. Home straight – 600m.

Inner dirt course of 2040m in length.

# CRISTAL

Diano de Noticias Avenue, Porto Alegre, Brazil.
www.jcrgs.com.br

### FEATURE RACE

| | | | | |
|---|---|---|---|---|
| GRANDE PREMIO BENTO GONCALVES | G1 | 2400M | AWT | 3YO+ | NOV |

Porto Alegre is the capital of the southern Brazilian state of Rio Grande do Sul, and is situated on the east bank of the Rio Guaiba.

The Hipodromo do Cristal opened in 1959 and is regarded as a masterpiece of modern architecture and a unique expression. The buildings were designed by renowned

Uruguayan architect Andres Roman Fresnedo Siri, and construction of the course took more than ten years to complete.

With its historic grandstands as the centrepiece, the hipodromo is also one of the main venues for social events in the area.

Racing is operated by the Jockey Club do Rio Grande do Sul and staged every Thursday, with the highlight fixture in mid November.

## THE TRACK

Left-handed. The main sand course has a circumference of 1928m. Inner turf course of 1780m in length.

# TARUMA

Avenue Victor Ferreira do Amaral, Taruma, Parana, Brazil. www.jockeypr.com.br

### FEATURE RACE

| | | | | |
|---|---|---|---|---|
| GRANDE PREMIO PARANA | G1 | 2000M | AWT | 3YO+ | OCT |

Taruma is situated in the state of Parana in the south of Brazil, 460km from Sao Paolo. The Hipodromo de Taruma was inaugurated in 1955. Operated by the Jockey Club of Parana, which was formed in 1874, the course is considered an important work of modern architecture. It was built to replace the course at Guabirotuba, which had been in operation since 1899.

Taruma is also a training facility with around 750 horses housed on the track. Racing is currently staged every other Friday with the highlight fixture in October.

## THE TRACK

Left-handed. Sand course of approximately 1700m.

# CLUB HIPICO

Avenue Blanca Encalada, Santiago, Chile.
www.clubhipico.cl

## FEATURE RACES

| CLASICO CLUB HIPICO DE SANTIAGO | G1 | 2000M | TURF | 3YO+ | MAY |
|---|---|---|---|---|---|
| PREMIO ARTURO LYON PENA | G1 | 1600M | TURF | 2YOF | JUN |
| PREMIO ALBERTO VIAL INFANTE | G1 | 1600M | TURF | 2YOC | JUN |
| PREMIO POLLO DE POTRILLOS | G1 | 1700M | TURF | 3YOC&G | SEPT |
| PREMIO POLLO DE POTRANCAS | G1 | 1700M | TURF | 3YOF | SEPT |
| PREMIO NACIONAL RICARDO LYON | G1 | 2000M | TURF | 3YOC&F | OCT |
| PREMIO EL ENSAYO | G1 | 2400M | TURF | 3YO | NOV |
| PREMIO LAS OAKS | G1 | 2000M | TURF | 3YOF | NOV |

The Equestrian Club of Santiago has a long and proud history. The first meeting was conducted at the Club Hipico course in 1870 and it is the oldest course in South America. As with many South American tracks, magnificent architecture is a feature and there is no finer example than Club Hipico, with the course listed in 1992 as a National Historic Landmark.

The buildings are absolutely splendid, complemented by beautiful fountains, manicured gardens, historic bandstand and a work by master Chilean sculptor, Nicanor Plaza. The scenery is also spectacular, with the Andes mountains in clear view.

The Equestrian Club has always catered for the high society of Chile and from abroad with former US president Theodore Roosevelt and Queen Elizabeth II among the many dignitaries to have visited the course.

The richest race on the calendar at Club Hipico is the Clasico El Ensayo. Staged in November, the El Ensayo is a leg of the Chilean Triple Crown and is South America's oldest stakes race.

## THE TRACK

Right-handed. The main turf course has a circumference of 2400m. Home straight – 600m.

# HIPODROMO CHILE

Avenue Hipodromo Chile, Independence, Santiago, Chile. www.hipodromo.cl

## FEATURE RACES

| GRAN PREMIO HIPODROMO CHILE | G1 | 2200M | DIRT | 3YO+ | MAY |
|---|---|---|---|---|---|
| PREMIO TANTEO DE PATRANCAS | G1 | 1500M | DIRT | 2YOF | JUN |
| CLASICO TANTEO DE POTRILLOS | G1 | 1500M | DIRT | 2YOC | JUN |
| PREMIO MIL GUINEAS | G1 | 1600M | TURF | 3YOF | SEPT |
| PREMIO DOS MIL GUINEAS | G1 | 1600M | DIRT | 3YO | SEPT |
| GRAN CRITERIUM MAURICIO SERRANO PALMA | G1 | 1900M | DIRT | 3YO | SEPT |
| PREMIO ALBERTI SOLARI MAGNASCO | G1 | 2000M | DIRT | 3YOF | NOV |

The Hipodromo Chile is located in the Chilean capital of Santiago.

The first meeting was held in 1906 and it is a very popular racetrack with the locals. Highlight races are the Gran Premio Hipodromo Chile in May and the Premio St Leger, which in 2013 is scheduled for November and is a leg of the Chilean Triple Crown.

Racing takes place every Saturday throughout the year with many fixtures also scheduled on Thursdays.

The Hipodromo provides plenty of action on race days with up to 20 races on the card.

## THE TRACK

Left-handed. The dirt course is a triangular oval with a circumference of 1645m.

# VALPARAISO

Avenue Los Castanos, Vina del Mar, Chile.
www.sporting.cl

## FEATURE RACES

| PREMIO EL DERBY | | G1 | 2400M | TURF | 3YO | JAN |
|---|---|---|---|---|---|---|
| COPA DE PLATA-ITALO TRAVERSO PASQUALETTI | | G1 | 1500M | TURF | 2YO | JAN |

The city of Vina del Mar is located on the pacific coast of central Chile.

The Valparaiso racecourse staged its first meeting in 1882.

Most of the founding members of the course resided in nearby Valparaiso, so while the actual location of the track is in Vina del Mar, the course adopted its name from the Valparaiso Sporting Club, which established and operates the venue.

Three years after its inauguration, Valparaiso became the home of the Premio El Derby – the Chilean Derby – which remains one of most prestigious and best-attended race days in the country.

The Triple Crown in Chile is conducted at three separate locations and unusually on different surfaces, with the St Leger run on the all-weather track at the Hipodromo Chile. Lighting was installed in 1982 to allow night racing.

The literal translation of Vina del Mar is 'vineyard by the sea' and as the name would suggest, it is one of the nation's premier wine regions.

## THE TRACK

Left-handed. Main turf course of about 2000m in circumference. The complex also features an all-weather track.

# CAMARERO

Route 3, Canovanas, Puerto Rico.
www.camarero-racepark.com

## FEATURE RACES

| | | | | |
|---|---|---|---|---|
| CLASICO DIA DE LA MUJER | G1 | 8½F | 3YOF | MAR |
| DERBY PUERTORRIQUENO | G1 | 8½F | 3YO | MAY |
| CLASICO GABERNADOR | G1 | 8½F | 3YO | MAY |
| COPA SAN JUAN | G1 | 9½F | 3YO | JUN |
| CLASICO LUIS MUNOZ RIVERA MEMORIAL | G1 | 6F | 2YO | JUL |
| JUL DAMA DEL CARIBE | G1 | 8½F | 3YOF | DEC |
| CLASICO CONFRATENIDAD | G1 | 10F | 3YO+ | DEC |
| CLASICO INTERNACIONALE DEL CARIBE | G1 | 9F | 3YO | DEC |

Canovanas is located in north-east Puerto Rico. The venue for racing here is the Camarero racecourse, 12 miles east of San Juan.

Originally known as the El Comandante Race Track, the name of the course was changed in honour of Camarero, the champion Puerto Rican racehorse from the 1950s who scored 73 wins from 76 starts and set the world record of 56 consecutive race wins. It is a record that still stands.

Bold Forbes was a champion 2yo in Puerto Rico and went on to win the Kentucky Derby and Belmont Stakes in 1976.

The course has well-kept grounds and the Terrace Room overlooks the track, providing great views and Creole cuisine.

Racing is conducted all year round with 28 Group 1 races on the schedule but the feature event is undoubtedly the Clasico Internacionale Del Caribe run in mid December.

## THE TRACK

Left-handed. One-mile sand oval.

## FEATURE RACE

### PUERTO RICO TRIPLE CROWN

The Triple Crown consists of the Derby Puertorriqueno, Clasico Gabernador and the Copa San Juan.

Winners of the Triple Crown include **CAMARERO (1954)**, **CARDIOLOGO (1961)** won 23 races in succession, **EL REBELDE (1966)**, **HURLY ROAD (1981)**, **VUELVE CANDY B (1991)**, **CHEROKEE PEPPER (1999)**, **ESTRELLERO (2001)** won 19 in a row, champion filly **MEDIAVILLA R (2002)** and **DON PACO (2011)**.

# MONTERRICO

Avenue The Derby, Santiago de Surco, Lima, Peru.
www.hipodromodemonterrico.com.pe

South American Jockeys' Championship

Racing in the Peruvian capital of Lima dates back to 1864 and a number of sites have been used to conduct race meetings. Such was the popularity of racing in Peru during the 1950s that the old San Felipe course was struggling to cope with the massive crowds on race days, so a new course was constructed.

The Hipodromo de Monterrico opened its doors in 1960. Initially all events were run on the dirt track but an inner turf course was installed shortly after.

Group 1 racing is almost exclusively for the 3yos in Peru, with only one open-age contest run at the elite level.

The richest race on the calendar is the Clasico Derby Nacional. Derby day in Peru is traditionally scheduled in the first week of November.

## FEATURE RACES

| | | | | |
|---|---|---|---|---|
| CLASICO GRAN PREMIO NACIONAL | G1 | 2600M | TURF | 3YO | JAN |
| CLASICO PAMPLONA | G1 | 2400M | TURF | 3YO+F&M | JUN |
| CLASICO JOCKEY CLUB DEL PERU | G1 | 2400M | DIRT | 3YO+ | JUN |
| CLASICO POLLA DE POTRANCAS | G1 | 1600M | DIRT | 3YOF | SEPT |
| CLASICO POLLA DE POTRILLOS | G1 | 1600M | DIRT | 3YOC | SEPT |
| CLASICO ENRIQUE AYULO PARDO | G1 | 2000M | DIRT | 3YOF | SEPT |
| CLASICO RICARDO ORTIZ DE ZAVALLOS | G1 | 2000M | DIRT | 3YOC | OCT |
| CLASICO DERBY NACIONAL | G1 | 2400M | DIRT | 3YO | NOV |

## THE TRACK

Left-handed. Main dirt course is an oval of 1800m. Inner turf course with a circumference of 1600m.

# MARONAS

Jose Maria Guerro, Montevideo, Uruguay.
|www.maronas.com.uy

Invasor

## FEATURE RACES

| | | | | |
|---|---|---|---|---|
| GRAN PREMIO PINEYRUA | G1 | 1600M | DIRT | 3YO+ | JAN |
| GRAN PREMIO JOSE PEDRO RAMIREZ | G1 | 2400M | DIRT | 3YO+ | JAN |
| GRAN PREMIO CIUDAD DE MONTEVIDEO | G1 | 2000M | DIRT | 3YO+F&M | JAN |

The Hipodromo Nacional de Maronas is a course with great character and the venue for racing in the Uruguayan capital of Montevideo. The course was established in 1874 in the neighbourhood of Ituzaingo.

In 1909 a new Members' Box was designed by Jacobo Vasquez Varela, which was refurbished in 1920. Famed architect Andres Roman Fresnedo Siri was appointed to design a new grandstand in 1940.

At its height, the Maronas course was one of the premier racecourses in South America, but encountered financial problems and mismanagement that saw the track flounder during the 1990s.

The government of Uruguay appropriated the site after its closure in 1997, as it was deemed a National Historical Asset. Over the next few years it successfully sought tenders to restore the course and establish new managers.

Maronas reopened in 2003 and racing in Uruguay was soon back in the world spotlight, courtesy of local champion Invasor, who swept the Triple Crown here before winning the Breeders' Cup Classic (2006) and the Dubai World Cup (2007).

Racing at Maronas is now conducted every Saturday and on most Sundays. The feature races are all run in early January.

## THE TRACK

Left-handed. Classic dirt oval with a circumference of 2065m.

# HIPODROMO PRESIDENTE REMON

A Way Jose Agustin Arango, Juan Diaz, Panama City, Panama. www.hipodromo.com

Jockey Laffit Pincay Jr records win 8833 to surpass Bill Shoemaker's record

Racing in Panama is conducted at the Hipodromo Presidente Remon. Located close to the heart of Panama City, the course

| FEATURE RACES | | | | | |
| --- | --- | --- | --- | --- | --- |
| CLASICO PRESIDENTE DE LA REPUBLIC | G1 | 13F | AWT | 3YO+ | JUN |
| CLASICO INDEPENCIA DE PANAMA | G1 | 10F | AWT | 3YO+ | NOV |
| CLASICO DIA DE LA MADRE | G1 | 9F | AWT | 3YO+ | DEC |

was opened in 1956 at the instigation of General Jose Antonio Remon Cantera.

Presidente Remon was assassinated the previous year in a hail of machine-gun fire at the Juan Franco racecourse, which the new venue was due to replace. During his reign, Remon famously refused to buckle during negotiations with the US government over aspects of a treaty regarding the Panama Canal and US military bases in Panama.

Not surprisingly the highlight event is the Clasico Presidente de la Republic, an open contest run in June.

Panama's Crown Casino is also located on the site.

## THE TRACK

Left-handed. The track features two sand courses. The main sand track is a classic oval with a circumference of 1600m. The inner sand course is 1400m in length.

# VENEZUELA

# LA RINCONADA

Final Avenida, Intercomunal de El Valle, Caracas, Venezuela. www.horseracingsouthamerica.com/hipodromo-la-rinconada-caracas-venezuela/

Opening day at La Rinconada

| FEATURE RACES | | | | | |
| --- | --- | --- | --- | --- | --- |
| CLASICO DE LA PRESIDENTE DE LA REPUBLICA | G1 | 2400M | DIRT | 4YO+ | APR |
| CLASICO HIPODROMO LA RINCONADA | G1 | 1600M | DIRT | 3YOF | MAY |
| CLASICO PRENSA HIPICO NACIONAL | G1 | 2000M | DIRT | 3YOF | JUN |
| CLASICO CIRA NACIONAL | G1 | 2000M | DIRT | 3YO | JUN |
| CLASICO HIPICA NACIONAL | G1 | 2000M | DIRT | 3YO+F&M | SEPT |
| CLASICO COPA ORO DE VENEZUELA | G1 | 2400M | DIRT | 3YO+ | SEPT |
| CLASICO JOCKEY CLUB DE VENEZUELA | G1 | 1800M | TURF | 3YO+ | OCT |
| CLASICO SIMON BOLIVAR | G1 | 2400M | DIRT | 3&4YO | NOV |
| CLASICO CIUDAD DE CARACAS | G1 | 1600M | DIRT | 2YOF | NOV |
| CLASICO ANTONIO JOSE DE SUCRE | G1 | 1600M | DIRT | 2YO | NOV |
| CLASICO COMPARICION | G1 | 1600M | DIRT | 3YO | DEC |

Situated in the suburb of Coche, 6km south of Caracas, the Hipodromo La Rinconada was opened in 1959. Originally designed by Arthur Froelich, the architect responsible for the Aqueduct racetrack in New York City, the course featured manicured gardens and magnificent murals during its heyday.

In recent times the course has been used to alleviate the critical housing shortage in Caracas, exacerbated by the floods of 2010 when many of the displaced were forced to take up residence underneath the grandstands at La Rinconada. While one can only be sympathetic to their plight, the situation has seen the deterioration of this once-great racecourse. Racing has managed to continue, with meetings held every weekend.

## THE TRACK

Left-handed. Classic dirt oval with a circumference of 1800m. Home straight – 400m.

# TOKYO

Chuo Expressway, Fuchu City, Tokyo, Japan. www.japanracing.jp

*T*he Tokyo course at Fuchu was originally constructed in 1933 and is the showcase racetrack in Japan with ultra-modern facilities that can cater for crowds in excess of 200,000 people.

Many of Japan's biggest races are staged here including the Japan Cup, which is one of the richest races in the world and one of the highlights on the international calendar.

The Japan Racing Association was formed in 1954 and its operations are overseen by the Ministry of Agriculture, Forestry and Fisheries. The JRA operates the major racecourses in Japan and with the exception of the Tokyo Daishoten, which is run at the Ohi track, stages all races in Japan that are graded at international Group 1 level.

All other courses in Japan are run by local government bodies under the authority of the National Association of Racing.

In the past four decades Japanese racing authorities have made an enormous investment in importing international staying bloodlines to improve the quality of their breeding and racing. For a time the most likely place to find an English or Kentucky Derby winner was on a stud farm in Japan, with the result that Japan is now viewed as one of the best producers of stayers in the world.

Prize money here is enormous and perhaps because of this the expansion of Japan onto the world racing stage has not been as rapid as predicted. When they do travel, Japanese horses have proved that they are more than capable of matching it with the best anywhere.

The Japan Cup has become a race that is increasingly difficult for the internationals to win, with none successful in the event since 2005.

Races in Japan are generally run on firm ground with the leaders setting a fast, strong gallop, so horses really do need to be able to get every centimetre of a distance and require a tremendous turn of foot.

While the racing is of the highest quality and on-course attendances are among the best in the world, at the same time Japanese authorities are acutely sensitive to the social problems that gambling can create and it is probably for this reason that racing receives scant publicity in the press.

The Tokyo track underwent a seven-year redevelopment, which was completed amid much fanfare in 2007. The course is also home to the JRA Racing Museum.

In short, Tokyo offers great racing, huge prize money, massive crowds and a state-of-the-art environment. If you are fortunate enough to be at Tokyo racecourse on a clear day, the sight of Mount Fuji towering in the distance is one to behold.

## THE TRACK

Left-handed. The course is a very wide oval circuit. The main turf track has a circumference of 2083m and a home straight of 525m.

Out of the straight, runners are on a bend to the 1600m. It is then a straight run to the home bend at the 1000m.

The inner dirt track is 1899m in length with a run home of 502m.

There is also a steeplechase track of 1675m.

| FEATURE RACES | | | | | | |
|---|---|---|---|---|---|---|
| JAPAN CUP | G1 | 2400M | TURF | 3YO+ | 1981 | NOV |
| FEBRUARY STAKES | G1 | 1600M | DIRT | 4YO+ | 1984 | FEB |
| NHK MILE CUP | G1 | 1600M | TURF | 3YO | 1996 | MAY |
| VICTORIA MILE | G1 | 1600M | TURF | 4YO+ | 2006 | MAY |
| YUSHUN HIMBA | G1 | 2400M | TURF | 3YOF | 1938 | MAY |
| TOKYO YUSHUN | G1 | 2400M | TURF | 3YO | 1932 | MAY |
| YASUDA KINEN | G1 | 1600M | TURF | 3YO+ | 1951 | JUN |
| TENNO SHO – AUTUMN | G1 | 2000M | TURF | 3YO+ | 1937 | OCT |

## FEATURE RACES

Inaugurated in 1981, the invitation-only Japan Cup is one of the richest races in the world and, with the standard of the locals, one of the toughest on the international calendar to win.

US mare **MAIRZY DOATES (1981)** won the first running.

Notable winners include **SYMBOLI RUDOLF (1985)**, who was the first winner of the Japanese 3yo Triple Crown to take out the race, and also won the Tenno Sho – Spring (1985) and twice won the Arima Kinen (1984, 85).

New Zealand mare **HORLICKS (1989)**; Australian **BETTER LOOSEN UP (1990)**; **TOKAI TEIO (1992)** won the Satsuki Sho, Tokyo Yushun (1991), Arima Kinen (1993); German star **LANDO (1995)**; **SINGSPIEL (1996)**; **PILSUDSKI (1997)**; **EL CONDOR PASA (1998)**.

**SPECIAL WEEK (1999)** won the Tokyo Yushun (1998), Tenno Sho – Spring, Tenno Sho – Autumn (1999); **TM OPERA O (2000)** won the Satsuki Sho (1999), Arima Kinen, Takarazuka Kinen, Tenno Sho – Autumn (2000) and was dual winner of the Tenno Sho – Spring (2000, 01); **FALBRAV (2002)**; **ZENNO ROB ROY (2004)**; and **ALKAASED (2005)**.

**DEEP IMPACT (2006)** won 12 of 14 starts including the Japan 3yo Triple Crown (2005), Tenno Sho – Spring, Takarazuka Kinen, Arima Kinen (2006); **ADMIRE MOON (2007)** won the Dubai Duty Free (2007); **VODKA (2009)** won the Hanshin Juvenile Fillies (2006), Tokyo Yushun (2007), Tenno Sho – Autumn (2008), Victoria Mile (2009) and scored successive wins in the Yasuda Kinen (2008, 09); **BUENA VISTA (2011)** won the Hanshin Juvenile Fillies (2008), Oka Sho, Yushun Himba (2009), Victoria Mile, Tenno Sho – Autumn (2010); and **GENTIL-DONNA (2012)** won the Oka Sho and Yushun Himba (2012).

First run in 1984, the race was upgraded to Group 1 status in 1997.

Winners since include **MEISEI OPERA (1997)**, winner of 23 of 36 including the Nambu Hai (1998) and Teio Sho (1999); **AGNES DIGITAL (2002)** twice won the Mile Championship (2000, 01) as well as the Tenno Sho – Autumn, Hong Kong Cup (2001), Yasuda Kinen (2003).

**ADMIRE DON (2004)** won the Asahi Hai Futurity (2001), Nambu Hai (2003) and the JBC Classic three times (2002–04); **KANE HEKILI (2006)** won the Derby Grand Prix (2005), Tokyo Daishoten (2008), Kawasaki Kinen (2009) and was dual winner of the Japan Cup Dirt (2005, 08).

**VERMILION (2008)** won the Japan Cup Dirt, Tokyo Daishoten (2007), twice won the Kawasaki Kinen (2007, 10) and three times won the JBC Classic (2007–09); **ESPOIR CITY (2010)** won the Japan Cup Dirt (2009), was dual winner of the Mile Championship

Deep Impact

(2009, 12), and three-time winner of the Kashiwa Kinen (2009, 10, 12); and **TRANSCEND (2011)** was a dual winner of the Japan Cup Dirt (2010, 11).

## NHK MILE CUP

First run in 1996, it has been won by **SEEKING THE PEARL (1997)**, who won the Prix Maurice de Gheest (1998); and **EL CONDOR PASA (1998)**.

## VICTORIA MILE

Run since 2006 and won by **VODKA (2009)** and **BUENA VISTA (2010)**.

## YUSHUN HIMBA

Otherwise known as the Japan Oaks, notable winners include **KURIFUJI (1943)**, undefeated in her 11-start career with wins in the Tokyo Yushun, Kikuka Sho (1943); **SWEE SUE (1952)** was a dual winner of the

Yasuda Kinen (1952, 53); **AIR GROOVE (1996)**; **MEJIRO DOBER (1997)** won the Hanshin Juvenile Fillies (1996), Shuka Sho (1997) and twice won the QE II Commemorative Cup (1998, 99); **CESARIO (2005)** won the American Oaks Invitational (2005); **BUENA VISTA (2009)**; and **GENTILDONNA (2012)**.

## TOKYO YUSHUN

Japan's equivalent of the Derby.

The 3yo Triple Crown consists of the Satsuki Sho (2000 Guineas), Tokyo Yushun (Derby) and the Kikuka Sho (St Leger).

Winners of the Triple Crown include **ST LITE (1941)**, **SHINZAN (1964)**, **MR C B (1983)**, **SYMBOLI RUDOLF (1984)**, **NARITA BRIAN (1994)**, **DEEP IMPACT (2005)** and **ORFEVRE (2011)**.

**HISATOMO (1937)** was the first filly to win the race. The only other fillies to win are **KURIFUJI (1943)** and **VODKA (2007)**.

Other notables winners are **HAKUCHIKARA (1956)**, who won 21 races including the Arima Kinen, Tenno Sho – Autumn (1957); **KODAMA (1960)** won the Hanshin Sansai (1959), Satsuki Sho, Takarzuka Kinen (1960); **KEYSTONE (1965)** won 18 of 25 starts; **TOKAI TEIO (1991)**; **SPECIAL WEEK (1998)**; **JUNGLE POCKET (2001)** won the Japan Cup that year; **MEISHO SAMSON (2006)** won the Satsuki Sho (2006), Tenno Sho – Spring, Tenno Sho – Autumn (2007).

## YASUDA KINEN

Named in honour of Izaemon Yasuda, who was the founding chairman of the Japan Racing Association, the race was inaugurated in 1951 and granted Group 1 status in 1984.

Notable winners since include **NIHON PILLOW WINNER (1985)**, a dual winner of the Mile Championship (1984, 85); Hall of Fame horse **OGURI CAP (1990)** won 22 of 32 starts including the Mile Championship (1989) and twice won the Arima Kinen (1988, 90); **HEART LAKE (1995)** for Godolphin.

**FAIRY KING PRAWN (2000)** became the first Hong Kong–trained horse to win a Group 1 outside Hong Kong; **AGNES DIGITAL (2003)**; **BULLISH LUCK (2006)**; **DAIWA MAJOR (2007)** won the Satsuki Sho (2004), Tenno Sho – Autumn (2006) and was dual winner of the Mile Championship (2006, 07).

**YAMANIN ZEPHYR (1992, 93)** and **VODKA (2008, 09)** both scored successive victories.

## TENNO SHO – AUTUMN

**SYMBOLI KRIS S (2002, 03)** is the only multiple winner to date.

Other notables include **HISATOMO (1938)**, **DAINANA HOSHU (1955)**, **HAKUCHIKARA (1957)**, **SHINZAN (1965)**, **MR CB (1984)**, **SUPER CREEK (1989)**, **YAMANIN ZEPHYR (1993)**, **AIR GROOVE (1997)**, **SPECIAL WEEK (1999)**, **TM OPERA O (2000)**, **AGNES DIGITAL (2001)**, **ZENNO ROB ROY (2004)**, **DAIWA MAJOR (2006)**, **MEISHO SAMSON (2007)**, **VODKA (2008)** and **BUENA VISTA (2010)**.

# NAKAYAMA

Funabashi, Chiba, Japan.. www.japanracing.jp

*T*he *Nakayama racetrack is located in Funabashi, which is part of the Greater Tokyo area.*

The course here was opened in 1920 and conducts some of the nation's top Group 1 races. Tokyo racing fixtures generally alternate between Nakayama and the Tokyo course at Fuchu.

It is the most undulating of any course in Japan, with the stiff uphill finish a feature.

Spring is undoubtedly the best time to visit the course, as cherry trees line the run into the home straight providing an absolutely spectacular sight when in bloom.

The most historic race here is the Satsuko Sho, run in April, which is the Japanese equivalent of the 2000 Guineas.

Nakayama is also the venue for two of Japan's great jumping contests – the Nakayama Daishogai and the Nakayama Grand Jump. The Grand Jump is one of the richest jumps events in the world. Australian chaser Karasi created history by winning the race three times in succession between 2005 and 2007.

The Arima Kinen has become one of the highlight races on the annual calendar. The majority of the field for the Arima Kinen is determined by public vote, with the remainder gaining entry through prize money won. The race generates enormous public interest and is often the highest betting turn-over race in the world.

## THE TRACK

Right-handed. The main turf course is 1840m in circumference with a home straight of 310m.

The track runs uphill to the 1600m and has a downhill run from the 1200m to the 600m. The track rises 2m in the final 200m.

The inner turf course is 1667m in length with a home straight also of 310m.

The dirt course is 1493m in length with a run home of 308m.

The steeplechase track has a circumference of 1456m.

## FEATURE RACES

### SATSUKO SHO

Japan's 2000 Guineas is the first leg of the 3yo Triple Crown.

Those to take out the Satsuko Sho–Tokyo Yushun double include **KUMONO HANA (1950), TOKINO MINORU (1951), KURINO HANA (1952), BOSTONIAN (1953), KODAMA (1960), MEIZUI (1963), TANINO MOUTIERS (1970), HIKARU IMAI (1971), KUBARAYA O (1975), KATSU TOP ACE (1981),** Japan Cup winner **TOKAI TEIO (1991), MIHONO BOURBON (1992), SUNNY BRIAN (1997), NEO UNIVERSE (2003)** and **MEISHO SAMSON (2006).**

Only two fillies have won the race: **TOKIT-SUKAZE (1947),** who won the Yushun Himba, and **HIDE HIKARI (1948).**

Other prominent winners include **TOSA MIDORI (1949),** who won 21 of 31 starts; **TM OPERA O (1999); DAIWA MAJOR (2004);** and **VICTOIRE PISA (2010)** won the Dubai World Cup (2011).

### SPRINTERS STAKES

The race was upgraded to Group 1 level in 1990.

Since then winners include **NISHINO FLOWER (1992); TAIKI SHUTTLE (1997),** who twice won the Mile Championship (1997, 98) and also took out the Yasuda Kinen (1998), Prix Jacques Le Marois (1998); **DURANDAL (2003);** Hong Kong hero **SILENT WITNESS (2005); TAKEOVER TARGET (2006); LORD KANALOA (2012)** won the Hong Kong Sprint (2012).

**BAMBOO MEMORY (1990), DAICHI RUBY (1991)** and **BLACK HAWK (2000)** all won the Yasuda Kinen; and **SAKURA BAKUSHIN O (1993, 94)** made it successive victories.

### FEATURE RACES

| SATSUKI SHO | G1 | 2000M | TURF | 3YO | 1939 | APR |
|---|---|---|---|---|---|---|
| SPRINTERS STAKES | G1 | 1200M | TURF | 3YO+ | 1967 | SEPT–OCT |
| ASAHI HAI FUTURITY STAKES | G1 | 1600M | TURF | 2YO | 1949 | DEC |
| ARIMA KINEN | G1 | 2500M | TURF | 3YO+ | 1956 | DEC |

### ASAHI HAI FUTURITY STAKES

A 1600m race for 2yos. Notables include **TOKINO MINORU (1950); MEIJI HIKARI (1954); TAKE-SHIBA O (1967); MIHONO BOURBON (1991); NARITA BRIAN (1993); GRASS WONDER (1997)** was a dual winner of the Arima Kinen (1998, 99); **EISHIN PRESTON (1999)** won the Hong Kong Mile (2001) and twice won the Hong Kong QE II Cup (2002, 03); **ADMIRE DON (2001);** and **ROSE KINGDOM (2009)** won the Japan Cup on protest (2010).

### ARIMA KINEN

Inaugurated in 1956 the race was renamed for its founder, Yoriyasu Arima, who passed away the following year.

As an all-star race it has been won by many top horses including dual winners **SPEED SYMBOLI (1969, 70), SYMBOLI RUDOLF (1984, 85), OGURI CAP (1988, 90), GRASS WONDER (1998, 99)** and **SYMBOLI KRIS S (2002, 03).**

Other notable winners include **MEIJI HIKARI (1956), ONSLAUGHT (1962), SHINZAN (1965), INARI ONE (1989), TOKAI TEIO (1993), NARITA BRIAN (1994), MAYANO TOP GUN (1995), TM OPERA O (2000), ZENNO ROB ROY (2004), HEART'S CRY (2005)** won the Dubai Sheema Classic (2006), **DEEP IMPACT (2006), DAIWA SCARLET (2008), VICTOIRE PISA (2010)** and **ORFEVRE (2011).**

# KYOTO

32-cho, Fushimi-ku, Kyoto, Japan. www.japanracing.jp

Triple Crown winner Orfevre

*T*he beautiful city and former imperial capital of Kyoto is situated in the central region of the island of Honshu.

Opened in 1924, it is the premier course in western Japan with most of the feature races conducted in October and November. It is also home to the spring version of the Tenno Sho, staged in April.

The tree-lined backdrop and the infield lake, which is home to a large population of swans, provide an elegant setting for some of Japan's best racing.

The track is connected to the Yodo railway station by an undercover pedestrian bridge, providing easy access on foot.

## THE TRACK

Right-handed. The main course is an egg-shaped oval.

Main turf course is 1894m in length. Home straight of 404m.

The course features the Yodo Slope, which rises just over 4m between the 1200m and the 800m then runs quickly back downhill by the same gradient from the top of the home bend at the 800m to the 650m.

Chute start for races over 1800m joins the back straight and gives a run of about 1000m before the home bend.

The dirt course is 1608m in circumference with a home straight of 329m.

The inner steeplechase turf course is 1414m in length.

## FEATURE RACES

### TENNO SHO – SPRING

While its autumn counterpart is run over 2000m, the spring version is a 3200m race and is the longest Group 1 race in Japan.

Dual winners include **MEJIRO McQUEEN (1991, 92)**, **RICE SHOWER (1993, 95)** and **TM OPERA O (2000, 01)**.

Other prominent winners include **REDA (1953)**, who remains the only mare to win; **TAKA O (1955)** won 31 races from 64 starts; **MEIJI HIKARI (1956)** won the Asahi Hai Futurity (1954), Kikuka Sho (1955) Arima Kinen (1956); **ONSLAUGHT (1962)** won 26 of 41 starts including the Zennihon Nisai Yushun (1959), Tokyo Daishoten (1960), Arima Kinen (1962).

**SPEED SYMBOLI (1967)** was a dual winner of the Arima Kinen (1969, 70); **TAKESHIBA O (1969)** also won the Sprinters Stakes to make him a Group 1 winner over 1200m and 3200m in the same year; **TAKE HOPE (1974)**; **SYMBOLI RUDOLF (1985)**; **INARI ONE (1989)** won the Tokyo Dias- hoten (1988), Takarazuka Kinen and Arima Kinen (1989); **SUPER CREEK (1990)**; **MAYANO TOP GUN (1997)** won the Kikuka Sho (1995), Arima Kinen, Takarazuka Kinen (1996); **SPECIAL WEEK (1999)**; **DEEP IMPACT (2006)** smashed the world record for 3200m; and **MEISHO SAMSON (2007)**.

### SHUKA SHO

Inaugurated in 1996 for 3yo fillies, notable winners include **MEJIRO DOBER (1997)**, who won the Hanshin Juvenile Fillies (1996), Yushun Himba (1997) and was a dual winner of the Queen Elizabeth II Commemorative Cup (1998, 99); **DAIWA SCARLET (2007)** won the Oka Sho, Queen Elizabeth II Commem- orative Cup (2007) and Arima Kinen (2008); **APAPANE (2010)**; and **GENTILDONNA (2012)**.

## FEATURE RACES

| | | | | | |
|---|---|---|---|---|---|
| TENNO SHO – SPRING | G1 | 3200M | TURF | 4YO+ | 1938 APR |
| SHUKA SHO | G1 | 2000M | TURF | 3YOF | 1996 OCT |
| KIKUKA SHO | G1 | 3000M | TURF | 3YO | 1938 OCT |
| QUEEN ELIZABETH II COMMEMORATIVE CUP | G1 | 2200M | TURF | 3YO+ | 1976 NOV |
| MILE CHAMPIONSHIP | G1 | 1600M | TURF | 3YO+ | 1984 NOV |

### KIKUKA SHO

Also known as the Japanese St Leger, it has been one by **ST LITE (1941)**; **KURIFUJI (1943)** was the first of only two fillies to win, **BROWNIE (1947)** was the other; **MEIJI HIKARI (1955)** won the Asahi Hai Futurity (1954), Tenno Sho – Spring, Arima Kinen (1956); **SHINZAN (1964)**; **TAKE HOPE (1973)**; **MR CB (1983)**; **SYMBOLI RUDOLF (1984)**; **RICE SHOWER (1992)**; **NARITA BRIAN (1994)**; **MAYANO TOP GUN (1995)**; **DELTA BLUES (2004)** won the Melbourne Cup (2006); **DEEP IMPACT (2005)**; and **ORFEVRE (2011)**.

### QUEEN ELIZABETH II COMMEMORATIVE CUP

Established in 1976 the race is the only Group 1 contest in Japan for 3yo fillies and older mares.

Dual winners include **MEJIRO DOBER (1998, 99)**; **ADMIRE GROOVE (2003, 04)** and **SNOW FAIRY (2010, 11)**.

Other prominent winners include **MEJIRO ROMANU (1986)**, who took out the then Fillies' Triple Crown by also winning the Oka Sho and Yushun Himba that year; **HOKUTO VEGA (1993)**; **HISHI AMAZON (1994)**; **PHALAENOPSIS (2000)**; and **DAIWA SCARLET (2007)**.

### MILE CHAMPIONSHIP

Dual winners include **NIHON PILLOW WINNER (1984, 85)**; **DAITAKU HELIOS (1991, 92)**; **TAIKI SHUTTLE (1997, 98)**; **DURANDAL (2003, 04)**; and **DAIWA MAJOR (2006, 07)**.

Other prominent winners include **NIPPO TEIO (1987)**, who won the Tenno Sho – Autumn (1987) and Yasuda Kinen (1988); **OGURI CAP (1989)**; **AGNES DIGITAL (2000)**; and **HAT TRICK (2005)**, who also won the Hong Kong Mile (2005).

# HANSHIN

1-1 Komanocho, Takarazuka, Hyogo, Japan. www.japanracing.jp

Transcend wins the Japan Cup Dirt

Hanshin Racecourse is located in Hyogo in the Kansai area of Honshu.

Opened in 1948, the Hanshin course, along with Kyoto, is considered one of the two feature racetracks in Western Japan.

Following a major refurbishment completed in 2006, the outer turf track is now one of the largest in the nation.

The course is fabulously appointed with ultra-modern facilities including a massive undercover parade ring. Hanshin offers top-class racing in a family-friendly environment with manicured grounds, a terrarium, and picnic areas to the east of the grandstand.

There is a play area for children, pony rides and a stage for character shows to keep the youngsters entertained.

Punters can enhance their luck by visiting the Lucky Shoe Spot, which features hoof imprints of some of Japan's most famous horses. Touching an imprint is said to bring good fortune.

The Oka Sho for the fillies is run at Hanshin, along with the Japan Cup Dirt and the Takarazuka Kinen, which, like the Arima Kinen at Nakayama, has the composition of the final field determined by a public poll.

## THE TRACK

Right-handed. The turf A-course is 2089m in length with a run home of 473m.

The course is mainly flat with a gradual downhill run from the 600m to the 200m, then a rise of 2m from the 200m to the winning post.

The inner dirt course has a circumference of 1518m with a home straight of 352m.

There is also a turf steeplechase track measuring 1367m.

## FEATURE RACES

### OKA SHO

Japan's 1000 Guineas.

Those to take out the Oka Sho–Yushun Himba double include **SWEE SUE (1952)**, **YAMAICHI (1954)**, **MISS ONWARD (1957)**, **KANE KEYAKI (1964)**, **TESCO GABY (1975)**, **TITANIA (1976)**, **MAX BEAUTY (1987)**, **VEGA (1993)**, **STILL IN LOVE (2003)**, **APAPANE (2010)**, and Japan Cup winners **BUENA VISTA (2009)** and **GENTIL-DONNA (2012)**.

Other prominent winners include **BROWNIE (1947)**, **YASHIMA DAUGHTER (1949)** won the Tenno Sho – Autumn (1950), **TANAMI (1970)** and **BROCADE (1981)** both won the Sprinters Stakes, **MEJIRO RAMONU (1986)**, **NISHINO FLOWER**

| OKA SHO | G1 | 1600M | TURF | 3YOF | 1939 APR |
|---|---|---|---|---|---|
| TAKARAZUKA KINEN | G1 | 2200M | TURF | 3YO+ | 1960 JUN |
| JAPAN CUP DIRT | G1 | 1800M | DIRT | 3YO+ | 2000 DEC |
| HANSHIN JUVENILE FILLIES | G1 | 1600M | TURF | 2YOF | 1949 DEC |

**(1992)**, **PHALAENOPSIS (1998)**, **TM OCEAN (2001)** and **DAIWA SCARLET (2007)**.

### TAKARAZUKA KINEN

All-star race with field composition determined firstly by public vote and the remaining places decided by prize money, similar to the Arima Kinen.

Notable winners include **KODAMA (1962)**, **SHINZAN (1965)**, **HIKARU TAKAI (1968)**, **SPEED SYMBOLI (1970)**, **KATSURAGI ACE (1984)** won the Japan Cup (1984), **TAMAMO CROSS (1988)** won the Tenno Sho — Spring and Autumn that year, **INARI ONE (1989)**, **MEJIRO McQUEEN (1993)**, **MAYANO TOP GUN (1996)**, **GRASS WONDER (1999)**, **TM OPERA O (2000)**, **TAP DANCE CITY (2004)** won the Japan Cup (2003), **DEEP IMPACT (2006)** and **ADMIRE MOON (2007)**.

**NAKAYAMA FESTA (2010)** and **ORFEVRE (2012)** both ran second in the Arc.

Only two females have won the race to date: **EIGHT CROWN (1966)** and **SWEEP TOSHO (2005)**.

### JAPAN CUP DIRT

First run in 2000, dual winners include **KANE HEKILI (2005, 08)** and **TRANSCEND (2010, 11)**. The Dirt Cup has also been won by **TIME PARADOX (2004)**, who won the Teio Sho, Kawasaki Kinen (2005) and was dual winner of the JBC Classic (2005, 06); **VERMILION (2007)**; and **ESPOIR CITY (2009)**.

### HANSHIN JUVENILE FILLIES

Notable winners include **NISHINO FLOWER (1991)**, **MEJIRO DOBER (1996)**, **VODKA (2006)**, **BUENA VISTA (2008)** and **APAPANE (2009)**.

# CHUKYO

1225 Magome-cho Shikita Toyoake, Aichi, Japan.
www.japanracing.jp

## FEATURE RACES

| TAKAMATSUNOMIYA KINEN | G1 | 1200M | TURF | 4YO+ | MAR |
|---|---|---|---|---|---|
| TOKAI STAKES | G2 | 1800M | DIRT | 4YO+ | JAN |
| CHUNICKI SHIMBUN HAI | G3 | 2000M | TURF | 3YO+ | MAR |
| FALCON STAKES | G3 | 1400M | TURF | 3YO | MAR |
| CBC SHO | G3 | 1200M | TURF | 3YO+ | JUL |
| SHO CHUKYO KINEN | G3 | 1600M | TURF | 3YO+ | JUL |
| AICHI HAI | G3 | 2000M | TURF | 3YO+ | DEC |

The bustling port city of Nagoya on the Pacific coast of central Honshu is the site for racing at the Chukyo course.

The track re-opened in 2012 after two years of renovations with over 17 billion yen spent on the redevelopment to provide first-class facilities for the public.

During this time works were carried out to extend both the turf and dirt tracks, with the home straights also redesigned to provide an uphill run to the winning post on all courses.

The new Pegasus grandstand was constructed to feature state-of-the-art architecture and facilities, along with an area for families and the Takamatsunomiya Kinen Memorial Garden to honour the winners of Chukyo's premier race.

The improvements also transformed the course for solar power and race-goers can now obtain an unobstructed view of the parade ring from the grandstand.

## THE TRACK

Left-handed. The turf A-course has a circumference of 1706m with a home straight of 412m.

Out of the home straight, runners are on a bend to the 1300m. It is a straight run until approaching the 800m for the home bend.

It is a gradual downhill run from the 1000m to the 350m. At this point the track rises by a gradient of 2m to the 250m mark.

Races over 1600m start from a diagonal chute that joins the top of the turn out of the home straight. This chute is also the release point for races over 3300m.

The inner dirt course is 1530m in length with a home straight of 410m

## FEATURE RACE
### TAKAMATSUNOMIYA KINEN

First run in 1971 and upgraded to Group 1 status in 1996, winners include **FLOWER PARK (1996)**, **BELIEVE (2003)**, **LAUREL GUERREIRO (2009)** and **CURREN CHAN (2012)** who were all winners of the Sprinters Stakes; **KINSHASA NO KISEKI (2010, 11)** won the race twice; and **KANALOA KING (2013)**.

# MORIOKA

10 Kamiyagita, Aza, Shinjo, Morioka-shi, Iwate, Japan. www.iwatekeiba.or.jp

Agnes Digital

## FEATURE RACES

| MILE CHAMPIONSHIP NAMBU HAI | JG1 | 1600M | DIRT | 3YO+ | OCT |
|---|---|---|---|---|---|
| MERCURY CUP | JG3 | 2000M | DIRT | 3YO+ | JUL |
| CLUSTER CUP | JG3 | 1200M | DIRT | 3YO+ | AUG |

Morioka is the capital city of the Iwate Prefecture in the Tohoku region of Honshu.

The Morioka racecourse, also known as Oro Park, is a very modern facility having opened its doors in 1996. With Mount Iwate as a backdrop it is a lovely setting for racing.

Calendar highlight is the Mile Championship Nambu Hai, a Group 1 race staged annually in October and won by some of Japan's best dirt-track horses.

Racing at Morioka is conducted by the Iwate Racing Association.

## THE TRACK

Left-handed. Main dirt course is a classic oval of 1600m. Home straight of 300m.

Out of the straight, runners are on a bend until the 1100m. It is then a straight run of about 400m to the home turn.

Races from 1200m to 1600m begin from a chute that links up with the top of the back straight. The chute doglegs to the left approaching the 1400m mark.

Release point for races over 2000m is from a chute that joins the top of the home straight.

Inner turf course of 1400m with a run home of 300m.

## FEATURE RACE
### MILE CAHAMPIONSHIP NAMBU HAI

**BLUE CONCORDE (2006–08)** won the race three times in succession.

Dual winners include **TOKAI NISEI (1993, 94)**; **UTOPIA (2004, 05)**; **ESPOIR CITY (2009, 12)**.

Other notable winners include top mare **HOKUTO VEGA (1996)**, who won the Queen Elizabeth II Commemorative Cup (1993), Teio Sho, February Stakes (1996) and was a dual winner of the Kawasaki Kienen (1996, 97); **MEISEI OPERA (1998)**; **AGNES DIGITAL (2001)**; **ADMIRE DON (2003)**; and **TRANSCEND (2011)**.

# OHI

2-1-2 Katsushima, Shinagawa-ku, Tokyo, Japan.
www.tokyocitykeiba.com

Hokuto Vega

## FEATURE RACES

| TOKYO DAISHOTEN | G1 | 2000M | DIRT | 3YO+ | DEC |
| TCK JO-O HAI | JG1 | 1800M | DIRT | 4YO+F&M | JAN |
| TEIO SHO | JG1 | 2000M | DIRT | 4YO+ | JUN |
| JAPAN DIRT DERBY | JG1 | 2000M | DIRT | 3YO | JUL |
| TOKYO HAI | JG2 | 1200M | DIRT | 3YO+ | OCT |
| LADIES' PRELUDE | JG2 | 1800M | DIRT | 3YO+F&M | OCT |
| TOKYO SPRINT | JG3 | 1200M | DIRT | 4YO+ | APR |

Ohi racecourse is situated in Shinagawa on Tokyo Bay.

Opened in 1950, racing here is operated by the Tokyo Metropolitan Racing Association.

The highlight race is the Tokyo Daishoten run in late December. It is the only international Group 1 race in Japan not organised by the Japan Racing Association.

In 2003 the new cutting edge L-Wing grandstand was added.

Night racing is conducted at Ohi from March until November, and the course is also host to one of Tokyo's biggest flea markets each weekend.

## THE TRACK

Right-handed. Classic dirt oval of 1600m in circumference. Home straight – 300m.

Out of the straight, runners are on a bend to the 1200m. It is a straight run until the home bend approaching the 700m.

## FEATURE RACES

### TOKYO DAISHOTEN

Notable winners include **ONSLAUGHT (1960)**, **INARI ONE (1988)**, **ABAKUMA PORO (1998)**, **GOLD ALLURE (2002)**, **BLUE CONCORDE (2006)**, **VERMILION (2007)** and **KANE HEKILI (2008)**.

Dual winners include **ADJUDI MITSUO (2004, 05)** and **SMART FALCON (2010, 11)**.

### TEIO SHO

First run in 1978; notable winners include **HOKUTO VEGA (1996)**, **ABAKUMA PORO (1998)**, **MEISEI OPERA (1999)**, **ADMIRE DON (2004)**, **TIME PARADOX (2005)**, **ADJUDI MITSUO (2006)**, **VERMILION (2009)** and **SMART FALCON (2011)**. **FURIOSO (2008, 10)** won the race twice.

### JAPAN DIRT DERBY

Run since 1999, prominent winners include **GOLD ALLURE (2002)**, **KANE HEKILI (2005)** and **FURIOSO (2007)**.

# NIIGATA

Sasayama, Kita-ku, Niigata, Honshu, Japan.
www.japanracing.jp

## FEATURE RACES

| NIIGATA DAISHOTEN | G3 | 2000M | TURF | 4YO+ | MAY |
| IBIS SUMMER DASH | G3 | 1000M | TURF | 3YO+ | JUL |
| LEOPARD STAKES | G3 | 1800M | DIRT | 3YO | AUG |
| SEKIYA KINEN | G3 | 1600M | TURF | 3YO+ | AUG |
| NIIGATA NISAI STAKES | G3 | 1600M | TURF | 2YO | AUG |
| NIIGATA KINEN | G3 | 2000M | TURF | 3YO+ | SEPT |

The port town of Niigata is situated on the north-west coast of the island of Honshu.

The Niigata racecourse staged its first meeting in 1965 with the course completely renovated in 2001.

It is a very spacious track in all respects and can claim three unique features. It is the nation's largest circuit, has the longest home straight and also has a straight sprint course – the only one of its kind in Japan.

The parade ring is covered but not enclosed with a huge marquee style roof. The finishing post is adorned with a colourful statue of the local symbol, the crested ibis.

Currently half-a-dozen races at Group 3 level are conducted at the track as well as one of Japan's feature jumps events – the Niigata Jump.

## THE TRACK

Left-handed. Classic oval. The turf A-course has a circumference of 2223m with a home straight of 659m.

Straight sprint course of 1000m.

Out of the straight, runners are on a bend until the 1800m point. It is then a straight run to the home bend at the 1000m.

The track is undulating in places and rises by about 2m between the 1400m and the 1000m then dips by 2m from the 1000m to the 800m.

Races over 2000m start from a chute that joins the back straight.

Inner dirt course of 1472m in length with a straight run home of 354m.

# HAKODATE

12-2 Homada-cho, Hakodate, Hokkaido, Japan.
www.japanracing.jp

## FEATURE RACES

| HAKODATE SPRINT STAKES | G3 | 1200M | TURF | 3YO+ | JUN |
| HAKODATE NISAI STAKES | G3 | 1200M | TURF | 2YO | JUN |
| HAKODATE KINEN | G3 | 2000M | TURF | 3YO+ | JUL |

The harbour city of Hakodate is located in Oshima on the island of Hokkaido. In 1854 it gained the distinction of being the first Japanese port permitted to conduct foreign trade.

Hakodate racecourse is the oldest in Japan with the first meeting staged here in 1896.

A two-year renovation was completed in

2010. The course was remodelled to give race-goers a close-up view of the action in a resort atmosphere.

The new grandstand has a rustic design and punters can view runners in the parade ring from the Dugout Paddock, which is a sunken area offering a hoof-level perspective of the horses. Competitors now make their way from the paddock to the track via a kabuki-styled runway through the crowd.

A rooftop observation deck offers spectacular panoramic views of Mount Hakodate and across the Tsugaru Strait to make it the only course in Japan that features an ocean outlook.

As with all modern redevelopments of Japanese racecourses, every effort has been made to provide a family environment with the infield containing a children's playground and amusement area as well as an athletics track.

The most valuable race on the calendar is the Hakodate Kinen, run in July.

## THE TRACK

Right-handed Classic oval. The turf A-course has a circumference of 1627m with a straight run home of 262m.

Out of the straight, runners are on a bend until the 1100m. It is a straight run of 400m to the home turn.

The course is quite undulating with a gradual downhill run between the 1600m and the 1200m. From that point the track rises steadily until the 500m, then runs gently downhill to the 100m.

The inner dirt track is 1476m in length with a home straight of 260m.

# KOKURA

4-5-1 Kitakata, Kokura Minami-ku, Kitakyushu-shi, Fukuoka, Japan. www.japanracing.jp

| FEATURE RACES | | | | | |
|---|---|---|---|---|---|
| KOKURA DAISHOTEN | G3 | 1800M | TURF | 4YO+ | FEB |
| KOKURA KINEN | G3 | 2000M | TURF | 3YO+ | AUG |
| SHO KITAKYUSHU KINEN | G3 | 1200M | TURF | 3YO+ | AUG |
| KOKURA NISAI STAKES | G3 | 1200M | TURF | 2YO | SEPT |

The ancient castle town of Kokura is situated in the industrial city of Kitakyushu on the island of Kyushu.

Racing here dates back to 1931 with the opening of the Kokura racecourse.

The naturally beautiful setting is enhanced by the addition of a fountain plaza and a lovely Japanese garden. The modern grandstand was constructed in 1994 and features a towering atrium and very good facilities for the public.

It is a very convenient course for race-goers to attend with a monorail line providing direct access.

Most of the main races at Kokura are staged in August and September, with the Kokura Daishoten run in February. The highlight of the steeplechase calendar is the Kokura Summer Jump.

## THE TRACK

Right-handed. Classic oval. The turf A-course has a circumference of 1615m. Home straight of 293m.

Out of the straight, runners are on a bend to the 1100m. It is then a straight run to the home bend at the 700m.

It is an uphill run from the winning post to the back straight at the 1100m, then the track falls gradually until the 400m point.

Chute start from the 1200m joins the top of the back straight.

The 2000m chute links up with end of the home straight.

The inner dirt track is 1443m in length with a home straight of 291m.

A diagonal strip of track across the infield gives the steeplechase course a total length of 1724m.

# SAPPORO

Kita 16 Jonishi, Chuo Ward, Sapporo, Hokkaido. www.japanracing.jp

Admire Moon

| FEATURE RACES | | | | | |
|---|---|---|---|---|---|
| SAPPORO KINEN | G2 | 2000M | TURF | 3YO+ | AUG |
| QUEEN STAKES | G3 | 1800M | TURF | 3YO+F&M | JUL |
| ELM STAKES | G3 | 1700M | DIRT | 3YO+ | AUG |
| THE KEENELAND CUP | G3 | 1200M | TURF | 3YO+ | AUG |
| SAPPORO NISAI STAKES | G3 | 1800M | TURF | 2YO | AUG—SEPT |

Sapporo is the largest city on the island of Hokkaido and is regarded as the capital of the north.

The city is famous for the Sapporo Snow Festival with an estimated 2 million tourists descending on the area every February. It is also well known as host city of the Winter Olympic Games in 1972 and many will be familiar with the premium local beer.

The course here was opened in 1907 and it is a picturesque setting for racing.

The turf surface is beautifully lush and the course is very family friendly with picnic grounds and an infield amusement park, pond and open-air stage for children's entertainment.

The highlight event on the calendar is the Group 2 Sapporo Kinen, run in August.

## THE TRACK

Right-handed. Classic oval with short straights and wide bends. The turf A-course has a circumference of 1641m. Home straight of 266m.

Out of the straight, runners are on a bend until the 1100m. It is a straight run to the home turn at about the 800m.

The inner dirt track is 1487m in length with a home straight of 264m.

Races over 1500m start from a chute that joins the turn out of the home straight.

# FUKUSHIMA

9-23 Matsunami-cho, Fukushima City, Fukushima, Honshu, Japan. www.japanracing.jp

### FEATURE RACES

| FUKUSHIMA HIMBA STAKES | G3 | 1800M | TURF | 4YO+M | APR |
|---|---|---|---|---|---|
| TENABATA SHO | G3 | 2000M | TURF | 3YO+ | JUL |
| RADIO NIKKEI SHO | G3 | 1800M | TURF | 3YO | JUL |
| FUKUSHIMA KINEN | G3 | 2000M | TURF | 3YO+ | NOV |

**Fukushima City is situated in Nakadori in northern Honshu.**

The racecourse at Fukushima conducted its first meeting in 1918. It is a gorgeous natural setting located near the hot springs resorts of the Tohoku region.

The course features a parade ring on the second floor of the grandstand.

A unique enhancement to the track is the model wooden horses that adorn the winning posts.

## THE TRACK

Right-handed. Oval-shaped course. The turf A-course has a circumference of 1600m. Home straight of 292m.

A chute for races over 1200m joins the back straight.

The 2000m races begin from a chute at the top of the home straight.

The inner dirt course is 1444m in length with a straight run home of 296m.

A diagonal strip of turf measuring 491m across the infield is used for steeplechase racing with runners joining the course proper at either end.

# KANAZAWA

1 Nishi, Hatta-machi, Kanazawa-shi, Ishikawa, Japan. www.japanracing.jp

### FEATURE RACES

| JBC SPRINT | JG1 | 1400M | DIRT | 3YO+ | NOV |
|---|---|---|---|---|---|
| JBC CLASSIC | JG1 | 2100M | DIRT | 3YO+ | NOV |
| JBC LADIES' CLASSIC | JG1 | 1500M | DIRT | 3YO+F&M | NOV |
| HAKUSAN DAISHOTEN | JG3 | 2100M | DIRT | 3YO+ | OCT |

Kanazawa in the Chibu region of central Honshu is situated between the Asano River and Sai River on the Sea of Japan. The city is bordered by the Noto Peninsula National Park and Hakusan National Park near the Japanese Alps and is the capital of the Ishikawa Prefecture.

The tree-lined Kanazawa racecourse is located in the Konan Athletic Park. The high-light races on the local calendar are all staged in early November.

The JBC Classic, JBC Sprint and JBC Ladies' Classic are all fairly recent additions to the annual fixture and are currently rated at domestic Group 1 level.

## THE TRACK

Right-handed. Classic dirt oval of 1200m in circumference. The home straight is 236m.

Out of the home straight, runners are on a bend until approaching the 800m. It is then a straight run of 300m to the home turn.

The 1500m start is from a chute at the top of the home straight.

Races over 1700m begin from a chute that provides only a very short run before linking up with the home bend.

The release point for races over 2300m is from a chute that jumps virtually onto the turn out of the home straight.

## FEATURE RACES

### JBC SPRINT

Run since 2001, notable winners include **BLUE CONCORDE (2005, 06)** and **SUNI (2009, 11)**, who have both won the race twice.

### JBC CLASSIC

**REGULAR MEMBER (2001)** won the inaugural edition.

**ADMIRE DON (2002–04)** and **VERMILION (2007–09)** both scored three consecutive wins, while **TIME PARADOX (2005, 06)** and **SMART FALCON (2010, 11)** both went back to back.

### JBC LADIES' CLASSIC

Established in 2011 **MIRACLE LEGEND (2011, 12)** won the first two editions of the race.

# KAWASAKI

1-5-4 Fujimi, Kawasaki-ku, Kawasaki-shi, Kanagawa, Japan . www.kawasaki-keiba.jp

## FEATURE RACES

| KAWASAKI KINEN | JG1 | 2100M | DIRT | 4YO+ | JAN |
|---|---|---|---|---|---|
| ZENNIHON NISAI YUSHUN | JG1 | 1600M | DIRT | DIRT | DEC |
| EMPRESS HAI | JG2 | 2100M | DIRT | 4YO+M | FEB |
| KANTO OAKS | JG2 | 2100M | DIRT | 3YOF | JUN |

The city of Kawasaki is situated in Kanagawa between Tokyo and Yokahama.

The racecourse at Kawasaki was opened in 1950 and this dirt course is a popular venue for night racing.

Racing here is operated by the Kawasaki Racing Association. The Super King Night Race and Kawasaki Kinen are both staged here.

A feature of the course is a gallery dedicated to former top jockey Takemi Sasaki, who rode more than 7000 winners during his career.

## THE TRACK

Left-handed. Classic dirt oval with a circumference of 1200m. Home straight – 300m.

Out of the straight, runners are on a bend until the 900m. It is then a straight run of 400m to the home turn.

A chute for races over 1600m joins the top of the home straight.

## FEATURE RACES

### KAWASAKI KINEN

Graded as a domestic Group 1 in 1998, notable winners since include **TIME PARADOX (2005)**; **ADJUDI MITSUO (2006)** was a dual winner of the Tokyo Daishoten (2004, 05) and won the Teio Sho (2006); **KANE HEKILI (2009)**; **FURIOSO (2011)** won the Zennihon Nisai Yushun (2006), Japan Dirt Derby (2007), Teio Sho twice (2008, 10), Kashiwa Kinen (2012); and **SMART FALCON (2012)** was a dual winner of the Tokyo Daishoten (2010, 11).

Dual winners include **ABAKUMA PORO (1998, 99)** and **VERMILION (2007, 10)**.

### ZENNIHON NISAI YUSHUN

First run in 1950, notable winners include **ONSLAUGHT (1959)**; **HIKURU TAKAI (1966)**; **AGNES WORLD (1997)** won the Prix de l'abbaye de Longchamp (1999) and July Cup (2000); **AGNES DIGITAL (1999)**; **UTOPIA (2002)** won the Derby Grand Prix (2003), twice won the Mile Championship Nambu Hai (2004, 05) and won the Group 2 UAE Godolphin Mile (2006); and **FURIOSO (2006)**.

# FUNABASHI

1-2-1 Wakamatsu, Funabashi-shi, Chiba, Japan.
www.f-keiba.com

| FEATURE RACES | | | | | |
| --- | --- | --- | --- | --- | --- |
| KASHIWA KINEN | JG1 | 1600M | DIRT | 4YO+ | MAY |
| DIOLITE KINEN | JG2 | 2400M | DIRT | 4YO+ | MAR |
| NIPPON TV HAI | JG2 | 1400M | DIRT | 3YO+ | SEPT |
| MARINE CUP | JG3 | 1600M | DIRT | 3YO+F&M | APR |
| QUEEN SHO | JG3 | 1800M | DIRT | 3YO+F&M | DEC |

The city of Funabashi is located in the Greater Tokyo area.

The Chiba Prefecture Horse Racing Cooperative Association oversees racing at the Funabashi racecourse, which has been in operation since 1950.

The highlight race on the calendar is the domestic Group 1 Kashiwa Kinen, staged in May.

## THE TRACK

Left-handed. Classic dirt oval. The main dirt course is 1400m in circumference. Home straight – 308m.

Races over 1200m start from a spur that provides only a very short run onto the bend out of the home straight.

A spur for races over 2000m allows only a very short run before runners are on the home bend.

A chute at the top of the home straight is the release point for races over 1800m.

## FEATURE RACE

### KASHIWA KINEN

Upgraded to domestic Group 1 status in 2005, notable winners since include **ADJUDI MITSUO (2006)**, **BLUE CONCORDE (2007)** and **FURIOSO (2011)**.

**ESPOIR CITY (2009, 10, 12)** was successful on three occasions.

# URAWA

1-8-42 Oyaba, Minami-ku, Saitama-chi, Saitama, Japan. www.urawa-keiba.jp

| FEATURE RACES | | | | | |
| --- | --- | --- | --- | --- | --- |
| SAKITAMA HAI | JG2 | 1400M | DIRT | 4YO+ | MAY |
| URAWA KINEN | JG2 | 2000M | DIRT | 3YO+ | NOV |
| OVAL SPRINT | JG3 | 1400M | DIRT | 3YO+ | SEPT |

The city of Saitama is located in the Kanto area, just north of central Tokyo.

The venue for racing is the Urawa racecourse under the auspices of the Saitama Prefecture Urawa Racing Association.

## THE TRACK

Left-handed. Classic dirt oval with a circumference of 1200m. Home straight – 220m.

Out of the straight, runners are on a bend until the 800m. It is then a run of approximately 300m to the home turn.

# SONODA

2-1-1 Tano, Amagasaki-shi, Hyogo, Japan.
www.japanracing.jp

| FEATURE RACES | | | | | |
| --- | --- | --- | --- | --- | --- |
| HYOGO CHAMPIONSHIP | JG2 | 1870M | DIRT | 3YO | MAY |
| HYOGO JUNIOR GRAND PRIX | JG2 | 1400M | DIRT | 2YO | MAY |
| Hyogo Gold Trophy | JG3 | 1400M | DIRT | 3YO+ | DEC |

The industrial city of Amagasaki is situated in the Kansai area on the island of Honshu.

The venue for racing here is the Sonoda Racecourse, north-east of downtown Amagasaki and adjacent to Osaka airport.

Course operations are managed by the Hyogo Prefectural Racing Association. The

Sonoda track is the only regional public track in the Kansai area.

## THE TRACK

Right-handed. Oval-shaped dirt course with a circumference of 1051m. Home straight – 228m.

Chute start for races over 1400m joins the top of the home straight.

# MOMBETSU

76-1 Toyokama-Komaoka, Hidaka-cho,Sara-gun, Hokkaido. www.hokkaidokeiba.net

| FEATURE RACES | | | | | |
| --- | --- | --- | --- | --- | --- |
| BREEDERS' GOLD CUP | JG2 | 2000M | DIRT | 3YO+ | AUG |
| HOKKAIDO SPRINT CUP | JG3 | 1200M | DIRT | 3YO+ | JUN |
| EDELWEISS SHO | JG3 | 1200M | DIRT | 2YOF | OCT |

Mombetsu is situated at the mouth if the Saru River on the coast of the Pacific Ocean in the Hidaka region of Hokkaido island.

The region is Japan's largest breeding centre with many of the nation's most prominent stud farms located in the area.

The Mombetsu racecourse was opened in 1997 and is operated by the local government of Hokkaido.

## THE TRACK

Right-handed. Classic dirt oval of 1600m in circumference. Home straight of 330m.

Out of the straight, runners are on a bend until the 1100m. It is then a straight run of about 400m to the home bend.

Races over 1200m begin from a chute joining the top of the back straight.

A chute for 2000m events links up with the top of the home straight.

# NAGOYA

1-1 Taimei-cho, Minata-ku, Aichi, Japan. www. nagoyakeiba.com

| FEATURE RACES | | | | | |
| --- | --- | --- | --- | --- | --- |
| NAGOYA GRAND PRIX | JG2 | 2500M | DIRT | 3YO+ | DEC |
| NAGOYA DAISHOTEN | JG3 | 1900M | DIRT | 4YO+ | MAR |
| KAKITSUBATA KINEN | JG3 | 1400M | DIRT | 4YO+ | APR |

Aichi is situated in the Chibu region of central Honshu.

The Nagoya track is also known as the Donko racecourse and is run by the Aichi Racing Association.

The highlight event is the Nagoya Grand Prix, staged annually on the club's Christmas Day fixture.

## THE TRACK

Right-handed. Classic dirt oval of 1100m in circumference. Home straight of 194m.

Races over 1400m and 2500m begin at the top of the home straight.

A chute for races over 1600m provides only a very short run before linking up with the top of the home turn.

# SAGA

3526-228 Nishitani, Aza, Ejima-machi,Tosu-shi, Saga, Japan. www.sagakeiba.net

| FEATURE RACES | | | | | |
| --- | --- | --- | --- | --- | --- |
| SAGA KINEN | JG3 | 2000M | DIRT | 4YO+ | FEB |
| SUMMER CHAMPION STAKES | JG3 | 1400M | DIRT | 3YO+ | AUG |

Saga is located in the north-west of the island of Kyushu.

Racing on this very tight dirt course is conducted by the Saga Racing Association.

## THE TRACK

Right-handed. Classic dirt oval of 1100m. Home straight of 200m.

Races over 900m and 2000m begin from a chute at the top of the back straight.

A chute that joins the top of the home straight provides the release point for races over 1400m and 2500m.

# KOCHI

2000 Nagahama-Miyata, Kochi-shi, Kochi, Japan. www.keiba.or.jp

| FEATURE RACES | | | | | |
| --- | --- | --- | --- | --- | --- |
| KUROFUNE SHO | JG3 | 1400M | DIRT | 4YO+ | MAR |

The city of Kochi is situated on the south coast of the island of Shikoku.

The Kochi racecourse is the only venue for racing on the island.

## THE TRACK

Right-handed. Egg-shaped dirt oval with a circumference of 1100m. Home straight of 200m.

Out of the home straight, runners are on a bend to the 800m before a run of 200m to the home turn.

Races over 1000m begin from a chute that provides only a very short run before joining the bend out of the home straight. It is also the release point for races over 2100m.

A chute for races over 1400m joins the top of the home straight.

The 1600m chute links up with the home bend.

# SHA TIN

New Territories, Sha Tin, Hong Kong. www.hkjc.com

*Sha Tin is the showpiece racecourse of the Hong Kong Jockey Club.*

Constructed in 1978 on reclaimed land, the course boasts first-class facilities to rival any course in the world and stages some very high-quality racing.

The Hong Kong Jockey Club holds a monopoly on pari-mutuel betting on racing which generates enormous turnover, usually in excess of HK$1 billion for a ten-race card at Sha Tin. It also conducts the lottery and football betting, in which locals also invest huge sums.

The HKJC is a not-for-profit organisation that annually donates HK$1 billion to charities and community projects. It is also the largest taxpayer in Hong Kong with around 12% of the government's total tax revenues contributed by the Jockey Club.

Racing is highly competitive with a star-studded array of trainers and riders always in residence. Big stakes are on offer for races in all classes and nowhere in the world do restricted horses run for the type of money commonplace here.

With its massive tote holds, Hong Kong is one of the great venues for the punter, and betting on the multiples is extremely popular. There are many bet options that can produce a life-changing dividend – including the double trio, triple trio and the six-up. Win pools are enormous but even then often outstripped by the quinella and quinella place.

Sha Tin is the training facility for 24 trainers and more than 1200 horses based in Hong Kong.

The course is considered a good galloping track and a very fair test with all runners generally having their opportunity. All of Hong Kong's major races are run here.

The highlight on the annual fixture is Hong Kong International Race Day, conducted on the second Sunday in December. This meeting has quickly built a reputation as one of the great race days on the world racing calendar, with four Group 1 races that attract the cream of the world's best gallopers to compete for the huge prize money on offer.

International Race Day has not only succeeded in putting Hong Kong on the world racing map but the addition of these races, and the scheduling of other lead-in races, has provided great incentive for local owners to import a better class of horse and has contributed to an overall raising of the standard of competition.

In the past decade the top Hong Kong horses have proved that they are not only capable of mixing it with the internationals at home but anywhere in the world.

While a large contingent of visitors to Hong Kong are always present for the show-case meeting, the most popular day remains

| FEATURE RACES | | | | | |
|---|---|---|---|---|---|
| HONG KONG CUP | G1 | 2000M | TURF | 3YO+ | DEC |
| HONG KONG MILE | G1 | 1600M | TURF | 3YO+ | DEC |
| HONG KONG SPRINT | G1 | 1200M | TURF | 3YO+ | DEC |
| HONG KONG VASE | G1 | 2400M | TURF | 3YO+ | DEC |
| QE II CUP | G1 | 2000M | TURF | 3YO+ | APR |
| CHAMPIONS MILE | G1 | 1600M | TURF | 3YO+ | MAY |
| HONG KONG CLASSIC MILE | HKG1 | 1600M | TURF | 4YO | JAN |
| STEWARDS' CUP | HKG1 | 1600M | TURF | 3YO+ | JAN |
| CENTENARY SPRINT CUP | HKG1 | 1000M | TURF | 3YO+ | JAN |
| HONG KONG CLASSIC CUP | HKG1 | 1800M | TURF | 4YO | FEB |
| HONG KONG GOLD CUP | HKG1 | 2000M | TURF | 3YO+ | FEB |
| QUEEN'S SILVER JUBILEE CUP | HKG1 | 1400M | TURF | 3YO+ | MAR |
| HONG KONG DERBY | HKG1 | 2000M | TURF | 4YO | MAR |
| CHAMPIONS & CHATER CUP | HKG1 | 2400M | TURF | 3YO+ | MAY |

the traditional Chinese New Year fixture, which draws crowds of up to 100,000 people.

Sha Tin is the weekend venue for racing, with meetings generally staged on Sundays between September and mid July.

## THE TRACK

Right-handed. Classic turf oval with a circumference of 1900m. Home straight of 430m.

Chute for races over 1600m and 1800m links up with the back straight.

The 1200m start provides only a short run to the home turn. Inside draws are an advantage.

Straight sprint course of 1000m. High draws are favoured.

The inner all-weather track of 1560m has a home straight of 380m.

## FEATURE RACES

### HONG KONG CUP

The world's richest 2000m race on turf has been won by **RIVER VERDON (1991)**, who was a three-time winner of the Hong Kong Gold Cup (1992–94), dual winner of the Champions & Chater Cup (1992, 94) and won the Stewards' Cup (1993). He remains the only horse to win the Hong Kong Triple Crown.

**FIRST ISLAND (1996)** won the Sussex Stakes (1996), Lockinge Stakes (1997); **VAL'S PRINCE (1997)** twice won the Joe Hirsch Turf Classic (1997, 99) and also won the Man O' War Stakes (1999); **JIM AND TONIC (1999); FANTASTIC LIGHT (2000); AGNES DIGITAL (2001); FALBRAV (2003); ALEXANDER GOLDRUN (2004); VENGEANCE OF RAIN (2005)** won the Hong Kong Derby, QE II Cup, Champions & Chater Cup (2005), Hong Kong Gold Cup, Dubai Sheema Classic (2007); **PRIDE (2006); RAMONTI (2007); VISION D'ETAT (2009); SNOW FAIRY (2010);** and **CALIFORNIA MEMORY (2011, 12)** became the first horse to win twice.

### HONG KONG MILE

The richest mile race in the world.

**GOOD BA BA (2007–09)** registered a hat-trick and Australian **MONOPOLIZE (1995, 96)** won twice.

Other notable winners include **SOVIET LINE (1994)**, who twice won the Lockinge Stakes (1995, 96); **CATALAN OPENING (1997)** won the Cantala Stakes (1997), Doncaster Hcp (1998); **JIM AND TONIC (1998); SUNLINE (2000); EISHIN PRESTON (2001); OLYMPIC EXPRESS (2002)** won the Hong Kong Derby, Hong Kong Classic Mile (2002), Hong Kong Gold Cup (2003); **ABLE ONE (2011);** and **AMBITIOUS DRAGON (2012)** won the Hong Kong Classic Cup, Hong Kong Derby, QE II Cup (2011), Stewards' Cup, Hong Kong Gold Cup (2012).

### HONG KONG SPRINT

Notable winners include **FAIRY KING PRAWN (1999)**, who won the Chairman's Sprint Prize twice (1999, 01), Yasuda Kinen (2000), Stewards' Cup,

Silent Witness

Established in 1975 to commemorate the Hong Kong visit of Queen Elizabeth and Prince Philip, the race became an international Group 1 event in 1995.

Winners since include **EISHIN PRESTON (2002, 03)**, who won consecutive editions. **VIVA PATACA (2007, 10)** also won twice, as well as the Hong Kong Derby (2006) and three Champions & Chater Cups (2006, 07, 09); **RED BISHOP (1995)** won the Hong Kong Vase (1994); **LONDON NEWS (1997)**; **ORIENTAL EXPRESS (1998)**; **JIM AND TONIC (1999)**; **SILVANO (2001)**; **VENGEANCE OF RAIN (2005)**; **PRESVIS (2009)**; and **AMBITIOUS DRAGON (2011)**.

## CHAMPIONS MILE

First run in 2001; dual winners include **BULLISH LUCK (2005, 06)**, who also won the Hong Kong Gold Cup (2004), Stewards' Cup (2005), Yasuda Kinen (2006); **ABLE ONE (2007, 10)** and **XTENSION (2011, 12)**.

**ELECTRONIC UNICORN (2003)** was a dual winner of the Stewards' Cup (2002, 03). **GOOD BA BA (2008)** and **SIGHT WINNER (2009)** are recent winners.

## HONG KONG DERBY

Established at the Happy Valley course in 1873, the race was transferred to Sha Tin in 1979. The conditions of the race were changed in 1981 to become a contest for 4yos only. It is the premier race on the domestic calendar and the race that every Hong Kong owner wants to win.

Winners since 1981 include legendary **CO-TACK (1993)**, winner of ten consecutive races; **RIVER VERDON (1991)**; **MAKARPURA STAR (1995)** twice won the Hong Kong Gold Cup (1995, 96) and won the Champions & Chater Cup (1995); **ORIENTAL EXPRESS (1997)**; **OLYMPIC EXPRESS (2002)**; **VENGEANCE OF RAIN (2005)**; **VIVA PATACA (2006)**; and **AMBITIOUS DRAGON (2011)**.

Bauhinia Sprint Trophy (2001) and dual-winner **FALVELON (2000, 01)**.

**SILENT WITNESS (2003, 04)** can lay genuine claim to being Hong Kong's greatest horse. He swept all before him, winning his first 17 starts in succession including the Bauhinia Sprint Trophy twice (2004, 05), Centenary Sprint Cup twice (2004, 05), Chairman's Sprint Prize (2004) and later won the Sprinters Stakes (2005). He was twice Hong Kong Horse of the Year and rated World Champion Sprinter three years running (2003–05). Such was his popularity that the HKJC set up a website dedicated specifically to him and erected a statue in his honour.

**SACRED KINGDOM (2007, 09)** was also a dual winner and also took out the Chairman's Sprint Prize (2008, 10) and Centenary Sprint Cup (2010, 11) twice, and won the KrisFlyer International Sprint (2009).

Other prominent winners include South African **JJ THE JET PLANE (2010)**, **LUCKY NINE (2011)** and **LORD KANALOA (2012)**.

## HONG KONG VASE

Races over longer distances are very few in Hong Kong. Consequently the Vase continues to be dominated by the international visitors.

Dual winners include **LUSO (1996, 97)** and **DOCTOR DINO (2007, 08)**.

Other prominent winners include **PARTIPRAL (1995)**, who was a dual Group 1 winner in Spain; **INDIGENOUS (1998)** twice won both the Champions & Chater Cup (1997, 98) and the Hong Kong Gold Cup (1998, 99) and is the only Hong Kong-trained horse to win; **BORGIA (1999)**; **DALIA-POUR (2000)** won the Coronation Stakes (2000); **ANGE GABRIEL (2002)** was a two-time winner of the Grand Prix de Saint-Cloud (2002, 03); **PHOENIX REACH (2004)**; **OUIJA BOARD (2005)**; **COLLIER HILL (2006)**; **MASTERY (2010)**; and **DUNADEN (2011)**.

# HAPPY VALLEY

2 Sports Road, Happy Valley, Hong Kong. www.hkjc.com

Happy Valley then and now

Happy Valley is the original racecourse in Hong Kong. It was constructed in 1845 on an area of swampland – then the only flat section of real estate on Hong Kong Island and deemed the only suitable site for a track. The first meeting was staged in December the following year.

The Hong Kong Jockey Club was formed in 1884 and maintains its administrative base at Happy Valley. Until the opening of the Sha Tin course in 1976, Happy Valley was the sole venue for racing in the country.

Racing only became professional in Hong Kong in 1971 and since then the Happy Valley course has been remodelled with the purchase of neighbouring properties, allowing the previously treacherous home bend to be extended and re-cambered. In 1995 renovations were completed to provide world-class facilities.

Meetings at the city course at Happy Valley are mainly conducted on Wednesday nights throughout the season. With the close proximity of the crowd to the racetrack and the surrounding wall of skyscrapers it is a unique and exhilarating racing environment that produces an electrifying atmosphere for spectators.

Happy Valley night racing is the social hub of Hong Kong and absolutely the place to be. The beer garden is always packed and is one big party with live entertainment, promotions and a close-up view of the oft-used 1650m start. A night at the races at Happy Valley is one of the great experiences in the world of horseracing and not to be missed.

Racing here is strictly for horses in the restricted grades with only one race staged at Group 3 level, and a handful of contests for Class 1 gallopers.

The tight, sharp turning circuit provides competitive racing with inside draws vital from most starting points. The further out the placement of the movable rail, the more runners who can travel against the inside fence are favoured. It is a very tough course to cover ground and still figure in the finish.

The highlight on the calendar is the International Jockeys Challenge meeting conducted on the Wednesday night before International Race Day. With many of the world's greatest riders in town to prepare for the weekend, a points-based competition is staged to enable the visiting hoops to compete against the best of the locally based riders, most of whom are top international jockeys in their own right.

Racing in Hong Kong is virtually all handicap based. Horses can only run in their designated class and are weighted strictly according to their handicap rating. For example, a 20-point spread in the handicaps will ensure a 20lb spread in the weights. Apart from the Derby and the Classic Mile for 4yos and a handful of races for griffins – all run at Sha Tin – races are not restricted by age or sex. Handicap ratings for each horse are adjusted after every race start and then reassessed at the end of each season.

All races at Happy Valley are ratings-based handicaps.

Worth a visit is the Hong Kong Jockey Club Archive and Museum, located on the second floor of the grandstand.

## THE TRACK

Right-handed. The course has a circumference of 1450m. The home straight is 310m.

Out of the straight, runners are on a bend to the 1150m. It is an uphill run of 150m to the sharp bend at the top of the track before a straight run of 500m, with the track rising on the approach to the home bend. It is then a downhill run to the hairpin bend onto the home straight.

Chute start for races over 1200m provides a run of almost 200m before the first turn.

# TAIPA

Estrada Governador Albano de Oliviera, Taipa, Macau. www.mjc.mo

*M*acau is situated 145km from Guangdong and 60km south-west of Hong Kong. The former Portuguese colony has been part of the People's Republic of China since 1999 but retains its autonomy.

The Taipa racecourse was originally established by the Macau Trotting Club as a harness-racing track in 1981, but failed to capture the imagination of the local public or adequately lure punters from Hong Kong.

The Macau Jockey Club was formed in 1989 and took over ownership of the site and replaced the existing left-handed track with right-handed turf and sand courses for thoroughbred racing. The sand track was completely rebuilt in 1999.

The transformation of the Macau waterfront into a massive casino precinct has presented a great challenge for racing. If the expectation was that the influx of big gamblers would translate into increased racing attendances then the reality has been to the contrary.

Instead, the Macau course has struggled to compete for the wagering dollar, experiencing a fall in revenues and now a dwindling of the horse population in this once-thriving racing centre.

The are two meetings every week: Friday night racing under lights and a day or twilight meeting held on Saturday or Sunday.

Prize money is good considering the general class of racing, and the course races year round.

## FEATURE RACES

| | | | | | |
|---|---|---|---|---|---|
| MACAU DERBY | G1 | 1800M | TURF | 4YO | APR |
| CHAIRMAN'S CHALLENGE CUP | G1 | 1200M | TURF | 3YO+ | APR |
| MACAU-HONG KONG TROPHY | G1 | 1500M | TURF | 4YO+ | APR |
| WINTER TROPHY | G2 | 1800M | TURF | 3YO+ | JUN |
| DIRECTOR'S CUP | G2 | 1500M | TURF | 3YO+ | JUN |
| SUMMER TROPHY | G2 | 1200M | TURF | 3YO+ | AUG |

## THE TRACK

Right-handed. Oval turf course of 1600m. Home straight of 370m.

Inner sand track of 1400m with a run home of 320m.

# KRANJI

1 Turf Club Avenue, Kranji, Singapore. www.turfclub.com.sg

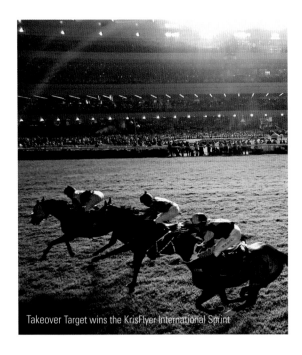
Takeover Target wins the KrisFlyer International Sprint

*The Singapore Sporting Club was formed in 1842 and organised the first official meeting the following year.*

The club was renamed the Singapore Turf Club in 1924 and the course constructed at Bukit Timah, which was the venue for racing from 1933 until 1999. Racing was then moved to Kranji, 22km from the city centre, following the completion of a new state-of-the-art facility.

The Singapore Turf Club was overseen by the Malaya Racing Association, which also manages the operations of the three major racing clubs in Malaysia.

The opening of Kranji saw the establishment of new international races open to competitors from outside of Singapore and Malaysia, including the Singapore International Cup and the KrisFlyer International Sprint – with both races immediately attracting top-line entrants from overseas.

Many horses are brought from Australia to race in Singapore, but following the outbreak of equine influenza there in 2007 Australian horses were precluded entry. Horses from Malaysia were similarly barred as a precautionary measure.

This forced Singapore to establish itself as a racing jurisdiction in its own right, and with the class of competition much stronger in Singapore than it is in Malaysia, the breakaway has been to the great benefit of Singapore, which continues to progress in leaps and bounds.

Racing here is professional, well run and very competitive. With its multiple layouts, Kranji is able to stage plenty of racing all year round with fixtures every week on Friday night and on Saturday and Sunday.

Prize money is very good and the personnel continues to grow in strength with many quality international trainers and riders relocating to Singapore. All contribute to the fact that Singapore, once incidental on the world stage, is now thriving as a racing nation.

## THE TRACK

Left-handed. The turf course features two home bends to provide a long course and short course.

The long course is 2000m in circumference with a home straight of 550m.

The short course is 1800m in circumference with a home straight of 450m.

A chute on the turf track links up with the top of the back straight to provide the release point for races over 1800m on the long round and 1600m on the short track.

Inner all-weather Polytrack is 1500m in length. The run home is 400m.

## FEATURE RACES

### SINGAPORE INTERNATIONAL CUP

Established in 2000 with the opening of the Kranji course, the race has been rated a Group 1 since 2002.

Winners since include **GRANDERA (2002)**, who won the Prince of Wales's Stakes, Irish Champion Stakes (2002); **MUMMIFY (2005)**; **JAY PEG (2008)**;

## FEATURE RACES

| FEATURE RACES | | | | | |
|---|---|---|---|---|---|
| SINGAPORE INTERNATIONAL CUP | G1 | 2000M | TURF | 3YO+ | MAY |
| KRISFLYER INTERNATIONAL SPRINT | G1 | 1200M | TURF | 3YO+ | MAY |
| PATRON'S BOWL | SG1 | 1600M | TURF | 4YO | JUN |
| SINGAPORE DERBY | SG1 | 2000M | TURF | 4YO | JUL |
| KRANJI MILE | SG1 | 1600M | TURF | 3YO+ | OCT |
| RAFFLES CUP | SG1 | 1800M | TURF | 3YO+ | OCT |
| SINGAPORE GOLD CUP | G1 | 2200M | TURF | 3YO+ | NOV |

and **GLORIA DE CAMPEAO (2009)** won the Dubai World Cup (2010).

### KRISFLYER INTERNATIONAL SPRINT

Notable winners include **TAKEOVER TARGET (2008)**, Hong Kong star **SACRED KINGDOM (2009)** and local sensation **ROCKET MAN (2011)** won the Dubai Golden Shaheen (2012) and the Lion City Cup on four consecutive occasions (2009–12).

### SINGAPORE GOLD CUP

Run since 1924; **THREE RINGS (1954, 56, 57)** and **EL DORADO (2008, 09, 11)** both scored three victories in the race.

Dual winners include **GRENADIER (1965, 66)** and **SAAS FEE (1978, 80)**.

Other prominent winners include **COLONIAL CHIEF (1989)**, who won the Hong Kong Cup (1989); **KIM ANGEL (2000)** won the West Australian Derby (1988); **KUTUB (2001)**; **ZIRNA (2003)** won the New Zealand Bloodstock Breeders' Stakes and Raffles Cup (2003); **SMART BET (2002)** won the Singapore Derby and the Singapore Triple Crown – Kranji Mile, Raffles Cup and Singapore Gold Cup (2002).

### SINGAPORE DERBY

Run under the current conditions since 1998 when it became a race for domestic 4yos.

Winners since include **OUZO (1998)**, who won the Raffles Cup (1999) Singapore International Cup (2000); **SMART BET (2002)**; and **JOLIE'S SHINJU (2009)**.

# MONGOL DERBY

*T*he Mongol Derby is a race covering nearly 1000km across the Mongolian Steppe – one of the harshest natural environments in the world.

Julie Barnicott is a former UK jockey now living in Singapore and married to champion trainer Steven Burridge. In 2009, Julie rode in the annual Mongol Derby – an experience she describes as life changing. This is her account:

The Adventurists is a charity organisation that invents crazy events for people to participate in as a way to raise money, including the Mongol Rally and the Rickshaw Run.

The Mongol Derby was initiated to replicate the messenger system established by Genghis Khan in the early 13th century. The messenger route was a series of outposts every 40km or so along the route where a 'Ger' or tent was set up, with horses tethered to a line outside. The messenger would carry his letters at a full gallop for the 40km, jump off his horse, take a fresh steed and gallop on with his mail until sunset.

When darkness fell, he would sleep in a tent or at a station until sunrise before continuing on. It was a very fast and efficient way of moving information across the massive empire, which spread across China, parts of Russia and most of the Middle East.

The Adventurists took a Land Rover and a GPS and followed one of the original routes across Mongolia, heading up to the Siberian border. They set up 'way points' along the route, which spans almost 1000km. Horse stations were also established every 40km to 50km.

Many local families and herdsmen were sponsored to assist with the race by providing 30 or so ponies for each station that were partly broken in and fit enough to cover the distance. It took an enormous amount of organisation and finance, and needed to be arranged more than a year before the first Mongol Derby was run.

The organisers set up tents at each station and provided a simple meal and local (dirty) stream water at each one. I rode 25 different horses over the eight-day journey.

Vets from all over the world were sponsored to steward the riders and oversee the treatment of the horses. At every station was a vet with clipboard and heart-rate monitor to check the horses. We could only return the horses once their heart rates were back to normal and were penalised if they were not. This ensured that the horses were ridden kindly and fairly.

Prior to the race we were instructed to bring a hand-held GPS. On arrival in Mongolia we met with a computer technician who downloaded the route and information about the local terrain.

Only 10kg of equipment is allowed, so most important were the water cleaning tablets, a very light tent, warm clothes, a tiny stove and some food.

Richard Dunwoody was supposed to ride in the race but was called back to the UK after only the first day due to commitments on *Strictly Come Dancing*.

Before the race we were lectured by the organisers and warned not to cross certain rivers and to go around mining areas, etc. The vets also lectured on horse welfare and how to ride the horses, which were semi-wild.

At the start of the event we all set off at a full gallop for the cameras and the press but after 20 minutes most of us were leading our mounts while trying to figure out how to use the GPS.

I had the GPS tied around my neck but somehow the strap broke during the first 10km and I lost the GPS, so I was really stuck. My horse gave me a really nasty kick to the knee while saddling up on the first day. I knew that it was bleeding but dared not look too closely or tend to it. I just rubbed some Dettol cream onto the outside of my riding pants and hoped it would soak through!

A girl called Rowan went somersaulting off her horse when it tripped down a marmot hole, so I helped her back on and we rode together for the duration of the race. She was quite savvy with her navigation skills but had no tent and no food, so we joined forces.

A chap called Julian, who was not such an experienced rider but had done a lot of mountaineering, also joined up with us. I had wanted to be independent and without anyone holding me back but in the end having them alongside me was the best thing that could have happened.

On average we covered 120km per day. The race spread right out from the very beginning with some riders wanting to follow the prescribed route exactly and some of us preferring short cuts by travelling as the crow flies. It's a good plan until one runs into a cliff, impassable mountain or un-crossable river.

Some of the horses were uncontrollable and not all riders were very experienced.

Consequently there were many falls and dramas. In general the horses were shy, flighty and spooky. They would buck when the equipment touched them – sometimes in places they had probably never been touched before! I was very quiet on them, daring not to make any sudden movements but many riders were not in tune with the young or unbroken horses and there were several horrible bucking incidents.

Rowan was not keen to race, which so irked me. I wanted to win but after four days was in the trailing bunch. She was late out of bed and in no particular hurry whereas I,

being an ex-jockey, was saddling in the dark and ready to go at 7am.

To protect the horses, the rules state that there is no riding before 7am and after 7pm. We were fitted with transmitters that relayed our position to the event organisers every hour. If movement was detected outside of the allowed hours, time penalties were applied. In the event of a fall that caused injury, a red button could be pressed to send an SOS, along with coordinates so that medical assistance could be despatched.

However it was made clear before the start that we would likely be many miles from

civilisation and help could take days to reach us. If the situation was critical a helicopter was available but even then it would still take at least 24 hours to arrive. Luckily on my ride there were lots of bumps and bruises but nobody was seriously hurt.

A US$600 deposit is required up front to compensate the owner if a horse is lost or the organisers for equipment not returned. A couple of riders lost their horses and belongings. One horse was recovered but someone had pinched the saddle and saddle bags!

Some of the competitors had a great time along the way, with a number of them enjoying the evenings drinking vodka with the local herders – if there were any around – and having plenty of laughs. We were so exhausted at the end of every day that we just slept and nursed our weary bones.

On one occasion we did not make it to a Ger before nightfall and were forced to set up a makeshift camp. It was frightening at night – below freezing, totally dark, lots of animal noises and no idea where we had pitched the tent until morning. My horse wandered off during the night but fortunately we were able to find him and could continue.

The food was terrible. Big, dirty tin saucers with a very poor soup of goat or lamb. Not many vegetables grow in Mongolia as it is too cold, so the soup had the odd potato or a very leathery piece of meat. There was a horrid fermented milk drink that made us westerners dry reach at the mere smell, but after a few miserably cold days I just had to swallow it to get some energy. Having lived in Asia for 20 years my guts are like iron, so I had no ill-effects from the food but some suffered bouts of sickness and dysentery and many lost weight quite dramatically.

We never undressed or cleaned our hands or teeth for the whole eight days – there was nowhere to do that and no time.

After four days our position in the race was about 15th of the 25 starters. I begged Rowan to race with me and told her that if I had wanted to go sightseeing I could have gone on a tour holiday. This prompted a falling out, but I needed her GPS so that was it.

The next morning Julian and Rowan were up at the crack of dawn and, to be fair, she really got into gear. For the next few days we rode like messengers and overtook a number of riders.

On the last day with 60km to ride we were amazingly in second place. While riding through some thick bushes, Rowan's horse came to a halt as it stood over a branch. I shouted "Back up! Back up! Get off!" Unbelievably her horse had become impaled on the branch. She backed him up and the horse freed itself but the wound was large and open and bled so fast that I was sure he wouldn't survive.

A local herdsman was passing by. With hand signals we asked him to ride back to the previous station and alert the vets. I was devastated as I was keen to get second place. Julian and I briefly discussed riding on but felt we had to honour Rowan and wait with her. It took ages for a replacement horse to arrive and riders went on past, which was bitterly disappointing.

We had to ride really hard now to reach the finishing line and even then it would be after dark and time penalties would be incurred but we just went for it. To make matters worse we took a wrong turn and the rain came down so heavily. It was absolutely freezing and I just wanted the whole thing to end!

We kicked on and made it to the finish line on three really lazy, exhausted horses that were very grumpy and no fun to ride.

At the end of the 1000km ride there was a mini-van waiting to take us to a resort, as promised. But the resort hadn't been finished yet and our suitcases with clean clothes, shampoo, etc had not arrived from Ulaanbaatar. There was no hot water, no shower and we were too late for food. The cabins were without electricity or heating and I was frozen, damp and couldn't dry off. The only thing that had kept me going for the last two days was the thought of a hot shower.

Luckily along the way Julian had insisted that I tend to my wound and gave me some antibiotic tablets, which I rubbed into it. I was so thankful to him and to Rowan, who had been so caring in helping clean and dress the wound. Rowan was grateful that I had given her a shake up and had really enjoyed getting into the race.

During this experience there were so many things to overcome. It was gruelling and tested every part of mind, body and soul. But it felt so fantastic to have come through it and in fifth position overall. And the scenery is just incredible.

Happily the impaled horse was saved.

After a few days drinking and sleeping at 'the resort that wasn't', we were driven back to Ulaanbaatar.

Best of all, I had managed to raise $20,000 for charity.

Mad as it sounds, I am actually contemplating another go at the race.

# GREYVILLE

150 Avondale Road, Greyville, Durban, KwaZulu-Natal, South Africa. www.goldcircle.co.za

*R*acing in South Africa has made significant inroads onto the world stage in recent times.

Owners have invested outside of the country to improve bloodlines, and riders Basil Marcus, Felix Coetzee and Douglas Whyte have proven top class in the ultra-competitive environment of Hong Kong, following in the footsteps of Michael 'Muis' Roberts and his European successes. The imposing international record being built by trainer Mike de Kock has also signalled the emergence of South Africa as a genuine racing nation.

While prize money remains comparatively low, the tracks here are large, extremely spacious and race very fairly.

Durban is a renowned tourist hot spot with its glorious stretch of beaches along the Golden Mile.

Racing in the Durban area can be traced back to 1844, with the Greyville racecourse staging its first official meeting in 1897.

Greyville hosts much of the country's finest racing and is the venue for South Africa's major open-age contest, the Durban July, which is the richest and most prestigious race in the nation. Run on the first Saturday of the month, it is also the premier race day in the nation with four Group 1 races currently on the program.

Durban July day is the highlight of the social calendar as locals take the opportunity to step out in the height of fashion and enjoy the champagne parties that continue well into the evening.

Floodlighting was installed in 1996, allowing it to become the first course in South Africa to stage night racing. An unusual feature of Greyville is the Royal Durban Golf Course located on the infield of the track.

## THE TRACK

Right-handed. Pear-shaped or triangular oval with a circumference of 2800m. The home straight is 500m.

Out of the straight, runners are on a bend until the 2500m. It is a slightly uphill straight run of approximately 800m to the top turn. Another bend takes runners past the 1400m then another straight run of about 600m to the home bend.

The course is fairly undulating with a testing uphill run from the 800m to the top of the home straight.

## FEATURE RACES

### DURBAN JULY

Considered South Africa's premier open-age contest, with a history dating back to 1897.

Dual winners include **CAMPANAJO (1897, 98)**, **CORRIECRIAN (1907, 08)**, **PAMPHLET (1918, 20)**, **MILESIA PRIDE (1949, 50)** and **EL PICHA (1999, 2000)**.

Notable winners include **TIGER FISH (1959)**, who won the South African Nursery Plate, South African Classic and South African Derby (1959); **COLORADO KING (1963)** won the Hollywood Gold Cup (1964); the great horse **SEA COTTAGE (1967)** won 20 of 24 starts including the Cape Derby, South Africa Guineas (1966) and was a dual winner of the Queen's Plate (1966, 67); **MAZARIN (1971)**; **IN FULL FLIGHT (1972)**; **YATAGHAN (1973)**; **JAMAICAN MUSIC (1976)**; **POLITICIAN (1978)**; **LONDON NEWS (1996)** won the South African Guineas, South African Classic, Cape Argus Derby, (1996), J&B Met and Hong Kong QE II Cup (1997);

## FEATURE RACES

| | | | | | |
|---|---|---|---|---|---|
| WOOLAVINGTON 2000 | G1 | 2000M | TURF | 3YOF | JUN |
| DAILY NEWS 2000 | G1 | 2000M | TURF | 3YO | JUN |
| PROVINCE STAKES | G1 | 1600M | TURF | 3YO+F&M | JUL |
| GOLDEN SLIPPER | G1 | 1450M | TURF | 2YOF | JUL |
| GOLDEN HORSESHOE | G1 | 1400M | TURF | 2YOC&G | JUL |
| DURBAN JULY | G1 | 2200M | TURF | 3YO+ | JUL |
| THEKWINI FILLIES' STAKES | G1 | 1600M | TURF | 3YOF | JUL |
| PREMIER'S CHAMPION STAKES | G1 | 1600M | TURF | 2YO | JUL |
| GOLD CUP | G1 | 3200M | TURF | 3YO+ | JUL |
| CHAMPIONS CUP | G1 | 1800M | TURF | 3YO+ | JUL |

IPI TOMBE (2002) won the Dubai Duty Free (2003); **DYNASTY (2003)**; **DANCER'S DAUGHTER (2008)**; and **IGUGU (2011)**.

## GREYVILLE GOLD CUP

Dual winners include **HUMIDOR (1933, 35)**, **WHAT NEXT (1940, 41)**, **CHEZ MONTY (1950, 51)**, **CUFF LINK (1965, 67)** and **HIGHLAND NIGHT (2002, 03)**.

OCCULT (1986) and **SPACE WALK (1993)** both also won the Durban July.

Sun Classique

# KENILWORTH

Rosemead Avenue, Kenilworth, Cape Town, South Africa. www.goldcircle.co.za

## FEATURE RACES

| | | | | | |
|---|---|---|---|---|---|
| CAPE GUINEAS | G1 | 1600M | TURF | 3YO | DEC |
| CAPE FILLIES' GUINEAS | G1 | 1600M | TURF | 3YOF | DEC |
| QUEEN'S PLATE | G1 | 1600M | TURF | 3YO+ | JAN |
| PADDOCK STAKES | G1 | 1800M | TURF | 3YO+F&M | JAN |
| CAPE FLYING CHAMPIONSHIP | G1 | 1000M | TURF | 3YO+ | JAN |
| SOUTH AFRICA MAJORCA STAKES | G1 | 1600M | TURF | 3YO+F&M | JAN |
| J&B MET | G1 | 2000M | TURF | 3YO+ | JAN |
| CAPE DERBY | G1 | 2000M | TURF | 3YO | JAN |

**YARD-ARM (2004)**; **RIVER JETEZ (2010)**; and **IGUGU (2012)**.

**K**enilworth is a suburb of Cape Town, the second-most populated city in South Africa.

The racecourse at Kenilworth is South Africa's oldest, with racing here dating back to 1883. It is a beautiful course with splendid views of Cape Town's famous landmark, Table Mountain.

Located close to the city centre, Kenilworth is the venue for many of South Africa's Group 1 races, with the highlight the J&B Met, run in January. The New Course was constructed in 1978 and a modern grandstand built in 1988.

The infield of the track is a very important natural conservation area as it is home to hundreds of indigenous plant species, many of them threatened or extinct in the wild. In addition, many rare varieties of birds, reptiles, amphibians and mammals inhabit the seasonal wetlands in the centre of the course, known as the Kenilworth Racecourse Conservation Area.

## THE TRACK

Left-handed. The course consists of three separate layouts.

The New Course has a circumference of 2800m with a home straight of 600m. It is considered a very fair course with all runners having an equal opportunity. Most summer meetings are staged on this course.

The Old Course is 2700m in length with a run home of 450m. On-pace runners can be better suited as the course is more of a circular oval. It is used predominantly for racing during autumn and winter.

The straight sprint course is 1200m and features an uphill run for the first 200m and the final 200m to the winning post.

## FEATURE RACES

### J&B MET

The race has had many multiple winners.

**POCKET POWER (2007–09)** made it a hat-trick and is the only horse to have won three times.

Dual winners include **SPRINGLAWN (1912, 13)**, **BATTLEPLANE (1919, 20)**, **CLARE CLAN (1922, 25)**, **ROAMER (1928, 29)**, **MOONLIT (1936, 38)**, **ROYAL CHAPLAIN (1941, 42)**, **ZAMORA (1943, 44)**, **THORIUM (1947, 49)** and **POLITICIAN (1978, 79)**.

Other notable winners include **BOVIDAE (1946)**, the first mare to win; **WILLIAM PENN (1968)**; **YATAGHAN (1974)**; **SLEDGEHAMMER (1975)**; **MODEL MAN (1987)**; **JUNGLE WARRIOR (1990)**; **OLYMPIC DUEL (1991)**; **EMPRESS CLUB (1993)**; **PAS DE QUOI (1994)**; **LONDON NEWS (1997)**; **HORSE CHESTNUT (1999)**;

### QUEEN'S PLATE

Dual winners include **SEA COTTAGE (1966, 67)**, **CHICHESTER (1970, 71)**, **SLEDGEHAMMER (1975, 76)**, **POLITICIAN (1978, 79)**, **YARD-ARM (2003, 04)** and **POCKET POWER (2006, 07)**.

Other notable winners include **WILLIAM PENN (1969)**, **IN FULL FLIGHT (1972)**, **YATAGHAN (1973)**, **QUARRYTOWN (1981)**, **EMPRESS CLUB (1993)**, **JET MASTER (1999)**, **FREE MY HEART (2002)** and **WINTER SOLSTICE (2005)**.

### CAPE DERBY

Prominent winners include **COLORADO KING (1963)**, **SEA COTTAGE (1966)**, **CHICHESTER (1979)**, **MAZARIN (1971)**, **JAMAICAN MUSIC (1974)**, **POLITICIAN (1977)**, **BOLD TROPIC (1979)** was a multiple G2 winner in the USA, **JUNGLE WARRIOR (1988)**, **PAS DE QUOI (1990)**, **RESFA (1998)** won the Hong Kong Steward's Cup (2000), **DYNASTY (2003)** and **JAY PEG (2007)** won the Singapore International Cup and Dubai Duty Free (2008).

### CAPE GUINEAS

Notable winners include **COLORADO KING (1953)**, **HAWAII (1968)**, **IN FULL FLIGHT (1972)**, **JAMAICAN MUSIC (1974)**, **POLITICIAN (1977)**, **WELCOME BOY (1978)**, **BOLD TROPIC (1979)**, **QUARRYTOWN (1980)**, **EMPRESS CLUB (1992)**, **JET MASTER (1998)** and **HORSE CHESTNUT (1999)**.

# TURFFONTEIN

Turf Club Street, Turffontein, Johannesburg, South Africa. www.phumelela.com

*Turffontein is a suburb of Johannesburg, the capital of Guateng province on the eastern plateau of Highveld. It is the largest city in South Africa.*

The historic Turffontein racecourse is situated only 5km from the Johannesburg CBD and staged its first meeting in 1887.

The track conducts some of country's most prestigious races, notably the South African Derby in April and the Summer Cup in December. The Summer Cup is one of the oldest races on the South African calendar and remains one of the most valuable and keenly contested open handicap events.

The course is considered the stiffest test of a thoroughbred in the nation with a relentless uphill run between the 1600m and the start of the home straight at the 800m. The course rises by a gradient of 12m during this time, followed by the long run to the finish. Consequently very few runners are able to make all at Turffontein and the cast-iron rule for riders here is to wait, wait and then wait again. Then when the waiting is over, count to 10.

A rationalisation of local racing clubs saw the course's operations transferred to Phumelela Gaming and Leisure Ltd in 1998.

## THE TRACK

Right-handed. The main turf course is oval shaped and 2700m in length. Home straight of 800m.

Chute start for races over 1400m provides only a very short run before linking up with the home bend.

A straight sprint course of 1200m joins the main track.

An inner turf track has a circumference of 2500m with a run home of almost 500m.

## FEATURE RACES

### SOUTH AFRICAN DERBY

Notable winners include **MOONLIT (1935)**, **LENIN (1940)**, **NAGAINA HALL (1954)**, **TIGER FISH (1957)**, **HOME GUARD (1968)**, **ELEVATION (1972)** won the Summer Cup on three consecutive occasions (1972–74), **WELCOME BOY (1978)**, **SUPER QUALITY (1996)**, **HORSE CHESTNUT (1999)** crushed his rivals by 10 lengths, and **GREY'S INN (2004)**.

### SA CLASSIC

Notable winners include **LENIN (1940)**; **NAGAINA HALL (1954)**; **TIGER FISH (1957)**; **HAWAII (1967)** won the Cape Argus Guineas, South African Guineas (1968) and in the USA won the United Nations Stakes and Man O'War Stakes (1969); **HOME GUARD (1968)**; **YATAGHAN (1972)**; **QUARRY-TOWN (1979)**.

Champion filly **EMPRESS CLUB (1992)** won the Cape Argus Guineas, South African Guineas, South African Fillies Guineas, (1992), J&B Met, Queen's Plate and Horse Chestnut Stakes (1993); **NATIONAL EMBLEM (1995)**; **LONDON NEWS (1996)**; **CLASSIC FLAG (1998)**; **HORSE CHESTNUT (1999)**; **SURVEYOR (2003)**; **GREY'S INN (2004)**; and **IRRIDESCENCE (2005)** won the Hong Kong QE II Cup (2006).

## FEATURE RACES

| | | | | | |
|---|---|---|---|---|---|
| SA CLASSIC | G1 | 1800M | TURF | 3YO | MAR–APR |
| HORSE CHESTNUT STAKES | G1 | 1600M | TURF | 3YO | MAR–APR |
| SOUTH AFRICAN FILLIES CLASSIC | G1 | 1800M | TURF | 3YOF | MAR–APR |
| EMPRESS CLUB STAKES | G1 | 1600M | TURF | 3YO+F&M | MAR–APR |
| SOUTH AFRICAN DERBY | G1 | 2450M | TURF | 3YO | APR |
| COMPUTAFORM SPRINT | G1 | 1000M | TURF | 3YO+ | APR |
| CHAMPION CHALLENGE | G1 | 2000M | TURF | 3YO+ | APR |
| SUMMER CUP | G1 | 2000M | TURF | 3YO+ | DEC |

# SCOTTSVILLE

45 New England Road, Scottsville, KwaZulu-Natal, South Africa. www.goldcircle.co.za

JJ the Jet Plane wins in Dubai

## FEATURE RACES

| | | | | | |
|---|---|---|---|---|---|
| GOLDEN HORSE SPRINT | G1 | 1200M | TURF | 3YO+ | MAY |
| SOUTH AFRICAN FILLIES SPRINT | G1 | 1200M | TURF | 3YO+F&M | MAY |
| GOLD MEDALLION | G1 | 1200M | TURF | 2YO | MAY |
| ALLAN ROBERTSON FILLIES' CHALLENGE | G1 | 1200M | TURF | 2YOF | MAY |

Peitermaritzburg is the capital of the KwaZulu-Natal province in South Africa.

The venue for racing is the Scottsville track, located only 2.5km from the heart of the city and 75km from Durban.

The course staged its first meeting in 1886 as the City Sporting Club.

The highlight of the racing and social calendar is undoubtedly the unique Golden Horse Sprint day on the last Saturday in May.

Fast horses and fast living are the order of the day. Four Group 1 events are conducted on the program – all run on the straight course over the sprint distance of 1200m – with races at the elite level for the 2yo fillies, an open race for 2yos, a fillies and mares contest, and the open Golden Horse Sprint. The latter was the first sponsored race in South Africa.

It is also a high fashion extravaganza with a difference. The usually conservative nature of racetrack fashions is totally dispensed with and the local designers encouraged to outfit their models for the event in the most avant-garde, head-turning, jaw-dropping creations imaginable – anything that would have the wearer barred from the enclosure at Ascot.

The public facilities are first rate and the Golden Horse Shoe Casino is also part of the complex.

## THE TRACK

Right-handed. Classic turf oval with a circumference of 2300m. Home straight – 550m.

Out of the straight, runners are on a bend until approaching the 1600m. It is then a straight run of more than 600m to the home turn.

The straight sprint course of 1200m is a stern test. From the 1200m start it is a downhill run to the course proper then a steep uphill run to the 200m where the track rises even more sharply.

Chute start for races over 1800m joins the top of the back straight.

# CLAIRWOOD

89 Barrier Lane, Clairwood, KwaZulu-Natal, South Africa. www.goldcircle.co.za

## FEATURE RACES

| | | | | | |
|---|---|---|---|---|---|
| GOLD CHALLENGE | G1 | 1600M | TURF | 3YO+ | JUN |
| MERCURY SPRINT | G1 | 1200M | TURF | 3YO+ | JUL |
| GOLD CIRCLE DERBY | G2 | 2400M | TURF | 3YO | JUN |
| GOLD CIRCLE OAKS | G2 | 2400M | TURF | 3YOF | JUN |
| TIBOUCHINA STAKES | G2 | 1450M | TURF | 3YO+F&M | JUN |

The suburb of Clairwood is situated approximately 10km from the centre of Durban.

Clairwood racecourse was originally built on an area of swampland and staged its inaugural meeting in 1921.

Referred to as the Garden Course, the track underwent a major renovation in 1982, which included the construction of a new grandstand to provide good facilities for the public.

The course currently conducts two Group 1 races, held in June and July.

Clairwood has been slated for sale in recent times and there is some doubt about the future of the track beyond the current-year lease. The course is the only green space in a mainly industrial area and residents appear to be taking up the challenge to ensure it is preserved.

## THE TRACK

Left-handed. Classic turf oval. The course has a circumference of 2500m. Home straight of 600m.

Out of the straight, runners are on a bend until about the 2000m point. It is a straight run of almost 800m to the home bend.

The straight sprint course of 1200m. High draws are favoured on the sprint course, especially when the track is rain affected.

Inside draws are an advantage from the 1400m and the 2400m starting points due to the short run to the first bend.

## FEATURE RACE

### MERCURY SPRINT

**FLOBAYOU (1995–97)** is the only horse to score a hat-trick.

Dual winner **JJ THE JET PLANE (2008, 10)** earned a reputation as one of the top sprinters in the world. He also was a dual winner of the Golden Horse Sprint (2008, 10), the Al Quoz Sprint (2009, 11) and was also victorious in the Hong Kong Sprint (2010).

Other notable winners include **SMACKEROO (1983)**, **ON STAGE (1986)** campaigned with success in the UK, **JET MASTER (2000)**, **NATIONAL CURRENCY (2003)**, **NATIONAL COLOUR (2006)** and **WAR ARTIST (2007)** also had success in Europe.

# VAAL

Ascot Road, Viljoensdrift, Free State, South Africa.
www.phumelela.com

## FEATURE RACE

| EMERALD CUP | G2 | 1450M | AWT | 3YO+ | SEPT |
|---|---|---|---|---|---|

Viljoensdrift is located in the Metsimaholo Municipality of the Fezile Dabi District in the Free State province.

Vaal racecourse is the venue for racing and the track is the largest in South Africa by circumference. It also features the longest home straight of any course in the nation.

Racing here takes place on the turf and the sand, with the highlight race the Emerald Cup. It is staged on the sand course, which was opened in 2001.

## THE TRACK

Right-handed. The oval-shaped turf course is approximately 3000m in circumference. The run home is 1000m.

Races up to 1600m are held on the straight course.

High draws can be an advantage, particularly when the track is rain affected.

The inner sand course is 2800m in length. Home straight – 1000m.

The 1000m start on the sand course is at the top of the home straight.

Races over 1200m start in the middle of the home bend, and the 1400m start provides only a very short run to the turn.

# ARLINGTON

Shoenmakerskop Road, Walmer, Port Elizabeth, South Africa. www.phumelela.com

## FEATURE RACE

| EAST CAPE DERBY | G3 | 2400M | TURF | 3YO | MAY |
|---|---|---|---|---|---|

The windy city of Port Elizabeth is situated in the East Cape Province of Cape Town.

The Arlington racecourse staged its first official meeting in 1950 under the auspices of the former St Andrews Racing Club.

Racing in the area can be traced back to the 1850s, and the original Jockey Club of South Africa was established in Port Elizabeth in 1882. In 2004 the ruling body voted to change its name to the National Horse Racing Authority.

Arlington is an undulating track that is known for its excellent drainage, ensuring a very good racing surface throughout most of the year.

The home straight is a downhill run so it is common for quick times to be registered for most distances.

Calendar highlight is the East Cape Derby in May.

## THE TRACK

Right-handed. Classic turf oval with a circumference of 2000m. The home straight is 600m.

A chute that links up with the back straight provides the release point for races from 1800m to 2000m.

The 1200m start provides only a very short run before the home turn.

There is a straight sprint course of 1000m that joins the home straight. The sprint course runs downhill for the entire trip.

# DURBANVILLE

Bowlers Way, Durbanville, Cape Town, South Africa.
www.goldcircle.co.za

## FEATURE RACES

| MATCHEM STAKES | G3 | 1400M | TURF | 3&4YO | OCT |
|---|---|---|---|---|---|
| DIANA STAKES | G3 | 1400M | TURF | 3&4YOF&M | OCT |

Durbanville is a mainly rural residential suburb of the Cape Town metropolitan area.

Racing and equestrian sports on the current site at Durbanville date back to 1898 when recreational meetings were staged to finance the upkeep of the hounds of the Cape Hunt Club.

The racecourse was officially established in 1922 as the Durbanville Gymkhana Club and operated under this banner until 1956. The club has been the subject of a number of amalgamations and name changes since but racing has remained constant.

Due to its very good drainage the Durbanville track conducts its meetings mainly during the winter months.

The course currently hosts two races graded at Group 3 level, staged on consecutive weeks during October.

## THE TRACK

Left-handed. Oval turf course of 2200m in circumference. The home straight is 600m.

The straight has a downhill run to the finish and generally favours on-pace runners.

Inside draws are considered an advantage from all start positions.

# FAIRVIEW

Draaifontein Road, Greenbushes, Port Elizabeth, South Africa. www.phumelela.com

## FEATURE RACES

| ALGOA CUP | G3 | 2000M | TURF | 3YO+ | NOV |
| Champion Juvenile Cup | L | 1400M | TURF | 2YO | JUL |

Fairview racecourse is located in Port Elizabeth, where racing was first staged by the Port Elizabeth Turf Club in 1857.

Racing at the current site commenced in 1977.

Following the completion of a new stable complex in 2007 Fairview became the central training base in the area with all trainers form Arlington relocating their operations here. Phumelela Gaming and Leisure Ltd now manage the courses here and at Arlington.

The course hosts a number of Listed races with the highlight fixture in November for the running of the Algoa Cup, currently rated at Group 3 level. Fairview is noted as a track with poor drainage that does not cope well with adverse conditions.

## THE TRACK

Right-handed. Pear-shaped turf oval of approximately 2750m in circumference. The home straight is 800m.

Out of the straight, runners are on a wide bend until approaching the 2000m. It is then a straight run of almost 800m to the tight home bend.

Inside draws are an advantage from the starting points at the 1400m and the 1600m.

Races up to 1200m are run on the straight sprint course that joins the top of the home straight. The run along the straight course is mainly downhill and high draws are generally preferable.

# INDIA

# MUMBAI

Mahalakshimi, Tulsiwadi, Mumbai, India. www.rwitc.com

## FEATURE RACES

| INDIAN OAKS | G1 | 2400M | TURF | 4YOF | JAN |
| INDIAN DERBY | G1 | 2400M | TURF | 4YO | FEB |
| BREEDERS' MULTI MILLION | G1 | 1400M | TURF | 3YO | FEB |
| INDIAN TURF INVITATIONAL CUP | G1 | 2400M | TURF | 4YO | MAR |
| INDIAN 1000 GUINEAS | G1 | 1600M | TURF | 3YOF | DEC |
| INDIAN 2000 GUINEAS | G1 | 1600M | TURF | 3YO | DEC |

Racing in Mumbai dates back to 1798 with a two-day fixture the first recorded meeting.

In its infancy, racing was generally staged using cavalry horses and chargers imported from the UK and Arabia.

The course on the current site was constructed following a donation of land by industrialist Sir Curnow N Wadia. The Maha-laxmi racecourse is based on the design of the Caulfield track and was opened in 1883.

Racing in Mumbai is operated by the Royal West India Turf Club, which leases the course. Mahalaxmi is the venue for the Indian Classic races.

Facilities are good, with a new club house opened in 2009.

Racing season is from November until April, with the Indian Derby run in February.

## THE TRACK

Right-handed. Turf course of 2400m in circumference.

# HYDERABAD

Bari Galla Colony, Malakpet, Hyderabad, Andhra Prakesh, India. www.hydraces.com

## FEATURE RACES

| GOLCONDA DERBY | G1 | 2400M | TURF | 4YO | JAN |
| PRESIDENT OF INDIA GOLD CUP | G1 | 2400M | TURF | 4YO+ | SEPT |
| DECCAN DERBY | G1 | 2000M | TURF | 3YO | OCT |

Hyderabad is the capital of the southern Indian state of Andhra Prakesh.

Racing in Hyderabad began at the Moula Ali racecourse in 1868 and was established at its present home at Malakpet exactly a century later.

The Hyderabad Racing Club became an independent turf authority in 1977.

Hyderabad stages one of the premier weight-for-age contests in India – the Presi-dent of India Gold Cup.

Racing is conducted on the Monsoon Track from July to October and then on the tan bark-based turf of the Winter Track from November to March. The highlight event is run in September.

## THE TRACK

Right-handed. Turf Monsoon Race Track has a circumference of 2250m. Home straight of 550m.

Winter Race Track has a circumference of 2150m.

# BANGALORE

Racecourse Road, Bangalore, India.
www.bangaloreraces.com

## FEATURE RACES

| | | | | | |
|---|---|---|---|---|---|
| BANGALORE DERBY | G1 | 2400M | TURF | 4YO | JAN |
| STAYERS' CUP | G1 | 3000M | TURF | 4YO+ | MAR |
| SPRINTERS' CUP | G1 | 1200M | TURF | 4YO+ | MAR |
| MAJOR MEHRA MEMORIAL SUPER MILE CUP | G1 | 1600M | TURF | 4YO+ | MAR |
| FILLIES' CHAMPIONSHIP STAKES | G1 | 1600M | TURF | 3YOF | JUN |
| COLTS CHAMPIONSHIP STAKES | G1 | 1600M | TURF | 3YOC&G | JUN |
| DERBY BANGALORE | G1 | 2000M | TURF | 3YO | JUL |

Bangalore is the capital of the state of Karnataka in the south of India.

The Bangalore course is situated on 34ha of land and is well designed to use the limited space as best as possible.

Racing is operated by the Bangalore Turf Club, which was formed in 1920 and has a perpetual lease for as long as the course is used to conduct race meetings.

It is noted as a very challenging course as the track falls sharply by a gradient of 13m between the 1800m and the 800m, then rises back up by 11m from there to the winning post.

Weather conditions are good in Bangalore and many trainers send horses from Mumbai and Kolkata for the summer.

There are around 70 race days split between the summer and winter seasons.

## THE TRACK

Right-handed. Turf oval with a circumference of 1950m. Home straight of 450m.

# TURKEY

## VELIEFENDI

Osmaniye Mh. 34144 Bakirkoy, Istanbul, Turkey.
www.tjk.org

Topkapi Trophy winner Musir

## FEATURE RACES

| | | | | | |
|---|---|---|---|---|---|
| BOSPHURUS CUP | G2 | 2400M | TURF | 3YO+ | SEPT |
| TOPKAPI TROPHY | G2 | 1600M | TURF | 3YO+ | SEPT |
| ANATOLIA TROPHY | G2 | 2000M | AWT | 3YO+ | SEPT |
| ISTANBUL TROPHY | G2 | 1600M | TURF | 3YO+F&M | SEPT |

Turkey is a thriving racing nation and the Veliefendi course in the capital of Istanbul is the principal of the eight tracks under the direction of the Jockey Club of Turkey.

Veliefendi is the oldest of Turkey's tracks, constructed in 1913 on pastoral land formerly belonging to Seyhulislam Veliyuddin Efendi.

Major races are held in the first week of September and offer excellent prize money. The meeting is strongly supported by international trainers and the feature events attract top-class fields.

The Jockey Club also oversees breeding operations in Turkey and regularly purchases top horses to stand at stud in Turkey, where many very well-known names are among the ranks.

The course is a major training centre and features a museum, apprentice training school and a picnic area.

## THE TRACK

Right-handed. Main turf course is oval shaped and is 2020m in length. Home straight of about 500m.

Inner all-weather track of 1870m.

# MAURITIUS

## CHAMP DE MARS

Port Louis, Mauritius. www.mauritiusturfclub.com

The island republic of Mauritius is situated 2000km off the south-east coast of Africa.

Racing here has a great history and is extremely popular. The venue is the Champ de Mars racecourse.

Colonel Edward Draper founded the Mauritius Turf Club in 1812, making it one of the world's oldest active race clubs. Established in the same year, the course is considered the oldest in the southern hemisphere.

While the Champ de Mars track may be very tight, the local riding ranks are constantly bolstered by the presence of international jockeys, with many taking up short- and long-term riding contracts.

There are four Classic races in Mauritius: The Duke of York Cup (1600m), The Duchess of York Cup (1400m), Barbe Cup (1600m) and the Maiden Cup (2400m).

## THE TRACK

The Champ de Mars course is an elliptical oval of only 1298m in circumference. The run home is 250m.

# SPECIAL THANKS

Kerrie Haire; Clare Forster – Curtis Brown; David Price; Graeme Poole; Damien Oliver; Steve Moran; Anthony Hogan; Antony Hill; Shane Templeton; James Earls – VRC; Jeff Haynes – Hawkesbury; Sarah Wills – Scone; Les Kilias; Garry Buckley – Country Racing Victoria; Colin Tuck – ATC; Belinda Glass - Ballarat;

At Hardie Grant – Sandy Grant, Pam Brewster, Oliver Raymond, Dale Campisi.

# FOR ASSISTANCE WITH SUPPLYING PHOTOS, THANKS TO:

William Derby & James Brennan (York)
Claire Fortescue & Angela Turney (Epsom)
Kerrie Haire (Siena)
Julie Barnicott-Burridge (Mongolia)
Haydn Thompson (Tailor Made Travel)
Mike Caldwell (Goodwood)
Olivia Hills (Ascot)
Haydock Park
Jessie Court (Chester)
Amy O'Regan (Limerick)
Kate Mckee (Beverley)
Richard (Pontefract)
Jeremy Martin (Salisbury)

Alyssa Piper (Bath)
Evan Arkwright (The Curragh)
Iain Ferguson (Ayr)
Danielle Skelton (Hamilton Park)
Donna Berry (Canberra)
Penny Tripp (VRC)
Luke King (Cranbourne)
Penny Reeve (Seymour)
Ian Hart (Bendigo)
Michael Craig (Kembla Grange)
Brody Russell (Bunbury)
Michael Lodding (Pinjarra)
Helen McCormack (Kalgoorlie)

Lyn Roberts (Morphettville)
Tim Smith (Birdsville)
TRK Photo (Pimlico, Laurel Park)
Mac McBride & Mary Shephardson (Del Mar)
Drubha Selvaratnam (Jebel Ali)
Gill Simpkins & Pam Wright (Golden Circle RSA)
Margaret Hellbeck (ATC Heritage Office)
Tim Auld (Warrnambool)
Ann & Horst Willers (Germay)
Glenyse Buckley (Kilmore)
Belinda Glass & Lachlan McKenzie (Ballarat)
Garry Buckley (Country Racing Victoria)
Colin Tuck (ATC)